MOLIÈRE

MOLIÈRE

John Palmer

with a new Index

BENJAMIN BLOM, INC.

PUBLISHERS

NEW YORK

1970

First Published 1930
Reissued 1970 by Benjamin Blom, Inc.
Bronx, New York 10452
with a new Index
© 1970 by Benjamin Blom, Inc., Bronx, N. Y. 10452
Library of Congress Catalog Card Number 65-16246
Printed in the United States of America

PREFACE

To survey the work of Molière, present the man, and recover the environment in which he lived is, perhaps, a task impossible in a single volume. The attempt had, however, to be made. Molière must be shown at work in a theatre with which it is essential to make ourselves familiar and fighting for the freedom of his art in a society whose views and prejudices must be clearly understood. No great genius was ever more deeply implicated in the life of his time, and his achievements cannot be considered in detachment. The work of Molière cannot be isolated from the man; still less can the man be isolated from his period.

The life of Molière is packed with obscure problems and the evidence is capable of many interpretations. The personal equation of the biographer must accordingly count for much; but he can at least present the facts in a way which allows his readers to form an independent judgment. There are no references and only one footnote in this book, but the authorities are presented and described as the story goes and such personal impressions as the author permits himself will be easily identified.

JOHN PALMER.

Petite Boissière, Geneva.
October, 1929.

CONTENTS

I.	The House of the Monkeys	9
II.	The Young Philosopher	21
III.	Sudden Conversion	35
IV.	The Illustrious Theatre	56
V.	The Actor at Large	75
VI.	The First Plays	100
VII.	The Return to Paris	122
VIII.	The Battle of the Exquisites	139
IX.	Gentlemen, the King!	159
X.	The Heroic Muse	179
XI.	The School for Husbands	195
XII.	Portraits	209
XIII.	The Marriage of Molière	222
XIV.	The School for Wives	253
XV.	The Comic War	265
XVI.	The Royal Diversions	293
XVII.	Tartuffe	332
XVIII.	The Wicked Marquis	361
XIX.	The Golden Mean	388
XX.	Impious in Medicine	409
XXI.	Auteuil	427
XXII.	The Death of Molière	460
	Bibliographical Note	493
	Index	495

I

The House of the Monkeys

I

T stood three hundred years ago at the corner of the Rue St. Honoré and the Rue des Vieilles Etuves. On the ground floor was a shop in which were exposed for sale tapestries and other wares for the decoration and furnishing of the fine houses of the period. Behind the shop extended a kitchen, used also as a dining-room. Above the kitchen, set in the angle of the roof, was a bedroom, and above the shop that gave upon the street was the principal apartment of the house—best bedroom and sitting-room combined. Finally, above all this, just under the roof, was the work-room of Jean Poquelin, upholsterer to the King of France.

Such was the house in which the son of Jean Poquelin known to posterity as Molière, spent the first impressionable years of his life.

The pillar supporting the house at the angle of the street was a sculptured column in the form of an orange tree, about which played a festoon of monkeys, whence the house was invariably described as the *maison des singes*. Monkeys were the symbol of the actor, to whom reputable society and heaven itself were closed, but in the early years of his tenancy Jean Poquelin, upholsterer to the King, son and grandson of an upholsterer, married to the daughter of an up-

9

holsterer, might pass his door to the Court, or on his way to attend some noble client, without misgiving. Descendant of a family with a respectable burgher ancestry, to be traced by scholars yet unborn back to the fourteenth century, he could have as yet no premonition of the disgrace that awaited him.

The house of the monkeys has since been destroyed, but the wall of the building which now stands on the site of it, No. 96 of the Rue St. Honoré, bears in letters of gold on black marble the following inscription:

Cette Maison a été construite sur l'emplacement
de Celle ou est né
Molière
Le 15 Janvier 1622

The inscription is possibly incorrect. In 1622 Jean Poquelin may have inhabited another house in the Rue St. Honoré and moved later to the house at the corner. For the biographer, however, the house of the monkeys, where Jean Poquelin was certainly living by the time his son was of an age to be intelligently aware of his surroundings is the birthplace of Molière. Any other possible address may be left to the antiquaries.

Jean Poquelin I was an alderman of Beauvais. His son, Jean Poquelin II, grandfather of Molière, came to Paris in the sixteenth century and prospered, establishing himself firmly as a burgess of the city. Jean Poquelin III, eldest of the ten children of Jean Poquelin II, followed his father's business. The *marchand-tapissier* or upholsterer of the seventeenth century dealt not only in tapestries, but in all that pertained to the furnishing and appointment of houses. He combined the trade of a modern furniture dealer with that of a decorator and collector of antiques. On April 27th, Jean Poquelin III, *marchand-tapissier*, married the daughter of Louis Cressé, *marchand-tapissier*, and within nine months the dynasty was assured. The first child of the marriage, born promptly but decently in the following January, was baptized on the fifteenth of the month, and received his father's name. In due course he would succeed his father as Jean Poquelin IV. No one as yet suspected that this was Molière.

Marie Cressé brought as dowry to her husband the sum of 2,200 *livres tournois*.* This was not a fortune; but the two families were people of substance and, as was the orderly habit of the French middle class, they recorded the least of their transactions one with another in due and proper form. No casual note of hand or gentleman's agreement was held to suffice as between husband and wife or between father and son. At every turn in their affairs we find the family council and the family lawyer. That is all to our advantage. The house, furniture, clothing and personal effects of Jean Poquelin, long since destroyed, may thus be described from inventories and contracts still extant. For the signing of the marriage contract between Jean Poquelin and Marie Cressé, there was convened an Homeric assembly. First came the bride, bridegroom and their parents. There

* The purchasing power of the *livre tournois* in the seventeenth century has been very variously estimated and is almost impossible to determine with accuracy owing to very appreciable changes in the comparative value of commodities. It was certainly not for any purpose less than the equivalent of five gold francs to-day, and for some purposes its purchasing power was considerably greater. References will also occur in this book to crowns (*écus*) and *pistoles*. The crown was an ambiguous coin. There was a large crown equivalent to six, and a small crown equivalent to three, *livres*. The *pistole* was equivalent to ten *livres*.

followed among the collected relatives, Daniel Crespy, the feather merchant; Toussaint Perier, the linen draper; Marin Gamard, the master tailor; Jean Autissier, builder and contractor to the King; Noel Mestayer, the hatter, and Denis Tostere, the stonemason. We look in vain among those assembled for any hint of abnormal inclinations or gifts. There is only one suspicious circumstance. Marie Cressé herself, rather surprisingly, could read and write.

Altogether nineteen people signed the marriage contract and nothing was left to chance. The interests of three generations were all clearly defined. There was to be community of goods between the parties. Marie brought into the common stock 1,800 *livres* in cash and 400 *livres* in furniture and linen. Jean Poquelin contributed the exact equivalent—2,000 *livres* in cash, and 200 *livres* in stock and fittings. The possibilities of death, divorce, bankruptcy, second marriage—all were provided for in terms that any lawyer may read with pleasure and respect. The details are of small importance, but the general conclusion is significant. The social history of France is largely embodied in such contracts. In February, 1621, when this particular document was signed by a family council of nineteen, the rulers of Paris were fighting for the King's ear. Only a year before the Huguenots had organized France into eight rebel departments. Louis XIII was a young man torn between many counsellors, all advising him for their own good. Richelieu was not yet in control of the government, which was almost equivalent to saying that there was as yet no government in France. High politics, however, passed well over the head of Jean Poquelin. He represented a class that had survived a hundred revolutions. The fortunes and aspirations of this family were built upon the substantial virtues of the middle state.

In the seventeenth century accommodation was limited. Meals were eaten in the kitchen, behind the shop where, in addition to the yellow and red copper utensils upon the wall, the pewter services, the great oak cupboards and tables of walnut and pine, were six armchairs of walnut, covered with tapestry *point de Hongrie*. During the day Jean Poquelin when at home remained in the shop or workroom. In the evening he would sit with his children in the room above the shop that gave upon the Rue St. Honoré. In the hearth was a handsome pair of copper fire-dogs, with balls of olive green. Beside the hearth were two comfortable chairs of the type known as gossip-stools (*caqueterres*), and these are inventoried as much worn. In the middle of the room was an imposing table of walnut, supported on seven columns and covered with a green flowered cloth. In one corner of the room stood a cabinet of pied walnut, and in another corner a large square bureau or dresser covered with an embroidered tapestry. Six high-backed chairs of walnut, covered with flowered needlework in silk, were ranked along the walls, which were hung with a tapestry of Rouen in seven pieces, with fine pictures and a mirror of Venetian glass. Finally there was the bed, a noble structure of walnut, with a coverlet of silk, draped in green serge with fringes and tassels of silk.

Jean Poquelin himself wears, perhaps his suit of Spanish cloth, black or grey, with buttons of gold, or, if this be a festival, his suit of black Neapolitan taffeta; while his wife, in her fine skirt of watered silk and her earrings of pearl, bends over her embroidery. Such was the room in which the

13

young Molière, sitting upon one of those gossip-stools, first made himself acquainted with the playhouse pleasures of Terence and the austere speculations of Lucretius on the nature of things.

Of the character and disposition of his mother very little is known or can be conjectured. Marie Cressé was twenty years old when she married in April, 1621; she had six children in ten years, of whom four survived; she was thirty-one when she died in May, 1632. She had an abundance of fine linen, beautifully kept; she had three handsome necklaces, two bracelets, four pairs of earrings; a brooch or medal of gold set with emeralds and rubies; two girdles of gold and a golden chain; fourteen rings, seven being set with diamonds, one with an emerald and two with opals; one gold and two silver watches. She could, as has been mentioned, read and write, and there were two books in the house—the Bible and *Plutarch's Lives*. The rest is inference. Molière was ten years old when she died; and we look in vain for any allusion to his mother, either definite or implicit, in any of his words or works.

Jean Poquelin, with four surviving children on his hands, married, in the year following the death of his first wife, Catherine, the daughter of Eustache Fleurette. Eustache was a neighbour of Jean Poquelin in the Rue St. Honoré. He was perhaps an ironmonger. Of Catherine, the step-mother of Molière, nothing personal can be ascertained. She was married in May, 1633; she had two children in three years, of whom one survived; she died in November, 1636.

It is a poor biographer who allows himself to be defeated by lack of evidence, and fancy has made remarkably free with the mother and step-mother of Molière. Marie Cressé could read and there was a Plutarch in the house. It was, therefore, from his mother that Molière inherited his love of books, and a leaning towards things of the mind. Marie Cressé was proud in linen and in costly but simple clothes. Her house was admirably furnished and richly hung. It was, therefore, from Marie Cressé that he inherited his pleasure in the splendid costumes of the actor and the pageantry of the stage. Marie Cressé had in her room a small coffer, covered with needlework, in which she kept the christening robes of her children. She was, therefore, an affectionate mother of an unusual religious sensibility. It is a pleasant reconstruction. There is no evidence, however, that Marie Cressé ever read the Plutarch; the desire to dress well is not uncommon in the mothers of quite ordinary children; and it is scarcely surprising that the daughter and wife of an upholsterer should be well provided with furniture. The small coffer with the christening robe is intimate and engaging; but there was hardly a mother in Paris who did not possess just such a coffer, and could not lay her hand upon just such a robe in time of need. Children were frequent in those days.

No less ingenuity has been expended upon Catherine Fleurette. The portrait of an ideal mother has been romantically contrasted with the portrait of a neglectful, or even odious step-mother. There is not a vestige of evidence this way or that. It is true that Molière at the age of fifty introduced a wicked step-mother into the last of his plays. But wicked step-mothers are more common in literature than in life. There is, in fact, nothing for or against poor Catherine except that she married the father of a genius and, therefore, had somehow to be interesting.

15

Molière was ten years old when his mother died. He was under the care of his step-mother only between the ages of eleven and fourteen. For any permanent relationship or influence during his childhood we must, therefore, look to his father. Jean Poquelin has fared ill at the hands of posterity. There can, nevertheless, be little doubt in the mind of a fair reader of the records that it was Jean Poquelin who was mainly responsible for the upbringing of his eldest son. Some time between 1631, when his mother was still alive, and 1636, when his step-mother died, it was decided that Molière should have the best education in France. The Jesuit college at Clermont was at that time a nursery of scholars and princes. Who decided that Molière should be entered? Unfortunately, it is impossible to fix the date. But whether the decision was taken during the life of his mother or after the death of his step-mother the attitude of Jean Poquelin is clear, and there is no reason why the father of Molière should not receive full credit. The Plutarch, after all, may have belonged to him, and he also had an excellent wardrobe. His suit of black Neapolitan taffeta is evidence as good as the seven handsome petticoats of his first wife; and if we are to search the plays of Molière for a wicked step-mother, it is lawful to note upon the way that there are to be found in them several excellent fathers, including a certain M. Jourdain, *bourgeois gentilhomme*, who had a touching faith in the value of education. Jean Poquelin, however, has had small sympathy from the lettered. He was an upholsterer. He successfully survived two wives, each of whom brought him a respectable dowry. In his business transactions he employed a solicitor. He lent money at interest to his friends and was thus a creditor. This is

16

not the portrait of a hero. Jean Poquelin has paid dearly in reputation for virtues that fail to be extraordinary.

In April, 1631, when Molière was nine years old and his mother still alive, Jean Poquelin became *tapissier ordinaire du roi*, and was sworn into office before the King's First Gentleman of the Bedchamber, Monseigneur de Souvré and Marquis de Courtenvaux. The post had previously been held by his brother Nicolas, who agreed to part with it for a consideration. Six years later Nicolas seems to have repented the transaction, and even showed a disposition to revive his claims. Whereupon Jean Poquelin, wishing to be sure of his title, very handsomely paid his brother the sum of three hundred pounds for a new agreement, "in order to avoid any litigation which might arise between them owing to the claims which the said Nicolas alleges in respect of the office." Thus Nicolas solemnly abandoned any right he might have imagined himself to possess.

The ultimate purpose of this transaction was soon to appear. Jean Poquelin, making sure of his title as *tapissier ordinaire du roi*, was thinking in terms of the dynasty. This was to be, with the King's permission, an hereditary perquisite. He had secured it for himself, and he now set about securing the reversion of it for his son. Heredity is a royal principle, and Jean Poquelin had his way. The second contract with Nicolas was signed on 29th March, 1637. Nine months later, in December of the same year, the son of Jean Poquelin was recognized as his father's heir in a royal letter of appointment dated 14th December. Four days later, Molière, then sixteen years of age, accompanied his father to Court and took the oath of service before the Marquis de Souvré.

Here, beyond any possibility of doubt, we have a firm basis for the relations of father and son. Jean Poquelin, to secure for Molière the reversion of this most respectable office bought the title twice over from his brother and used his credit with the Court to obtain a letter signed by the King himself. Meanwhile, his son, at Clermont, was enjoying the best education that money or influence could procure, and there was nothing in that education which, in the mind of Jean Poquelin, appeared to be at all inconsistent with the future place and position for which the heir of the Poquelins was intended. Jean Poquelin, returning home on the evening of December 18, 1637, in his Neapolitan taffeta, with his son beside him, might congratulate himself on a worthy ambition successfully fulfilled, and the monkeys that clambered about the pillar of his house in the Rue St. Honoré could suggest nothing to his mind except that they were a most inappropriate form of decoration for the residence of a respectable burgess of Paris. His heaven was for the moment without a cloud.

In the sixteen odd years since his first marriage Jean Poquelin had continuously prospered. The stock in his shop, valued in the marriage contract of 1621 at two hundred pounds, was inventoried on the death of his first wife in 1632 at ten times that amount. He had even begun to invest in house property, having purchased on 30th September, 1633, for 8,500 *livres* a famous house under the pillars of the market, opposite the pillory, which for over two centuries was wrongly accepted as the birthplace of Molière. To that house he would ultimately move. There, it was hoped, his son would succeed him as head of the family. The image of St. Christopher, patron of wayfarers, hung down in front of it—an excellent sign for such as might have at any moment to go on progress with the King.

The post so carefully acquired by Jean Poquelin at Court was one of consideration and honour. It carried a salary of 300 *livres* for a period of service not exceeding three months of the year. The *valet-tapissier* was a member of the King's household, lodged and fed at the King's expense. He superintended the making of the King's bed, and accompanied the royal person on its travels. He was responsible for the royal furniture and effects. His status to-day would be that of a high official in the Office of Works, with the added prestige of a post near the person of the King at a time when it was the royal policy to domesticate the high nobility of France and to convert the intimate needs and refreshments of Majesty into a magnificent and public ritual. To offer the King's shirt was to become a privilege exclusive to the best families of France. Such was Jean Poquelin and such were his ambitions. In 1637 when he took his son to Court to be sworn of the King's household, he was forty-two years of age, successful in his business, in favour with the King, and resolute that his son should carry on the family tradition. His friends and relatives, like himself, were successful tradesmen. He had been twice married—on each occasion to women of his own class. His house was not larger than his means. He had ambitions, but they were in every way appropriate to his condition. He was just in his dealings and careful to have them, even with members of his family, recorded in black and white.

It is the portrait of a normal member of the French middle class in the seventeenth century. To the son who worked beside him in the shop, who sat with him at the day's end

19

in the house of the monkeys on one of those gossip-stools inventoried as much the worse for wear, and who accompanied him to the Court in 1637 to be sworn into a decent inheritance, he presented a constant example of the virtues of moderation.

We shall discover in Molière, a name as yet unknown to father or son, the genius of good sense:

La parfaite raison fuit toute extremité
Et veut que l'on soit sage avec sobriété.

That is to be his final word on the conduct of a wise man in society. Not for nothing was he the son of Jean Poquelin III. Molière, perhaps, would have been less entirely Molière, if he had not so narrowly escaped being Jean Poquelin IV.

II

The Young Philosopher

T HE initial task of the biographer of Molière is to recover him from the mass of legend that has accumulated about his name for the last three hundred years. Every stage in his career is encumbered with anecdotes, conjectures, libels, and constructions. The ingenuity of a thousand scholars has for three centuries been applied to every reported or misreported event or saying, every inference, right or wrong, that may be related, however distantly, to his life and works. The detective interest will here be reduced to a minimum. It cannot be wholly eliminated, but only those controversies will be indicated which lead us directly to the man.

There are two biographies of Molière which can claim to be original sources. The first is the preface to the edition of his plays collected and published in 1682, nine years after his death by La Grange and Vinot. La Grange was the friend of Molière for over thirty years. He was a competent actor, a loyal and industrious colleague, a man of regular habits and scrupulous honesty. To him we owe the famous Register, in which he kept a list of the plays produced by Molière at his theatre, with a record of the receipts from each performance. This record, though scarcely more than a ledger, shows a kind heart and domestic inclinations, for among the

entries we find every now and then brief notes of the mar-
riages, births, christenings and deaths which befell the members of the company. La Grange became in later years its
orator or spokesman, and he undoubtedly relieved Molière
of much of the work and worry of management. The
preface of 1682 is brief and reticent. The good faith and
intelligence of its authors are beyond suspicion, and it is
to be implicitly trusted unless there is clear evidence that
they were in any particular instance mistaken or wilfully
misled.

Twelve years later appeared the only other biography of
Molière which can claim to be a contemporary source, the
Vie de Molière of Grimarest, first published in 1698. It
was largely based upon information obtained from Baron,
the brilliant young actor whom Molière took late into his
company and treated, towards the end of his life, almost as
an adopted son. Grimarest, however, wrote over twenty
years after the death of Molière. He listened to anyone with
a story, and enlivened his narrative with scenes, conversations and anecdotes which are obvious literary confections.
Grimarest would always believe any tale which ought, in his
opinion, to be true. He is a faithful reflection of what people
believed about Molière in 1698, but he is seldom to be
trusted as a witness either at first or second hand.

The only other contemporary sources are legal and official
documents of the period—contracts, inventories, receipts,
certificates, leases and affidavits, which a tactful biographer
will consult but forbear to intrude upon his readers; references to Molière scattered through the lives, letters and
memoirs of the time; and, most valuable of all, the contemporary libels. The libels upon Molière were infamous,

22

but they were circumstantial. The enemy was wisely exact
in details which were known or could easily be checked, and,
though ingenious in the slander of inference, he was careful
to season plausible fiction with hard fact. Often we must
refuse to believe the friendly Grimarest and wring the truth
from the heart of malice and misrepresentation.

The education of Molière is a case in point. Grimarest
relates that Molière up to the age of fourteen remained in
his father's shop, and that his parents deliberately refrained
from giving him an education which might unfit him for his
modest inheritance. The boy, however, had a maternal
grandfather with a passion for the stage, who inspired his
grandson with a distaste for upholstery. Molière was thus
provoked to beg his father for a more liberal education, and,
with the help of his grandfather, finally persuaded Jean
Poquelin to release him from the shop and send him to the
college of Clermont. This decision, according to Grimarest,
was taken in 1636.

The story is improbable in itself and makes complete non-
sense of the facts. The maternal grandfather of Molière,
Louis de Cressé, was himself an upholsterer, and had blessed
the marriage of his daughter with an upholsterer. *Noblesse
oblige.* That he should recommend his grandson to commit social suicide by becoming an actor is most unlikely.
That, as a preparation for the stage, he should recommend
the most respectable college in France is even more astonishing. But the fact that bluntly contradicts the whole story
of Grimarest has already been indicated. Jean Poquelin,
who, according to Grimarest, was persuaded to send Molière
to college in 1636 so that he might become an actor, arranged
in December of that year for his son to succeed him as *valet-*

23

tapissier du roi. It is accordingly clear that Jean Poquelin regarded his son's education at Clermont as an appropriate preparation for the office of *valet-tapissier*, or, at least, saw nothing incongruous in sending to Court a young man well-found in Latin and philosophy.

The story of Grimarest is of importance, since it affords a clue, and as it happens, a false clue, to the relations of father and son. This commonplace anecdote of a humdrum father, overborne by a boy with visions and an old man with second sight, deprives the sequel of all human significance. Truth will prove in this case to be more dramatic than fiction—more dramatic, at any rate, than the fiction of Grimarest.

The college of Clermont, founded by the Jesuits in 1551, was at the height of its fame. The Jesuits were the pioneers of modern education, the first teachers who consciously made it their aim to fit their pupils for this world rather than the next. Not only had they introduced new methods of teaching old subjects, such as Greek, Latin and rhetoric. They had also begun to insist on the importance of the modern side, including in their syllabus mathematics, physics and chemistry. They even went so far as to give prominence to the last and rarest subject to be taught in schools, intelligent reading and competent writing in the vernacular.) Nor were social accomplishments neglected. Dancing and fencing, the turning of epigrams, the composition and presentation of tragedies and ballets—all were included. The tragedies were in Latin, but the ballets needed no interpreters. In the words of a seventeenth century gossip (1658):

> La verité, sortant du puit,
> Par ses pas et ses pirouettes,
> Ravit et prudes et coquettes.

Truth issuing from her well to pirouette under the skilful direction of the reverend fathers is in pleasant accord with the Jesuitical tradition. Note, also, that ladies were present.

The Jesuits were unpopular. Their successful combination of worldliness and piety exposed them to the envy and suspicion of their competitors. But even those who publicly criticized them did not hesitate to send their sons to Clermont. The education was good and the company was better. At Clermont the sons of a burgess like Jean Poquelin, who was merely respectable, sat in the same classes with the nobility, an opportunity which wise parents, then as now, were unable to resist. The Jesuits, taking the world as they found it, made a skilful use of its social ambitions and inequalities. Blood, brains and wealth—of such was their kingdom of heaven, and they used each of these assets to attract the other. "The Jesuits," said Chateaubriand, "contrived to establish between pupils of different rank and fortune a system of patronage which turned to the advantage of science and learning." Men might be equal before the throne, but at Clermont their inequality in all other respects was candidly recognized. The sons of the nobility had each a private tutor. The Prince de Conti, socially the most distinguished of the contemporaries of Molière, had more than one. It is not recorded whether, like the Duc d'Enghien, his desk was separated from those of his fellow pupils by a gilded rail, but he was doubtless quite adequately protected from too promiscuous contacts with the sons of those who had not in the real sense of the word been "born," and whom he would meet only in the general classes and competitions. The editors of the preface of 1682 tell us that Molière "followed the Prince de Conti in all his classes." That may or may not be true. The Prince was nearly eight years younger and graduated three or four years later than Molière. We may be sure, however, that, if the son of Jean Poquelin "followed" the Prince, it was arranged that he should do so at a respectful distance.

Molière was presumably a day-boy, as Voltaire definitely asserts. The college at that time consisted of about four hundred boarders, and the day-boys were at least four times as numerous. The Jesuits liked to catch their pupils young. Normally a boy when he entered would be not more than eight years old, and he was expected to be already able to read and write. For two years he was instructed in the first principles of grammar (infima grammatica). He passed to the middle and higher grammar in his third and fourth year. Another two years were devoted to the humanities, ending with a class in rhetoric. The classical course thus lasted for six years, and was normally completed at the age of fourteen. The pupil might then take a course in philosophy, which ran for another two years. The Prince de Conti, who entered Clermont in 1637 at the age of eight, graduated in 1644 in classics and philosophy, and was at fifteen a master of arts and a little monster of learning.

Molière, according to Grimarest, was fourteen when he went to Clermont. In other words, he was entered in 1636. The authors of the preface of 1682 mention no date, but tell us that he "followed" the Prince de Conti in all his classes and won his esteem. The Prince, as we have seen, was entered in 1637. Such evidence should be conclusive, but is really very hard to accept. We are asked to believe that Molière began his studies in the humanities at an age when most scholars were completing them, and that the normal

26

procedure of a great college was substantially modified to meet the special convenience and aptitude of the son of a *marchand-tapissier*. Grimarest, on the education of Molière, is obviously astray, and for once the honest editors of 1682 appear to be endorsing a legend which is extremely doubtful. The Prince de Conti was afterwards the patron of Molière, and the Prince was at Clermont during part of the time that Molière was also present. Our biographers accordingly assume that Molière "followed the Prince in all his classes" and "won his esteem"; in other words, a boy of fourteen, the son of a tradesman, won the esteem of a boy of seven, who was, if anything, more advanced in his studies, a Prince of the House of Condé, who graduated in the presence of a cardinal. Incidentally, we shall find that the Prince, on meeting Molière in later life appeared to have little or no recollection of the boy who had "followed" him at Clermont.

If it is difficult to determine exactly when Molière entered Clermont, it is possible to ascertain more or less accurately when he left. Among the enemies of Molière who will enliven the later chapters of our story was Le Boulanger de Chalussay, petty author of a libellous comedy, *Elomire Hypocondre*, written in 1870. The play is packed with reckless slander, which extends to the birth, education, professional initiation and marriage of its victim. Chalussay has thereby achieved a dubious immortality. The education of no French schoolboy is complete till he has by heart some of the more notorious passages in which Molière is libelled as actor, author and man. Chalussay informs us that Molière left college in 1640, or a little before—in other words at the end of the college year in 1639. The normal classical course of studies at Clermont was, as we have seen, a course

27

of six years, and it was followed by a further course of philosophy which lasted for two years. "If he was a good humanist, he was an even better philosopher," declare the editors of 1682. Molière, therefore, took both courses, which normally required eight years. This would mean that he entered Clermont at the beginning of the college year in 1631, when he was eight years old, and while his mother was still alive, and not, as Grimarest asserts, in 1636, when he was fourteen and at the instance of his grandfather. His years at Clermont would thus be 1631 to 1639. This is unorthodox as biography, but it is in accordance with the curriculum and practice of the college.

Reference has been made to the plays and ballets performed at Clermont. We naturally wonder whether Molière took any part in them, and whether his mind was thus directed to the stage. The plays were from the works of Plautus, Terence and Seneca, freely adapted and interlarded with original acts by masters and pupils. Chappuzeau, in a famous history of the French Theatre published in 1674, devoted a special chapter to these fashionable entertainments and he very credibly relates that Louis XIV once witnessed a tragedy at Clermont. "All this is admirable," exclaimed one of the spectators. "I quite agree with you," responded the King, "this is my own college." The Jesuit fathers caught the saying as it flew, and the Collège de Clermont promptly became the "Collège Louis-le-Grand." Was Molière, perhaps, among the scholars who contributed to these admirable dramatic exercises? Tradition has for once neglected to improve the occasion. The editors of 1682 tell us that Molière loved and mastered the poets, reading them with particular care, especially Terence,

28

but nothing is said of any nascent inclination for the stage. Molière, at Clermont, was in love with scholarship and ardent in philosophy. The professorial tragedies, except as a means to latinity, apparently found and left him indifferent.

Needless to say, the plays at Clermont did not pass uncensured in an age when the theatre was infamous. The Abbé Voisin in a pamphlet, published in 1671, expressed the orthodox view: "It is indeed no small evil thus to encourage in young people a taste for the pleasures of the stage," and a later master of Clermont, Father Jouvency, put his foot very firmly down upon a practice which "could not fail to enervate the minds and corrupt the morals" of the young.

The philosophic studies of Molière were thorough and individual. The atoms of Epicurus and the vortices of Descartes will figure among his comic characters. But his chosen philosopher was Lucretius, and Lucretius, in the opinion of the early seventeenth century divines, was bad company. At some time in his career, beginning perhaps at Clermont, Molière translated portions of the *De Natura Rerum* into French verse, and it is believed that the editors of 1682 at first proposed to include this translation in their edition of his collected works. The publisher, however, found the Lucretian doctrine to be "opposed to the immortality of the soul," and the discreet editors not only dropped the translation, but made no reference to the matter in their biographical preface. What became of the manuscript? Grimarest affirms that Molière, fallen into a fit of passion with his cook, who had used some of it for curl-papers, thrust the remainder into the fire. Others assert that

29

his widow sold it to a publisher for 600 *livres*. Almost
certainly the translation still existed in 1682. It was in verse
of varying measures, not a continuous work, but a collection
of favourite passages. It was cordially praised by a rival
translator but all the evidence we have of its merit is a few
verses on the blindness of love incorporated by their author
in the fifth scene of the second act of *Le Misanthrope*.

Among the great masters in philosophy of the day was
the celebrated Gassendi. Gassendi was audacious in speculation and a teacher whose pupils all witness to the vital
influence of a free spirit. He was a champion of Epicurus, a
severe critic of the pedantic exercises in Aristotle which still
prevailed in many schools, and a formidable rival of Descartes. His defence of Epicurus laid him open to charges of
libertinism and his criticism of Descartes, though it was aimed
at the Cartesian method and not at its Christian conclusion,
invited the anathema of the pious. The charge of impiety
was in no way justified. Gassendi subscribed to the existence
of God and the immortality of the soul. He insisted, however, that man, though he was spirit, did not thereby cease
to be flesh. His epicureanism went no further than his
retort upon Descartes: *en m'appelant chair, vous ne m'ôtez
pas l'esprit; vous vous appelez esprit, mais vous ne quittez
pas votre corps.* This is the language of a practical philosopher and it has a familiar ring. The philosophical references of Molière all reflect this sturdy compromise between
soul and sense. Molière certainly studied and admired the
work of Gassendi and, directly or indirectly, Gassendi, the
disciple of Epicurus, completed the work of the Jesuit
fathers.

Was Molière, in fact, his pupil? Grimarest is circumstantial. While Molière was at Clermont or somewhere about that time—the dates, however, are extremely precarious—Gassendi was acting as tutor to a young man who was to be a lifelong and intimate friend of Molière. It was said in later years that Molière could scarcely live without Chapelle and that Chapelle never really recovered from the death of Molière. He was the natural son of François Lullier, a gentleman high in the public administration. He inherited from his father a Rabelaisian spirit and a wit which he reserved almost entirely for his friends. At twenty he was locked up at the instigation of two pious, but alas! natural aunts in the prison of St. Lazare for scandalous behaviour. Chapelle lampooned the aunts and wrote some admirable verses on prison life. Contemporaries all insist on the vivacity of his intelligence. He had a delicate nose for a fool, and a very resolute love of good company. He ran to philosophy in his cups and when drunk became eloquent upon the system of his master. Lyre in hand and Gassendi in his pocket,—so Voltaire pictured him. Racine, La Fontaine and Boileau were among his familiars.

Gassendi, teaching Chapelle, admitted other pupils to his class. Among them was Bernier, another friend of Molière in later life. Bernier was the least flamboyant but the most faithful of these young philosophers, and some forty years later he published a summary account of his master's doctrine. He became a great traveller, and a quarter of a century later diverted Molière with stories of Persian manners and the great Moghul.

The story of Grimarest is based upon no other evidence than the friendship of Molière for these two men. Molière, says Grimarest, met them both at Clermont, and Gassendi, struck with his "docility and penetration," admitted him to his class. The tale is further adorned by the swaggering intrusion of Cyrano de Bergerac with his broken nose, swearing horribly that he, too, will be a philosopher. Wounded in two sieges, a fearsome duellist and a notable musketeer, he was henceforth to devote himself to letters. Perhaps already he had in his pocket a copy of *Le Pédant Joué*, the play in which he mocked his previous master, Jean Grangier, principal of Beauvais, terrible to the youth of the period, a redoubtable performer with the rod and a great believer in Latin. It is recorded by Boileau that Molière loved Cyrano, and the friendship is authentic whether they met under Gassendi or not. It is a high tribute to the teaching and personality of Gassendi that he secured the respect of this turbulent spirit. The *Voyage dans la Lune* of Cyrano bears the stamp of the philosopher. The lunacy is Cyrano, but the doctrine is Gassendi.

The legend of Gassendi and his class of free spirits is attractive, and with a little shuffling of dates and straining of the evidence it is just possible to accord it the benefit of the doubt. The rigid seeker after truth, however, will regard the whole story as one which had to be invented because it so obviously ought to be true. Gassendi was the first philosopher to popularize the application of commonsense to abstract speculation. His pupils were all of a Bohemian turn —Chapelle, who caught his glimpse within the tavern; Bernier, the traveller in outlandish parts; Cyrano, the brilliant adventurer who imported into letters the manners of the guardroom. What was more natural than to add Molière to the list—especially as Molière was familiar with the doctrines of Gassendi, the friend in later life of all

32

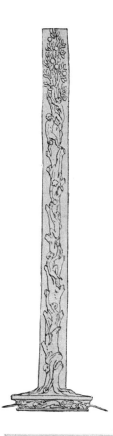

*J'ay receu de Monsieur de penautier la somme de
quatre mille liures ordonnées aux comediens par
Messieurs des Estats. faict a pezenas ce 17ᵉ
decembre mil six cent cinquante.* Moliere. /

pour 4000ᵗᵗ

three of his pupils and a crowning example to his contemporaries of the awful results of evil communications in youth.

On leaving Clermont, or, if you will, the seminar of Gassendi, Molière studied the law. He appears to have been called to the bar, and even to have practised on one occasion. All the contemporary authorities agree, while Grimarest is unusually categorical. He tells us that, certain persons having denied that Molière was ever a barrister, he had consulted the family who had positively assured him of the fact. These legal studies, however, may have been as summary as we care to make them. Chalussay implies they were serious, but at that time the law was undoubtedly an ass. Any young man who could smatter in Latin and pay the necessary fees might be called. Charles Perault, the contemporary of Molière, who took his degree in law in 1651, has written an amusing account of how he received his licence. Arriving at Orléans at ten o'clock in the evening, along with two other candidates, he beat up the examiners. A servant demanded from the window whether they had brought their fees with them, and, on receiving assurances in the affirmative, roused the learned doctors, three in number, who at once with robes hastily thrown over shirts and nightcaps admitted the young men and submitted them to a brief oral examination. Marriage, hazarded one of them, is a legal union between man and woman. The doctors were satisfied, the fees were paid, and three happy barristers retired. This, of course, does not mean that a mastery of law was a small matter under Louis XIV. It took, indeed, three years to make a competent barrister. It did mean, however, that anyone who desired to write himself a barrister might

33

do so without breaking his young wits upon the mysteries of the profession.

Matrimonium est ligitima maris et feminae conjunctio— Molière obviously took his legal studies further than that. In his plays he deals familiarly with legal mysteries and he never makes a mistake.

Molière was now nineteen years of age. He had served as his father's apprentice in the workshop of the Rue St. Honoré, and was the sworn successor to his father's office at Court. He had received a thorough grounding in classics and philosophy. Latin was his second language. He had Terence by heart. He had witnessed and perhaps participated in the college entertainments. He had studied the law even more than was necessary, and been called to the bar. Molière from the age of ten to the age of twenty was, in a word, being thoroughly well educated and acquainting himself with the nature of things. The rest is legend. The stories that associate him closely in boyhood with his future patron the Prince de Conti, or his future comrades, Chapelle, Bernier and the rest, are in all probability constructive fictions. More especially there is not a shred of evidence that he had at this time any sense of his vocation for the theatre. There is as yet nothing to suggest that the son of Jean Poquelin at twenty was not prepared to fulfil his father's ambition.

III

Sudden Conversion

NOT far from the house of the monkeys, Rue St. Honoré, in the same parish of St. Eustache, lived a family in striking contrast with that of the prosperous and respectable Jean Poquelin. Joseph Béjart, an official in the Department of Forestry, was a man of easy manners and uneasy circumstances. He had married in 1616, and on his death in 1642 left to his widow, Marie Hervé, an inheritance which with great presence of mind she very promptly renounced as likely to be richer in liabilities than in assets. Eleven children had been born of the marriage —more than Joseph could either discipline or afford. These young people, or as many of them as survived, were fending for themselves in various ways, but all had a passion for the theatre. Even Joseph is suspect. In moments of expansion he called himself the Sieur de Belleville, which may imply that at some time or other he had been, or had believed himself to be, an actor.

The Béjarts made no secret of their delinquencies. They flaunted their misdemeanours at the parish font, and recorded them in certificates drawn in good and proper form.

The eldest daughter of the house was Madeleine. At eighteen she was addressing verses to Rotrou, dramatic author, the most considerable of the predecessors of Corneille, assuring him that his dying Hercules would render him immortal. At nineteen she was the mistress of the Comte de Modène, soldier and sonneteer, political adventurer and amateur of the stage. When, at twenty, she became a mother, there was no apology. On the contrary, there was a handsome christening, at which the Count's paternity was publicly acknowledged, and the child received for godparents her natural grandmother and the legitimate son of her own illegitimate father. Such a ceremony, to say the least, was lacking in reticence. It indicated, moreover, that Madeleine's behaviour was viewed with complacency not only by the Count and his legitimate heirs, but by the mother of Madeleine herself—who, by the standards of Jean Poquelin and the decent burgesses of Paris, should have been hiding a diminished head. We will not plead the licence of the times or urge that conduct might in the seventeenth century be published which in a less candid society is decently obscured. Jean Poquelin was of the middle classes, and the middle classes are insensitive to moral variations.

Madeleine Béjart, born in 1618, and four years older than Molière, was a mother and a woman of experience at a time when he was still thumbing his philosophers at Clermont. She was handsome in her reddish way, more than commonly intelligent, with a genius for friendship. She had been the mistress of the Comte de Modène, and in all probability became the mistress of Molière. In neither case, however, was the amatory relationship of vital importance. Her loves were for a season, but her affections were for life. She was the friend for over thirty years both of her undoubted and of her hypothetical lover. Madeleine was of an even and tolerant disposition, facile, perhaps, in gallantry,

36

but steadfast in companionship. Her passion—if she had one—was for the theatre; the abiding care of her life was for the interests and happiness of Molière. Posterity owes her a debt which it has frequently misinterpreted. Too often it has preferred to emphasize the charms which seduced a respectable young man to follow an infamous profession and neglected to discover the friend and colleague whose affection and competence were his strongest and most reliable support from the moment when their fortunes were first united.

When and where did she first encounter Molière? There were a hundred ways and places. Sooner or later everyone in Paris must cross from the right to the left bank of the river; and, for the actress as for the schoolboy, the fine new bridge of Henri Quatre—still the Pont Neuf—with its demilunes, in the shelter of which mountebanks and pedlars, famous throughout France, exhibited their wares and their talents, would be the chosen route. This was the cynosure of vagrant Paris, and Madeleine, strikingly red, undoubtedly handsome, covertly observed by all her neighbours, splendidly indifferent to all eyes and whispers, moving across the bridge to the great fair of St. Germain was not a person to be missed. Molière without any pointing of the gossips, might well have pursued her—at least with his eyes. Tallemant de Réaux, a contemporary gossip, is explicit on the subject: "a boy named Molière left the benches of the Sorbonne to follow her; he was for a long while in love with her and married her in the end." The boy was not yet named Molière; he was never at the Sorbonne; he was not long in love with Madeleine, and he never married her. But there is a kernel of truth in the statement.

37

The autumn of 1641 was clearly a critical moment. The son of Jean Poquelin was ready to face the world. He was nineteen; his education was complete; he was a barrister and the King's *valet-tapissier* elect, with a respectable trade at his fingers' ends. He had earned the right to breathe a while before serious employment. There had not, so far, been any authentic whisper of the stage. But Madeleine was passing and within a year Molière had decided to become an actor.

That Madeleine counted for something in this event is clear. She revealed to him that irresistible vocation which was to be evident in every subsequent action of his life. But the vocation had always been there. The editors of 1682 are explicit on the subject: "On quitting his legal studies he chose the profession of an actor owing to the irresistible vocation which he felt for the theatre." That the son of Jean Poquelin became Molière for love of a handsome woman is a legend, which could be cherished only by a nation which makes it a point of honour to practise a literary eroticism which seldom accords either with its temperament or its history.

What persuasions, previous to his acquaintance with Madeleine, had Molière received? All is conjecture. It is impossible to do more than portray the influences at hand and imagine the effects for ourselves. The legendary grandfather addicted to the theatre and secretly encouraging his grandson to aim at the stage has been already rejected, and there is no record of young Poquelin showing any special interest in the theatrical performances at Clermont. Neither at home nor at school was Molière prepared for an apparently sudden conversion at nineteen years of age. The

libellous author of *Elomire* suggests a third possibility.
Molière on his way to Clermont must often have loitered
upon the Pont Neuf before the booths of the showmen,
have paused amid the crowded alleys of the Fair of St.
Germain, or have stood in the Place Dauphiné where
Mondor was conjurer and Tabarin was making his name a
synonym for disorderly enjoyment. Was it thus, from the
mountebanks of the fair and the market, that Molière received his first impressions? The libellist is circumstantial.
He affirms that Molière, on completing his studies, solicited
employment from Bary and Orvietan, who were the most
popular of the mountebanks of St. Germain; that he was
even ready to appear before the public as a snake-swallower;
that he was called by the brothers of Madeleine *le mangeur
de vipères*. All this is pure malice. It is true that the
father of Molière inherited two boxes within the enclosure
of St. Germain, home of the Théâtre de la Foire where Bary
and Orvietan were accustomed to perform; but Molière was
drawn, not to the farce of the fair, but to the tragic theatre
of Bellerose and Mondory, and there is here a world of influences to explore.

Molière, born in 1622, could hardly have frequented the
theatre before 1635, and the utmost we can say of him in
boyhood is that he had special opportunities of doing so.
One of the friends of Jean Poquelin, also an upholsterer,
was a master of the *Confrérie de la Passion* and in the theatre
of the Hôtel de Bourgogne, owned by the *Confrérie*, the
masters had a private box reserved for them and their
friends. In all probability it was from this box that Molière
first looked down upon the stage.

The *Confrérie de la Passion* was a survival from the Middle Ages, which somehow contrived to live for at least a hundred years after it had ceased to be anything but a privileged nuisance. It cannot, however, be neglected by the historian of any phase of the French theatre for the Comédie Française is to-day its heir. As its name implies, it had first been organized as an association for the performance of mediæval mysteries—a guild of amateurs, acting for their own pleasure and the public edification, who paid their own expenses and managed their own affairs under an elaborate system of regulations. Its charter served as a model for the contract under which Molière first entered the profession, and that contract became in turn the basis of the constitution, many times revised, of the Comédie Française as it exists to-day.

Miracle plays, which after the renaissance became offensive to public taste, had been prohibited by Act of Parliament in 1548. This should have been the end of the *Confrérie*, but it was only the beginning of a long struggle with the professional theatre which lasted until three years after the death of Molière. The *Confrérie* abandoned its own performances in 1578, but kept a firm grip of its privileges. These included a monopoly of the control of public theatrical performances in Paris. The submission of public amusement to a system of monopoly survived well into the seventeenth century, and the privileges of the *Confrérie* were confirmed by the Kings of France successively from Henry II to Louis XIII. No company, unless the King or some powerful patron took it under his special protection, might lawfully settle in Paris without permission of the brotherhood. A troop desiring to perform in public was thus compelled to lease the Hôtel de Bourgogne at a fair rent—two crowns to the brotherhood per day—or, if it dared to compete with the lessees of the brotherhood, might find itself subject to prosecution and arrest. The professional actors naturally resented a monopoly for which no reasonable pretext could be found, except that they were rogues and vagabonds and must, therefore, in mediæval fashion, have a respectable surety for their good behaviour. Unauthorized companies disputed the monopoly; the company enjoying it tried always to suppress the interlopers. For a hundred years there were petitions, protests, riots and open breaches of the law, so that Henry IV, a friend of the theatre, found it necessary to prohibit persons quite explicitly from throwing stones, powders or other missiles upon the stage.

Various companies came and went at the Hôtel de Bourgogne during the seventy or eighty years that followed the abolition of the mysteries in 1548. Finally, however, we find in more or less permanent occupation of the theatre a group of players which early in the seventeenth century began to call itself the *Troupe Royale*. This company was in 1629, by an express order of the King in Council, accorded a lease for three years of the Hôtel de Bourgogne, subsequently renewed from time to time, at a yearly rental of 2,400 *livres*. Thus were established the royal players, whose performances Molière saw as a young man and with whom he was to enter upon a bitter rivalry in after years.

In the period immediately preceding its permanent establishment, the Troupe royale had alternated at the Hôtel de Bourgogne with another company under the Cornelian actor Mondory which subsequently settled at the Théâtre du Marais. In law there should have been only one theatre in Paris—the Hôtel de Bourgogne. In fact there were several of which only the Théâtre du Marais need for the moment be mentioned. It owed the toleration it enjoyed to the two men who had done most for the redemption of the stage—Corneille whose *Melite* produced at the Marais was his first success in Paris and Richelieu who esteemed Mondory, the leader of the company, above all other players. The Marais is of special interest to the biographers of Molière. Madeleine Béjart was familiar with several of its actors and authors and possibly she had even appeared in its productions.

What would be the impressions of the young scholar of Clermont sitting in the box of the *Confrérie* at the Hôtel de Bourgogne in about the year 1635? He would enter the theatre in the early afternoon; the fashionable hour of performance was beginning to advance, but the authorities still insisted upon the play concluding before darkness fell. The room was a long and narrow rectangle. Two galleries ran around the walls upon three sides of it, and on the fourth side was the stage. The floor was an open space, a large pit where the bulk of the audience stood during the performance or wandered restlessly about during the intervals.

The performance has not yet begun. The late arrivals are entering the boxes and galleries. These are respectable burgesses, or even noble lords, who have not yet contracted the bad habit of sitting upon the stage. These privileged ones have paid perhaps twenty *sols* for their seats, unless, claiming to be of the King's household, they have, under protest from the doorkeeper, ruffled their way in for nothing. The people packed together in the pit have paid ten *sols* for admission by Act of Parliament. They are restless and uncomfortable. The stage is not easily seen, for there is no slope to the floor. The hall is ill-lighted with a huge chandelier of tallow candles, hanging before the curtain. No respectable women are present and the jests which fly about the crowded floor are of a masculine persuasion. The audience is in a holiday mood, but a quarrel may break out on the smallest provocation and the good people in the pit must look well to their pockets. Plying their wares in the hall and the corridors are the licensed vendors of wine, drinks cold or hot according to the season, sweetmeats and oranges. Standing against the wall near the stage, beside a group of barrels full of water, is a man in livery with a pair of snuffers. He is the fireman, in charge of the lighting, and, if the candles are burning badly, he will lower away the great chandelier, suspended over a pulley in front of the stage, and snuff them carefully in order to avoid an ill odour in the house.

The audience is impatient and the tragedy is not yet ready. Nor would it be possible to start a tragedy before these ribald folk. From between the curtains advances a single figure. This is the orator of the troop. He comes to deliver the prologue or harangue, which soon will be out of fashion, but which still delights a generation which has listened to such masters in that kind as Bruscambille. With a tactful impudence he rallies the people upon their behaviour. Will the gentlemen who have apparently come for exercise go for a walk elsewhere? Will those who desire to listen prepare to do so, and those who seem bent upon enjoying their own wit now give way to the players? A tragedy is to be performed—a very serious matter. The author is praised; the piece is outlined; announcements are made concerning the actors who are about to take the stage. Then, perhaps, prior

to the play, as between the Acts, there is music—two violins,
a drum and a flute.

The audience at last is quiet and ready for the play. The
tragedy itself is still, perhaps, by Alexander Hardy, the first
secular dramatist of France, but more likely by one of the
authors who led the tragic muse through Rotrou to Corneille. It is a fine robustious performance—stuffed with
kings and princes, ladies in a fine passion, agonies of mind
and the major interests, such as love, death, the conquest of
self or of the world. The actors fight in that narrow room
for an effective hearing. Perhaps it is Bellerose—elegant,
inclined to be lachrymose but necessarily loud. As a physical feat alone his performance is remarkable. Mondory,
the tragic actor of the Marais, burst a blood vessel and died
of paralysis as the result of his efforts, and Montfleury, the
successor of Bellerose at the Hôtel de Bourgogne, was described by his contemporaries as dying not of fever or the
gout, as the doctors alleged, but of *Andromaque*.

Was the young Molière, watching this performance, swept
away on the high tide of tragic passion, or was he, even as
a boy, inclined to mock at the emphasis and exaggeration
of the royal troop? Possibly he listened even as early as this
with reservations. That, however, was of small importance.
He had looked, albeit from the front of the house, upon
the mimic world of the stage, and these first impressions
could not fail to be vivid and enduring. It would be still
more interesting to know what thus early he made of the
King's tragedians, when, upon the conclusion of the serious
play, they put on, as custom required, the motley of popular
farce so that the audience might be sent away in good
humour. The founders of the royal troop had, at the be-

ginning of the century, been more celebrated for their farce than for their tragedy. Robert Guérin, tragedian, with his comrades Hugh Guéru and Henri Legrand, were more popular among the burgesses of Paris in the first quarter of the seventeenth century as clowns than as heroes. Corneille had not yet lifted tragedy to its pride of place; and, in order to win the affections of the public, these actors must discard the buskin for the comic mask. Robert Guérin, clad in a tunic drawn tight about the waist that gave him the appearance of a cottage loaf, his face like a full moon, trousers that stopped short at the ankles, shoes with enormous rosettes and a little round hat worn coquettishly on one side would set the house upon a roar, while Hugh Guéru, veritable enemy of sadness, as he is styled in a famous broadsheet, launched his witticisms from a mask impressively immobile, and Henri Legrand, whose humour was of a sour and elderly complexion, in keeping with his slender legs, mouth drooping at the corners and suit of solemn black, completed the picture. For laughing purposes these actors discarded their tragic names. Thousands who cared little for Guérin, Guéru and Legrand adored them as Gros Guillaume, Turlupin and Gaultier-Garguille. Another famous figure was Bruscambille, master of the harangue, in whose orations to the unruly public, preserved for posterity, are embalmed all the woes and tribulations of the actor before the theatre became respectable, his epigram on the life of a comedian being the last pre-Cornelian word upon these pioneer years of the stage: *une vie sans soucis et quelque fois sans six sous.* Finally, there was the Capitaine Fracasse, ancient Pistol of France, with his tall bonnet, enormous ruff, sword thrust aggressively behind him, fierce

moustache, a veritable army in buckram. The shades of
these famous clowns still lingered about the Hôtel de Bourgogne, and Molière, who may even have seen them as a boy,
certainly beheld the inheritors of their tradition.

During the first quarter of the seventeenth century the
French theatre was in transition. Little had as yet been
done to raise it in public esteem or procure for it the brief
period of splendour in the course of which Corneille, Molière
himself and Racine made it the principal glory of France.
The critical years lay still in the immediate future. Fortunately for the stage, however, the great Richelieu, in the
intervals of statecraft, had assumed the quill of a tragedian.
Not only did he write plays but he built a theatre for their
becoming presentation—the first theatre constructed expressly for dramatic performances in France,—destined, as
we shall see, to be the first house of Molière. This was
the *Palais du Cardinal*, afterwards the *Palais Royal*, in
which all the masterpieces of Molière from *L'Ecole des
Maris* to *Le Malade Imaginaire* were first given to the
public and whence he was carried to die within a few hours
of his last appearance upon any stage. The enthusiasm of
Richelieu for the theatre was soon to be embodied in a public
act. Clearly a profession which included the master of
France among its authors and to which the great Corneille
was beginning to contribute his masterpieces could no longer
be execrated even in theory, and in 1641, four years after
the first performance of *Le Cid*, Louis XIII, taking the
Troupe Royale under his protection and according it a pension of 1,200 *livres* a year, published a famous edict in
which the theatre was acknowledged to be a reasonable form
of diversion and in which the royal desire was expressed that

46

the calling of an actor should no longer be deemed to prejudice his standing and honour as a possibly respectable member of society. This curious edict, however, though it formed a landmark in the progress of the stage, proclaimed rather than abolished the strange anomaly of the actor's position in face of society and the church; and, in appreciating the step which Molière was about to take, it is essential to realize that the status of the actor, honoured and cherished by the Court, adored from this time forward by the public, remained ambiguous. Molière, deciding to become an actor, could be under no illusion. The theatre, theoretically infamous, might be tolerated by the King's lieges with a quiet mind after 1641, but the attitude of the church, of local authorities and of the respectable public could not be changed in a generation or even in a century.

The attitude of the church, in particular, was never really modified, though from time to time it was more indulgent than the canon prescribed. The actor was an excommunicated person. He was only admitted to the sacraments as an act of indulgence. Upon his death bed he was required formally to renounce his profession before he was allowed to receive them. If he died unable or unwilling to comply with this formality, he was in law deprived of Christian burial, which could only be accorded him by connivance or special dispensation. Full advantage was taken of the canonical regulations by the more fanatical clergy, more especially in the provinces; and the severest penalties were exacted in any case where the players offended clerical prejudices, where they competed in any way with ecclesiastical diversions, or where, as might well happen, their performances had little relish of salvation. Thus in 1666 at Narbonne it was announced from the pulpit that there would be no sacraments or sermons for any persons who attended the performances of a company which had been rash enough to open a theatre in Lent. The clergy in Paris, in view of the increasing toleration of the Court, were less drastic, but in 1624 the Archbishop of Paris declared in full synod that players according to the canon stood deprived of the sacraments and of Christian burial. Nor was this attitude of the church in any way softened out of consideration for the known piety and good works of individual players. The supreme instance of Christian zeal misapplied in a particular case was that of the pious actor Rosimont, who died towards the end of the century. He was a man of exemplary life, more than ordinarily devout, and in 1680 he had published a *Life of the Saints for Every Day of the Year*. To remove any possible stumbling-block for the orthodox, he had issued it under a pseudonym; and so well did he conceal his pious act that not even the priests whom he edified were aware of his authorship, with the result that upon his demise they promptly refused him Christian burial, as the canon prescribed—a conspicuous demonstration that it is not always safe for a Christian to conceal from his right hand what his left may be doing. Bossuet, the most illustrious enemy of the theatre—who, on the passing of Molière, declaimed from the pulpit "woe unto them that laugh for they shall weep" —categorically affirmed that it was the constant practice of the church to deprive of the sacraments during life and in death all those who acted upon the stage unless they renounced their profession, adding that these unfortunate persons might only be admitted to communion as public sinners.

Molière, choosing to be a professional actor, could not

48

fail to be thoroughly familiar with the clerical point of view and even more intimately acquainted with the attitude of the respectable middle classes of the town. Hitherto he had known the theatre only from outside, seen it with the eyes of his father, felt no irresistible premonitions. He had not yet passed the fatal proscenium whence for the born actor there is no return. It was Madeleine, the admirer of Rotrou, ambitious to shine in tragedy, already committed to the mimic world, who led him to take the irrevocable step. The conviction was probably as sudden as it was irresistible. There came perhaps a moment when, potentially the lover of Helen, the friend of Alexander, the disciple of Socrates, he saw the varied pageant of life narrowing down to the sole existence of Jean Poquelin IV, *valet-tapissier du roi;* and just at that moment the stage was revealed to him as a lively mimicry of the thousand frustrated lives that are carried within the breast of a single spectator. He was a born actor, and for the born actor the mood in which the public intensifies and extends its emotions through the glamour of the stage is the condition of his being. It invests every sordid or childish detail of his profession with a passionate significance. The son of Jean Poquelin had suddenly to make a choice: Jean Poquelin IV *valet-tapissier du roi,* sitting at ease in the box of the *Confrérie,* occasionally diverting himself with the joys and distresses of that mimic world, or the thousand men he had it in him still to be—he did not know their names as yet—Sganarelle, Harpagon, Alceste, Tartuffe, Don Juan. They are with him as he climbs the stage to meet, perhaps, Floridor at the Marais, or Montfleury at the Hôtel de Bourgogne. The candles are put out one by one, and the long hall is full of shadows. The

49

voices of the players, behind the partition, discarding their splendid dresses, are heard in jest or lamentation. The leader of the company is giving his instructions for the morrow to the musicians, to the mistress of the robes, to the actress who is to die for him shortly in the presence of a hundred spectators. The son of Jean Poquelin, *valet-tapissier*, has, not yet consciously, perhaps, made his choice, but it was said of Chatham that his first glimpse into the royal closet intoxicated him—which was only fitting in a King's minister. For the man who would be Molière one glimpse within the green-room would suffice.

Meanwhile, his father, though as yet unaware that his plans were doomed, had begun to take alarm. This association of his son with the Béjarts was most unfortunate. Madeleine was notoriously of an easy disposition, and there was every prospect of a serious entanglement. Jean Poquelin had not sent his son to Clermont and had him sworn of the King's household that he might consort with a family which was socially indiscreet and notoriously far from prosperous. During all that winter of 1641-1642 the intimacy with the Béjarts was, nevertheless, increasing, and it began, perhaps, to be hinted that the boy's infatuation for the actress might become a passion for the stage.

What was to be done? King Louis XIII in the winter of 1641-1642 was at Narbonne, where he was likely to remain for the next six months. Normally Jean Poquelin should have gone south in April to take his term of service as *valet-tapissier*, which ran from April to June. Why not send as deputy his young successor in office? His son would thus be well out of the shot and danger of desire and perhaps acquire an interest in the work for which he had been so

carefully prepared. The alarms and pleasures of Court
and camp could scarcely fail to hold and interest a young
man of nineteen, new to incidents of travel. The appeal
of the booths and playhouses of Paris and the scandalous
prestige of the Béjarts, a fine theme for the gossips of St.
Eustache, would seem of small account after three months
in the royal household.

The prescription was excellent. The scholar of Clermont,
on service with the King in the spring of 1642, must have
had his fill of political excitement. The King's army was
besieging Perpignan, and in June, 1642, came the sensational
conspiracy and arrest of Cinq Mars. Tradition assigns
Molière, without a shadow of foundation or probability, an
active part in these tragic incidents, alleging that he con-
cealed the hunted nobleman in a cupboard within a few yards
of the King's bedchamber. All this is purely legendary and
profoundly false. Molière was to spend the better part of
his life in close touch with the Court and within the shadow
of high political decisions. But he remained profoundly
indifferent to politics as professionally understood. The
events at Perpignan were as the passing of Fortinbras.

The office he held was no sinecure. The King on progress
took with him two complete sets of furniture, and the *valet-
tapissier* combined the duties of a billeting officer with
those of a quartermaster. "When the Court is in progress,"
ran the royal book of household instructions, "the first and
second bedchamber follow each other alternately. There
are two complete bedchambers—two beds, two sets of furnishings and appointments. The first bedchamber is despatched on the day before the Court sets forth, so that
the King, arriving the next day at his destination, finds his

room already prepared; the second bedchamber meanwhile goes forward to the next place of halt—and so forth. Thus of the two officers who are serving their quarterly term of office, there is always one who is responsible for the first bedchamber and one who accompanies the second."

All this was invaluable experience. Molière, *valet-tapissier du roi,* was learning to organize a provincial tour. From camp to camp, from one small town to another, he must shift the royal scene. The properties were more substantial, but was the play, for him, more real than those with which he was not long afterwards to tour the long white roads of Provence? Jolting over these same roads, with horses and waggons impressed for the royal service, he had leisure to reflect upon the decision that lay before him on his return. This, perhaps, was his last effort, made in good faith, to meet the wishes of his father. There was much to observe, new types of men in this generous south, a landscape that surprised the townsman at every turn; men of authority about the King and his ministers; the fortunes of war and policy; the gossip of the Court; the life of the camp; a scene that changed with every day that passed. His father might well have hoped that his son's fancy would be caught and held; that after such an experience he would not readily surrender his birthright. Madeleine and her brothers, down at heel, living on the edge of Bohemia, hungrily following the fortunes of their handsome sister, should compare but ill with the splendour of Louis, and the ruffling lords who had not yet felt effectively the hand of Richelieu. Passing from spring to summer were the vines and olives of France; the young man was witnessing an abundant, unfamiliar life in a new setting. Yet, as the sequel showed, he was undeterred,

52

almost untouched, by this experience. He observed the great men and their foibles; they were to be his subjects. He consorted in good fellowship with the people of the country; they were to be the first of his friends in front. He might even pause with approval on his way from town to town to admire the disposition of hill and stream. But certainly, when he paused, you may be sure that the landscape had somewhere a man in it. Inanimate nature remained for him, then as ever, inanimate. The only scene he would ever really love was a scene that could be shifted. Nature, for Molière, first to last, was a backcloth. We are not to imagine him held breathless by wide horizons, or creeping river or the shapes of hills. It was, rather, at such a moment that suddenly, perhaps, he would remember the Pont Neuf and the pillars of the market.

Molière returned to Paris in the late summer of 1642. The experiment had failed, and the failure was in a few months to be confessed. For a short while yet appearances were saved, but Jean Poquelin must already have seen how things were going. There began to be long, and for the moment mysterious, councils at the house of the Béjarts; all through that autumn projects must surely have been aired and means discussed. Finally, in December, the decision was taken, and Jean Poquelin was informed. His son had decided to go upon the stage, and was not to be moved from his purpose. The necessary plans had been laid. He was proposing to enter into partnership with the Béjarts and their friends, to form a company, to assist in financing it, to assume joint responsibility for a theatre, to identify himself with the hazards and disabilities of a group no member of which had much or anything to lose. For Jean

53

Poquelin this was the end of hopes which he had nursed for many years. His son was proposing to abandon an honourable position in order to become a social outlaw, very possibly a beggar.

The first reaction is easily inferred. Jean Poquelin, the whole family of the Poquelins, two sets of maternal relatives, all the survivors and descendants of the Homeric gathering that had witnessed the marriage contract of Marie Cressé in 1621, tried by every possible means to turn the young man from his purpose. Tradition credibly affirms that Poquelin turned in his distress to Georges Pinel, friend of the family, who, it is said, had taught his son to read and write, and that the good man, accepting the mission, was sent to continue the persuasions which Poquelin had himself exhausted. The sequel was the first of the comedies by Molière. The master, sent to convert his pupil, was himself converted. He joined the troop that was assembling at the house of the Béjarts, and his signature, some months later, was duly affixed to the contract under which it was constituted.

The way in which father and son met this crisis in their relations is a credit to them both. There is no evidence of any bitterness or estrangement on either side. The position had somehow to be faced and regulated—reduced to black and white, as was the custom in any orderly and responsible family. Jean Poquelin might, if he had wished, have opposed his son's project and refused him the means of carrying it into effect. The boy was only twenty-one, still, therefore, a minor, the legal majority being at that time twenty-five. For the moment, however, Poquelin acquiesced, though he had doubtless not abandoned all hope of ultimately retrieving the prodigal. In six months the company would probably be bankrupt, and the young actor would tire rapidly of the false glitter and shrill accents of the stage; while Madeleine, who had seduced him from respectability, would, if report was to be relied upon, soon be looking elsewhere for the protection she so badly needed.

Jean Poquelin affected, therefore, to yield, and the result was a legal document duly signed between father and son on January 6, 1642. Molière surrendered the reversion of the office of *valet-tapissier du roi* in favour of such other of his father's children as the latter might select. To this renunciation stood appended a receipt for 630 *livres*. The son acknowledges that he has received this sum from his father on account of monies which may be due to him from his mother's estate, or which he may ultimately inherit. The money is to be devoted to a purpose unspecified in the document, but referred to as something already agreed upon.

The purpose of this advance was declared for posterity six months later on June 30, 1643, in the articles of association whereby the son of Jean Poquelin became one of the founders of the Illustrious Theatre.

IV

THE ILLUSTRIOUS THEATRE

THE company of which Molière definitely became a member in the summer of 1643, in calling itself the Illustrious Theatre, could scarcely have suspected, however young and ardent its members, that its name would thereafter be so seriously justified. The hyperbole of its title was purely formal, the word illustrious being at that time a modish epithet which might be assumed in all modesty by any public enterprise. The articles under which it was constituted, modelled upon those of the *Confrérie de la Passion*, perpetuated a system of management and finance which survived even the Revolution and the hand of Napoleon. Its statutes were in all essentials similar to those of the Comédie Française to-day. Few governments have been able to resist tinkering with the constitution of the French national theatre. But the main principles have never been seriously altered. When Molière died in 1674, his company, still organized on the same lines as the Illustrious Theatre, was an association of players, each of whom was entitled to a share of the proceeds of their work, and all of whom were subject to a discipline administered by general agreement in the common interest. Its members had definite rights and obligations, such as the right to a pension on retirement, or the obligation to accept such acting parts as were assigned to them. It was also, by that time, a pensioner of the State and subordinated in certain respects to a representative of the head of the State. The young people who assembled to sign the contract of June 30, 1643, were laying the foundations of a theatre which was to form an historic link between the *Confrérie de la Passion,* which had been under royal protection from the beginning of the sixteenth century, and the Comédie Française of the Third Republic.

What are the main provisions of this historic deed? Each of the associates contributes to the funds of the company and enjoys in return a share of the profits. No member may withdraw or be dismissed except at four months' notice. Plays are cast and all business decisions are taken by a majority vote of the company. Anyone who leaves the company by friendly arrangement, after giving the necessary notice, is entitled to withdraw his contributions to its funds and to receive a sum representing the value of his share in the properties; anyone expelled from the company for insubordination or negligence forfeits his interests. A player who deserts the company or refuses to carry out his undertakings under the contract is bound to provide compensation for any prejudice it may thereby sustain and to pledge his property as security for such compensation. Finally, the signatories engage to pay to the company the sum of 300 *livres* if they should withdraw before the theatre is actually opened.

This, then, was a joint and corporate undertaking, financed by its members, who were bound by articles safeguarding them from the desertion or indiscipline of their colleagues. Of special and personal interest is a provision that Madeleine is to choose her own part. It places her quite definitely as the leading spirit. Another purely personal provision is that the heroes shall be impersonated alternately by Poquelin (Molière) and two other members of the company. There is also a special clause providing that all the signatories shall subscribe to their undertakings as though they were legally majors. Molière himself was a minor, so was one, at least, of the Béjarts.

The company which signed this contract on June 30, 1643, was assembled in the house of Marie Hervé in the Rue de la Perle. There was not a member of whom Jean Poquelin could approve, with the exception, perhaps, of Maître Mareschall, *avocat en Parlement*, who was there for the merely professional purpose of seeing that the document was drawn, signed and witnessed in due and proper form. Denys Beys, first of the signatories, was the brother of Charles Beys, author of tragi-comedies. He died five years later of over-drinking. Germain Clerin was the brother of an actress and Catherine des Urlis was the sister of an actor, both at the Théâtre du Marais. Nicolas Bonnenfant had twice belied his name by failing to give satisfaction to the two successive employers with whom his family had placed him. Finally, there was Georges Pinel, the renegade writing master, and Madeleine Malingre the daughter of a carpenter.

Determined efforts have been made to give to this small band of adventurers an air of respectability. The lame, the halt, and the blind, says the libellous author of *Elomire*. No, say the apologists, this was a company of young gentlemen amateurs who, having acted for their own amusement, now decided to adopt a profession which was within the next generation to be held in honour. *"Enfants de famille,"* says

58

the Preface of 1682, thereby suggesting that these young people had been in the real sense of the word "born." "*Quelques bourgeois de Paris*," says Grimarest, using a title which was not quite so easily earned as all that. These are praiseworthy but wholly misguided efforts to break the social fall of our hero by means of discreet implications. The son of Jean Poquelin was no gentleman amateur engaging in a pastime or, still less, embarking upon a reputable career. Nor had these associates of his any claims to gentility. All were clinging to the skirts of a profession whose members were tolerated by society if they were amusing, petted if they were fair, and ranked by the reputable burgesses of Paris with sword swallowers, pedlars and rat catchers, with the additional qualification that they were almost certainly damned. Molière was henceforth of the fraternity. He was renouncing name and position, abandoning the stage of the world for the world of the stage, a deliberate professional, with all the contempt of the professional for the casual interloper into his mystery. The son of Jean Poquelin first signed himself the Sieur de Molière upon a contract engaging a dancer for the Illustrious Theatre on June 28, 1644. For us, however, he is Molière from the moment of his decision taken in the previous year. Thenceforward he never once looked back.

The contract between the members of the Illustrious Theatre presupposes that the company was already formed, and that the contributions had been already paid. Molière had already left his father's house. His address upon the contract is Rue de Thorigny, where in January, 1636, Madeleine Béjart, just eighteen years of age, had bought a house and garden for 2,000 *livres*, of which she had already paid half the amount. It is to be presumed that it was in this house that she had lived under the protection of the Comte de Modène, whom in July, 1636, she had presented with the daughter to whom allusion has already been made, and it is to be further presumed that it was to this house that she returned with Molière on the evening of June 30, 1643. Her own address is entered on the contract as the house of her mother; but Marie Hervé was always prepared to lend her address for legal purposes. That Molière did not give his father's address was only natural. Father and son had, presumably, decided that perhaps it would be wise not to see too much of one another during this present crisis. What Jean Poquelin had to say about Madeleine and her trail of needy young adventurers would hardly be pleasant hearing, and Molière would wish to spare the sanctity of the paternal hearth, just as a year later he decided to renounce his father's name so that his family might be saved the indignity of seeing it flaunted upon the playbills.

Of the young people present in the house of Marie Hervé that summer afternoon, some would desert the ship as soon as it appeared to be sinking, but others would remain loyal to the death. Madeleine, leader of the enterprise, as one by one the members of the troop came to the table and affixed their signatures, watching them with shrewd, indulgent eyes, would have more faith in Beys, who would bring her into touch with the fashionable authors of the day, or in Clerin, who would keep her on friendly terms with the Théâtre du Marais, than in the young man who, so far as she knew, brought to the enterprise only his infatuation for the stage, his affection for herself and a modest contribution of 600 *livres* to the common funds. The smile with which she watched him take up the pen was less shrewd, perhaps, and more indulgent. She may even have thought it was rather a shame. This young man had a sound inheritance and brilliant prospects. What was he doing with the tribe of Ishmael? Probably, however, he would tire of the adventure, as his rather pompous but quite sensible father evidently hoped. Meanwhile, he was very young and she had leisure to be kind. He was a serious and dependable young man, with more brains than all the rest of them put together. But would he ever really come up to professional standard? He had immortal longings, as she had, to excel, and one could only excel in tragedy. She could not, with all her indulgence, avoid misgiving as to his tragic powers. He was not sufficiently emphatic; had not yet learned to roar with conviction. Nor was he by any means cast in the heroic mould—only moderately tall, his nose a little thick, his mouth large, with full lips. He had, however, a noble mien, a good leg, and he walked slowly—an excellent carriage for the stage. He had fine eyes, but scarcely the eyes of a successful actor—too serious altogether, contemplative eyes with an inward look, the eyes of a dreamer.

However, the next few months would test his powers and the quality of his enthusiasm. For him, perhaps, the whole enterprise would be an episode. For Madeleine and her brothers it was life or death.

But first it was necessary to find or build a theatre. It was the habit of the companies which had previously come to Paris from the provinces to hire for their spectacles a tennis court. The Théâtre du Marais, for example, had taken up permanent quarters in a court not far from the house of the Béjarts. The Illustrious Theatre went further afield and found a court near the Porte de Nesle, known as the *Jeu de Paume des Mestayers*. This was to be no fleeting enterprise. On 12th September, 1643, the company signed a lease for three years for the sum of 1,900 *livres*. Marie Hervé stood security for the rent, pledging her house in the Rue de la Perle and her personal property—indeed everything that she possessed.

The new company was ambitious and not to be satisfied with a makeshift. The tennis court was to be suitably adapted and equipped. Incidentally, the road in front of it was in need of repair, and Léonard Aubry, contractor to the King, was entrusted with the work. Pending these operations, the new company decided to go to Rouen, the city of Corneille, and it was there, in the autumn of 1643, that the founders of the Comédie Française first lit their candles and Molière first faced the public as a professional actor. Not a whisper has come down to us of that event, except that it did really occur. Probably the play was a tragedy of Corneille, and possibly Madeleine was praised.

All hearts, however, turned to Paris, where the journeymen were being urged to press forward with their work at the *Jeu de Paume des Mestayers*. The impatient young comedians authorized one of their number in due and legal form, by power of attorney, to constrain by every judicial means the proprietor of the tennis court and the masons and carpenters to make all possible speed, and in December the whole company, back in Paris, was urging its good friend Léonard Aubry to complete the repair of the road in front of the theatre. Aubry duly undertook that all should be finished, weather permitting, by the last day of the month. Aubry will come again into the story. As a contractor he

62

paved the way for the Illustrious Theatre. As a friend he would smooth the path of Molière in other ways.

The Illustrious Theatre opened its doors, probably, on New Year's Day in 1644. The audience, it seems, was in holiday mood. Never was there more hilarity in the pit, and never was it more thoroughly misplaced, says the author of *Elomire*. Whence we may infer that the play was a tragedy, and that the audience found it amusing. The libellist goes on to assure us, a fact which became only too obvious in the sequel, that, as the next days were neither holidays nor Sundays, the money taken by the troop did not inconvenience the pockets of its members.

> Car alors, excepté les exempts de payer,
> Les parents de la troupe et quelque batelier,
> Nul animal vivant n'entra dans notre salle.

In other words, the audience consisted of relatives, friends and professionals who did not pay for their seats.

The Illustrious Theatre, beginning with high hopes, has, so far as its histrionic achievements are concerned, left not a wrack behind—not a word of comment by any contemporary critic, not a syllable of reference, apart from the libellist already quoted, respecting the first appearance of the Sieur de Molière. What was the repertoire? The tragedies of Corneille were, of course, included. The company of Molière was never during his whole career without one or more of them in rehearsal. Then there was the *Scévole* of du Ryer and *La Mort de Chrispe* of Tristan l'Hermite. We know of these plays from the fact that the company had to borrow money to pay the authors. The title page of *L'Artaxerce* by Magnon records that it was performed by the

Illustrious Theatre. The company, moreover, had been joined by a new recruit, Nicholas Desfontaines, author of several tragedies, into the titles of which the word "illustrious" was pertinently slipped: *Eurymédon ou l'Illustre Pirate* (1644), *Perside ou la Suite de Illustre Bassa* (1644), *Saint Alexis ou l'Illustre Olympie* (1644), *L'Illustre Comédien ou le Martyre de Saint Genest* (1645). It may be inferred, however, that the most successful, or the least unsuccessful, of its productions was another play of Tristan l'Hermite, *La Mort de Sénèque*. Tallemant de Réaux, a storehouse of contemporary gossip, tells us that the best part of Madeleine was that of the unfortunate Epicharis tortured by Nero: *Epicharis, fille égale de Minerve en beauté de visaige, divine Epicharis. . . . O beauté sans seconde.* She braves the tyrant and insults his mistress, a most satisfactory part.

These few names sufficiently indicate the nature of the adventure on which Molière had embarked. He was drawn to the theatre not, as the libellists assert, by the buffoonery of Gaultier-Garguille or the grimace of Scaramouche, but by the heroic tantrums of the royal tragedians and the actors of the Marais. His immortal longings were to excel as a tragic hero.

Tristan l'Hermite, interested in the domestic and professional affairs of Madeleine, was a follower of Gaston de France. He was thus in a position to obtain for the company the protection of a prince, and when, in September, 1644, it had acquired the right to perform *La Mort de Chrispe* it was able to describe itself as *entretenue par son Altesse royale*. His Royal Highness, however, did nothing for the support of his comedians beyond lending them his name,

64

MOLIÈRE

From the portrait attributed to Pierre Mignard, in the collection of the Duc d'Aumale.

and even that privilege was withdrawn when they fell upon evil days. Of more profit to the young tragedians was the favour of the Duc de Guise, which Tristan, as a gentleman of his suite, was also in a position to obtain. When in the spring of 1644, the Duke went to the wars, he distributed his rich apparel among the actors of Paris. Molière and his friends came in for a share of it, together with the actors of the Hôtel du Bourgogne and the Théâtre du Marais. The Duke's finery was at any rate of more value than the Prince's favour. Here at least was something that might be worn by the company, or, in the last resort, used as security for its debts.

The documentary history of the Illustrious Theatre is a record of financial embarrassment. Under the contract of association members of the company might on withdrawal at four months' notice claim a repayment of their contributions to its expenses. On July 1, 1644, six months after the opening of the theatre, the contract was modified; henceforth no one might withdraw his money for the simple reason that there was no longer any money to withdraw. Two months later, on September 9th, Marie Hervé pledged her house in the Rue de la Perle, already mortgaged for 2,400 *livres*, as security for 1,100 *livres* borrowed by the troops. On December 17th the company acknowledged debts to Sieur Pommier, amounting to 2,000 *livres*, and a debt to Sieur Baulot of 600 *livres*, and it agreed that all the receipts of the theatre, after expenses had been met, should be paid over to these gentlemen. Already the scenery and equipment of the theatre had been pawned. Each member of the company had been asked to find a guarantor for his share of the debt, and Clerin was the only one of them, apart

65

from Molière and the Béjarts, who succeeded in finding a guarantor. Marie Hervé stood security for her daughters and for Molière, whom she apparently now regarded as one of the family. Joseph had, meanwhile, abandoned the sinking ship, together with Bonnenfont, and Catherine des Urlis.

The Illustrious Theatre was now in a pretty pickle— its capital exhausted and a debt of at least 2,600 *livres* to be met. Jean Poquelin might reasonably feel himself justified in his policy of expectation. But the end was not yet. The Illustrious Theatre, in its adversity, found in Molière a responsible representative. On December 14th he cancelled the lease of the *Jeu de Paume des Mestayers,* and on the following day all that was left of the company contracted with a master carpenter to remove its theatrical fittings and equipment to the tennis court of the *Croix Noire,* on the Quai des Ormes near the Port Saint Paul. Molière at the same time moved his quarters and took lodgings with a linen-draper near at hand. The new theatre was to be ready on January 8, 1645.

The creditors of the company followed these proceedings with very natural misgivings. For a time, however, they held their hands. In the theatre one never knows. One never has known. But the new venture was not more successful than the old; and in May François Pommier, creditor for 2,000 *livres,* began to show his teeth, haling the tragedians before *les Sieurs de Requêtes du Palais.* The magistrates were kind and granted a respite. Now, however, came the master-chandler, Antoine Fausser, with bills for 142 *livres.* Molière, cited to appear before the magistrates a second time, was arrested and committed to the Châtelet, then the Newgate of Paris. Thence on August 2nd he addressed a request to the Lieutenant-civil, Preux d'Aubray, asking to be set at liberty on the ground (1) that the debt was small, and (2) that he did not personally owe the money. The lieutenant gave orders for Molière to be released on bail for six months so far as that particular debt was concerned. Meantime, however, François Pommier had appeared once more, claiming his 2,000 *livres* and asking that Molière, as representative of the company, should be locked up till payment or some earnest of payment had been received, while M. Dubourg, a linen-draper, also came forward with a warrant. The company pleaded for its representative, and the magistrate decided that Molière should again be released on condition that he undertook to pay 40 *livres* a week for three months or 340 *livres* in all, which represented the share of the debt for which he was personally liable. The magistrate required a guarantor of this arrangement, who was found in the person of Léonard Aubry, the King's contractor, who had paved the way in front of the *Jeu de Paume des Mestayers* in December, 1643. Aubry assumed responsibility for the whole debt, and what was left of the troop made itself responsible to Aubry. Its members may not now venture to describe themselves as the *comédiens de son Altesse royale*. Gaston de France no longer lends these bankrupts so much as his name. They had been lucky, indeed, to procure the assistance of Aubry.

Clearly it was high time that Jean Poquelin appeared upon the scene. His liveliest expectations had been fulfilled. His son was not merely an Ishmaelite but apparently their scapegoat.

To understand the relations of father and son we must

67

cast forward for a moment to the month of December in the
year 1646.

The Illustrious Theatre had perished and Jean Poquelin,
with seeming indifference, had seen his son arrested for debt
and harassed continually by importunate creditors. On
Christmas Eve, 1646, however, we find him undertaking to
pay Léonard Aubry the sum of 320 *livres* if his son should
be unable to do so, and five years later, on 14th April, 1651,
Molière signed an admittance of debts to his father amounting in all to 1,965 *livres*. The attitude of Jean Poquelin is
clear from these transactions. He would not assist the
Illustrious Theatre to live a day longer than was, in his
opinion, necessary. His son had chosen to act as its representative. To help the Illustrious Theatre and thereby to
prolong its days, was throwing good money in highly in-
definite quantities after bad. Besides, there was a principle
at stake, and Jean Poquelin, third of the dynasty, was a man
to whom principle was dear. He had known, perhaps he had
openly prophesied, how this sorry business would end, and
the sooner it ended the better. His son had gone over to the
house of Béjart. Let him realize exactly where these folk
had landed him.

In December, 1646, however, the Paris adventure had
been liquidated, and his son had emerged with definite liabilities which represented his own personal share of the joint
responsibility. There was no longer any question of pulling
chestnuts for the sons and daughters of Béjart. Jean Poquelin, therefore, came to the rescue, guaranteed his son's debts,
and in the sequel paid them off as and when they became due.

The attitude of Jean Poquelin is even more clearly shown
by his action in regard to the post of *valet-tapissier*. Molière

68

in January, 1643, had formally abandoned all claim to the
reversion and placed it at the disposal of his younger brother.
Jean Poquelin, however, took no further steps. The prodigal
might yet return. Molière's renunciation remained a private
arrangement between father and son, and was not made
publicly effective. Molière, in documents and notes, continued to sign himself *valet-tapissier*. There was a short
period, possibly not more than a year, in which his brother
held the post and when Molière must write himself, as in
1659, *"bourgeois de Paris,"* or *"comédien de la troupe de
Monsieur, ci-devant valet du roi."* But on the death of his
brother he again assumed the office. Only for a brief interval
during his career did Molière cease to be *valet-tapissier du
roi*, in spite of his initial act of renunciation. In his certificate
of burial and in the inventory of his property after death,
he is still described as *valet-tapissier*, and in that quality he
was carried to the grave under the pall of the honourable
corporation of *tapissiers*.

The point is of importance. It bears directly on the status
of Molière as an actor and helps us to appreciate his relations with his father. The young man who was writing himself Molière; making himself responsible for desperate contracts with chandlers and linen-drapers; cohabiting with the
most notorious woman in the parish, or living away from his
father's house in obscure lodgings; getting himself arrested
three times over in as many days; shouldering debts which
he could not pay, secured on the property of a lady who was
presumably the mother of his mistress; provoking unexpected laughter in the pit by exhibiting himself in a profession for which he was apparently quite unsuited; doing
violence to his character and education by associating with

69

people who were incompatible with his quiet disposition and sensitive scholarship—this young man was still, in the view of Jean Poquelin, *valet-tapissier du roi*. This theatrical adventure was a violet in the youth of primy nature—nurtured by the very capable and seductive woman with red hair, who was learning to her own cost that enticing the son of a prosperous tradesman to follow a dubious profession was, though it might be more diverting, less profitable, than ministering to the pleasures of the high nobility.

The prodigal would undoubtedly return. Meanwhile, perhaps Jean Poquelin found consolation in the fact that his son was apparently born to supremacy. He had joined the Illustrious Theatre as one of a company of ten. All his colleagues had the advantage of him in age and experience. Within a few months, however, he had begun to act as its representative and to sign important documents in its behalf. It was the privilege of this young man, with the quiet disposition and melancholy eyes, to take the lead always and everywhere. Thus might Jean Poquelin, discreetly awaiting the issue, watch the proceedings of the Illustrious Theatre with one auspicious and one dropping eye. The blood of the Poquelins and the learning of the Jesuit fathers must tell. The qualities that had brought his son so rapidly to the front among these queer companions and had finally landed him in the Châtelet were an earnest of what he might do in a more honourable and satisfactory occupation.

Jean Poquelin in these anticipations was deceived. Molière was released from the Châtelet in August, 1645. For a moment he disappears, then, suddenly, we find him again, not as we might reasonably expect at his father's house under the pillars of the market, but at Narbonne, towards the end of the year, in the service of the Duc d'Epernon. He had played for Paris and failed, but there still remained the provinces, then as always the nursery of young comedians.

Thus began the second act of the adventure, leaving us scarcely time to bid farewell to the Illustrious Theatre, bankrupt and defeated. Its documentary history, meagre in itself, is to be filled in as we please. There is a story here as rich in emotion and incident as fancy cares to make it, full of measured hopes and quick reverses, of endless counsels and hasty expedients. The young actor was living in a world in which the best laid schemes go suddenly awry, in which every hour may be the eleventh, in which victory has often to be improvised from defeat, in which there is only one fixed and unalterable law—to ring up the curtain at a given hour. The routine of it has not changed in the three hundred year's history of the modern stage: the choice and reading of the play; the distribution of the parts; the rehearsals that begin so lightly and become so grim; the assembling of properties; the drafting of the bills; the dressing, furnishing and lighting; the endless discussions of possible success or failure; the cutting and emendation of the text; the acceptance of good "business" and stern suppression of bad; the gradual identification of the players with their parts so that they must quote their tags and endlessly go over every detail of the piece at supper or in the wings between exits and entrances; the reports from the front as to who, if anyone, is at the door; the hour of suspense that precedes the performance of a new play; the first contact with an audience, friendly or hostile; the swift message from the house that all is well, unnecessary because the actor already knows; the flush of a victory earned and the counting of the spoils; the realization, as it may be, of a defeat that can, nevertheless, be explained or retrieved. For the Illustrious Theatre alas! defeat was the customary issue. Nevertheless, for two years tragedy after tragedy was presented, Molière playing every hero in three and busying himself with the implacable routine of rehearsal and management. His duties were varied. The players shared among themselves the minor duties. Mondory, the leading actor at the Marais, for years took the money at his own doors. One or other of the acting members of the company must be gate-keeper, treasurer, property-man, stage-manager, acting-manager and publicity agent. A zealous member might choose to be all in one, and there is no doubt as to the zeal of Molière. He was one of ten members of the company but, be it remembered, he was the member who went to prison on behalf of them all.

More important than any of the practical details of this apprenticeship was the fact that Molière had found his vocation. Where Jean Poquelin saw failure and an awful warning, Molière found himself once and for all committed. He had entered the small world of the stage which for him contained the greater world of reality. "Four boards and a passion" was for the moment his device, not yet *l'étrange enterprise de faire rire les honnêtes gens*. But though he was far as yet from suspecting in himself the author of *Tartuffe,* he had already felt a passion stronger than authorship, stronger than anything he had yet learned to feel or think, the pure passion of the stage. He had entered a mimic world in which alone he would henceforth live at a maximum. On New Year's Day, 1644, he had stepped from the wings into an unknown play and the step was irrevocable. Molière had taken the stage. The curtain falling on the

72

first tragedy of the Illustrious Theatre had cut him off from the world. Henceforth he would remain on an enchanted platform where, like Pompey, with the stamping of his foot he was able to raise an army. He had felt it as a void that waited to be filled with scenes and heroes to whom the flesh and blood of his comrades had lent, and would lend again, virility and substance. He had felt the lure of an empty stage in an empty house.

So it came about that Jean Poquelin, waiting in his fine apartment under the pillars of the market for the bankrupt who was bringing with him airs from the prison house, was to hear with stupefaction one summer night that the Sieur de Molière, far from abandoning the career he had chosen, was on the morrow of his defeat making arrangements with Madeleine to leave Paris to tempt misfortune in the distant provinces. That must have been a remarkable interview between father and son. Jean Poquelin assuredly did his best. This second madness was worse than the first. It destroyed, moreover, all hope of penitence. Eighteen months of ill-success, ending in bankruptcy and arrest, had failed to discourage the young man. This, then, was no mere infatuation. Molière, in that talk with his father, cannot fail to have made some effort to explain himself. We can imagine Jean Poquelin, in his Neapolitan taffeta, striding restlessly about the great walnut table with seven columns, trying, not very successfully, to take it in. For him the only clear thing that emerged was that his son, amiable and easily impressed in other ways, was in this matter implacable. He had not, it seemed, been led ignobly away by the red-haired woman. He was fulfilling some queer destiny of his own.

Molière was to wander through the provinces for thirteen

years. Meanwhile, Jean Poquelin paid at intervals the debts
of his son, and when, at long last, Molière returned to Paris,
his father had become definitely reconciled to his son's career,
and had even consented to accept the Béjarts. Madeleine,
still the business man of the company, negotiating a lease
for the Théâtre du Marais in October, 1658, will give the
house of Jean Poquelin under the pillars of the market as her
legal address.

V

The Actor at Large

MOLIÈRE left Paris at twenty-three and returned at thirty-six. The interval is mostly legend. He wrote at least two plays during that period; he visited certain towns; he was successively under the protection of the Duc d'Epernon and the Prince de Conti. Those are the facts, but it is essential to look beyond them and, with the help of such traditions as are not contradictory or historically unacceptable, to follow him as closely as possible and form as vivid an idea as we can of the life he was leading, the people he met, the position he was making for himself and the direction in which his genius was being urged.

But first we will leave to the local topographers, jealous for the renown of their cities, and to the scholars for whom small points are precious because they are small, the exact itinerary of Molière during these years. Almost every town in southern France of any size or consideration has naturally wished to claim a piece of him, and is ready to contend even for the honour of having pelted him from the stage. His movements have been arduously reconstructed from the marriage and baptismal certificates of friends or members of the company, from applications for licences to perform, from receipts given on account of contributions for the poor, from evidence of his association with noble protectors or local authorities. The question whether the company of Molière played in any particular town in any particular year is of small importance, and does not help us to clear up any of the major mysteries of his life, or get any nearer to the man himself. There is a vast literature on the subject, but only the results need detain us. The following is a list of the places which were almost certainly visited by Molière in the years indicated: Narbonne, 1645; Toulouse, Albi, Carcassonne, 1647; Nantes, 1648; Toulouse and Narbonne, 1649; Narbonne and Agen, 1650; Grenoble and Lyon, 1652; Lyon and Montpellier, 1653; Montpellier, 1654; Montpellier, Lyon, Avignon and Pézenas, 1655; Pézenas, Narbonne, Bordeaux and Béziers, 1656; Béziers, Lyon, Dijon, and Avignon, 1657; Lyon, Grenoble, Rouen, 1658. The above list comprises only the towns for which documentary proof can be quoted.

How did Molière, lost to view when he left the prison of the Châtelet in August, 1645, contrive to reappear at Narbonne towards the end of the year in the service of the Duc d'Epernon, Governor of Gauyenne? The answer, alas! is Madeleine. We have noted among the authors of the Illustrious Theatre the poet Magnon. Magnon in October, 1646, dedicating his tragedy of *Josaphat* to the Duc d'Epernon extols among the noble deeds of his patron the protection and help which he has recently afforded to the most unlucky, but one of the most deserving, actresses of France:

"You have rescued this unfortunate lady from the abyss into which her talents had precipitated her, and restored to the theatre one of the finest actresses that ever adorned the stage."

76

The Duke's achievement is described as not the least meritorious act of his distinguished life—one which is doubtless highly satisfactory to the Duke in person and to Parnassus in general. Satisfactory also to the author of *Josaphat*, who thereby secured in Madeleine a leading lady for his play and possibly some little credit with his Grace for an arrangement which he had doubtless contributed to bring about.

The position is made still clearer from another dedication. Among the witnesses of the original act of association of the Illustrious Theatre was André Mareschall, described as a parliamentary lawyer. This worthy amateur of the stage committed in 1646 a tragedy, entitled *Papyre ou le Dictateur Romain*, which he dedicated to the Duc d'Epernon. The tragedy, says its author, is to pass "from your liberal hands to those of your comedians who, wholly devoted to the entertainment of your Grace, and enriched not only by your generous gifts but by the accession of illustrious players, will, subject to your favour and support, achieve such excellence and fame that no one will venture to deem them unworthy of your protection." Whence it may be inferred (1) that the Duke already had a troop of players; (2) that the friends of Madeleine interested the Duke in her misfortunes; and (3) that the Duke thereupon decided to enrich his company with all that remained of the Illustrious Theatre. In other words, Madeleine, Joseph and Geneviève Béjart, with Molière in attendance, were duly incorporated. Du Trallage, in his contemporary notes on the theatre, completes the picture. He informs us that in 1644 or 1645 Molière acted at Bordeaux and that M. d'Epernon "held this actor in esteem as a man of wit and intelligence." All honour to the

Duke. It was Madeleine he rescued from the abyss, but he appears to have been the first person in France to realize that Molière was possibly worth encouraging for his own sake.

The titular leader of the new company was a veteran actor of the southern provinces, Charles du Fresne. Du Fresne had in 1643 given performances in Lyon with Nicolas Desfontaines, one of the authors of the Illustrious Theatre, who thus supplies another link between Paris and the provincial adventure. The company which du Fresne was directing in 1645 was admitted to be one of the best in France. The Duke was the first provincial Governor to regard a company of players as almost indispensable to the state in which he lived. He required it for his festivals, public and domestic. When the Estates assembled or a political event needed special emphasis, when a marriage was to be celebrated, or a great lady to be amused, the Duke's players were in special request and their efforts suitably rewarded.

Molière quickly assumed a position of responsibility. The citizens of Bordeaux in 1648 were in rebellion against the Duke, who then had no feeling or leisure for distraction. The company moved accordingly to Nantes. On Thursday, 23rd April, Molière appeared at the town hall in advance of his companions. The town records are explicit: "There came to-day to the office the Sieur Morlierre, one of the comedians of the company of the Sieur du Fresne, who informed us that the rest of the company would be arriving on that day in the town and who very respectfully asked us to permit them to appear upon the stage and to present their comédies." Molière was merely one of the members of the company, and the clerk at Nantes does not even know how

78

to spell his name; but, as previously in Paris, he was already acting for business purposes as its spokesman and representative. The entries at Nantes are particularly full and informing. While Molière was dealing with the town authorities, du Fresne was making himself responsible for the lease of a tennis court at Fontenaye for a period of three weeks, thus showing that he was not only on the spot with the Sieur Morlierre, but that here was a company which looked ahead and organized its tours with efficiency. This was no wandering troop that arrived at hazard and set up its booths in the market place. Very conveniently, a few days later, a member of the company, Pierre Réveillon, had a daughter. Du Fresne, du Parc, Marie Hervé and Madeleine Béjart all signed the baptismal certificate, thus enabling us to identify the company beyond all possible doubt. Note that the mother of Madeleine was present. The Béjarts were always a united family.

The biographers of 1682 contribute little either to the history or legend of Molière in the provinces. Molière having failed in Paris, "was obliged to tour the provinces of the realm where he began to make for himself a great reputation." Such is the summary of his first biographers. They merely add that Molière was for some time under the protection of the Prince de Conti; that *L'Etourdi* was produced at Lyon in 1653; and that *Le Dépit Amoureux* was presented shortly afterwards before the Estates of Béziers. Grimarest contributes nothing that is either correct or of consequence.

The classic picture of the life of the wandering player towards the middle of the seventeenth century is the *Roman Comique* of Scarron. It is a picture consecrated by tradition, a first essay in the literature of Bohemia. The players move

79

from town to town. They may play here but not there. They may be welcomed or cast out. Their properties are threadbare, the purse is empty. They will steal anything and call it purchase. It is a life from pillar to post, frequent in uproar, in sudden intimacies, in relationships easily formed and as easily broken. They cannot see beyond the next inn upon the road, the next pitch in the market square.

All this, however, bears but a very faint resemblance to the life led by the players of the Sieur du Fresne. It is only true in the sense that there is a fraternity of spirit and disposition between the highest and lowest of those who must make themselves a motley to the view. Scarron was describing earlier conditions and at this stage in its history the theatre was rising rapidly in esteem; he was describing, moreover, a small and undistinguished company; and he was writing to stagger and amuse his readers. The company of the Sieur du Fresne did not play in barns or in the city square, but in the houses of the nobility, in municipal halls or in the local tennis court, hired and adapted in advance. These were not the vagrants of popular legend. Their status, despite its theoretical infamy, was more that of a civil servant than a gipsy. Their engagements to perform when the Estates were in session were in the nature of public contracts, and on these occasions they received substantial public grants, which more than covered their expenses.

Molière has been much commiserated for his provincial years. Emphasis is laid upon the physical fatigues of the road, the competition of unworthy rivals, his financial worries, the tyranny of local authorities, the humiliations that attend service with the great, the insolent toleration or open contempt of the devout. Such is not the impression left by a careful reading of the records. This, on the contrary, was perhaps the happiest period in the life of Molière. Admittedly he was thinking of Paris and impatient to return. But, meanwhile, he was succeeding in the profession he loved. The road had its pleasures as well as its hardships, and competition only emphasized that the troop of the Sieur du Fresne was the best touring company in France. As to his financial worries, they were wholly imaginary. No one was making a fortune, but the troop paid its way and lived upon the fat of a generous land. Local authorities might be capricious and apt to stand upon their dignity; but tactfully handled—as Molière knew how—they were courteous and forthcoming. They might prohibit the players from charging more than ten, twelve or fifteen sous for a place, stipulate that the proceeds of the first performance or a proportion of the ordinary receipts should be given to the poor, require rent for a public hall, prohibit a performance owing to hard times or the illness of a notable. But the company of Molière, unlike some others which unwisely tried to dispense with the necessary formalities or failed to show sufficient respect for public persons, rarely had any difficulties with the municipal authorities. By its noble patrons the troop, during his terms of service, was welcomed and respected, and by the devout it was not yet seriously incommoded. Molière, moreover, was still young and in excellent health. Every day had its interests and experiments.

The Duc d'Epernon, Governor of Guyenne, lived in semi-royal state at his magnificent château de Cadillac or at Agen, and his players were expected to contribute to sumptuous festivals for the entertainment of his celebrated mistress, Nanon de Lartigue. The company, when it was not in actual service with the Duke, was free to accept other engagements equally distinguished. Thus in July, 1647, when the King sent the Comte d'Aubijoux, his lieutenant general, into Languedoc, there were viceregal receptions at Albi, and the players were invited thither at the expense of the town to assist in entertaining the royal envoy. The town, as it happened, forgot to pay the bill, and no less a person than the intendant of the province, the Comte de Breteuil, wrote to the magistrates of Albi in the following October, reminding them that the comedians of the Duc d'Epernon had come to Albi by special request and upon a promise of free transport for their effects and the sum of 600 *livres*. The fathers of the city are firmly reminded that the company "is composed of persons of the highest respectability and very excellent artists, who deserve to be rewarded for their pains," and the intendant intimates that he will be personally grateful if this small matter is promptly settled. The letter was written from Carcassonne on October 9th, and the bill was paid on October 24th. Other indications of the assured position of the company are not lacking. Allusion has already been made to the fact that at Nantes in 1648 a daughter was born to one of the actors of the troop. Among the signatures of the baptismal certificate was the president of the Parliament of Brittany and an auditor general. These were obviously no vagabonds whose christenings were so impressively attended.

The Duc d'Epernon, then an excellent and enthusiastic patron of the players, who had made the discovery that Molière was intelligent, was not a successful prince. There was much disorder and distress throughout the country, culminating, now and then, in flat rebellion. Thus, in No-

vember, 1647, the town council of Poitiers, discussing a
letter from the "Sieur Morlierre" asking permission for
the company of the Sieur du Fresne to settle in the town
for two months, decided at the instance of the mayor and
the lieutenant general to refuse the necessary permission
"in view of the hard times and the dearness of corn."
But public distress rarely interferes with private pleasure,
and the Duc d'Epernon, living in Agen with his mistress,
had frequent need of distraction. In February, 1650, he
had a special theatre prepared for his players in a tennis
court, with a private gallery for his friends, where he
might console himself with the lovely Nanon and forget
the curses of the city. Fortunately the players who profited
from his protection did not suffer from his unpopularity
and when, in the summer of 1650, the Duke decided to
retire from the province, they passed into the service of the
Estates of Languedoc. There was in the autumn a three
months' session of the Estates at Pézenas, and for the whole
of that time, the company was employed under a special
contract, for the sum of 4,000 *livres*, paid over by a decision
of the Estates themselves.

Thereby hangs the most celebrated of the provincial
legends, for Pézenas makes a more audacious claim than
any of its rivals to a share in the history of Molière. It
has even succeeded in producing a chair, subsequently acquired as a relic by the Comédie Française, in which Molière
sat for long hours observing men and manners in the shop
of one Gély, a barber, whose saloon, as was then usual,
fulfilled socially the office of a *café*. There is alas! not a
scrap of evidence for the story, but it is a good example of
the legends which must be ignored within the limits of a

83

reasonable biography. A volume would be needed to set them forth and a library for their assessment.

In the following year Moliére paid a flying visit to Paris. It was a personal visit and not, therefore, included in the itinerary of the company. He had been absent for nearly six years. Was he perhaps already making efforts to return? The attempt would at that moment be natural, since the company had lost its first protector and had not yet found a second.

Jean Poquelin himself is our witness to the presence of his son in Paris, for on April 14, 1651, Molière signed a recognition, before two notaries of the Châtelet, of sums paid on his account or to him personally by his father. Jean Poquelin had continued to prosper in his house under the pillars of the market. He was now a leading man in the guild of *tapissiers* and had been appointed one of the experts entrusted with the inventory and valuation of a portion of the royal furniture. He must still be regretting his son's infatuation for the stage, though Molière, discussing with his father the fatal step taken eight years ago, had now something to show in justification. He was not yet the titular leader, but he was the most important member of the best touring company in France. He was, as we shall shortly see, beginning to discover his talents as an author, and he had made the discovery, bitter at first, that the public which refused to accept him as a tragedian could not have enough of him as a comic actor. It was true that he was not yet in a position to pay his debts. But the day would come. The profession he had adopted was rising rapidly in the social scale. One day—the moment, it seemed, was not yet—he would return to Paris and challenge the supremacy of the royal company at the Hôtel de Bourgogne. Jean Poquelin could hardly as yet be reconciled, but it was impossible for him not to be interested. This young man could talk. His account of life in the towns and castles of the south was worth hearing—humours and misadventures of a roving existence lived on the edge of political events that were transforming the country; accidents of the road and traffic of the stage; sketches of people and places; plans for the future; and, almost certainly, the most cherished plan of all—the return to Paris, not yet practicable but ultimately to be managed.

We obtain at about this time glimpses of Molière and his way of life in two contemporary sources. Nicolas Chorier, writing a life of Boissat, a very respectable gentleman of letters, member of the Academy, and vice-bailiff of the city, has described a meeting of Boissat with Molière at Vienne. Boissat was at Vienne in 1651—his biographer misdates the occasion by at least ten years—and to him came Molière:

"Jean-Baptiste Molière, excellent actor and author of comedies, came at about this time to Vienne. Boissat received him with honour. He did not anathematize him after the fashion of those who affected a stupid and insolent severity. Boissat was a frequent spectator of some of the plays which Molière presented. He even invited to table this man who had achieved distinction in his art and gave him an excellent dinner. He did not class him with persons excommunicated, impious and criminal, as is the habit of certain fanatical creatures."

Note that Molière is described both as actor and author; that he is singled out for special favours; and that the status of the actor is rising fast enough to flutter the consciences of the pious.

Our second witness is d'Assoucy, poet, musician, gamester and an excellent correspondent. Needy and loquacious, he first encountered Molière at Carcassonne in July, 1651. On leaving the town he wrote to Molière excusing himself, in terms that point to a certain intimacy, for not having taken leave of his friend. Four years later d'Assoucy came to Lyon where for three months he spent his days gaming, feasting and frequenting the theatre, finally embarking with the company to go down the Rhône to Avignon. D'Assoucy found the people of Lyon cordial to his muse. What charmed him most, however, was the society of "Molière et Messieurs les Béjarts." D'Assoucy had an opportunity at Lyon of witnessing *L'Etourdi*, the first substantial revelation of Molière as a dramatic author, but, being d'Assoucy, he has more to say of the good fare and easy living of his friend than of his acting and authorship. D'Assoucy must live either upon his wits or upon his friends. At Avignon he lost heavily at play, but that was of little consequence, "since a man is never poor so long as he has the esteem of Molière and the Béjarts for his friends in despite of the devil. . . . I might count myself richer and happier than ever before." Molière and the Béjarts were already sufficiently prosperous to attract a parasite. That Molière esteemed d'Assoucy is doubtful; but d'Assoucy had a vein of hearty pleasantry and could tell a story. He was an amusing and tenacious companion, and there was no particular reason why Molière should shake him off. Molière forgave any man whose faults were open, and d'Assoucy confessed later that the love was all on one side:

86

> Pour moi je l'aime et le revère,
> Oui sans doute et de tout mon cœur;
> Il est vrai qu'il ne m'aime guère.
> Que voulez-vous?   C'est un malheur.

It is unfortunate, perhaps, that the most continuous witness to the kind of life lived by Molière in the provinces was a man whose works were mercilessly satirized by Boileau, whose vices were cheerfully exhibited by himself, and whose compositions were praised by Corneille, who had no ear for music.   D'Assoucy followed Molière from Avignon to Pézenas in 1655 and adhered to the company throughout the winter.   His motives are revealed with an engaging frankness.   The lure was sweet company and good food:

> Au milieu de sept ou huit plats,
> Exempt de soin et d'embarras,
> Je passois doucement la vie;
> Jamais plus gueux ne fut plus gras
>
> .   .   .   .   .
>
> A cette table bien garnie
> Parmi les plus friands muscats
> C'est moi qui souffloit la rôtie
> Et qui beuvoit plus d'hypocras.

The company of Molière, when it left Lyon in 1653, was enriched by the accession of two actresses to whom a long succession of his characters was soon to be entrusted.   Of the Illustrious Theatre Molière himself, Joseph Béjart (returned), Madeleine Béjart and her sister Geneviève still remained.   Louis Bèjart the younger brother of Joseph, had also been recruited and with the other members of his family was there for life.   The first of the new actresses,

87

born Le Clerc, entered the profession as Catherine de Rosé. She joined the company in 1650 and married one of its actors, Edme Villequin ou de Brie, and as Mademoiselle de Brie she became for Molière one of the most intelligent and steadfast of his interpreters. Three years later, in 1653, came Marquise Thérèse de Gorla. She was the daughter of a peddling druggist and showman, a nimble dancer and perhaps the loveliest woman of her time. She, too, married one of the troop, and as Mademoiselle du Parc achieved ambiguous fame. The relations of Molière with the three principal women of his troop, Madeleine Béjart, Mademoiselle de Brie and Mademoiselle du Parc are almost wholly legendary. Biographers and critics have naturally found it difficult to forgo so obvious an opportunity for the sexual complications which must somehow enliven their literary adventures. Molière, it is alleged, sighing in vain for the favours of the lovely but unimpressionable Mademoiselle du Parc, was driven for sympathy to the less outwardly imposing but more sympathetic Mademoiselle de Brie; who, from pitying his infatuation, became by insensible degrees its remedy. The authority for this allegation is a pamphleteer, who thirty years later published an anonymous libel upon the wife of Molière entitled *La Fameuse Comédienne*. We shall meet again this anonymous gentleman. Suffice it for the moment that Grimarest so far supports him as to inform us that even, after marriage, Molière was accustomed to look for sympathy to Mademoiselle de Brie. He even reports a hypothetical conversation between Molière and one of his friends in which the dramatist, deserted by his wife, explains that he turns naturally to Mademoiselle de Brie for consolation, being accustomed to her defects, and,

88

therefore, able to endure them better than the imperfections
of a stranger—an explanation such as a literary confectioner
might cleverly attribute to a satirist, but which accords extremely ill with the generous and fair spirit of Molière.
The anonymous author of *La Fameuse Comédienne* is false
in his facts, for he implies that Mademoiselle de Brie and
Mademoiselle du Parc both joined the company in 1653,
and Grimarest is false in his characters. An anonymous
libel, supported by an anecdote in which the charming creator
of Agnes and Isabelle is described as thin, plain and lacking
in sense, have left an impression which no amount of critical
scholarship has been able to destroy. Nothing whatever is
known of the amative relations of Molière with any of the
women into whose arms he has been impelled by the imaginative eroticism of his biographers. We may think what
we please according to temperament and inclination. But let
the evidence at least be weighed. The contemporaries of
Molière believed that he was the lover of Madeleine during
the early days of their association and in all human probability they were right. Only one contemporary witness of any
credit—and he is a witness at second hand—includes Mademoiselle de Brie among the women beloved of Molière.
This was Brossette, who quotes Boileau as saying that Molière
was "enamoured of the actress Béjart and subsequently of
the actress de Brie." No witness of any credit at all includes Mademoiselle du Parc or whispers of any other entanglement. The utmost that the most voluptuous seekers
after a feminine interest may be justly allowed are the three
women who came nearest to Molière in his daily work—
Madeleine, Mademoiselle de Brie, and his future wife.

The two new actresses of the troop were sufficiently un-

89

like to avoid a serious rivalry. It was the privilege and perhaps the pleasure of the lovely Marquise de Gorla, Mademoiselle du Parc, to inspire livelier emotions than she was ever able to return. She was of a cold disposition, consistently followed her own interests, and was never wholly at ease in the troop of Molière, being the only faithless member. On two occasions she deserted her comrades. Tempted perhaps by the great Corneille in 1659 she went over to the Théâtre du Marais shortly after the arrival of Molière in Paris. Tempted quite certainly by Racine in 1667 she went over to the Hôtel du Bourgogne. On the first occasion she returned within a year, but her exit on the second occasion was final. Contemporary witnesses refer often to her perfections, and yet somehow leave an impression of nullity. The proofs of her attraction are illustrious. The two Corneilles, father and son, both sighed in vain, the first being more melodious but the second more convincing. In 1659 Racine, on the threshold of his career, was not so easily denied. He was young, ardent and already marked for fame. To consent was not only kind but good policy. He bore away his conquest to play in *Andromaque*, and was inconsolable when a little later she died. So bitter was his despair that the gossips of the day, in face of its extravagance, spread the legend that he had poisoned her. That, however, is unlikely. Racine, though capable of repenting such a deed in sweet anguish, was hardly capable of the deed itself. The destiny of Mademoiselle de Brie was happier. Many years after the death of Molière she continued to play in his comedies; and when at last the rulers of the Comédie Française, thinking she was too old for the part, presented another Agnes to the public, the audience drove her successor from

90

the stage and clamoured for the return of their favourite, whose vivacity and intelligence could in the part of a child still oblige them to forget that she had grown grey in its portrayal.

On the departure of the Duc d'Epernon from Guyenne in 1650 the company had lost its first protector, but in 1653 it found a second and a more illustrious patron. Prince de Conti, the young prodigy of Clermont, was now a conspicuous figure in the political world. His nature and education pointed to the church, but he had rebelled—unwisely as the sequel showed—against his destiny. In 1649, at the age of twenty, he had been one of the leaders of the rebel Fronde in Paris. But treason was lightly punished in those days. Not yet was Richelieu in a position to hang a gentleman for breaking the law. The Prince was imprisoned for a year and then released—to engage again in civil war and contempt of the monarchy. His brother, the great Condé, a still more distinguished rebel, confided to him in 1652 the direction of affairs in Guyenne. Conti, however, bored with rebellion in the provinces, soon began to intrigue with the Court for forgiveness, and was lavish in his promises of good behaviour. In July, 1653, he successfully made his peace and was permitted to withdraw to such of his country estates as he might be pleased to select. He chose the beautiful château of La Grange in the vicinity of Pézenas, and, feeling that he was now entitled to the classic relaxation of the warrior, he retired thither with his mistress, Madame de Calvimont. The lady begged of him a company of players. Cosnac, in charge of the Prince's lighter moments—he delicately describes himself as responsible for the *menus plaisirs du Prince*—suggested Molière, and wrote on his own responsibility inviting the troop to come at once to the château. The lady, however, was impatient, and there happened to be another company near at hand. It was led by a certain Cormier, a celebrated mountebank, whom Molière as a boy may often have seen in front of his booth on the Pont Neuf where the arts of the showman were in the fashion of the day used to advertise the wares of the pedlar. Conti, anxious to please his mistress without delay, engaged Cormier, and when Molière arrived, refused to pay even the costs of his journey. Thereupon Cosnac, considering that his honour was involved, paid Molière and his companions out of his own pocket and arranged for them to play in the town.

The sequel is unedifying. The Prince, put to shame by the generous act of Cosnac, or being, perhaps, reminded that he had been "followed in his studies" at Clermont by a certain Jean-Baptiste Poquelin, at last consented to receive the Sieur de Molière at La Grange. A play was presented, but Madame de Calvimont, brainless as she was fair, preferred the mountebank of the Pont Neuf to the future author of *Le Misanthrope*. The Prince was accordingly bound to declare himself in favour of Cormier, though the rest of the audience was unanimously for the company of Molière, which infinitely surpassed its rivals both "in the excellence of its actors and the magnificence of their attire." The Prince, however, had a secretary who, like many a better man before and after him, fell a victim to the lovely Marquise, Mademoiselle du Parc, and who gave no rest to his master or his master's mistress until he had persuaded them to acknowledge that Molière was more worthy of protection than the rival company. Thus was genius detected and encouraged at a time when the favour of princes was of more account than the applause of the vulgar. Conti took Molière under his protection and dismissed the juggler. The company received a pension and the right to describe themselves as *comédiens du Prince de Conti*. Doubtless the Prince was well satisfied with the exchange. The pleasure to be derived from a stupid woman is limited, and the Prince was a man of more than ordinary intelligence. Molière, indeed, was shortly upon such good terms with his new protector that he is said to have been offered the post of the amorous secretary, who died shortly after his timely infatuation.

For the next four years Molière remained in high favour with the Prince. Conti, in 1653, had already in view his marriage with the niece of Mazarin which was to take place in the following year. There was accordingly a season of high festival at Montpellier during which the Prince prepared himself for the married state with banquets and comedies. Incidentally, he felt it desirable, in order to fit himself for the companionship of the princess-elect, to take a more intelligent mistress. Madame de Calvimont was accordingly dismissed with 1,000 *pistoles*. The Prince, inconstant in love, politics and religion, was admirably consistent in economy. These weeks of festivals at Montpellier, in which the Prince surprised even his boon companions, must have left a profound impression on Molière. For the first time he was intimately in touch with the high nobility of France. First impressions are deep, and tradition has cast the Prince de Conti for the model of Don Juan. Certainly there was more than a hint of the cynical hero of *Le Festin de Pierre* in these strange preparations for

93

marriage with the niece of a cardinal. Happily for Molière, Conti, once he was married, treated his wife at least as handsomely as his mistress, and when the princess joined him in Montpellier in the winter of 1654-5, her arrival, which coincided with a session of the Estates, was the signal for another brilliant festival. Molière, on this occasion, appeared in a species of ballet that was beginning to be fashionable, in which professional actors shared the stage with distinguished amateurs.

The Estates rose in March, and Molière left Montpellier for Lyon. It was his second visit. Everyone agrees that it was in Lyon that Molière produced his first play of importance, but the evidence is conflicting whether this event, one of the most critical of his career, took place during the first visit in 1653 or the second visit in 1655. The balance is in favour of the second visit. *L'Etourdi* would thus be produced by Molière in the spring or summer of 1655 in the intervals of his service with the Prince de Conti.

In November the Prince summoned him back to a meeting of the Estates in Pézenas. Conti was staying with the Grand Provost of Guyenne, whose rooms were large enough to house a theatre. Three bishops, in full canonicals, and three barons representing the Estates, called upon him to present their compliments. Conti met them on the doorstep. He excused himself for receiving them in such a place, but the players had arrived and his rooms were in extreme disorder. Protests were doubtless raised. These were persons just sufficiently exalted to stand upon their dignity; and it was, perhaps, not altogether an accident that the austere bishop of Aleth shortly found occasion to wait upon the Prince. The prelate was fortunate enough to find him a little sick, and, therefore, piously disposed, and his vivid exhortations, for the moment apparently ineffective, were shortly to bear historic fruit.

For the moment, however, Molière was in the highest favour. The Prince not only had a passion for the stage and attended all the representations, but discussed with Molière the principles and practice of the art of the theatre, and read with him all the best plays, ancient and modern.

It will have been noted that the periods of service of Molière with Conti usually coincided with a session of the Estates. The protector who refused to reimburse Molière and his company for their travelling expenses when first they came to La Grange, who cashiered his mistress for 600 *pistoles,* which Cosnac for very shame had increased to 1,000, was not unwilling that the worthy deputies of Languedoc should pay for his pleasures. On the ground that his players were invited for their distraction, the expenses were charged to their account. Thus on February 4, 1656, at Pézenas the Prince, as generous with the public funds as he was careful with his own, assigned his players the sum of 5,000 *livres* charged upon the provincial budget.

From Pézenas, in February, 1656, the company proceeded to Narbonne, where the town council met to discuss a request that they should be authorized to perform. The magistrates of Narbonne, remembering their Roman origin, wrote themselves as consuls of the city. The first consul informed his colleagues that the players of His Highness the Prince de Conti, arriving from Pézenas, where they had played during the session of the Estates, desired to pass a fortnight in the city of Narbonne to the public satisfaction. As there was no place suitable for such performances other than the great hall of the consular palace, the players, supported by all the worthy people of the town, had requested permission to make use of it. The consuls decided to thank the players and to grant them the hall. Such entries in the official records of the city clearly show that the popular idea of Molière as a strolling player of the kind described in the *Roman comique* of Scarron has little relation to truth.

Next to Lyon, as a town prosperous and enlightened, came Béziers, then as now, a rich city of the vine where the traveller from the West first feels that he has reached the South. Lyon saw the first production of *L'Etourdi*, Béziers of *Le Dépit Amoureux*. On November 17, 1656, the King's commissioner was holding the Estates in Béziers, and the presence and conduct of the players became a question of public importance. They were apparently accustomed to give the deputies free passes to the theatre on the understanding that the company would not in the long run lose financially by the arrangement. This practice was strictly prohibited as the result of a decision taken by the Estates on December 16th. The players were forbidden to distribute free tickets to the deputies, the financial authorities to make them any grants from the public funds, or the treasurer to pay them. This appears to have been more a measure taken in the interests of a reasonable control of the public purse than from any hostility to the theatre. The rich wine-merchants of Béziers were not the sort of men to be un-protestingly fleeced. In February, 1656, Joseph Béjart had ingeniously exploited their innocent snobbery by rubbing up his heraldry and bringing out a *Recueil des Titres et Blazons* for which he was accorded by the deputies a grant of 1,500 *livres*. He repeated the performance at Béziers

96

in April, 1657. But once was enough; and this time he received only 500 *livres*, with a note in the minutes to the effect that no such book as he might present in future would be considered unless he had previously received explicit orders to compile it.

Meanwhile, Molière was again losing his protector. The festival of the Prince de Conti at Pézenas had been his carnival. He had since had leisure, on a bed of sickness, to realize the force of the pious remonstrances of the Bishop of Aleth and to realize the enormity of the sins which his constitution was no longer able to support. From being the patron of Molière, Conti was henceforth to be the scourge of the contemporary theatre. Ten years later he published his *Traité de la Comédie,* a histriomastrix which entitles him to rank with our own Jeremy Collier as a prosecutor of public amusement. There is no explicit record of the effect upon Molière of the Prince's reformation, but his feelings are not difficult to infer. Conti had read with him the comedies of Terence; he had kept bishops and burghers at the gate while he saw to the comfort of his players; his life had precociously been one long series of disorders. The change was disconcerting, abrupt, certainly impressive. Nor could it be dismissed as mere hypocrisy. The Prince's conversion, though to the young actor who had seen him in the prime of his delinquencies it must have seemed uncommonly shallow, was undoubtedly sincere, which only made it the more profoundly treacherous. This was an event of abiding effect, and it is difficult to avoid the conclusion that the famous scene in which Don Juan adds the grimace of piety to his other sins was indirectly inspired by this illustrious example. There are also certain scenes in *Tartuffe* to which the conversion of Conti may have deviously contributed; but that is dangerous ground. Suffice it to note that Molière early in his career lost a friend and a champion of the stage as the unexpected result of pious persuasions.

The Prince in reformation was merciless. From Paris, where he lay sick in 1656, he passed by way of Lyon to the south to take up his responsibilities as commander of the army in Italy. Arriving at Lyon he wrote to the Abbé de Ciron on May 15, 1657: "There are some players here who went formerly under my name. I have taken steps to inform them that they must no longer make use of it and, as you may well believe, I have taken good care not to see them." It was some consolation perhaps to our players, on moving from Lyon to Dijon, to find in residence their old friend the Duc d'Epernon, who, since 1651, had been Governor of Burgundy. The Duke was more constant in his pleasures than the Prince. Nanon de Lartique was still his mistress. Molière obtained the permission of the municipal council to play in Fishmongers' Hall.

From Dijon Molière passed to Avignon, and there he met the painter Mignard. This was a happy event for posterity. But for Mignard, who became his lifelong friend and remained intimately interested in his fortunes and affairs, we should have no authentic picture of Molière. The famous portrait of the tragic actor, crowned with laurels, in the part of Cæsar in the tragedy of Pompey possibly belongs to this period. The attraction between the two men must have been real and spontaneous. The sensitive nature and delicate perceptions of Mignard are clearly shown in the picture that hangs to-day amid the horrors of Versailles, and all that we know of him reveals a kind and loyal disposition. But though Molière secured Mignard for himself, he apparently owed his first acquaintance, like so many things else, to Madeleine. Mignard had recently painted the portrait of the Duc de Guise, and in the suite of the Duke was the Comte de Modène, now at Avignon, and thus able to serve as a link between the parties. The link was strong enough to serve. Mignard in 1662 signed the marriage certificate of Geneviève, sister of Madeleine, and, years later, Madeleine in her will entrusted the painter with the management of her estate. It is significant that, in so many cases, even the men who loved Molière for his own sake were usually brought by others within his circle. He was by nature seclusive. He did not seek men out or impose himself upon their affection.

The long odyssey was drawing to an end. Molière was now the acknowledged leader of the best provincial company in France. He had a high reputation as an actor and powerful friends. The way back to Paris lay through Rouen, and it is there that we find him in May, 1658. This was his Rubicon. For the moment we must leave him there and deal with a person whom we have hitherto neglected—not Cæsar crowned with laurels as painted by Mignard at Avignon, but the apprentice author of *L'Etourdi* and *Le Dépit Amoureux*.

VI

THE FIRST PLAYS

OF the many legends we have systematically neglected, the most famous, perhaps, though it is
purely local and has no serious foundation, is that
of the lost valise. It is said, that, riding along the dusty
roads of Languedoc, Molière dropped his valise by the way.
A peasant woman, seeing it fall, promptly covered it with
her ample skirts and, when Molière returned to look for it,
sympathized with him very candidly in his loss and hoped
that he would eventually recover his property. Molière
rode off unsuspectingly after his companions, who rallied
him for his simplicity and urged him to return. *"A quoi
bon?"* he replied. *"Je viens de Chignac, je suis à Lavergnac,
j'aperçois le clocher de Montagnac: au milieu de tous ces*
gnacs *ma valise est perdue."*

What did the valise contain? Tradition, ever prompt with
an answer, says it held the MSS. of the plays and sketches
with which Molière had begun to enrich the repertoire of
his company. That Molière during his provincial years
wrote such plays and sketches, apart from those which have
come down to us, is undoubted. When in October 24,
1658, he first appeared before King Louis, we shall find
him referring to the *"petits divertissements qui lui avaient
acquis quelque réputation et dont il regalait les provinces,"*

and on that occasion he presented a play, not now extant, entitled *Le Docteur Amoureux*. There were undoubtedly others. La Grange in his Register mentions eleven such pieces produced during the first years after the return of Molière to Paris, all probably written during the provincial period of his authorship. The Editors of 1682 regarded these plays as juvenilia which the authors would not wish to preserve, and we may infer from the titles that their themes and situations were afterwards used by the author in later pieces. *Le Fagotier* and *Gorgibus dans le Sac* were presumably early versions of *Le Médecin malgré Lui* and *Les Fourberies de Scapin;* and there are some half dozen titles which indicate that the author was upon ground which he was afterwards to make more peculiarly his own. *Les Trois Docteurs Rivaux, Le Docteur Pédant, Le Maître d'Ecole*—all these are obviously essays in the fustigation of the learned professions which was to be one of the brighter aspects of his comic theatre.

There is a vast literature on the subject of the plays that Molière may or may not have written, ranging from the pleading of bibliophiles with doubtful MS. in which they presume to detect the hand of the master to the commentaries of severely sceptical critics who refuse to admit a single line as authentic previous to *L'Etourdi*. As usually happens in such cases, the particular controversies are long and complicated in proportion as the issue is insignificant. Whether the apocryphal *Joguenet ou les Vieillards Dupés*, piously embalmed by an eighteenth century *moliériste*, is a preliminary sketch for *Les Fourberies de Scapin* or a shameless imitation by another hand is a question of small importance, unless the investigator is bent on proving that a great dramatist may write an indifferent play. And that can usually be better shown from his authentic works.

Suffice it that Molière in the provinces was author to his company, and supplied it with a number of farces which his best friends did not wish to perpetuate. Grimarest assures us that everyone in Languedoc, "including persons of the severest disposition never wearied of seeing them enacted," and the striking success of these early farces with the public is beyond dispute. De Visé, writing as an enemy in 1663, must confess: "Molière wrote farces which were something more than farces and which were esteemed in all the towns he visited above those presented by any other actor." Neither the subjects nor the characters were, however, in any way original. The themes were those of the popular Italian pieces of the day, partly written, partly improvised by the actors in accordance with the indications of the author: surprises, mystifications, trickeries and disguises. The characters were those of the *commedia dell' arte:* old gentlemen outwitted, loquacious doctors of learning, resourceful valets, impertinent maids and young lovers. Two of these apocryphal works, *La Jalousie du Barbouillé,* and *Le Médecin Volant,* have for the last sixty years been included in the standard editions. *La Jalousie du Barbouillé,* with which all complete editions now begin, contains at least one incident which Molière repeated in the immortal *George Dandin—* the scene in which Angelique, barred from the house by Barbouillé, succeeds by a skilful manœuvre in locking out, in turn, her jealous lord. The incident, however, is from Boccaccio and the play itself can scarcely claim to be really written. It is a mere sketch which in performance must have been generously expanded and developed by the actors.

The doctor, who persistently demands explanations but never stays for an answer and is finally dragged from the stage feet-foremost still discussing the nature of things, is the traditional pedant of the *commedia dell' arte,* whom Molière, when he came to write from nature, would bring to life in a dozen incarnations. *Le Médecin Volant,* is an embryonic version of *Le Médecin Malgré Lui.* The wit and humanity of the great farce is to seek, however, and there is at least one passage in which Molière has neglected to mitigate the grossness of his Italian model. The resourceful valet who impersonates a physician in order that his master may obtain access to his lady is another traditional character. To prevent discovery he has to appear as man-servant and doctor in rapid alternation, and is at last required to produce both characters at once. All this is pure harlequinade— though it is none the worse for that.

The recent reaction against the excessive realism of the modern stage and against the intrusion of the man-of-letters into the theatre has resulted in a good deal of misconception about the artificial and improvised Italian comedy of the early seventeenth century. There are even misguided people who look back to it as to a summit in theatrical history. The *commedia dell' arte* was in sober reality an extremely simple form of entertainment in which half-a-dozen traditional stage characters, playing to half-a-dozen stock situations, amused the public with jokes which must needs be taken by the simplest auditors. Such plays depended more on the actor than the author, and the actor was free to develop or vary his part as he pleased. It has been wrongly inferred that such plays were not written at all. We are asked to believe that the actors, by some miracle, came together, agreed upon a subject, entered upon the stage, and relied upon their wit and inspiration of the moment to carry them through. All this is modern invention. Somaize, another enemy of Molière—we shall soon be meeting them all—says that he adapted *Le Médecin Volant* from *Il Medico Volante* of Dominique, a celebrated Harlequin of the seventeenth century, adding, in his anxiety to prove that Molière was in all things the sedulous ape, that he imitated the Italians not only in their plays but in their postures and conduct of the scene. There is no extant version of *Il Medico Volante*, but a scenario was left in MS. by Dominique, who, writing in the first person, describes the scenes in which he figures, the principal turns of the dialogue and the places in which he reserves for himself an opportunity to extemporize. It is clear from these notes that the *commedia dell' arte* was not the happy-go-lucky institution of popular tradition. The actors knew exactly how the play would run. There were places, however, where they were permitted to extemporize, and it is extremely doubtful whether even the extemporization was genuine. Each actor must have had his repertoire of jests and devices. The famous improvisations of the *commedia dell' arte* could in the majority of cases have been little more than a systematic disregard of the advice of Hamlet to the players at Elsinore: And let those that play the clown speak no more than is set down for them.

However much we may respect the vigour and vitality of the *commedia dell' arte*, its limits should be recognized. It eliminated the merely literary play and ensured that the art of the theatre should be first to last a traffic of the stage. But those who look wistfully back to Harlequin for their inspiration and denounce the dramatic author as a cuckoo in the nest wilfully misread theatrical history. The theatre has always flourished in proportion as the dramatic author has predominated. The dramatic author in France first emerged in the latter half of the sixteenth century in the person of Alexander Hardy. His position was at first precarious, and for many years ignoble. Hardy wrote eight hundred plays, and he lived and died in poverty. He did little for himself, but he prepared a way for his successors, demonstrating in a very practical fashion that a company which had a fertile dramatic author in its service outlived its rivals and did better business than the companies which relied upon the common stock. French tragedy was the fruit of that discovery, and the successors of Hardy—Rotrou, Mairet, Magnon and the rest—prepared the way for Corneille, who, while Molière was still at school, had achieved a position of ease and honour.

Comedy, however, is a later growth than tragedy, and, when Molière sketched his early farces, the comic author had still to earn his place in the story. Comedy still stood in modest hesitation between the scenario of the Italians, planned and rehearsed into being on the stage, and the finished composition of the dramatic author, to which the tragedies of Rotrou and Corneille had pointed the way. Molière, at the outset of his career as an author, provided his company with farces borrowed from any source, fitted to the needs of the moment, hastily written or not in the real sense of the word written at all. He was the "factotum or shakescene" of Elizabethan England. To bring such pieces to judgment is a waste of criticism. The original owner of the MS. from which *La Jalousie de Barbouillé* and *Le Médecin Volant* were printed for the edition of 1734, at first very rightly refused to allow their publication: "As to the plays which our author produced in the provinces," he wrote, "it is true that two of them have fallen into my hands. It is easy to see, however, that Molière did not *write* them. They are sketches such as he gave to his actors, who filled in the outlines for themselves, in the manner of the Italians, according to their capacity. It is certain that Molière never digested them on paper."

The position of the comic author during the early seventeenth century must be kept in mind, not only in relation to these early sketches, but equally in relation to the first authentic plays which we are about to consider. *L'Etourdi* and *Le Dépit Amoureux*, in which the genius of Molière was first declared, were unoriginal in subject, incident and character. Molière throughout his career was to be charged with imitation and theft. The charges were bad criticism and worse faith. Molière was a great reader, and he remembered instinctively anything that might serve his turn. The traditional saying with which he met the charge of having borrowed from Cyrano de Bergerac a famous scene in *Les Fourberies de Scapin* was his own first and last word on the subject of his adaptations: *Je prends mon bien où je le trouve.* There is not a play of Molière for which a dozen sources have not been discovered, and it will be necessary to deal now and then with specific cases. All these charges of repetition or plagiary, however, must be read in the light of his position as a comic author of the seventeenth century. Molière followed the practice of the time. The subjects and characters of the comic theatre, when Molière began to write, belonged to any actor or author who could turn them to good account. There was no law of theatrical copyright, no recognized system of royalties. There was a certain custom of the profession which was beginning to develop towards the modern view of literary property, but throughout the life of Molière any play after its first run might be performed or adapted by anybody. A brief survey of this evolution is necessary to an understanding of the controversies in which Molière will shortly be involved.

The position of the dramatic author had, until quite recently, been that of the hired poet who, in consideration of a retaining fee, contracted to supply his company each year with so many plays. Hardy, retained by Valleran at the Hôtel de Bourgogne in the first years of the century, provided the troop with as many plays as it required, and he abided by that contract till the day of his death in 1628. This was the system under which Marlowe and Shakespeare came to maturity, and in France it constituted an intermediate stage between the Italian school of improvisation, where plays were written, in so far as they were written at all, by the actors, and the modern system of independent authorship, according to which a play is the property of the playwright and the actor is only permitted to perform it upon certain conditions. The hired poet wrote to the pleasure of his employers. He was in constant touch with them, and produced for them a rapid succession of plays in which appropriate parts must be available for every member of the cast. In the first quarter of the seventeenth century the successors of Hardy, culminating in Corneille, had changed all that so far as tragedy was concerned. The tragic author was no longer a hired servant, but the proprietor of his works for which he had to be paid a fair price. His tragic texts had a recognized value apart from anything its inter-

107

preters might do with them. His name began to figure upon playbills and to be noted by the public. The modern system of royalties first began clearly to emerge towards the middle of the century. Corneille, who made the profession of a dramatic author respectable (provided, of course, that he wrote tragedies in verse), made it also lucrative. The practice was introduced of paying to the author either a portion of the receipts of each performance or a fixed sum for the right to produce his play for as long as the play might still be regarded as a novelty. The author, however, lost all rights in his play after its first run was exhausted, and any producer might annex it after publication.

The actor at first distrusted these developments. He regarded the author as a dangerous interloper, and the Cornelian actress, Mademoiselle La Beaupré, complained bitterly of his encroachments: "Monsieur de Corneille," she writes, "has done us a great mischief; formerly we could get plays at three crowns a piece, written in a single night. That was the custom and it worked extremely well. Now, however, the plays of Monsieur de Corneille cost us dear and we make very little out of them." The lady neglects to observe that the author who was becoming a person of consideration and dignity in the theatre was also rising remarkably in the social world and carrying along with him all his interpreters. True, the actor was losing the prerogatives of purchasing a play for three crowns or tossing his author in a blanket (apparently a frequent practice), but Monsieur de Corneille was raising the whole status of the theatre and in the long run no one benefited more from this development than the actor himself.

The hired poet of Hardy's day was, during this intermediate stage of authorship, the least regarded member of the company. Tristan l'Hermite in his autobiography relates how in 1608, being at the Louvre in the service of the Duc de Verneuil, he would escape from his tutor to consort with a company of players who came occasionally to the Court. One day he found some eight or ten of them in the garden riotously engaged. They were carrying between them a young man, clad in a dressing gown, his slippers and nightcap already sown in various alleys. Tristan asked one of them who the young man might be. He replied that he was a poet whom the actors had hired and that he did not wish to play at bowls, being in the vein to write. Small wonder that Chapelain, over twenty years later, writing of the young Rotrou, predecessor of Corneille, expressed astonishment that so promising a young man should have undertaken so shameful a service. By the middle of the century the actors had, however, learned to treat their authors with respect and in proportion as they did so became themselves more respectable. And the reason for the change was simple. They found that it paid.

It will be noted that royalties, when first introduced, were received by the author only so long as the play was a novelty. In respect of a play already produced and printed neither producer nor author was in any way protected. A play, once acted, was common property. That was hard upon the author, but the producer was equally liable to suffer. The author, having given his play to one producer, might immediately seek another if the performance displeased him. We shall deal later with classic instances of the wrongs suffered by Molière both as an author whose plays were pirated by publishers and as a producer whose play might

109

be taken away from him and given to a rival theatre during the first week of its run.

The actors and dramatists of the early seventeenth century thus had an entirely different view of authorship from ourselves, and the whole question of plagiary was on quite a different footing. Any play that had run its course in any theatre was anybody's property. This applied even to the texts of plays and it applied even more forcibly to subjects and situations. Once Dominique had sketched *Il Medico Volante* the subject belonged generally to the theatre, and a popular company was not only permitted but expected to make the most of it. The royal troop at the Hôtel de Bourgogne, as well as Molière, had its *Médecin Volant,* written in verse by Boursault and produced in 1661. It was one of the duties of an enterprising manager to ensure that the fashionable subject of the day was not omitted from his repertoire. Now it was *Le Médecin Volant.* A little later it will be *Le Festin de Pierre.* Originality and the personal touch were a matter of treatment and presentation. Style was the man; the subject was neither here nor there. Molière, writing *L'Etourdi,* which in treatment is the first strikingly individual play he produced, took his characters and situations from at least half a dozen authors. There is hardly a line of the farce which could in a modern playbill be described as "new and original" without risk of an action for breach of copyright.

Molière, writing *L'Etourdi,* was thirty-three years of age. He had passed more than ten years of his life in varied association with men and women of every class—authors, poets, princes, men of the Court and the town, soldiers, deputies. Still, however, he remained a little remote from them all.

He lived as yet only in the theatre. His first two authentic plays were those of a young man who derived his inspiration from the literature and practice of his profession rather than from life. Personal observation yet counted for little or nothing. There was hardly a touch of the comic realist in these early plays. That is the first important point to be noted in respect of *L'Etourdi* and *Le Dépit Amoureux*. To brighten the repertory of his theatre and to justify the leadership he was assuming, Molière turned a little negligently to authorship, drawing on the common theatrical stock for the lost preliminary sketches which unexpectedly and perhaps to his mortification—for he was a serious young man—were received with uproarious delight by his provincial audiences. Encouraged by these experiments, he wrote at last a comedy in five acts and in verse. But it was still an actor's play. It assembled the stock characters of the contemporary theatre. For Molière reality lay still with the tragic heroes of Corneille and, when Mignard painted his portrait at Lyon, it was as Cæsar crowned with laurels that he desired to go down to posterity, not as the author of the best comedy of artifice that had yet been written.

The full title of this comedy of artifice is *L'Etourdi ou les Contretemps,* and its character is better defined in the subtitle than in the title. It consists of a series of episodes in which Mascarille tries ingeniously to win for his master possession of Célie, the beautiful slave of Trufaldin. Mascarille invents one ruse after another, but each in turn is defeated owing to his master's untimely and innocent intervention. The interest grows by repetition. What will be the next device of the clever rascal with whom it is a point of honour to succeed in his disinterested stratagems, and

III

how will his unfortunate master contrive, as he infallibly
must, to bring about his own discomfiture? The play was
produced at Lyon in 1653 or 1655. The controversy as to
its date is tedious and of small importance. The modern
critics, after much scholarly hesitation, have finally decided
in favour of 1655, the conclusive argument being that among
the sources from which Molière so freely borrowed was
Le Parasite of Tristan l'Hermite, published in 1654 and
produced at the Hôtel de Bourgogne at the beginning of
that year.

L'Etourdi is in plot a free adaptation from Beltrame's
L'Inavvertito. Molière has suppressed parts of his original, regrouped scenes and incidents, added certain episodes,
mostly borrowed from other authors, and provided the
play with a conclusion of his own. This same conclusion,
Molière's only original contribution to the plot, is the one
serious blemish on the play. Molière frequently borrows
like a genius and invents like a simpleton. Among the
dramatists who minister so brilliantly to his occasions we
find, in addition to Beltrame and Tristan l'Hermite, Plautus,
Luigi Groto, Terence and Fabritio de Fornaris, while scattered throughout the five acts are tricks and echoes of Italian,
Spanish and French authors who would have been entirely
forgotten had Molière neglected to lay them under contribution. It must be further confessed that in many important
respects Molière has not improved upon his originals.
L'Inavvertito is in some ways a better play than *L'Etourdi*
—clearer, more logical, more evenly balanced, more convincing. Nor can it be maintained that Molière has improved on his models in the presentment of his characters.
The unwary reader, yielding to his admiration of Mascarille,

will naturally applaud the soliloquy in which this prince of valets pays tribute to his own exploits:

> Je veux que l'on s'apprête
> A me peindre en héros, un laurier sur la tête,
> Et qu'au bas du portrait on mette en lettres d'or:
> Vivat Mascarillus, *fourbûm imperator.*

Mascarille has an artist's pride in his virtuosity. All this is admirable, but justice compels us to admit that Mascarille, knave on principle, is equally admirable in his Italian setting. He is the familiar rascal invented by the Greeks, borrowed by the Romans, inherited by the Italians, imitated by the French, and handed on by Molière to Beaumarchais. He has lived on the European stage for nearly two thousand years, though in life he never existed at all. The same is true of the other figures of the farce. All are traditional and in no way extended or refreshed. Some of them, yielding to the exigencies of the plot, are not even consistent with themselves, which in farce is a serious fault and one to which the Italian models of Molière were seldom liable.

Molière has not, in the sense of Bottom the Weaver, "translated" his characters, and he has certainly not improved upon his models in construction. He has, on the contrary, shown an almost insolent disregard for the technical conduct of his play. He brings his characters on to the stage as and when he needs them with a magnificent disregard of time, place and probability. He leads his action along from one coincidence to another. Mascarille must have speech with Célie: *Oh! bonheur! la voilà qui paraît à propos.* Mascarille has need of money: enter Anselm with 2,000 *livres.* Mascarille contrives a plan to outwit the credulous

113

Pandolfe: *Bon! voici mon homme justement.* These instances might be indefinitely multiplied, but all pale their
ineffectual fires in comparison with the amazing conclusion
in which Turkish pirates, long lost sons and daughters,
brothers meeting sisters unawares and the whole apparatus
of the romantic theatre of the renaissance is suddenly flung
at the heads of a bewildered audience in order to clear up
a confusion which a more careful dramatist would never have
permitted to occur.

Where, then, is the genius? What are we to infer from
this preliminary reading of the first authentic play of Molière
in the light of its models? The incidents are borrowed;
the characters are conventional; the construction is careless.
L'Etourdi, nevertheless, is the second imperishable comedy
written in the French language, and if Corneille, in one of
his lighter moments, had not written *Le Menteur*, it would
have been the first.

Note, first of all, that Molière, breaking every rule of
orthodox construction, is faithful to the principle that governs
them all. He is in living touch with his audience from first
to last. There is only one rule which this actor, experienced
in dealing with every kind of audience, rustic or polite, infallibly observes. Later, as the experienced author of several masterpieces, he will explain and defend the system
which by instinct he practised from the outset. The aim of
the dramatist is to please. Whether he pleases in contempt
or in respect for the rules is no matter. So much the worse
for the rules. Molière, passing from incident to incident
in *L'Etourdi*, constantly has in mind, by no conscious effort
of his own, but because he has lived for years in living contact with them, the spectators who sit or stand about him.

114

So long as he holds their interest and can carry them along, he has no academic misgivings as a constructive playwright. For him the well-made play is a play that an audience will gladly accept as it goes. Every moment "serves for the matter that is then born in it." Mascarille invents a stratagem. Molière knows that his audience is impatient to see the stratagem carried into effect and defeated by the master whose turn it is meant to serve. He knows exactly how much his audience, in that mood and expectation, will stand in the way of coincidence; and he strains its credulity just as far as it will go. The reader in his library will note the improbabilities of time and place; he will see exactly where the ice is thin and deplore the author's neglect of details which a dramatist less vital and robust would never venture to allow himself. But Molière is writing for the man in the theatre who is prepared to meet him more than halfway. He presumes on the fact that, if the man in the theatre sufficiently desires certain things to happen, the dramatist may bring them about when and how he pleases. His art often consists less in avoiding improbabilities than in getting his audience in the mood to disregard them. There had been, previous to *L'Etourdi*, many a farce better constructed according to the rules; there had never been a farce better constructed according to the principal end and object of dramatic authorship.

The outstanding blemish of the play, the fumbling-up into a loose adieu of its conclusion, is a case in point. The conclusion of many of the plays of Molière—but not the great plays of character—is often a sorry business. In this he resembles Shakespeare, and the reason in the two authors is identical. The play has served its turn. The end is in sight. The interest of the audience drops and that of the author, writing in touch with the audience, drops to an equal degree. Let the story come to an end and the curtain fall as quickly as possible. Almost anything will serve so long as most of the characters are present and can be more or less neatly disposed of at the finish. The conclusion of *L'Etourdi* is admittedly poor, but no poorer and no more scandalous to the producer than the conclusion of *Twelfth Night*. The audience is ready to depart, and the instinct of the author in both cases is to cut the knots which still remain untied. We are not defending the method. In a lesser dramatist it would be fatal. But masters such as Shakespeare and Molière can break with impunity rules which are necessary to the salvation of his pupils.

The constructive defects of *L'Etourdi* need not, therefore, detain us. Molière, later on, will present his own triumphant apology. The lack of originality in the matter of incident and character is a more serious matter. The immortal comedian is still to seek. Molière at thirty-two is younger than his years, still more interested in literature than in life. He goes to the established theatre for his subject, and does not look beyond. He has, as we shall shortly realize, observed and reflected much. But he is not yet tempted to relate these observations and reflections to his art. So long as he remains in the extravagant, romantic South he holds at arm's length the realities which will claim him as soon as he returns to Paris. In the dry air of the capital, where all extravagance expires and where it is impossible to escape the pressure of contemporary life, he will take from the society about him the themes and characters which for the moment he draws exclusively from tradition. Mean-

while, he expends his genius upon a comedy of marionettes, content with the familiar gesticulations of the classic
stage.

The comedian abides his time and inspiration, but observe that the stylist is already complete. The exuberance
of the dialogue, its amazing volubility—inexhaustible and
yet never forced or inappropriate—brilliantly indicates what
may be expected of the author when he turns to the portrayal
of the human comedy. By turns he is formal and familiar,
exalted and colloquial, vivacious and precise. Within the
limits of this play, despite its artifice and the narrow range
it offers, there is every variety of mood and effect in the
writing. Victor Hugo declared the dialogue of *L'Etourdi*
to be the best that Molière ever wrote. The irresistible
movement of the play is, in fact, verbal rather than substantial. How these people talk! That is our first reflection.
We are carried along from felicity to felicity. There is here
a writer who already knows how much, as yet unsaid, it is
possible to say in a language, rooted like his own in scholarship, but renewed and enriched by a perpetual accommodation with the social needs of a race for whom speech is as
necessary as light and air. *"Beaucoup de fautes contre la
langue,"* said Voltaire, *"vices de constructions . . . mots
impropres et surannés"*; and he might have urged, in support of this judgment, similar strictures by La Bruyère and
Fénélon. But this only meant that Molière had a wider
range of speech than the academies and that even Voltaire,
free spirit and revolutionary, was in matters of style and
expression subdued to the classical pedantry of his generation. Molière, for all his creatures, finds the appropriate
expression and finds it without any searching, lighting upon

it like bird on bough. He speaks in turn the language of sense and sentiment, tenderness and malice, indignation and detachment, peasant and prince, realism and romance. He has a ready word for all things that concern the commerce of man with man.

Le Dépit Amoureux, first produced before the Estates of Languedoc at Béziers in 1656, is, like *L'Etourdi,* freely adapted from an Italian model. Molière took both his subject and his characters from a play of Nicolo Secchi, entitled *L'Interresse*—a romantic comedy of intrigue which had been popular in the Italian theatre for over fifty years. The plot is intricate and preposterous. Its heroine has contrived to live from birth as the son of her father, and to marry the man she loves without revealing her sex. That is the least of the complications. The perverted skill with which its acrobatic twists are managed is wholly Italian. Molière has introduced only a few minor variations and chastened the grossness of his original in which the latent indecencies of the situation were thoroughly exploited. The construction, in view of the nature of the plot, had to be more carefully organized than in the case of *L'Etourdi,* but the same indifferent, careless hand is apparent. The introduction of the main plot is deliciously naïve:

> . . . vous savez la secrète raison
> Qui cache aux yeux de tous mon sexe et ma maison;
> Vous savez que dans celle ou passa mon bas âge. . . .

It recalls inevitably the burlesque of Sheridan:

> You know, my friend, scarce two revolving suns,
> And three revolving moons have closed their course. . . .

118

and the reply of Molière to anyone who objected that, if the lady knows all this, there is no necessity for her to be informed, would be, quite shamelessly, the answer made by Mr. Puff to Mr. Dangle. The lady may know it well, but the audience has still to be instructed.

Molière, in addition to taking an Italian play for his model, has again borrowed broadcast from his extensive reading. Plautus, Terence, Erasmus, Cyrano, Rotrou, Bracciolini and Horace are all laid under contribution. His genius is still nourished upon literature rather than life. There is in the play as a whole no advance upon *L'Etourdi*, but rather a retrogression. The author is not always felicitous and sometimes fails to avoid obscurity in his handling of the romantic involutions of the intrigue.

There is, however, a group of scenes and characters which, abstracted from the play as a whole, declare the future comedian who would shortly turn from literature to life; and posterity, which outgrew the artificial comedy of intrigue imitated from Nicolo Secchi, was unable to let these isolated scenes fall into oblivion. The play as a whole retained its popularity, as did *L'Etourdi*, through the reigns of Louis XIV and Louis XV, *L'Etourdi*, well in front, however, scoring 359 against 244 performances. It was then discovered that, though *L'Etourdi* might still hope to survive as an ingenious exercise in the antique mode, its successor was doomed to an increasing neglect. The Comédie Française thereupon took a brave and wholly justifiable decision. Valville, one of its principal actors under Louis XVI, detached from the play half a dozen scenes which were beyond the reach of fashion and inserted a few connecting lines here and there, with the result that two acts of imperishable comedy replaced, in the repertoire of the house of Molière, the original five acts of romantic farce. The justification for this innovation can be read in the subsequent record of the first two plays of Molière. From 1814 to 1870 there were only 51 performances of *L'Etourdi*, while of the abridged version of *Le Dépit Amoureux* there were no less than 372. This abridged version has retained its popularity to the present day.

The scenes which have thus survived the revolutions of taste and fashion for over three hundred years comprise the whole of Act I; Act II, Scene 4; and Act IV, Scenes 2, 3, and 4. These scenes, which can happily be disengaged, without any loss of significance, from the intrigue in which they are embedded, are linked together with verses taken from other parts of the play or interpolated by the editor. They show us master and man quarrelling with mistress and maid upon a misunderstanding, swearing they will never forgive or forget, but gradually relenting and renewing their vows. *Amantium iræ, amoris integratio.* These passages belong to Molière alone, and are the first to declare his comic genius as distinguished from his literary and theatrical dexterity. Thousands of scenes have since been written on the lines which here were traced for the first time. How many heroines of the comic stage have we not seen following faithfully this progress of Lucile, the mistress, and Marinette, the maid, through all the prescribed stages of indignation, defiance of the gentle passion and reconciliation sweetly deferred. The thing has been done a thousand times since Molière, but it has never been better done. Into a conventional comedy of intrigue, the work of a skilful artificer who knew his public and had learned how to manipulate his puppets for their diversion, there slips a touch of nature that is to transform the comic theatre of France, and the hand of the comedian is already as light and firm as ever it will need to be. These scenes are for ever fresh and true. This was the comedy of Molière himself, for which he was indebted to no predecessor.

VII

THE RETURN TO PARIS

W E left Molière, concluding a provincial pilgrimage of thirteen years, in the city of Rouen, home of Corneille, where the Illustrious Theatre had made its first appearance before the public in the winter of 1643. Speculation turns at once to the meeting of the two dramatic authors. Molière, professionally devoted to the Cornelian theatre, had loved it from early youth, and Corneille had also written a play entitled *Le Menteur*, the first polite comedy of France. Molière would be eager to make his better acquaintance, and Corneille could hardly fail to have heard of *L'Etourdi* and *Le Dépit Amoureux*, though he had not, perhaps, begun to suspect that here was a man destined to raise the comic to the level of the tragic muse. Alas! there is no record of any encounter between them. We look in vain for the impressions made on the great Corneille by Molière, and we find in place of it a vivid record of the impression made by his leading lady, the lovely Marquise, Mademoiselle du Parc. Pierre Corneille, fifty-two years of age, not only fell a victim to her good beauties, but recorded his infatuation with a grave dignity, as befitted a creator of classic heroes:

> Allez, belle Marquise, allez en d'autres lieux
> Semer les doux périls qui naissent de vos yeux.

He admits that grey hairs and a wrinkled brow give to the most cordial sentiments a charm that is sad rather than effective. He has loved too long to be still a candidate for love, and he writes his epitaph in a spirit of charming resignation:

> Il vécut sans la dame et vécut sans ennui,
> Comme la dame ailleurs se divertit sans lui.

Thomas Corneille, his younger brother, even more heavily smitten, confessed the smart in an elegy less deserving of quotation. The rivalry between the brothers was without rancour—a fine, generous affair worthy of two very noble kinsmen. We may regret that the distinguished brothers preferred to record their appreciation of a pretty actress than to tell us of their meeting with the author of *Le Dépit Amoureux*; but the choice was not unnatural.

> There's your Venus—whence we turn
> To yonder girl that fords the burn.

How exactly was the return to Paris finally arranged? Our sole authority is the Preface of 1682. Molière, we are informed, came to Rouen in the spring of 1658 to explore the situation:

"His friends had advised him to draw nearer to Paris and for this purpose to bring his company to a neighbouring town. Thereby he would be able to turn to good account the reputation which he had acquired in the eyes of several persons of influence who, being interested in his career, had promised to introduce him to the Court. . . . He accordingly came to Rouen. There he remained during the summer, and after making several secret journeys to Paris, succeeded in recommending his services and those of his comrades to Monsieur, the only brother of His Majesty, who accorded him his name and protection, and presented him to the King and the Queen mother."

There is no means of knowing who were the "persons of influence" who finally induced Monsieur to take the company under his protection. Possibly it was Mazarin, who might have heard of Molière through his son-in-law the Prince de Conti, or the painter Mignard. All that we know for certain is that Molière was not counting exclusively upon his introductions, for, while he was negotiating for a hearing at Court, Madeleine was negotiating for a theatre. With or without a protector of the royal house, they were determined to have an autumn season in Paris, and on July 12, 1658, Madeleine signed a contract with the Comte Louis de Talhouet for the lease of the *Jeu de Paume des Marais* with all its furnishings and equipment. The lease was to prove unnecessary and was allowed to lapse; but it is, nevertheless, precious to the biographer, for Madeleine, in signing it, gave as her address the house of Jean Poquelin under the pillars of the market. The Béjarts, nomadic for the last thirteen years, had no address in Paris. Marie Hervé had followed the fortunes of her children from city to city. And now Madeleine, requiring a fixed legal abode, ventured to take the house of Jean Poquelin. It is the first indication that the father has not only forgiven his son, but accepted his son's career. Molière during his "secret" visits to Paris presumably lodged with his father, discussing with him his projects, infecting him, perhaps, with his enthusiasm. Times were changing. The young king and his younger brother were known to be interested in the theatre. Mazarin was notoriously a patron of the arts. The great Richelieu had

124

himself tried his distinguished hand at dramatic authorship. For thirteen years Molière had paid his way in the provinces, consorting with princes, a public servant of the Estates. Jean Poquelin might well begin to think that his son had after all not done so badly. The time had come, in any case, to put away regret; and for Madeleine, when she came to Paris, there would be a resigned welcome at the house under the pillars of the market.

Molière was to have opened at the Marais in September, but by that time he had secured his protector, and on 24th October, 1658, the company of the Sieur du Fresne, henceforth the *Troupe de Monsieur*, made its first appearance before King and Court in the guardroom of the Vieux Louvre.

The audience on that occasion included a group of spectators more formidable than the King himself. Gentlemen from the south had doubtless brought back to Paris from time to time stories of the glittering festivals of the Duc d'Epernon and the Prince de Conti. Merchants from Lyon and Béziers may have begun to speak of the young author of *L'Etourdi* and *Le Dépit Amoureux*. Molière, who was accused by his enemies, among other things, of being most apt to speak the right word in the right ear at the right moment, had doubtless not been idle during his secret visits to Paris in the summer. There must have been considerable gossip in the town of these new players from the provinces who had secured the interest of the King's brother, and no one would be more interested than Montfleury and the royal players of the Hôtel de Bourgogne. The Hôtel de Bourgogne was now without a rival, for the Théâtre du Marais, after the death of Mondory in 1637, had ceased to be a formidable competitor. Richelieu, the old protector of the Marais, had even proposed that the company should be incorporated with the royal troop. Distinguished audiences had flocked to the Marais to witness *Le Cid* and *Le Menteur;* but the elder Corneille was now giving his plays to the rival company. Even Jodelet, its most faithful comedian, to whom Corneille had entrusted *Le Menteur,* had played from time to time at the Hôtel de Bourgogne, and, when Molière came to Paris, the fortunes of the Marais had sunk so low that the proprietor of the theatre, as we have seen, was ready to dispose of the lease.

The Hôtel de Bourgogne was thus at the height of its prosperity. It was in 1658 the only protected theatre. It received from the King a pension of 1,200 *livres.* It had "created" most of the great tragedies of Corneille. It had imposed on the public its own ways and methods. There was only one way of playing tragedy, and that was the royal way. It was a little the way of the periwig-pated fellow who, if he did not tear a passion to tatters, at least sounded his verses like three heroes in one and left his audience in no doubt as to when he considered himself to be saying something that called for emphasis and applause.

Montfleury, watching the début of Molière before the King on 24th October, 1658, if he felt at all alarmed at the appearance of these new competitors, must have been speedily set at ease. The play was *Nicomède*—the Cornelian tragedy in which everyone present had seen Montfleury himself. Let us, therefore, look at the performance for the moment with his professional eyes. Obviously this Molière would never be a serious rival. The fellow had no notion how to act a tragedy. This was neither nature nor art. He spoke his lines with discretion, but where was the sound and fury? And that eternal *hoquet* was unfortunate. Moreover, he carried himself abominably—feet all over the place, nose in the air, head twisted queerly back, one shoulder perpetually in advance of the other, eyes restless and wandering, hands thrust against his ribs. The women, on the other hand, were not so bad. The elder Béjart could act, had a fine presence, spoke well, played with conviction. And the du Parc was a lovely creature—disposition of an iceberg and not very intelligent, but they often made the best actresses. Old du Fresne was getting past his work, but he had learned his business in a hard school and was cool as a cucumber, though he had never before played in Paris in his life. Not a bad performance, but clearly the *Troupe Royale* had nothing to fear from the *Troupe de Monsieur*.

The tragedy drew to an end and the curtain fell. Montfleury need not hesitate to applaud, for the players must be feeling a little low. None could know better than they that the tragedy had missed its mark. They must have realized from the start that it was one thing to amuse provincials and quite another pair of shoes to move the capital.

But what was this? The curtain was up again; and there, alone upon the stage, was the Sieur de Molière. He had come forward and louted low to the royal group. Shades of Bruscambille! the fellow was going to make a speech, and that was a practice going rapidly out of fashion. It was all very well for a travelling showman or a mountebank on the Pont Neuf, who must cry his wares or the public would pass him by. But the theatre was moving up in the world, and the harangue was nearly obsolete.

It must be admitted, however, that he did it rather well.

127

The Sieur de Molière was clearly more in his element as the orator of his company than as a heavy lead. He held himself with dignity and an air of rather melancholy grace; his manner was courteous and yet with a hint of pride, serious and yet with a suggestion that somewhere, if you sought it out, there lurked a pleasant irony. And he could turn a speech as well as any courtier:

"M. de Molière came upon the stage. After thanking His Majesty in modest terms for the kindness with which he had overlooked the deficiencies of his company, which had appeared only with the greatest misgivings before so august an assembly, he assured His Majesty that the desire which they all had to amuse the greatest King in all the world had caused them to forget that His Majesty had in his service excellent originals of which they were but feeble copies. Since, however, His Majesty had been so good as to suffer their country manners, he begged very humbly to be permitted to present one of the small diversions which had acquired him a certain reputation and with which he had been accustomed to amuse the provinces" (Preface of 1682).

Montfleury must acknowledge that the speech was well turned—especially the bit about the tragedians of the Hôtel de Bourgogne. "Feeble copies" was good, though he had said it with a twinkle and had not seemed very clearly desirous of copying anybody. Excellent originals . . . feeble copies . . . country manners . . . small diversions which had acquired him a certain reputation—all that was in the right tone and manner. Even the reference to the greatest King in all the world would pass—a trifle forced, perhaps, but it was said that the young Louis had an exalted view of his position, and that such compliments would soon be current coin.

For if the King like not the tragedy, why, then, methinks he likes it not perdy. The Sieur de Molière was not going to leave it at that; he was resolved to snatch a victory from the jaws of defeat. For the first time there was an outburst of genuine applause. But Montfleury was shaking a dubious head. These tactics were old as the hills. It had been the fashion in the infancy of the tragic theatre to play a farce at the end. Send the people away in a good humour—that was the idea. But tragedy should now be able to stand alone.

The small diversion that followed *Nicomède* on this occasion was entitled *Le Docteur Amoureux*, evidently one of the lost sketches of the provincial period. Molière played the doctor and his success was immediate. Montfleury, watching the little play and noticing its reception, must have wondered what on earth had induced his rival to come before the King with a tragedy. For this was obviously a comic actor. Not Jodelet himself had such gaiety or was so swift in word and gesture. There was more of the comic spirit in his left eyebrow than in the whole company of Scaramouche. And there was at the same time something oddly appealing. This was pure farce, mostly grimace, with little suggestion of humanity, and yet it somehow affected you as not entirely the gesticulation of a clown. This Sieur de Molière, with the comic eyebrows and flexible mouth was, it seemed, a sad fellow at bottom. All that gaiety was upon the surface only. The dark eyes dancing with fun and the nimble tongue—how the fellow talked—carried you along on a tide of laughter, and yet there was a suggestion that even the poor pedant he so extravagantly mocked was somehow lamentable. Could it be that comedy and tragedy were two aspects of the universal fate?

129

The Sieur de Molière had saved the situation, and Montfleury had for the moment no reason to grudge him his
success. This was no serious competitor for the royal
tragedians. But Jodelet, at the Marais, had better look to
his laurels and Scaramouche himself might find it difficult
to stand up against so good an actor in the same line of
business.

Friends and enemies alike agreed that the first appearance
of Molière and his company at Court was not strikingly
successful. "These new actors," says the Preface of 1682,
"were not displeasing." The first editors of Molière can
go no further than that. They add that the audience "was
especially satisfied with the charm and acting ability of the
women." Charles Perrault bluntly declares: "It is true
that the company did not succeed on this first occasion." All
this, however, applied only to the tragedy. The speech of
Molière was received with acclamation and the comic sketch
that followed it amused, as much as it surprised, everybody
present (Preface of 1682). What was the impression of
the King himself? Undoubtedly he was amused. There
is no record of what the King said; but his action speaks
for itself. Scaramouche, his favourite actor, was then at
the Salle du Petit Bourbon. His Majesty arranged that
Molière should share this hall with the Italians, and he was
authorized to make such terms with Scaramouche as might
seem fair to both of them.

The room was spacious and elegant, the vaulted ceiling
painted with lilies, the sides broken up with small recesses
and doric columns. It communicated by means of a series
of long galleries with the palace, so that its tenant might
feel himself to be virtually in the King's house. Once it

130

had been the property of the Constable of Bourbon, confiscated for treason by François I. The yellow daub of the executioner, with which the house of a criminal must traditionally be splashed, might still be seen above the door, and the arms of a noble house everywhere broken and defaced. But the proud motto remained intact, and Molière entering his new quarters would read the word *"Espérance"* in big letters above the portal.

Molière, under his arrangement with Scaramouche, agreed to pay to the Italians the sum of 1,500 *livres* as a contribution to the expenses which they had incurred in equipping the theatre, and it was further agreed that, as first comers, the Italians should retain for their performances Tuesdays, Fridays and Sundays, which were the "ordinary" or most profitable days of the week. Molière for the moment must be content with the "extraordinary" days—Mondays, Wednesdays, Thursdays and Saturdays.

Scaramouche, born Tiberio Fiorelli, had now for many years been the comic darling of the Court—especially dear to the King. Tradition insists that this famous master of the *commedia dell' arte,* on an occasion when the young Louis had fallen into a fit of temper, so that his nurse was unable to deal with him, had taken the child in his arms and turned the cataract of tears to laughter so uncontrolled that the jester provoked to his own discomfiture a cascade of another sort. The King would sometimes invite Scaramouche to amuse him at table, and is said to have poured out for his jester two glasses of wine with the royal hands.

Of what kind and degree were the relations of Scaramouche and Molière? The evidence, alas! is small. Angelo

131

Constantin, writing a life of Scaramouche, engraved a famous stanza beneath his portrait:

> Cette illustre comédien
> Atteignit de son art l'agréable manière;
> Il fut le maître de Molière,
> Et la nature fût le sien.

The affirmation that Molière was the pupil of Scaramouche was frequently made by his enemies. Every French schoolboy can recite the lines from the *Elomire Hypocondre* of de Chalussay, most spiteful of all the libellists:

> Chez le grand Scaramouche il va soir et matin.
> Là, le miroir en main, et ce grand homme en face,
> Il n'est contorsion, posture, ni grimace,
> Que ce grand écolier du plus grands des bouffons
> Ne fasse et ne refasse en cent et cent façons.

Molière would be the last to deny his debt to the Italians, and that debt has been freely acknowledged in a previous chapter. Of the personal relations of the two great actors, however, there is no record, though they were meeting constantly upon intimate and difficult occasions, rivals in the same house and in the most jealous of all professions. Twelve years later a certain M. de Palaprat records that during the winter of 1671, he used to meet Molière at the house of Vario, a painter from Florence: "This great actor," he writes, "and infinitely greater author, lived in close familiarity with the Italians, for they were good players and very excellent fellows. There were always two or three of the best of them at supper. Molière was often present but not as often as we desired." There is still, however, no word of Scaramouche, and there could hardly have been any real friendship between two men so utterly different in genius and temperament. Scaramouche, though undoubtedly a genius in his kind, was the clown of an older generation. His principal assets were flexibility in grimace and an agility which enabled him to kick himself soundly at an appropriate moment. Soon his jests would go out of fashion as too gross for a public which had learned to appreciate *Tartuffe* and *Le Misanthrope*. He died in 1685 in the full tide of his sins, still apparently able to kick himself—and usually he deserved it—at eighty years of age.

Molière opened his first public season at the Salle du Petit Bourbon on 2nd November, 1658, and, amazingly, he continued during its first weeks the tactics which had brought him within an inch of disaster at the royal performance, producing in succession five tragedies of the elder Corneille, none of them successful. Finally, with a strange reluctance, he decided to do at last what he should have done at first. *L'Etourdi* was produced in November, followed in December by *Le Dépit Amoureux*. Their success was immediate and unparalleled. The editors of 1682 register the profits with a legitimate satisfaction—70 *pistoles* for each player from *L'Etourdi*, 7,000 *livres* net from each of the plays.

Why for the first few weeks of his season did Molière persist in his fidelity to the tragic muse? Why, indeed, had he not chosen to come at once before the King with one of the two plays which he had already tested in the provinces? The choice may to some extent have been imposed upon him by his company. Charles du Fresne was still the *doyen* of the troop. Madeleine was still its leading lady. Mademoiselle du Parc desired always to shine with her own

light. Of the other members, Joseph and Louis Béjart
would support Madeleine in her tragic leanings; Geneviève
Béjart never appears to have had views of her own upon
any subject; du Parc would go with his wife. Mademoiselle
de Brie, the only born comic actress of the troop, had yet to
discover her powers. Molière was not yet master in his
own house. *Primus inter pares* was the utmost he could be
under the act of association which remained always the
charter of the company, and he lacked as yet the overwhelm-
ing prestige which he was shortly to acquire.

Molière, in fact, might still have trouble with his players.
Chapelle, writing to him on 13th April, 1659, sympa-
thetically likens him to Zeus distracted with the claims of
Hera, Aphrodite and Pallas on behalf of their Greeks and
Trojans. He hopes that Molière will issue successfully from
his embarrassments, and contrive a distribution of parts which
shall please everybody and do justice to the play of the
moment. Thus, the troop was rebellious to discipline; and,
since its affairs were managed by a majority vote, it is unsafe
to assume that its policy was necessarily that of its leader.
The points in dispute at this time were clearly serious and
hotly debated. Mademoiselle du Parc in the spring of 1659
temporarily abandoned Molière for the Théâtre du Marais,
and Charles du Fresne, retiring from the stage altogether,
returned to the provinces.

Nevertheless, though Molière was not yet altogether
master in his own house, there is no doubt that his own inclinations were still strongly in favour of tragedy—still the
only respectable branch of dramatic art. Paris had rejected
him as a tragedian fourteen years previously. Perhaps it
would accept him now. But in vain—it is again an enemy,

134

the malicious Chalussay who writes—did he persist in tempting fortune:

> Mais inutilement je tentai la fortune.
> Après *Heraclius*, on siffla *Rodogune;*
> *Cinna* le fut de même et *Le Cid*, tout charmant,
> Reçut, avec *Pompée*, un pareil *traitement.*
> Dans ce sensible affront, ne sachant où m'en prendre,
> Je me vis mille fois sur le point de me pendre.

That is correct history, though spitefully delivered and in very execrable numbers.

The production of *L'Etourdi* and *Le Dépit Amoureux*, however, completely changed the fortunes of the company. That, confesses Chalussay, was a "wonder." The spectators were transported: *Ce ne fut que ah! ah! dans toute l'assemblée.*

The King during the winter was absent from Paris, in search, among other things, of a queen, but he had not forgotten the Sieur de Molière, and, on his return, hearing of the success of *L'Etourdi* and *Le Dépit Amoureux*, summoned the *Troupe de Monsieur* in April, 1689, to the château de Chilly. The play presented was *Le Dépit Amoureux.* Loret in his rhyming gazette and again in his *Muse Historique* tells us of the fine company, the hunting, the delicious food and rich apparel of the ladies in waiting. He mentions also that there were violins and a comedy. But who acted and what was the play was as yet of no consequence to the gazeteer. This same Loret had been equally negligent on a previous occasion. On February 15th Monsieur, the King's brother, had visited the Petit Bourbon to see how his comedians were faring. There was a representation, Loret tells us, of a comical subject. The "subject" was

deemed to be excellent, and was highly praised by the
gentlemen present. Molière had seized the occasion to
make one of his famous harangues and had turned a pleasant
compliment to the address of his protector. But Loret does
not even refer to him by name. He is merely "the
leading actor in that place." Loret speaks only to the fashion
and Molière is not yet the talk of the town. Thus we have
no record of how *Le Dépit Amoureux* was received by the
King in April. Certainly, however, he was again amused,
for on May 10th he summoned Molière to the Louvre for
a command performance of *L'Etourdi*, and a week later he
witnessed two other provincial sketches of Molière, *Le
Médecin Volant* and *Gros-René Ecolier*. During April and
May, 1659, Molière appeared five times before the King.

During the next six months the *Troupe de Monsieur* became firmly established at the Petit Bourbon. Scaramouche
went in June to Italy, and Molière thenceforward had the
theatre to himself. He at once began to give his performances on the ordinary theatrical days—a change which
brought him into more direct rivalry with the Hôtel de
Bourgogne. This rivalry was intensified by the fact that
Molière, though he relied for success on his farces, alternated comedy with tragedy and took the whole theatre for
his province. In the course of the year he revived twenty-
one plays of his own repertoire, including several tragedies
that belonged also to the repertory of the royal troop. He
also produced two new tragedies—*Pylade and Oreste*, by
Coqueteau de la Clairière and *Zénobie* by Magnon, thus
showing that as a producer he did not intend to abandon the
tragic music. Both were failures. He accorded Madeleine
an opportunity to revive her old successes in *Scévole* and

La Mort de Chrispe and gave to Jodelet, his new recruit from the Marais, an opportunity to distinguish himself in three of the farces of Scarron.

The accession to the troop of Jodelet who died, unfortunately, in the following year, balanced the secession of Mademoiselle du Parc and her husband. Of more importance to posterity was the recruiting of a new and lifelong member in Varlet de la Grange, who joined the company as an actor new to the stage in 1659. Like his friend, du Croisy, recruited at the same time, he belonged to the new generation of actors, orderly and respectable, men of education and substance. La Grange died in 1692 much esteemed to the end of his career, while his friend, du Croisy, outliving him by three years, was at the last so distinguished for good works in the parish of Conflans-St.-Honorine, to which he had retired shortly after the death of Molière, that the vicar was too much affected by his death to preach the valedictory sermon.

Meanwhile, in the pauses of these activities, Molière, back in Paris after fourteen years of absence, was seeing with the eyes of maturity people and things which he had previously observed only with the eyes of youth. More especially was he noticing the new society in the midst of which he was finding himself more and more securely at home. This son of a *valet-tapissier*, grandson of an alderman, who had passed his boyhood under the paternal supervision of a burgess of industry and substance, who had passed from the serious circle of his father's friends to the looser company of the theatre, was observing the manners of the Court and of those who stood well within or upon the edge of the social life of the time. Now and then a flicker of amusement would gleam

137

in the melancholy eyes and the suspicion of a smile wrinkled the full flexible mouth for an instant ere it passed.

Why go to the Italians and endlessly repeat the comic heroes of tradition? Here was the comedy of life. The thought came, went, and finally persisted—till one day Molière took up his pen and wrote the title of a new comedy in one act. The smile deepened as the facile pen slipped over the sheet, and on November 28, 1658, with the production of *Les Précieuses Ridicules* the modern comedy of manners was born.

VIII

THE BATTLE OF THE EXQUISITES

THE first and perhaps the most famous *salon* in history is best known to most amateurs of literature through the memoirs and letters of Madame de Sévigné. In the first years of the seventeenth century, when the gentlemen of France were as rude in their society as in their politics, Catharine de Vivone, daughter of the Marquis de Pisani, ambassador of France at Rome, married Charles D'Angennes, the Marquis de Rambouillet. To the Marquise, then only twenty-two years of age, but a woman of character and taste, the French Court, a bivouac between two campaigns, was tedious and disorderly. She was seldom seen at the palace, but collected and entertained her own circle of friends at her house in the Rue St. Thomas du Louvre. Towards 1624 a chronic indisposition confined her even more strictly at home than she wished, but by that time the friends she needed had already found the way to her door, and the Hôtel de Rambouillet was soon the social and intellectual centre of France.

The Marquise, in her famous blue drawing-room, was at home to anyone who was or might be interesting. Merely social distinctions were ignored. Princes of the blood, if they deserved it, were expected to meet with pleasure sons of people who had not in the true sense of the word been "born." Distinction of mind or manner was the acid test, and it was applied with supreme discretion by a great lady, utterly fearless of political or social tyranny. Voiture, Corneille and Bossuet were frequent visitors. The memoirists were legion, including Segrais, Bussy-Rabutin, Ménage and, of course, Madame de Sévigné. The *salon*, which began as a protest against the bad manners of the time, was the beginning of a new period in social history, and was particularly important owing to the impulse it gave to all forms of literary accomplishment.

The Marquise de Rambouillet herself escaped the ridicule which was to fall so swiftly and unexpectedly upon the exquisites of a younger generation. She was of a kind, hospitable, and genuinely cultivated disposition, and she set out to teach the society of her time a lesson which it really needed. Her social power was enormous, and in the prime of her influence was always well used. She was a great lady and an incomparable hostess. Richelieu, seeking to employ her prestige for his political purposes, sent to her house a messenger suggesting that the Marquise should inform him privately of the views expressed in her *salon* upon his policy. The Marquise replied that her guests were so well aware of the high consideration in which she held his Eminence that no one would ever have the audacity to speak ill of him in her presence and that she would, therefore, never have any reason to perform the service for which he had petitioned. The Marquise thus evaded the request of his Eminence and secured his friendship with a delicate rebuke.

When Molière came to Paris in 1658 the Hôtel de Rambouillet, which had been famous for over thirty years, had already outlived its purpose. It had started as a protest against the bad manners of the time. It had become a conventicle of good taste. Good taste is an excellent critic; but it leads swiftly to impotence and destroys itself by inbreeding. The people who frequented the blue salon in the Rue St. Thomas, in the fastidious presence of their hostess, refined upon their sentiments and etherealized their wits till nothing was left but affectations of feeling and expression uncorrected by any reference to genuine emotion or common sense. Love itself became a metaphysical abstraction; each separate hair on the head of every possible emotion was numbered; conversation became virtually unintelligible except to the initiated. Wit was the measure of a man, and this seventeenth century wit was little more than the application of a practised verbal dexterity to the simplest matters. Mere refinement speedily gave way to downright affectation. The daughter of the Marquise de Rambouillet, breathing this tenuous atmosphere from childhood, is said to have fainted upon hearing a vulgar word, and Monsieur de Montausier, the unfortunate gentleman who married her, was required to spend fourteen years in overcoming one by one the scruples and alarms which were held to be right and necessary in such cases. Her admirers had by that time decided that Catharine, the Christian name of this sensitive paragon, was not sufficiently poetical, and Malherbe had taken upon himself to repair the blunder of an unromantic godfather. Arthénice, Eracinthe and Carinthée were felt to be sufficiently mellifluous anagrams. Meanwhile, Mademoiselle de Scudéry had also appeared, and her famous Saturdays were spreading the exquisite infection. It was she who invented the Map of the Tender Passion with its Village of Gallant Addresses, its Hamlet of Sweet Letters and Castle of Small Attentions.

141

This was the map which gave the poor Monsieur de Montausier so much trouble. Map in hand he must find his way to the city of Sensitive Esteem through forty leagues of Friendly Sentiment, at the risk of losing his way and finding himself at the Lake of Indifference. The devotees of the Hôtel de Rambouillet, isolating themselves from the common world had no standard whereby to correct their own absurdities. No one of any consequence escaped their influence. La Rochefoucauld adored the novels of Mademoiselle de Scudéry and could draw from memory the Map of the Tender Passion. He came daily to the blue room of the Hôtel de Rambouillet where the romances of the sect were read, where serious discussions were held upon imaginary problems of sentiment, where riddles were propounded and the latest epigrams and portraits in verse were produced. "These people," wrote La Bruyère, "left to the commonalty the art of speaking intelligibly. One thing, expressed with no great clarity, led to another even more obscure, which was in turn improved upon by the delivery of riddling redes which were always greeted with prolonged applause. From an exaggeration of what they described as delicacy of feeling and refinement of expression, they finally reached the point of being entirely ambiguous and of failing to understand even one another. For these conversations there was no need of good sense, a reliable memory or the least ability. Only wit was necessary—a wit which was not of the best but false in kind and at the mercy of imagination."

The nearest approaches to this particular vein of preciosity in English literary history were the Elizabethan Euphuists, who followed Lyle, and the poets of conceit who followed the marvellous Dr. Donne, while within living memory a

faint analogy may be sought in the "souls" of Carlton Ter-
race. The exquisites of the Hôtel de Rambouillet were also
"souls," and the word "darling" was almost a compulsory
form of address within the circle. One could scarcely be a
précieuse without being also a *chère*.

The exquisites, to receive their guests, went usually to
bed. The bed was prepared in an alcove or *ruelle*. Each
of the ladies who pretended to the rank of a true exquisite
had at her constant disposal a gentleman who described himself as her *alcoviste*. He did the honours of the house, directed the conversation and was responsible for the instruction of neophytes who desired to enter the circle. The devotion of the alcovist to his lady was a purely abstract passion. Never the slightest scandal attached to these refined
activities. The exquisite was expected "tenderly to entertain
her lover without enjoyment and substantially to enjoy her
husband with aversion."

Though in 1658 the exquisites had degenerated from
leaders of a literary movement to corrupters of form and
fashion, there had as yet been not the slightest suggestion
that they were in any way ridiculous. All the best people
were exquisites. Not to be an exquisite was social obliter a-
tion. The wisdom of La Bruyère was wisdom after the
event, and the members of the sect who, like Ménage and
Segrais, describe the *précieuses* in their memoirs with a
smiling indulgence are saving their faces with posterity by
postdating a discretion which prior to Molière they had not
yet attained. No one had effectively mocked the exquisites
or troubled their supremacy. Society would no more have
dreamed of smiling at the "enigma" or "portrait" of the
alcove in 1658 than it would dream to-day of smiling at

Derby day or the induction of an Archbishop. Scarron, it is true, disappointed at the reception of his *Sapho*, had addressed to Mademoiselle de Scudéry an epistle alluding to the false exquisites who clumsily imitated their illustrious models, but Scarron lauded with enthusiasm the author of *Clélie* and the cartographer of the Tender Passion. In 1656 St. Evremond had gently rallied the sect upon its metaphysical affections and the Abbé de Pure had in the same year published a romance in four volumes in which the camp-followers of the movement were the victims of an irony so gentle, and incidentally so involved, that the author's preciosity was more apparent than his intention to castigate the offence in others. To modern ears it may seem pure malice in the Abbé when he tells us that the exquisite is "not born of a father or mother but secreted by the alcove as an oyster secretes the pearl." But the Abbé, though he derided the excesses of the sect, was himself an exquisite, known among the alcovists as Prospero, and his romance was inspired more obviously by the resentment of the real exquisites that their mysteries should be imitated and profaned by intruders than by any profound conviction of the mischievous absurdity of the precious persuasion.

These were straws, but the wind had scarce as yet begun to blow. Mademoiselle de Scudéry, with La Rochefoucauld in attendance; Madame de Sévigné with her retinue of precious folk; the solemn Bossuet; the illustrious Corneille, with Ménage, Segrais and the rest, were still untouched. The Map of the Tender Passion was·the Michelin Guide to society, and in 1658 it was still as much as one's social life was worth to smile at the exquisites.

Twelve months later everyone of account within twenty

144

leagues of Paris was laughing heartily, and the wisest of the exquisites made merry with the rest. *Les Précieuses Ridicules,* a comedy in one act, destroyed the fashion in a single afternoon. There was clearly no appeal against this devastating verdict of commonsense. Either the exquisites must laugh with the vulgar or be damned forever in their absurdity. The great lady, who at the height of her fame had snubbed the mighty Richelieu, was equal to this even more dangerous crisis. During the early run of the play she invited Molière to perform it on no less than three separate occasions for her own special benefit. Let the gallèd jade wince, our withers are unwrung. Molière met this skilful manœuvre by solemnly asserting in his preface that, in portraying his exquisites, he had intended to satirize only a vicious imitation of excellent originals. The statement deceived nobody, save certain laborious critics of a later generation. It was an example to the world how a defeat should be accepted and a victory enjoyed by persons of goodwill.

The Marquise was followed by the more discreet of her admirers. Ménage, writing his memoirs after the event, tells us that in leaving the theatre he took his friend Chapelain by the arm: "Sir, said I to him, yesterday we admired all the absurdities which have just been so delicately and sensibly criticized; but, in the words of St. Remy to Clovis, we must now burn what we have adored and adore what we have burned." The more intelligent exquisites could not have acted otherwise in face of the instant success of the play. Merely as a matter of tactics they must acquiesce; but there is also no doubt that there were many cases of sudden conversion. Boileau in his tenth satire could scarcely be more explicit in his reference to the sect:

Reste de ces esprits jadis si renommés
Que d'un coup de son art Molière a diffamés.

The poor comedian from the provinces, depending for liveli-
hood and favour on a spoiled public of doubtful taste, had
struck in a moment at the heart of an evil fashion which the
great ones had not thought, or, perhaps dared, to challenge.
He reaped richly the reward of his courage. The general
verdict was that of the apocryphal gentleman in the pit who
rose in his enthusiasm and cried: *Courage, courage, Molière,
voilà de la bonne comédie.* During the next few months
people came from within sixty miles of Paris to see the play.
Loret, the gazetteer, must now devote a page of his rhymed
chronicle to the production, and carefully records that, hoping to be admitted for thirty *sols*, found himself obliged to
pay ten pistoles for a seat. Never, he tells us, had any play
enjoyed so great a vogue; the masterpieces of Corneille had
not received so much applause; the audience was in laughter
from start to finish; never had so many distinguished people
been seen together; wise and foolish made merry one with
another. His allusion to the fact that, hoping to laugh for
thirty *sols*, he was not permitted to unbend for less than ten
pistoles is a reference to one of the most gratifying aspects
of the event so far as the players were concerned. At the
second performance, on December 2nd, the prices of admission were doubled.

The first performance took place on 18th November, and
the second performance on 2nd December. That interval of
a fortnight is significant. Not all the exquisites were as wise
as Arthénice and the inner circle. Somaize, whom we shall
find impenitent, informs us in his *Dictionaire des Précieuses*,
or Who's Who in the Alcove, that immediately on the pro-

146

duction of the play "an alcovist of quality prohibited its
further performance for several days and Segrais, also of
the clan, relates that a copy of the play was sent in haste to
the King, who was then in the Pyrenees." But the alcovist
of quality found small comfort there. By His Majesty, the
piece was "very well received." Within a year there had
been forty-four performances of the play, including command performances before the Secretaries of State, Messieurs de Guénégaud and Le Tellier, and the Chevalier de
Grammont. A grateful company in December, 1658, paid
500 *livres* in royalties to the author, and a further sum of
499 *livres* in January, 1659.

The feelings of the author himself lie warm between the
lines of his joyous preface to the first edition of the play.
Segrais reports him to have said: "No longer need I take
Plautus and Terence for my masters or despoil Menander.
I have only to study the world." The witness is suspect but
the saying is not inappropriate. The author himself is more
modest. He would, he tells us, claim for his comedy, if
he had time to argue the matter, that he had kept it within
the limits of an honest and allowable satire, and he affirms
that "the correction of social absurdity must at all times be
the matter of true comedy." Here, for the first time, is a
declaration of faith. Hitherto Molière, except for a few
scenes of nature in *Le Dépit Amoureux*, had kept within
the limits of the comic theatre of tradition. He was
inditing now a preface to the first modern comedy of
manners.

Publication of the play was forced upon him by the first
of his enemies—no less a person than Somaize of the Dictionary. On the Quai des Augustins, the Paternoster Row

of seventeenth century Paris, a certain Jean Ribou, calling himself a publisher, conducted a trade, mainly piratical, under the sacred sign of Saint Louis. The new play was an excellent property. Ribou with the help of Somaize procured a copy of the piece, and Somaize undertook to write a parody entitled *Les Véritables Précieuses*. Ribou then applied to the authorities for a double privilege or publishing licence. The play of Molière was to be slipped unobtrusively into the projected volume and offered for sale with the parody.

But Molière was warned in time. The licence of Ribou was cancelled, and Molière was given a privilege to publish his play exclusively for five years. The preface, written in haste, hardly conceals beneath its smooth irony the triumph of the successful warrior. Strange, he writes, that one should publish a man in spite of himself, but this was no time to play the modest author. He would be insulting all Paris quite unreasonably if he should accuse it of having applauded a foolish play and he would not be so impertinent as to gainsay the verdict of those who had found it worth while. He obstinately maintains, however, that he had not intended to print his play. It owed much of the favour it had found to the delivery of his actors and he felt that it should not be deprived of these accessories. He would, he affirms, have been satisfied if its success had been confined to the theatre. His hand, however, had been forced and, with embarrassment, he had accepted his destiny. He must publish and if necessary be damned, since he had not had leisure to take the precautions usual in such cases. There had been no time to find a distinguished person to protect, willy-nilly, his modest work, no opportunity to canvass his friends for verses in commendation of his play, though he might easily have found such as could furnish him in French, Latin or even Greek— and everyone knew that a tribute in Greek could be marvellously effective at the head of a book. Thus runs the pen of an obviously happy man. The author who had struggled for fifteen years in obscurity had come at last within reach of his desire. He was forced to publish his play, but how sweet was the enforcement!

There remains the conclusion of the preface in which the author suggests that his play was aimed at the false and not at the genuine exquisites. The most excellent things, he pleaded, are liable to be foolishly aped and all such vicious imitations which deserve to be chastised are at all times matter for the comedian; it would be wrong of the genuine exquisites to take offence because the ridiculous people who copy them so ill are put upon the stage. Posterity, reading these observations, has persistently wondered whether Molière was or was not aiming at the exquisites themselves. The answer is contained in the comedy itself. There is hardly a stroke of it which cannot be matched from the precepts and examples of the sect. Madelon and Cathos are not "vicious imitations" but faithful protraits of the fashionable exquisites of the day. Wisely they refused to recognize themselves and laughed at their undoing. But that was simple policy. It is equally true that Molière handsomely apologized to his victims. But that was simple courtesy. The ironic disclaimer of the preface can be safely disregarded. It is only in works quite obviously based on the observation of living originals in which the author's familiar note is to be found on the title page: this book contains no reference to any existing persons or institutions.

Grimarest tells us that *Les Précieuses Ridicules* "though it had been played for some time in the provinces, enjoyed in Paris all the sensation of a novelty." There is no evidence for this astounding declaration. It is merely one of the many blunders of a biographer who is a perpetual illustration of the fact that there is no worse historian than the witness once removed. Certain critics have found in the statement of Grimarest support for the view that Molière in his play was satirizing a provincial imitation of the real thing, and not the thing itself. The documentary answer is explicit. La Grange in his Register describes *Les Précieuses Ridicules* as a new play in 1659, and there is no previous contemporary reference. The answer from internal evidence is equally clear. Molière could no more have written his satire on the exquisites before he came to Paris in 1659 than Shakespeare could have written his comedy on the euphuists before he came to London in 1592. There is another legend equally misleading and unnecessary. It has been argued that Molière, between the first performance of his play on November 18th and its revival on December 2nd, revised his text, with the result that the farce became a comedy and was rendered less offensive to the genuine exquisites. The arguments on either side lead us by tedious ways to a general conclusion that the documentary evidence for any such hypothesis is too slender to justify it even if it were intrinsically probable. There is no real reason to doubt that, though Molière may have made a few cuts and changes as a producer often will upon a second performance, the play witnessed by the Marquise de Rambouillet, Ménage and the rest on November 18th was substantially the play as we read it to-day and there is no good reason to believe that one

syllable of that brilliant indictment was ever in any way re-
tracted or amended.

The first encounter of Molière with the polite world resulted in a victory so swiftly won, that we may easily be led
to underestimate the audacity of his attack, the very real
resistance with which he met, and the even more dangerous
jealousy which he provoked. The "alcovist of quality" who
is said to have very nearly secured the suppression of the
play was not alone. The whole literary world, though it
must "burn what it adored," was not in all cases able to do
it with so good a grace as the Marquise de Rambouillet.
Thomas Corneille plainly showed his ill humour in a letter to
the Abbé de Pure. These gentlemen of the Palais Bourbon, he complains, having ruined an excellent tragedy—he
is referring to their "detestable production" of the *Oreste et
Pylade* of Coquetean de la Clairière—went on to perform
their farce upon the exquisites, thus making it abundantly
clear that "they were only equal to trifles of that kind, and
that the best plays must necessarily fare but ill at their
hands." Meanwhile, lesser men hastened to exploit the subject which Molière had made the talk of the town or to
angle for the favour of those whom he had secretly mortified.
J. de la Forge wrote a rejoinder in heroic verse entitled *Le
Cercle des Femmes Savantes* and a comedy by Chappuzeau,
entitled *L'Académie des Femmes*, was performed at the
Théâtre du Marais in 1661. All this was in the way of good
and legitimate business. The manœuvres of Somaize of the
Dictionary, on the other hand, to whom the gratitude of posterity is due for having pushed Molière into print, were less
ingenuous. He was determined to make the best of both
worlds. He picked his subject to the bone, making merry

151

with the exquisites, but apologizing at every turn to the illustrious persons whom he had no wish to offend; stealing with both hands from Molière, but accusing his original of every crime that an author could commit. Molière was a plagiarist. All his wit was derived. The man had nothing of his own. He had recently bought from the widow of Guillot-Gorju the memoirs of her husband wherewith to stock the farces that had since become so popular with the town. Not one of his plays would stand for an hour upon its merits. He owed his success to the arts of the showman. He was an expert in publicity which included private readings of his plays, with much removing of the hat in distinguished company and a skilful packing of his theatre. His success in farce was, of course, notorious, but neither the author nor his company could cope with plays of any merit or of a serious intention. Somaize, in fact, was setting out to do two not very consistent things: first to show that the play of Molière was of no account whatever, and secondly to produce in rapid succession a series of imitations. First came *Les Véritables Précieuses*. This was closely followed by *Le Procès des Précieuses*, the famous *Grand Dictionnaire des Précieuses*, *Les Précieuses en Vers, Dialogue de Deux Précieuses sur les Affaires de Leur Communauté* and *La Pompe Funèbre d'une Précieuse*.

Les Précieuses en Vers was no more than the play of Molière rendered into verse. Somaize was hard put to it to abuse an author and versify his play, but he contrived it very successfully. "It may seem strange to you," says our ingenuous pirate, "that, having dealt with Mascarille (Molière), as he deserved in *Les Véritables Précieuses*, I should now be taking the trouble to put into verse a play of which he claims to be the author." Strange indeed, but the play, it seems, was "stolen from the Italians." Molière had added a few small touches to an old script and was able successfully to profit from his theft by reason of his acting, which pleased a sufficiently large number of people to justify him in claiming to be the most popular clown in France. "It is always something," concludes our author, "to excel in any walk of life."

Molière, according to Somaize, was reviving in *Les Précieuses Ridicules* a play, produced a short time previously by the Italians, based on a scenario written by the Abbé de Pure. This scenario of the Abbé de Pure has for generations haunted the footnotes and appendices of the more devout biographers. There is no evidence, however, of any substantial derivation. We have already found the Abbé de Pure in correspondence with Thomas Corneille, who praised a second rate tragedy which had failed at the Petit Bourbon owing to the "detestable acting of Molière and his company" and dismissed *Les Précieuses Ridicules* as a trifle undeserving of serious attention. There were several reasons which predisposed the Cornelians to range themselves, even in defeat, with the exquisites. There was, first, the issue of tragedy versus comedy as a polite accomplishment, which was soon to be fought to a bitter and unsavoury conclusion between the old tragedians and the new comedians. There was, secondly, the infatuation of the illustrious brothers with Mademoiselle du Parc, who just at that moment had deserted the company of Molière to go to the Théâtre du Marais. Thirdly, there was the fact that both the Corneilles were themselves frequenters of the alcove. The letter of Thomas Corneille to the Abbé de Pure, however, is less interesting for what it says than for what it omits to say. He is writing, he remembered, to a man who, according to Somaize, should be regarded as the real author of *Les Précieuses Ridicules*. He refers to *Les Précieuses Ridicules*, but, though the world is ringing with its praises, he makes no allusion to the allegation that it has been stolen from his correspondent. If Molière had copied in any vital respect a play which the Abbé had written for the Italians, his friend could hardly have failed to comment on the fact, and it is even more remarkable that the Abbé should have neglected to put in a claim for himself. The charge of plagiary began, and should have ended, with Somaize.

The charge will recur. All the Greek dramatists from Æschylus to Euripides were plagiarists in the sense that their themes were common property. Molière, in that sense, was invariably guilty; Shakespeare more often than not. But the charge in the present instance was not even seriously intended. *Les Précieuses Ridicules* opened a new chapter in the history of the comic theatre. It was in style, treatment and substance, for all its slightness of texture and its brevity, the most profoundly original comedy since Aristophanes. It was in no way imitated, and could be referred to no previous model or school. It was different both in origin and intention from any of the previous work of Molière. Unlike *L'Etourdi* and *Le Dépit Amoureux* it depended in no way on theatrical situation or surprise. The plot of the play was the common property of contemporary farce—a valet who counterfeited his master. The interest of the play lay, however, not in what would happen, but how the characters would conduct themselves according to their lights, no longer the footlights but the lights of nature and disposition. The two gentlemen disclosed at the rise of the curtain, heartily indignant but amused; Gorgibus, the first of a long line of city fathers; his daughter and niece, ungracious and impertinent, filling the stage with their exquisite airs, painted to the life without effort or exaggeration—here was something very different from the high passions, surprises and hazards of a world in masquerade, something that the polite world had not yet seen, for which a name had not yet been invented. Some day it would be described as realism. For the moment it was merely obvious that the theatre had suddenly stepped nearer to life. Here was a mirror thrust at the face of society, and it was a mirror that gave style and significance to its reflections. It was like and yet unlike. Each word and gesture was true, but it was at the same time more comprehensive and more inevitable than the truth of every day. These exquisites were not only true to the period but true of all the exquisites who ever lived.

It may be felt that Molière pushed too far his satire against the foolish cousins. To be deceived by a brace of valets in masquerade is cruelty indeed. But the punishment is fitted to the crime and is scarcely excessive. The affectation of these precious ladies is more than skin-deep. It has begun to spoil their natural affections and render them odious. "For my part," says Madelon, in disdain of her excellent father, "I live in astonishment that you should ever have been able to produce so refined a daughter as myself," and when the good man has withdrawn, swearing they shall marry decently or go to a nunnery, she improves upon the text. "Some day," she says, "it will, I think, be discovered that I owe to some fortunate adventure a more illustrious birth." Such sentiments were not uncommon among the devout readers of *Clélie* and frequenters of the alcove. The genuine exquisites of the Hôtel de Rambouillet, like Cathos and Madelon of the play, also dreamed of possibly romantic origins, scorned to use names received in baptism, rejected honest lovers who failed to woo them by the Map of the Tender Passion—in short had got so completely out of touch with nature and commonsense that only a very stern lesson would suffice them.

In the scenes which exhibited the two valets masquerading as exquisites of the period, there were necessarily touches of farce. These were servants aping their masters, and they must, therefore, occasionally blunder. But the habits and performances of the true fops of the period were drawn with but little exaggeration, even in detail. Mascarille, with his riddles, impromptus, portraits, madrigals and artificial exercises in gallantry was anyone of the fine gentlemen watching him from the side of the stage. The language and manners of the play were certainly not more extravagant than those of the blue room at the Hôtel de Rambouillet. The footman who is a "requisite," the looking glass which is a "counsellor of the graces," the chairs which are "commodities of conversation," one of which extends its arms to the visitor who is begged to satisfy the longing it feels to embrace him—all this is soberly of the alcove. The repeated references by Mascarille to the peril in which he stands from the bright eyes of "Polyxene" and "Araminte" and the notorious thievery of fair ladies in the matter of hearts were drawing-room commonplaces of the period. The heart which has been skinned alive, which has a mouth that cries and subsequently takes to its legs is a mild example of the mixed metaphors which occur broadcast through the works of Somaize, the Abbé Cotin and the rest. The tribute paid to Mascarille by Madelon herself is topically just: "How *natural* is everything he says!" Molière might have gone infinitely further without becoming liable to any charge of caricature. Equally pertinent was the attack of Molière upon the literary *snobisme* of the day. The word was as yet unknown, but Molière had discovered the thing. The man of fashion must know of every book, play, sonnet, portrait and lampoon. Not to be in at the birth was to lose caste with a coterie that lived in an atmosphere of mutual appreciation and compliment.

It may be objected that too much importance must not be ascribed to a play that satirized a movement peculiar to the period. But that is to mistake the nature of this achievement. A satire aimed at a specific fashion may be of general application. So long as complicated fashion is liable to corrupt natural simplicity, these exquisites of Molière will remain amusing and intelligible. The author has avoided too rigidly dating his comedy. The process of instinctive selection, which is half the secret of genius, has kept him from multiplying his local and personal allusions and from the ultra-preciosity which rendered the work of his imitator Somaize, for example, unreadable, except by an historian of the period, within twenty years of its publishing. One can read *Les Précieuses Ridicules* to-day without a footnote and without having heard of the Hôtel de Rambouillet or studying the Map of the Tender Passion. Knowledge of the originals adds to our appreciation of the comedy; but it is not essential to our enjoyment.

Technically, the play, in substance a comedy, was, in form, a farce. The counterfeiting valets were farce, and had been exploited in several contemporary plays of the period,

notably in *Jodelet ou le Maître Valet* of Scarron. The
names of Mascarille and Gorgibus were names frequently
used in the farces of Molière himself. The play ends, in
the manner of farce, with the classic bastinado. Now and
then the dialogue, as when the two valets emulously display the wounds of their valour, declines from the comic
level. But the substance of the play prevails over the form.
It is a comedy of manners. Its appeal lay in the faithful
portrayal of the exquisites and in their undoing. Molière
had freed his comedy from the classic mask. *Les Précieuses
Ridicules* was the first of his comedies of satire and observation and its success was a critical event in the career of
its author, which would henceforth be mainly a record of
bitter controversy and of his heroic struggle for the freedom
of the comic art.

IX

GENTLEMEN, THE KING!

GENTLEMEN, the King! The doors of the long Gallery stand open and His Majesty enters. For a moment he looks down the double row of bent figures. These are the noblemen of France, many of whom can remember when the King ruled upon sufferance and rebellion in arms or policy was a country diversion. But all are now glad to crook the knee and hat in hand catch a reflected glory from the royal face. The King pauses an instant. This is a solemn moment of the day. He has been clothed, fed, and variously tended by gentlemen still flushing with the honour of his more intimate presence. Already a long succession of ministers, marshals and high-officials have been informed that anon he will speak with them. Now he emerges from the ritual of preparation and stands aware of his high office and significance. This is Louis no longer but the King of France, and he reads the identification in the humble eyes and sudden silence of the room. He is still young and of a friendly impressionable spirit, but even now he cannot long forget that he fills a throne and must be in the eyes of the world the virtue, wisdom and solace of a nation. Even in his pleasures and his comforts the King must prevail over his person. Secretly he may have slipped that night from the room of de la

Vallière, but his gentlemen must find him conjugally in the apartments of the Queen before they may venture to presume acquaintance with his movements. He has built himself at Versailles a palace of ease, but it will be for centuries an expression of the mind and spirit of France. He may unbend in laughter, but when the King laughs he must find a worthy comedian so that the world may laugh with him for generations to come. To warm the royal heart with a noble passion he has already the great Corneille, and to bring him to the melting mood he will require wonders from the young Racine.

The King will hereafter be the necessary protector of Molière through the most critical years of his career, and the question arises how far his comprehension of the greatest genius of his reign in fact extended. The character of Louis —his abilities, motives and inclinations—have remained, and will probably continue to remain, an enigma to posterity. He was the most public person who ever lived, but this very publicity defeats the private enquirer. He ate in public. His toilet was a public ritual. He even sat in public upon the stool. He was bled, purged and put to bed in the eye of France. Privately, he soon ceased to exist. The man was merged in the institution. He became a legend, to which all must subscribe and from which at the last he never permitted even himself to escape. For the revolutionary historians, he naturally figures as a monster of royal egoism, but the candid inquirer remains perplexed. Was this a man who, by a miracle of devotion, obliterated himself and lived only for his office, or did the office serve merely to enlarge his person? In organizing his elaborate apotheosis, to which all the most famous men of his genera-

160

Le vray Portrait de Mr de Moliere en Habit de Sganarelle.

MOLIÈRE IN THE COSTUME OF SGANARELLE
From the original engraving by Simonin in the *Bibliothèque Nationale*.

tion contributed, did he feel himself to be a cipher to this
great accompt or the total sum? Remembering the childhood of Louis Dieudonné, a long record of humiliation,
poverty and neglect, one is tempted to find in him an illustrious example of a man driven by a sense of inferiority in
childhood to assert and extend himself abnormally in later
life. Was the magnificent parade of Versailles the symbol
of an inverted diffidence? Playing as a boy with his lacquey,
he wished always to reverse the rôles—the prince would
be lacquey and the lacquey prince. He loved his mother
passionately, but saw her wholly devoted to Mazarin. By
the untamed and noble adventurers of the regency he was in
early youth regarded as almost an idiot. Even his mother's
ladies in waiting, the only society he knew, refused him a
reverence, and it was some time before the young King,
come to years of discretion, dared to put on his hat in the
presence of the notables. Meanwhile he was inscribing in his
copybook—the first royal autograph that has survived—
L'hommage est dû aux rois. Ils font ce qu'il leur plaît.
Are we to seek among these early humiliations, in such
strong contrast with his birth and pretensions, the origins
of a policy which finally reduced the nobility of France to
crave the honour of valeting the royal person? Was the
splendid pageant of Versailles the expression of a secret distrust which, for the glory of the realm and the honour of
the dynasty, must be perpetually denied and overcome?
There is more than a hint of morbidity in the splendid figure
which issued daily from its bedchamber to greet the lieges
of France—a picture, carefully composed, of quiet majesty
and absolute will, that was yet a man of devious impulses
and affections, suffering from a ludicrous disease, gro-

tesquely tortured and misused by his physicians, working indefatigably for his country and concentrating upon himself all its vitality and aspiration.

These are problems for the general historian. It is essential, however, for the biographer of Molière, who so often hung perilously upon the King's favour, to appreciate the royal motives and form some idea of the King's competence and taste. He was, perhaps, the most splendid patron of literature who ever ruled a modern State. All the arts ministered to his pleasure or to the glory of France. The French language and civilization during his reign obtained a hold upon Europe whereby it is still, for international purposes, supreme. How much this systematic protection of every form of artistic achievement was deliberate policy and how much of it was private pleasure? What, in any case, were the personal preferences of Louis XIV? Here an obvious distinction must be drawn between the young King, who still permitted himself to be diverted, and the emblem or figure of State which he finally became. Molière died in 1673 before the man was merged in the monarch. He caught the sunrise, for Louis was still in these early years accessible to genius. But Molière passed away not a moment too soon. Within a few years Corneille was dying in poverty. Racine was wasting his genius as historiographer royal, while the King sat solemnly before an interminable series of pastorals and operas in which his glories were monotonously hymned. The royal favours were at the last concentrated upon Lulli, an avaricious clown, of whom more hereafter, and the gracefully insipid Quinault, whose gods and shepherdesses dragged down the theatre of Corneille and Molière to the function of a looking-glass in

162

which the Roi Soleil might be perpetually dazzled by his own reflection. With Louis XIV, grown devoutly royal, sunning himself in the rays of his high office, to all outward seeming using the arts, as he used his hall of mirrors at Versailles, to give back multiple images of the royal person, we have fortunately little to do. The shadow of the coming change, perhaps, darkened the closing years of Molière, but the King who was shortly to defend the author of *Tartuffe* against his enemies, was not yet the King who, from deliberate policy or yielding to an instinct which he could not control, finally enforced from the poets, painters and architects of France the posture which he had successfully exacted from her nobility.

To the young King we must, in fact, accord the merit of having appreciated the comic genius of Molière sooner and more effectually than many of his subjects. We shall find him, when *Tartuffe* was condemned as impious and its author described as a devil in human form, arranging for it to be performed for the edification of a papal legate—which is as though Queen Victoria, when the *Ghosts* of Ibsen was being likened by her more respectable subjects to an open drain, had commanded a special performance of the play at Buckingham Palace before the Archbishop of Canterbury. Louis XIV, as we shall see, supported Molière as author and man against persistent calumny and misrepresentation; and their relations were as familiar and friendly as the relations of subject and prince could be. But it is essential not to exaggerate. Posterity has emphasized the royal favours to Molière, and too often neglected to observe that, in cases where these favours were real and effective, they were by no means exclusive. The King ultimately pensioned the

163

company of Molière, but the pension never exceeded 7,000 *livres*, while the pension accorded to the tragedians of the Hôtel de Bourgogne was 12,000 and the Italian comedians received 15,000 *livres*. The King frequently invited Molière and his company to Versailles, but he invited also his rivals. The King stood godfather to the child of Molière in July, 1668, but he also stood godfather to the son of Dominique, the famous Harlequin, in the year 1669, and for the children of Lulli he was in later years to create posts, clerical or musical, before they were old enough to leave the nursery.

The King esteemed and supported Molière, but the tradition of a special and exclusive regard is hardly acceptable. In particular, the story of the supper-tray, consecrated by posterity in poem and picture as *La Légende de l'En-Cas de Nuit* is almost certainly apocryphal. The story runs that the King, to give his gentlemen a lesson in courtesy, reproved them for refusing to make his bed with a comedian. Opportunely at that moment arrived the *en-cas de nuit*. The King invited Molière to sit down, carved him the wing of a chicken and called in the courtiers to witness Majesty supping with an actor. This is the invention of an age— the story dates only from 1823—which had forgotten the severity of an etiquette which never varied. For Molière to sup with the King would have caused more excitement in France than the battle of Namur or the revocation of the Edict of Nantes. No man was ever permitted to sit at the royal table and the highest nobility of the land stood to respectful attention while Majesty dined. The young Louis was still subject to fits of friendly expansion. He might pour out a glass of wine for Scaramouche or kiss the gardener

(Le Notre) in a moment of enthusiasm, but he certainly never ate with Molière.

The King's expressions of personal opinion concerning the work of Molière do not, moreover, lead us to suppose that he fully understood its importance. Boileau always regarded Molière as unique in his genius. One day the King asked him who was the most rare of the great writers who had rendered his reign illustrious. Boileau named Molière. "I was not under that impression," said the King, "but you are better able to judge than I am." This anecdote is given in the memoirs of Louis Racine. Another saying recorded by Grimarest is equally significant. "A year ago," says Grimarest, writing in 1698, the King had occasion to say that he had lost two men whom he would never be able to replace: Molière and Lulli. The simultaneous reference indirectly throws a light upon the King's esteem. The collaboration of the dramatist and the musician was for years the most distinguished feature of the royal festivals at Versailles and St. Germain. Molière fitted, in fact, into the royal scheme as a principal organizer of His Majesty's pleasures, one among the many men who contributed to the royal splendour and thus to the glory of France. The King's tribute was to Molière, author of *Les Amants Magnifiques*, rather than to Molière author of *Le Misanthrope*.

Posterity must view the patronage of Molière by Louis with mixed feelings. Without the royal protection Molière could never have ridden the whirlwinds he continually raised. But he paid for that protection a price which can only be viewed with indignation and dismay. The author of *Le Misanthrope* was obliged to spend largely of the years of his prime in organizing entertainments for the Court which he should have been free to employ in other ways. The King overworked and misused his genius with the same unconscious insolence which towards the end of his reign culminated in the reduction of Racine to an ignoble silence.

The King, as we have seen, was absent from Paris when *Les Précieuses Ridicules* was first produced. He did not return until July, and within a few days, on July 29, 1660, he invited Molière to bring his company to the Bois de Vincennes, where the famous act was played as a postscript to *L'Etourdi*. The King saw both plays again at the Louvre on August 30th in the presence of his brother. Five days later there was yet a third performance at the house of Mazarin. Mazarin was sick. The King, as an act of respect to his dying minister, stood *incognito* through the performance, leaning on the back of the Cardinal's chair, and upon its conclusion Molière received a very practical expression of the royal favour in the shape of a grant of 3,000 *livres*, paid to him by Mazarin on the King's account. There was henceforth no doubt that Molière was to be the King's man, and Loret, the gazetteer, hastened to remedy his previous omissions. For the first time he refers to Molière by name, and celebrates him in the doggerel which made so sweet a music in the ears of society. Loret admits that he has himself been diverted by *L'Etourdi* on several occasions, and then informs us (Muse Historique, letter of 30th October, 1660), that not only the Cardinal but several great persons —an allusion to Louis XIV *incognito*—found the two plays excellent:

> Et, par un soin particulier
> D'obliger leur auteur Molier,
> Cette généreuse Eminence

166

> Leur fit un don en récompense,
> Tant pour lui que ses compagnons,
> De mille beaux écus mignons.

Molière is moving up in the world. Some day Loret will even learn to spell his name correctly.

Molière soon had urgent need of his royal friend. The alcovist of quality, who is reputed to have procured the suspension for a fortnight of the performances of *Les Précieuses Ridicules*, though he may not be in person historic, stood for a number of people who were now beginning to be thoroughly disconcerted by the sudden success of its author. More particularly the actors of the Hôtel de Bourgogne, with whom war to the knife would soon break out, were profoundly disturbed. For behold, the great Cardinal was sick; and, instead of calling for the royal tragedians, he had sent for the *Troupe de Monsieur*, and Loret, as we have seen, though astonished, had hastened to greet the rising sun:

> Car Monseigneur le Cardinal
> Qui s'étoit un peu trouvé mal,
> Durant un meilleur intervalle
> Les fit venir, non dans sa salle,
> Mais dans sa chambre justement,
> Pour avoir le contentement
> De voir, *non pas deux tragédies,*
> *Mais deux plaisantes comédies.*

It was evidently high time for all good men to come together for the defence of society, high art and their legitimate interests, and a rare opportunity occurred in the autumn of 1661.

The Salle du Petit Bourbon, under the exclusive manage-

ment of Molière since the departure of Scaramouche, was
part of a building already condemned by the architects of
the Louvre. Sooner or later it was to be demolished to
permit of a partial reconstruction of the royal palace. The
overseer of works, M. de Ratabon, either from negligence
or malice, suddenly began the work of demolition on 11th
October, 1661, without a word of warning to Molière and
his friends. Our best authority for the incident is La Grange,
already keeping his famous Register, and La Grange inter-
prets the conduct of the King's overseer not only as a deliberate act of hostility but part of general conspiracy to
strangle the growing reputation of Molière while yet it was
possible to do so:

"On Monday, 11th October," he writes in his Register,
"the demolition of the theatre of the Petit Bourbon was
begun under the direction of M. de Ratabon, overseer of
works to the King, without warning to the company, which
was disagreeably surprised to find itself suddenly without a
home. A complaint was made at once to the King, to whom
M. de Ratabon represented that the site of the building was
required for the building of the Louvre and that, since the
interior of the hall had been constructed for the King's
ballets and belonged to His Majesty, he had not thought it
necessary, in advancing the work upon the Louvre, to consider the claims of comedy. The bad faith of M. de Ratabon was evident."

The attitude of M. de Ratabon and certain other intrigues
set on foot at this time point to a degree of hostility against
Molière sufficiently intense to drive his enemies to manœuvres that must have been highly displeasing to the
King and his brother. Monsieur asked that the wrong done

to his comedians should be instantly repaired, and the King, out of personal regard for Molière, assigned him the Salle du Palais Royal which was to be his permanent home to the end of his career. The company then asked permission to remove their interior furnishings and properties. The request was granted. Certain decorations, however, were reserved at the wish of the Sieur de Vigarani, who alleged that he needed them for the palace of the Tuileries. Vigarani was evidently another of the conspirators, for, having obtained the properties he promptly burned them in a fine contempt of everyone concerned. Meanwhile, the tragedians of the Hôtel de Bourgogne and the Marais, seeing Molière without a stage as the result of proceedings for which they were probably not altogether unresponsible, made a determined effort to deprive him of his troop, each of the rival companies making advantageous offers to his colleagues. Their efforts, however, were unavailing. "All the actors," says La Grange, "loved the Sieur de Molière, their chief, who, in addition to his extraordinary merit and capacity, was of so charming a disposition that one and all were moved to protest that they would remain faithful to his fortunes and would never leave him whatever proposal might be made to them or whatever advantages they might expect to find elsewhere."

These incidents are of importance as showing that already the King was prepared to be a friend in need. The preface of 1682 is explicit on the subject:

"The esteem in which M. de Molière was held by His Majesty increased daily, as did that of the most enlightened men about the Court, his merit and his excellent qualities swiftly prevailing with all whom he encountered. His work

169

as an actor did not prevent him from serving the King in his capacity as *valet-de-chambre* and he faithfully performed the duties of that office. He was thus able to distinguish himself at Court as a man of good address and worthy of all respect, not presuming on his capacity or credit, suiting his conduct to the humour of those with whom he was obliged to live and showing a fine and liberal disposition: in a word, he showed that he possessed and knew how to exercise all the qualities of a man thoroughly deserving of respect."

The testimonial is not, perhaps, the kind we should, in the best of all possible worlds, wish to receive for Molière from the editor of his immortal comedies. It suggests a desire, very natural in the friends of a man who had been refused Christian burial, to record of Molière that he was not only a comic genius but a man of some repute in the splendid world in which it was an hereditary privilege to present the King with his shirt. The Editors of 1682 here showed their discretion. The genius of Molière might be left to look after itself. His respectability was rather more open to dispute, and they accordingly were at some pains to place it unmistakably upon record.

Meanwhile, the author had not been idle. The zest of the Burgundians for his destruction had been sharpened by the success earlier in the year of *Sganarelle ou Le Cocu Imaginaire*. The play had been produced on May 28, 1660, at the Petit Bourbon. Posterity feels it to be a retrogression. Here again were the traditional figures, coincidences, surprises and misunderstandings. Sganarelle is the comic husband of classical farce. He sees his wife inspecting the portrait of a personable young man. Therefore he is betrayed. Every character immediately misunderstands every situation and suspects everyone else of impossible misdemeanours. Sganarelle suspects his wife; his wife suspects her husband; the lover suspects his mistress; the mistress suspects her lover. The lady drops a portrait so that it may be immediately picked up, in the interests of a general mystification, by exactly the right person, and faints with emotion just in time to be aided in her indisposition by exactly the wrong one. The hero, not to be outdone, conveniently swoons at a similar crisis. There has been a good deal of scholarly depreciation of these performances. Coincidence, repetition, symmetry—these are the necessary features of such a play. It is no detriment to an artificial plot to be artificial. Our perception of the artifice, if we appreciate the pattern, is part of the fun.

To ask why the successful author of *Les Précieuses Ridicules* should have chosen to return to his earlier manner is another matter. All kinds of deliberate and ingenious motives have been invented, but all such speculations are labour lost. Molière had no fixed programme or policy. He was a man of the theatre who practised, as the occasion called, every style and form of play. He never wholly abandoned the Italian manner, and some of his later examples in that kind are among the best of his works. He had written his first comedy of observation. The mood had passed. Meanwhile, the run of *Les Précieuses Ridicules* was exhausted and he had presented from his repertoire a number of plays which were not conspicuously successful. The public must receive a further stimulus. The result was *Sganarelle ou Le Cocu Imaginaire.*

The old theme, however, has suffered a change, and the author wears his previous manner with a difference. This new farce, based on purely theatrical coincidences and mis-

171

understandings, has, nevertheless, here and there, touches of character which are not to be found in *L'Etourdi*. The *suivante* who sings the praises of matrimony, though it serve only to keep the bed warm in winter and provide one with a companion to say "God Bless You" when one sneezes, is more than a figure of farce; and there are moments when the wife of Sganarelle assumes a comic life of her own as when, though incorrigibly virtuous, she nevertheless dwells with complacency on the picture of the handsome gallant of the piece. There is, moreover, one scene of the play which, though the manner is farcical, turns to pure comedy in substance. Sganarelle, obsessed with his own grievances, assumes that Célie his interlocutor, thinking of something else, is wholly preoccupied with him. The scene rests upon a misunderstanding, artificially maintained in accordance with the most ancient practice, each character misinterpreting what the other says. But the impression it gives of the egoism of the man with a grievance, of his readiness to believe that it is equally everybody's business with his own, is essential comedy. While Célie indicts her faithless lover, Sganarelle accepts her railing as an expression of sympathy for his own very similar misfortunes. Even when the lady says she is ready to die for grief apparently at the woes of a perfect stranger, Sganarelle is still undeceived, though he begins to be a little surprised, it is true, at the violence of her fellow feeling. The scene between these two characters, each following a separate line of thought and insensible to the other, suggests the comic method of Tchekhoff, whose dialogue so often takes the form of as many soliloquies as there are persons to the play.

Finally, there is the famous scene in which Sganarelle rests

172

for a moment in the shadow of Falstaff—the long soliloquy in which he debates the value and quality of honour. "Can it mend a leg?" demanded Falstaff. "Will the leg be less unshapely?" inquires Sganarelle, wondering whether he shall avoid an attack upon his rival. Incidentally, there are in this speech reflections on the point of honour as between the sexes which are shortly in *L'Ecole des Maris* and *L'Ecole des Femmes* to be audaciously developed, and to become a cause of battle and offence to antagonists infinitely more formidable than the exquisites. Why should the honour of a wise man be made to depend on the conduct of a frivolous woman? Why should a wife commit the folly and the husband be the fool? Sganarelle rages against the assumption that a deceived husband is necessarily absurd, and there is sufficient method in his madness to disturb the orthodox. Sganarelle is admittedly ridiculous. He hesitates to avenge his fancied wrongs, not because he is genuinely unconventional on the point of honour, but because it is better as he tells us, to be a cuckold than to be a corpse. But his observations are sounder than his conclusions, and here, for the first time, the moralist looks for a moment through the mask of the clown, allowing us a glimpse of the dramatist who was to use for his comic purposes the most pitiful and profound of the social passions.

The contemporaries of Molière did not entirely miss these serious implications. The play was a laughing success, but it was, nevertheless, recognized that it had a quality which put it in a different class from the popular farces of the period. Where modern critics are struck by its resemblance to the Franco-Italian comedy of intrigue and dwell upon its artifice, the audiences of 1661 were struck by the qualities

which were peculiar to Molière. They find nature and
character in the play to an extent which for them was novel
and exhilarating. Sganarelle and his wife, the young lovers,
Gorgibus and the rest, were not, for them, mere ciphers to
the situation, but genuine products of observation. The
audiences of 1660 were struck by the reality of the play
—a grimacing, extravagant, deformed reality, fantastically
presented, but making an appeal hitherto unprecedented on
the comic stage.

Even its enemies must join the chorus. Chalussay affirms
that Molière might have charged a crown for a place in the
pit, to such an extent had he found the secret of pleasing
his public. Donneau de Visé—whose better acquaintance we
have yet to make—confesses in the *Nouvelles Nouvelles*
that *Le Cocu Imaginaire* is, in his opinion, and in the opinion
of many others, the best of all the plays of Molière and the
most admirably written. He goes on to say that, though
Les Précieuses Ridicules had brought Molière into notice
with persons of quality, it was only after the production of
Sganarelle that he was overwhelmed with their attentions.
They even invited him to dinner, and what was still more
remarkable, allowed themselves to be invited in return. The
result, suggests the libellist, was deplorable—Molière being
"vain enough to regard himself, in matters of hospitality,
as the equal of persons much above him in station."

We have also the evidence of those who, as in the case
of *Les Précieuses Ridicules*, attempted to rob the author of
his work. Of these the most engaging and instructive is
the mysterious Sieur de Neufvillaine. Molière, remembering *Les Précieuses Ridicules*, on this occasion intended
to be beforehand with the book pirates, and to secure his

174

copyright had, on the 31st May, three days after its production, obtained a privilege that covered not only *Le Cocu
Imaginaire* but *L'Etourdi, Le Dépit Amoureux* and *Don
Garcie.* Molière was in no hurry to make use of his right.
Jean Ribou, on the other hand, of the Quai des Augustins,
was waiting to pounce, and on July 26th the Sieur de Neufvillaine, his man of straw, obtained a privilege for a book
entitled *La Comédie de Sganarelle avec des Arguments sur
Chaque Scène* which he handed over at once to Jean Ribou
for 220 *livres. La Comédie de Sganarelle* was, word for
word, *Sganarelle ou Le Cocu Imaginaire.* Ribou printed
it quietly and with speed; obtained a privilege on 31st
August just as he was ready to go to press; and, on the same
day, put the book on sale. Molière, warned only three
days before, at once lodged a complaint with the Lieutenant-
civil of the Provost of Paris, who descended upon the printer
and the bookshop. The books, however, were flown. Jean
Ribou smilingly met his inquisitors, denied their competence
and bade them to do their worst. The lieutenant seized
the only four of the 1,200 copies which he could find. The
customary appeals and counter appeals lasted till 2nd
November, when a final ruling was obtained from the Privy
Council that the privilege of the Sieur de Neufvillaine was
invalid, and that Jean Ribou must hand over to Molière the
1,201 copies of the book he had printed or its equivalent.
Molière seems, in the meantime, to have made a friendly
arrangement with the pirates, for he not only allowed the
whole edition to be exhausted, but adopted its text for subsequent impressions of the play.

Somaize had robbed his victim and abused him at the
same time. The Sieur de Neufvillaine, on the contrary,

was lavish with tributes to the genius and capacity of his author. He had seen the play five or six times. He had it almost by heart. He had written it down from memory out of pure admiration and attached to it a commentary drawing attention to its beauties. In a covering letter to a friend in the country, this gentle pirate advises his imaginary correspondent to come to town and see the piece for himself, as "only by seeing Molière is it possible to appreciate how the playing of the actor illuminates the wit and verity of the author." It would need, he exclaims, the brush of Poussin, Le Brun or Mignard to do justice to this incomparable actor; his face and bearing so well express the jealousy of Sganarelle that his emotions and thoughts would be plain to everyone though he never uttered a word. No actor ever had so expressive and variable a countenance, which in the course of this particular play was more than twenty times transformed.

To the Sieur de Neufvillaine Sganarelle was clearly not a figure of farce. There is, he tells his friend, nothing in it that is forced; everything is natural; *the comedy rests entirely upon observation;* it is the product of reflection and a profound knowledge of men:

I venture to maintain, he continues, that Sganarelle exhibits no symptoms of jealousy, nor expresses any feeling, that the author has not personally observed in the men about him, so naturally are all these things expressed. So true is the picture that the author may be said to have read the world as a preliminary to his revelations—a procedure which cannot successfully be followed unless the practitioner has as fine a gift of observation as Molière himself and as fine a discretion in the selection of what is best suited to his purpose.

176

The modern critic, defending the construction of the play, as in the symmetrical fainting of Célie and Lélie, must emphasize that it carries forward an artificial tradition. The Sieur de Neufvillaine, on the contrary, denies the artifice altogether. Lélie, he contends, does not faint at the critical moment because the plot requires him to do so, but because he has just come from a long journey and has had nothing to eat for several hours. So thorough a defence is admittedly embarrassing, and Molière himself must have smiled at an exposition of the fainting episode as a triumph of realism. But the old artifice was less obvious to the public of 1660 than the new nature and to that extent the Sieur de Neufvillaine was justified.

Other piracies and imitations bear witness to the popularity of the play, but the most valuable because the most disinterested witness was the anonymous author of the *Songe du Rêveur,* a pamphlet in verse attacking Somaize of the Dictionary for his many offences against the illustrious authors of the day. The dreamer wakes upon Helicon where the Muses are complaining to Apollo of the disorder produced in the realm of letters by the lesser pamphleteers. The Muses are especially indignant with the enemies of Molière, "our dear friend whom we most entirely love." The crimes of Somaize are solemnly recounted, including his theft of *Les Précieuses Ridicules* and *Le Cocu Imaginaire.* Somaize is brought to Helicon bound upon the horse Æolus and there is ordered by Apollo to present his apologies to Molière in the traditional white shirt of the penitent. Molière, reluctant to humiliate his enemy, declares that he is more than satisfied. Apollo, however, is inexorable, and there is loud laughter on Helicon at the expense of the miserable victim, in which Molière is at last himself forced to join. The pamphlet is significant as evidence of the position won by Molière within two years of his arrival in Paris, and it is even more interesting as an indication of his character. He is "gentle" and he is "modest," and, though he joins in the laughter against Somaize, he is by nature serious:

> Molière, qui n'est pas rieur,
> En rit aussi de tout son cœur.

It was some time before Molière could effect the necessary alterations at the Palais Royal; but the leaders of society, taking their cue from the King, helped the company over this difficult period by inviting it to give private performances. The King and Mazarin called it to the Louvre or to Vincennes on no less than six occasions. The fees paid to the company for these visits amounted to 2,500 *livres*, a sum which completely covered the establishment expenses at the Palais Royal.

Thus the year drew to an end. The comic genius of Molière was acknowledged even by those whom it had put out of fashion. He had won the public and he had won the King. The attacks so far made upon him had brought him public support and friends for his defence. He had defeated the pirates and placated the alcovists. The crisis which had threatened him with the loss of his theatre and his company had shown that he could rely on the practical support of Louis and the devotion of his comrades.

Meanwhile, the new theatre of the Palais Royal was being made hastily ready, and the author of *Les Précieuses Ridicules* was preparing to challenge unfortunate comparisons in another field.

178

X

The Heroic Muse

MOLIÈRE qui n'est pas rieur—the phrase rings strangely in the ear of the reader who has disinterred from the contemporary pamphleteers the *Songe du Rêveur* to which allusion was made in the last chapter. Nor is this a solitary verdict. In the year of the production of *Sganarelle* Scarron, author of the *Roman Comique* and of several popular farces of the day, died, and more than one contemporary scribbler hastened to celebrate the event, among them the anonymous author of the *Pompe Funèbre de Scarron* in which most of the famous men of letters of the day are shown disputing the right to succeed the dead poet. Molière is rejected by Scarron himself on the ground that he is too *serious* a jester.

Turning, moreover, to the Preface of 1682 we read of Molière: "Though he was extremely agreeable in conversation when with people he liked, he scarcely spoke at all in company unless he happened to find himself with persons for whom he had a special regard. It was accordingly said by those who did not know him well that he was of a contemplative and melancholy disposition."

The boy who at eighteen was captivated by the austere beauty of Lucretius, who had been drawn to the theatre by the appeal of heroic tragedy, who had suffered defeat in his

179

first dramatic adventures as the interpreter of the great Corneille, who had been painted by Mignard wearing the laurels of Pompey and had made his first appearance before the King in the solemn history of *Nicomède* was still, at the age of thirty-eight, in the flush of his comic triumphs, with Paris laughing at his feet and the great King smiling at his elbow, dreaming as he had always dreamed of achieving an admitted excellence in tragedy. He had won his place in the story, but it was not the place he desired. The players of the Hôtel de Bourgogne were still secure in the heroic field. The season of Cornelian tragedies in 1658-1659 at the Petit Bourbon had been a record of disaster only at last retrieved by the comic triumphs of *L'Etourdi*, *Le Dépit Amoureux*, and *Les Précieuses Ridicules*.

But Molière had not yet yielded to his destiny. While Paris laughed at *Sganarelle*, the author of that astonishing success—imitated, exploited, criticized and admired, in the street as in the alcove—was reading privately to his friends a MS. nearer to his heart. He had written his first and only heroic play and, so firmly did he believe in it, that, several months before its production, he had secured a privilege for its publication. The new play was completed in the autumn of 1660 and was intended to be the first of the new productions at the Palais Royal.

Nothing in the history of genius is more striking than the preoccupation of Molière at this moment of his career with the heroic muse. Deaf to the applause that was ringing daily in his ears, untroubled by the excitement he had caused, he retired, in the intervals of productions and visits that were the theme of fashionable Paris, to write the solemn story of *Don Garcie de Navarre ou le Prince Jaloux*. The Cor-

nelians had dismissed his satire upon the exquisites as an
agreeable trifle; Montfleury and his companions can never
have made any secret of their contempt for Molière in
tragedy, and the pamphleteers who later on, in their description of Molière as a heroic actor, so cruelly ridiculed even
his physical peculiarities and imperfections were merely re-
peating what must have been freely uttered by his rivals
from the first. The scorn of the tragedians and an assumption, perhaps, even in those who praised him, that a comic
success, though well enough in its way, was no real pass-
port to Helicon, found the heel of Achilles. The brilliant
humanist of Clermont, who was the creator of so much
merriment and who himself was seldom merry, accordingly
spent his first months of victory and success, not in speed-
ing along the path so clearly indicated, in taking possession
of the realm in which he was Molière, but in a pathetic
endeavour to show himself the equal of Magnon and
Coqueteau de la Clairière.

There is even more striking evidence of this first recoil
of Molière from his comic success. It was probably about
this time—though the evidence as to date is conflicting—
that he was completing and reading to his friends the lost
translation of Lucretius. In April, 1661, the Abbé de
Marolles, in a preface to one of his own classical transla-
tions, tells us that "a famous comedian will perhaps meet
with equal success in a similar design which he has undertaken on behalf of the six books of Lucretius." The Abbé
has heard some of the verses and they are "magnificent."
Chapelain, writing a year later to Bernier, also informs him
that Molière has translated the greater part of Lucretius
in prose and verse, and that the version is excellent. Molière

181

gravely translating Lucretius while Paris laughed at *Sganarelle* is a picture to be retained.

The Palais Royal, the new and permanent home of Molière, though mighty inconvenient for actors and spectators alike, was the first hall built especially for dramatic performances in France. The first round theatre with a sloping floor would not be constructed for another thirty years. This Salle du Palais Royal, expressly built for the production of *Mirame*, a tragedy by Richelieu, was the usual long rectangular room, with a stage at the far end and galleries upon three sides of it. The galleries, superimposed and two in number, were divided into boxes. Most of the spectators were thus obliged to sit sidelong to the stage and to relieve their discomfort a balustrade, known as the elbow-rest, or *accoudoir,* was provided. The pit was still an open space, in which the persons nearest the stage stood throughout the performance. There was a raised amphitheatre behind the pit, and further standing accommodation under an arcade of three arches at the back of the room. The spaces under the galleries served as corridors. The roof was of lead supported on eight great beams, sixty feet long. When Molière first came to the Palais Royal the evil custom had taken firm root of permitting members of the audience to sit upon the stage—a practice which, as we shall see, had a very marked effect upon the form and spirit of the contemporary play. Perhaps already the actors had erected a railing upon either side of the stage so as to reserve for themselves at least sufficient room to move. The hall is recorded to have held 3,000 to 4,000 spectators, but this appears to be an exaggerated estimate. A careful and conservative calculation, based upon the actual measurements of the hall, gives the following results: pit, 300; amphitheatre, 700; boxes in the galleries, 330; under the arcades, 70; on the stage, 50. This gives a total of 1,450 persons, which agrees very well with the receipts given by La Grange in his Register. The takings for a full house amounted to about 2,000 *livres*. The public paid 15 *sols* for admission to the pit and 5 *livres* for a box. The average price was thus about 1.5 *livres*, which would mean an audience of less than 1,400 people. The stage and the auditorium were lit after the same fashion as the Hôtel de Bourgogne, described in a previous chapter.

All Paris was curious to see how the comedian who seldom laughed, the too serious jester of the pamphleteers, would acquit himself in what was still regarded as a nobler form of entertainment. His friends hoped for a success that would put the ungenerous Cornelians to shame. His enemies prayed that he would deliver himself into their hands. Private readings of the MS. had whetted a fashionable curiosity, and the play, whether a success or a failure, would be the one topic of the alcoves for many days to come. The first audience was accordingly brilliant, and *Don Garcie* was produced before a crowded house on February 4, 1661. It was the only complete and unambiguous failure of his career. Molière stubbornly repeated the play, but at the seventh performance the receipts fell to 70 *livres*. In the theatrical slang of the day: *c'était un four*. Nearly two years later, in September, 1662, Molière revived the play in an effort to ascertain whether the King and the Court would endorse the verdict of the general public. It was subsequently played twice at Versailles and once for the King's brother at Chantilly. The King's sympathy—he saw the play three times and could do no more—encouraged Molière to revive it at the Palais Royal in the autumn of 1663. He was then in the most bitter flush of his quarrel with the tragedians of the Hôtel de Bourgogne, and the audience which flocked to his theatre on the first evening of the revival went to see, not *Don Garcie*, but *l'Impromptu de Versailles* in which the author mocked his fashionably heroic competitors. Even the sensation of seeing an unsuccessful tragic author hit back at his successful rivals failed, however, to compensate the spectators for five heroic acts of the jealous prince. The play ran for two performances only. The novelty of realizing that even Molière could be tedious was an inadequate inducement. The silence of the friends of Molière on the subject is even more eloquent than the open satisfaction of his enemies. La Grange in his Register mentions only the receipts. The Editors of 1682 do not even mention the play.

Molière finally accepted the verdict of his contemporaries. He allowed the privilege which he had secured for the publication of *Don Garcie* to lapse. He never published it, and later he embodied one or two of its speeches and fragments in *Tartuffe, Amphitryon, Les Femmes Savantes,* and, more particularly, in *Le Misanthrope.*

Let us be grateful to the contemporaries of Molière for rejecting him as an actor and author in the heroic style. Whether in other times and circumstances, as, for example, in Elizabethan England, he might have become a successful author of tragedy is an interesting speculation, but it is clear that in seventeenth century France he was merely wasting his genius in the heroic field. Molière in tragedy might successfully have led a romantic revival in a period of revolu-

184

tion, but the whole bent of his genius was in opposition to
the formal tendencies of French tragedy which were to prevail for the next hundred and fifty years. His lifelong fidelity to the heroic plays of Corneille and the fact that he was
the first to discover and stimulate the young Racine show
that he was intimately moved by excellence in tragedy, emo-
tionally sensitive, with an imagination quickly fired with a
noble passion. But the man who in his comedies was to
chasten and correct all forms of extravagance could hardly
in his creative work fail to apply the same tests of reality
and commonsense. He was completely out of tune with
the public which applauded Montfleury.

Don Garcie was from the first a mistaken enterprise—an
essentially false type of play—composed upon the tragic
level but declining to a happy and conventional conclusion.
It presented the fashionable characters of the day—impossible warriors, princes in disguise, great ladies whose emotions were refined out of all semblance to humanity. The
only quality that saved a play of this kind with an audience
bred in its traditions was a passionate fidelity to its assump-
tions and demands. The first person to be convinced and
borne away into this peculiar world must be the author himself. The first to weep for Hecuba must be the man who
veritably sees her with a clout upon her head where late
the diadem stood. And Molière was the last person in the
world to make milch the burning eyes of heaven in the
manner of Montfleury and the popular tragedians of the
day. Nor did he attempt it. The interest of *Don Garcie*
for the critic lies in the fact that it betrays a comedian introducing into a play of heroic artifice touches of character
and observation which in the result completely destroy its

appeal. The passages in *Don Garcie* that ensured its failure were precisely those which Molière preserved in *Le
Misanthrope*. The whole spirit of the play was thus at
issue with its form.

The subject is taken from *L'Heureuse Jalousie du Prince
Rodrigue* of the Florentine dramatist Cicognini, who in turn
derived it from a Spanish original. There is the familiar
lady who survives a fictitious death in male disguise; the
hardly less familiar brother who fails to recognize his sister
till the curtain falls; the customary dynastic policies of infinite complication and of no particular interest. Into this
framework, quite unnecessary for his purpose, Molière, instead of introducing the high passions, extravagant motives,
and fanciful situations of the orthodox heroic play of the
period, projects a serious and dispassionate study of the subject whose comic aspects he had just so triumphantly presented in *Sganarelle*. *Don Garcie de Navarre ou le Prince
Jaloux* is a cool and reasoned indictment of an extremely
painful emotion. The exposure is systematic; the analysis is
precise. There are passages in the play which for their
wisdom and justice lift it high above the heroic commonplaces
of the period. But the setting is all wrong. The dramatic
apparatus of *Don Garcie* is one that requires blind passion,
exquisite pathos and the slow breaking of hearts. There is
nothing of this in the play of Molière. It is a dramatic
essay in which he discusses in detail a situation which arises
in each of the five acts. It is never at any single moment
either moving or even dramatic. *Don Garcie* first to last
is jealous and it is all one to his audience whether his jealousy
is due to the deciphering of a torn letter, the visit of a rival
or the entertainment by his lady in disguise.

Molière, in fact, is interested only in his theme; and, working in an essentially false environment, he has concentrated upon it so intently that he has forgotten the first principles of the art of the theatre which he was so brilliantly to expound on a more fortunate occasion. All the rules of dramatic art, he will shortly explain, are derived from the sovereign necessity to please, and, hitherto, reading the plays of Molière, we have recognized them for the work of a man who lived continually in the presence of his public. But the author of *Don Garcie* has forgotten his public entirely. He leaves it unprovided and unpacified, without plot or passion, while his hero exhibits himself as an epitome of the jealous state and his heroine, with much regret and an immovable dignity, diagnoses and expostulates upon his case. There is only one dramatic moment in the play, when Don Garcie is invited to make his famous choice. Will he consent to believe in his lady without proof, upon her word alone that she is loyal, or must she satisfy him with clear and certain evidence that he is in the wrong? If he will accept her word, she will forgive his jealous doubts; if he demands an explanation he shall have it, but he must then renounce her for ever? That is a very pretty dilemma, not only dramatic in itself, but epitomizing the point of view of the proud Elvire who consistently argues that jealousy, being a distrust of the beloved, is an offence against her honour and, therefore, betrays a condition of mind incompatible with true affection. The scene also brings to a climax the hero's jealousy. He *must* be satisfied. Even though he loses his betrothed, he will have proofs of her disloyalty. Unfortunately, the rest of the play is dramatically nowhere near the level of this particular scene. Inci-

187

dentally, it should be noted that this scene, which alone is theatrically effective, is not itself in the heroic vein. It is in substance and effect an act of high comedy. It presents a comic antithesis between Elvire, excessively proud and obstinately faithful to her own point of view, and Don Garcie, helplessly sick of his malady, whose progress we watch, not with the vivid anxiety of a friend, but with the cool interest of a physician. We are not touched by the woes and passions of the protagonists. Neither of them at that moment engages our sympathy. There is nothing here of the pathos of Hermione or the tragic ruin of Othello. The scene is not, in fact, written on the heroic plane, and our emotions are not involved. The hero finds us impatient, and the heroine leaves us cold. Our interest lies in a point of view, in a situation where a problem of conduct is posed, in an analysis of a human failing which is being reasonably presented and discussed. We coldly incline to consider that the heroine, here as in the previous scenes, is a little severe on the unfortunate prince. Her conduct is ambiguous; she thinks too much of her own pride and too little of her lover; she is never sufficiently candid and not even sufficiently hurt. We cannot accept her on the heroic plane. Offended dignity is inadequate as a tragic theme, or even for the pathetic appeal of serious romance. The best scene of the play, successful as high comedy, fails as heroics by very reason of its qualities.

This is equally true of all the passages and incidents in the play that make it here and there quite excellent reading, not only for the light it throws on the genius of Molière but for its own sake. The sudden pause of Don Garcie in his magnificent oaths that never again will he suspect the

188

fidelity of his lady and his immediate headlong relapse into the jealous fit when a letter is brought to her; his refusal to read the letter when Elvire presses him to do so followed by his dissembled eagerness to see it as soon as she no longer insists; his declaration, a little later, that he will not listen to the insinuations of his false friend, followed as soon as his friend changes the subject, by an insistence that he shall be told the worst; the noble irony of Elvire at his expense; his piteous pleading that his jealousy is a proof of his affection; his struggle with himself, ending at the last in resignation and a partial victory over his unfortunate monster; the final relenting of Elvire despite all her previous expostulations; the quiet, persistent analysis of the jealous motive and the essential justice and reason of the author's attitude to the passion—all this is of the substance and tissue of high comedy such as Molière was to bring to perfection in *Le Misanthrope*. But it was precisely these passages and incidents that sorted so ill with the heroic trappings and romantic conduct of the play. *Don Garcie* might easily have been a masterpiece of comic irony. It was, unfortunately, and must in the theatre forever remain, an essay in romantic failure.

Many ingenious reasons have been invented to account for the disaster. It is argued that the public, expecting to be amused by a comic author, was naturally disconcerted at meeting him in another capacity or, again, that the play is of an indeterminate type which necessarily puzzled its audience. Such pleadings cannot be sustained. The public which had applauded *Le Cid* had not failed to appreciate *Le Menteur*, and the audiences who were shortly to weep at *Medea* would laugh as heartily at *Les Plaideurs*. *Don Garcie,* moreover, far from being an unpopular type of play, was strangely fashionable both in England and France throughout the seventeenth century. Molière, author of *Sganarelle*, in writing *Don Garcie*, was as obviously subscribing to the taste of the period as was Congreve, author of *The Way of the World*, in writing *The Mourning Bride*; and it is interesting to compare these two frigid exercises in the heroic vein by the two greatest comic authors of England and France. There is no reason to look for any recondite or mysterious reason for the failure of *Don Garcie* either in the defeated expectations of an audience that awaited a comedy or in the fashion of the day. *Don Garcie* failed because it was, from the theatrical point of view, a bad play. It called for emotion and failed to arouse it. It held out promises of a dramatic development which it never fulfilled. The characters, instead of winning our hearts, were exposed to judgment, and the action, instead of advancing to a dramatic crisis, presented essentially the same situation from start to finish. Don Garcie is jealous without cause in Act I. He is rather more jealous with rather less cause in Act V. *Don Garcie* is a heroic play without a hero, a romantic play without a romance. It is a play about a marriage that very nearly did not take place—an excellent theme for a comedy, but hardly for a drama in the heroic style. The hero does not move us with his jealousy; he is merely irritating; while Elvire moves us even less with her very just and pertinent reproaches. Everything she says is right, but so much commonsense, so admirably delivered, is hardly acceptable in a heroine of romance or even in a merely human woman sincerely afflicted.

The failure of Molière in *Don Garcie* was even worse for the actor than for the author. The noble princes of the

heroic drama were expected to roar according to their station.   An actor who declaimed in his natural voice and
manner could not hope to find favour with the admirers of
Montfleury.   Molière, who never made any reference in
his plays or prefaces to his failure as an heroic author, com-
ments indirectly upon his failure as an heroic actor both in
Les Précieuses Ridicules and *L'Impromptu de Versailles.*
He defends his own easier and more natural habit of playing by attacking the manner of his rivals.   His reference in
Les Précieuses Ridicules to the tragedians of the Hôtel de
Bourgogne is our first positive indication of their hostility.
Mascarille has written a play.   To whom, inquires the exquisite Cathos, will you entrust it?   Need you ask? says
Mascarille.   To the players of the Hôtel de Bourgogne to
be sure: "*Il n'y a qu'eux qui soient capables de faire valoir
les choses; les autres sont des ignorants qui récitent comme
l'on parle; il ne savent pas faire ronfler les vers et s'arrêter
au bel endroit: et le moyen de connoître où est le beau vers
si le comédien ne s'y arrête et ne vous avertit par là qu'il
faut faire le brouhaha?*"   The allusion was still comparatively good humoured, but the quarrel was swiftly enven-
omed, and *L'Impromptu de Versailles,* written four years
later, contained, among other things, a direct parody of the
fashionable style of declamation—its exaggeration and emphasis, its studied pauses and magnificent demeanour on even
the most trivial occasions, so that a King, addressing a simple
order to his captain of the guard, must speak as though he
were possessed with a devil.   *L'Impromptu de Versailles*
was written two years after the failure of *Don Garcie,* but
Molière in 1663 was still sensitive and rebellious.   It is significant that the only occasion on which he ever refers, in

the gross fashion of the day, to the physical peculiarities of
an opponent was in his parody of Montfleury, where, in
allusion to the immensely fat tragedian, he demands for the
heroic theatre a King of vast circumference who can fill a
throne in the grand manner. *L'Impromptu de Versailles*
is an important document and will be discussed in its proper
place. For the moment we merely note that the public,
though possibly amused, was not converted. The extent of
Molière's failure as an heroic actor is shown by the fact
that it refused to accept him in his own play. The author
of *Le Vengeance des Marquis*, one of the numerous dramatic contributions to the comic war which is shortly to
break out, tells us that the author of *Don Garcie* was "obliged
to give the part of the jealous prince to another actor because the public could not endure to see him."

The allusion of Molière to the girth of Montfleury was
his solitary lapse from the rules of generous controversy.
He was, in his own day, unique in the delicacy of his re-
joinders. Within the next few years he was to be reviled
and slandered in his person and private life. But the worst
he ever said of his worst enemy was that he was large enough
to fill a throne. The son of Montfleury, who contributed
to the comic war a play entitled, *L'Impromptu de l'Hôtel
de Condé* retorted with a famous description of Molière in
the rôle of Cæsar:

> . . . il vient le nez au vent,
> Les pieds en parenthèse, et l'épaule en avant,
> Sa perruque, qui suit le côté qu'il avance,
> Plus pleine de laurier qu'un jambon de Mayence,
> Les mains sur les côtés d'un air peu négligé,
> La tête sur le dos comme un mulet chargé,

MOLIÈRE IN THE RÔLE OF CÆSAR

From the portrait attributed to Pierre Mignard in the *Comédie Française.*

Les yeux fort égarés, puis débitant ses rôles,
D'un hoquet éternel sépare ses paroles. . . .

The reference to the famous *hoquet* cries quits for the *roi entrepaillé* of Molière and the description, though malicious, suffices to show why Molière did not appeal to his contemporaries in the heroic vein. The only other description we have of Molière as an heroic actor, that comes anywhere near to being contemporary, is that of *La Serre* written in 1734. Molière had been dead for over fifty years, but La Serre had talked with actors who had received minute descriptions from their predecessors:

Nature, says La Serre, which had been so generous to him in gifts of the mind, had refused him the external graces so necessary to the actor, particularly in tragic parts. His voice was heavy, with hard inflexions, and he had a volubility of utterance that ran away with his speeches and made him in this respect greatly inferior to the actors of the Hôtel de Bourgogne. He could only correct this volubility, so contrary to good articulation, by constant attention, which resulted in a *hoquet* which he kept until his death and which on certain occasions he contrived to use to good effect. In order to vary his inflexions he resorted to certain unusual intonations, which laid him open to charges of affectation, but to which his hearers became accustomed.

Thus might an admirer of Charles Macready describe the acting of Henry Irving, and, if we set against his portrait in tragedy by La Serre, his portrait in comedy by the Sieur de Neufvillaine in *Sganarelle,* we begin to get a fairly accurate appreciation of his playing. Undoubtedly, Molière was a great comic actor. Clearly he was in love with tragedy and had very original and persistent ideas as to the delivery of

193

heroic parts. But physically he was not built for the tragic stage, and his realistic conception of tragedy was in his own day impossible of acceptance.

We have so far avoided the comparison, so dear to critics, of Molière and Shakespeare. In the failure of *Don Garcie*, however, we may discover a point of comparison that has so far been overlooked. Molière, the contemplative observer, whose comedies are the highest expression of human intelligence in the theatre, failed in the heroic field because in his art intelligence must be always supreme. He sets out to present a hero, but brings him in the end to judgment; he makes as though he would appeal to our emotions, but ends by appealing to our commonsense. Shakespeare failed in his satirical comedies for an opposite reason. He set out in *Troilus and Cressida* and in *Measure for Measure* to correct and to satirize; but almost at once his detachment broke down; he identified himself with his victims; and, in the end, we find ourselves in love with Cressida and distressed for Lucio. The antithesis between the two greatest dramatists of the modern world is thus complete; for, just as Shakespeare's satirical comedies contain some of his most moving tragic utterances, so does the one heroic play of Molière contain some of his shrewdest observations on human weakness.

Don Garcie was publicly presented nine times in two years. It was then consigned to oblivion.

XI

The School for Husbands

DURING the Easter holidays that followed the
failure of *Don Garcie* at the Palais Royal it is
noted of Molière in the Register of La Grange
that he came before the company and asked for two shares
in place of the one which he already held. La Grange goes
on to record that the company granted him the two shares
"for himself and his wife if he should marry." Thus
Molière, when he began to write *L'Ecole des Maris* in the
spring of 1661, was already providing for his marriage
with Armande Béjart and arranging with his colleagues for
the terms of her admission to the troop, and no biographer
of Molière is permitted to read the play without wondering to what extent it is to be regarded as a personal document.

Nothing is more dangerous or misleading than to look for
an author in his works. Each case must be judged upon its
merits, and in the case of Molière the merits are extremely
difficult to assess. His subjects are often intimately connected with the events and emotions of his life. But all
suffers a transformation which is more than a mere matter
of form and selection. The plays of Molière, read in the
light of his experience as a man, are a strange paradox. He
creates in reaction from his personal misadventures rather
than in an effort to perpetuate or record them. No man, for

example, was ever more intimately exposed to the passion of jealousy; and yet no man has written more wisely or in a finer detachment concerning it. No man was ever more melancholy and seclusive; and yet no writer was ever so abounding in gaiety and in his work so prevailingly sociable. There was never so dauntless and extreme a fighter than the man who persistently challenged the society, religion and learned professions of his time; and yet no writer was ever so moderate, so conservative, so measured in the portrayal of men and manners. These paradoxes, which will be multiplied as we proceed, are reflected in his personal destiny as well as in his works, and they culminated in a last anomaly which has rarely been exceeded. The dramatist, who has been admired for three hundred years as the champion in all things of the golden mean, of the virtues of prudence and moderation, was refused Christian burial as an impious revolutionary.

The failure of *Don Garcie* took the company by surprise. To meet the emergency Molière resorted hastily to his provincial sketches, like *Gorgibus dans le Sac, Les Trois Docteurs, Le Médecin Volant,* and quickly produced two new contemporary plays, since forgotten. These were desperate measures and did not bring back to the theatre a public which had decided to applaud Molière in his own comedies and to accept him either grudgingly or not at all in anything else. *L'Ecole des Maris* was not ready until 24th June, 1661.

L'Ecole des Maris is a play with a thesis. Ariste and Sganarelle, two elderly brothers, have been entrusted with the education and future destiny of Léonor and Isabelle. Ariste is in favour of a reasonable indulgence. Sganarelle

196

is the advocate of an unreasonable repression. The brothers expect to marry their young wards. Ariste secures the affection and esteem of Léonor and will continue as her husband to allow her the liberties which he is confident she will not abuse, whereas Sganarelle by his severities and suspicions drives Isabelle into the arms of a rival.

The moral of the play is stated at the outset:

Ariste. Leur sexe aime à jouir d'un peu de liberté;
   On le retient fort mal par tant d'austérité;
   Et les soins défiants, les verrous et les grilles
   Ne font pas la vertu des femmes ni des filles. . . .
Sganarelle. Chansons que tout cela.
Ariste.   Soit; mais je tiens, sans cesse,
   Qu'il nous faut en riant instruire la jeunesse.

Ariste develops his theme at length. Good company, balls, plays and other diversions—these help to form and enliven the mind. The best of all schools is the world. Finally, to the amazement and scandal of his brother, he affirms that he will be as faithful to his views after marriage as before and Sganarelle predicts for him the fate that in the sequel befalls himself. Sganarelle intends to look better after his wife. Dressed in good plain serge, with a black dress for festal occasions, she shall keep the house, look to its affairs and mend her linen.

There has been a good deal of high writing concerning the doctrines of Ariste. Certain critics have found here a whole philosophy of nature: let the young grow as they please; honour and virtue being spontaneous and from the heart will of themselves be triumphant. There is, however, very little philosophy of nature in *L'Ecole des Maris,* though there is abundance of commonsense such as Molière invariably applies to all matters of social conduct. The less, indeed, we say of nature in this connection, the better. Marriage between a man of sixty, for Ariste is alas! a sexagenarian, and a girl of eighteen is an arrangement which nature might be expected to regard with at most a qualified approval, and it should be observed that nature, if she prompts Léonor to marry Ariste for his kindness and instructs her in all the honourable virtues, also teaches Isabelle to be something of a minx. We readily forgive her ingenious duplicities; they are a legitimate defence against the tyranny of her guardian. But the critics who have read this play as an ode in celebration of the simple virtues of the human heart, would have done better to observe that Isabelle owed to nature and to nature alone a genius for complicated intrigue rarely equalled upon any stage. There is, in fact, just enough, but no more, of the philosophy of nature in Ariste to correct the lack of it in Sganarelle. Ariste expressly allows that nature in the young must be corrected, but corrected in such a way that virtue does not inspire them with reprobation and fear. He is advocating not licence but a reasonable freedom. His views on education are merely one aspect of his general contention: *l'un et l'autre excès choque*. He stands for the conduct of an average man in a reasonably ordered society.

L'Ecole des Maris is a genuine comedy of character. Though the incidents of the play tend to farce, and the character of Sganarelle, who retains a generic name inherited from the comic old men of the Italian theatre, inclines at moments, towards the fantastical, neither the subject of the comedy nor the veracity of its portraiture is for a moment compromised. The extravagant absurdity of Sganarelle towards the close of the play is a logical consequence of the fixed ideas and emotions by which he is from first to last inspired. The situations in which he becomes involved are extravagant, but their extravagance is an expression of his own distorted inspiration. He becomes continuously more egocentric, and his gullibility arises in every case from a blind preoccupation with his own interests and desires. Molière here first reveals his comic genius at the full. The comedy of Sganarelle is a sublimation of the comedy of the drunken man, a source of infinite delight to his sober fellows because he has ceased to be one of them and is now a being, set apart, with a surprising logic and a procedure peculiar to himself. Unsuspectingly he acts as go-between between Isabelle and his rival, conveys their messages, fosters their intrigue, and finally himself conducts her to the arms of her lover—a figure of farce in his conduct, but saved for comedy by the fact that the ease with which he is deceived is due to the strongest and most persistent passion of his nature. He misleads himself more than he is misled. His egoism is so monstrous that it becomes at times pathological, and it is precisely at such moments that the genius of the author transforms what might so easily have been an exaggeration of farce into a profound and genuine stroke of character. The climax of the farce is also a climax of comic delineation. Turn, for an example, to Act II, Scene 14. Sganarelle, tremulous with delight at the fancied discomfiture of his rival falls, apparently, into a sudden pity for the young man:

> Pauvre garçon! sa douleur est extrême.
> Tenez, embrassez-moi . . .

That is the *coup de génie*—a supreme touch. The drunken egoist embraces in his rival an embodiment of his own triumph; his sudden sympathy is due to a vivid sense of the defeat which he believes himself to have successfully escaped. The pity of the egoist for others is never more than a vicarious compassion for himself.

Molière's Sganarelle, to the careless eye a figure of farce, is, indeed, the first of his masterpieces of comic portraiture. It survives the most modern tests. The creator of Sganarelle knew nothing of complexes which are now a commonplace of popular psychology, but for those whom it amuses to apply modern terminology to a classical subject, Sganarelle of *L'Ecole des Maris* is an excellent victim. His attitude to society, apparently so insolent, is due to a constitutional diffidence. His contempt for the amenities of human intercourse is sheer timidity. His aggressive misanthropy is mere avoidance. The scheme whereby he seeks to win a wife who shall be entirely devoted is inspired by a persistent sense of his own inferiority. He rails at virtues in others in which he instinctively feels himself to be deficient, and the malicious joy which he feels in his own apparent triumph is sheer reaction from his normally downcast condition. His brief intoxication, when he thinks himself beloved of Isabelle, is the new wine that bursts the wineskin of a temperament fundamentally unexpectant of success in any form. In the manner of his kind he harps continually on the misfortunes and disabilities of others—his brother's age or the infidelities of his neighbour's wife—merely to keep his spirits up. He must be seeking continually to prove himself the better man, and this is no more than an anxiety to assert a superiority which he feels to be constantly in peril. His resolute disregard of fashion, culminating in his proud declaration that those who find him ill to look upon have only to shut their eyes, is the defiance of a nervous distemper.

Note how the skill of the practical man of the theatre in dealing with an audience, so strangely lacking in *Don Garcie*, is in this play apparent at every turn. Observe especially the care he takes to prevent our delight at Sganarelle's discomfiture being impaired by any compassion for his undoing. Sganarelle is as odious in defeat as in prosperity. He brings about his disgrace by the eagerness with which he desires to exult over the disgrace of his brother. He has a genius for the mean word and is inspired by an egoism so monstrous that our sympathy is at every turn estranged. Even the gentle Ariste declares at the last that no one can pity a man who rejoices so spitefully in the misfortunes of others:

> Et je vois votre sort malheureux à ce point,
> Que, vous sachant dupé, l'on ne vous plaindra point.

Ariste, even when he believes himself to be deceived, remains true to his principles. He is disappointed, but there is no rancour or malice in the man, and he does not regret the generosity which has been, so he imagines, so ill repaid. Sganarelle is equally consistent. He cannot learn from his misfortunes. He has put his system to the test, and it has failed. But the failure, instead of convincing him of his error, merely confirms it. The fault lies not in himself or his opinions, but in the wickedness of the sex in general and of Isabelle in particular:

> Malheureux qui se fie à femme après cela!
> La meilleure est toujours en malice féconde;
> C'est un sexe engendré pour damner tout le monde.

201

J'y renonce à jamais, à ce sexe trompeur,
Et je le donne tout au diable de bon cœur.

Such is his conclusion which precisely reverses the moral of his defeat.

The critics who amuse themselves with derivations have in *L'Ecole des Maris* an excellent theme. Terence and Boccaccio share the honours with Lope de Vega, Dorimond and Boisrobert. The central idea, which is to contrast two different systems of education, based respectively upon indulgence and severity, is from the *Adelphi* of Terence. The Third Novel of the Third Day of Boccaccio supplies the ingenious ruse, already a commonplace of the contemporary theatre, in which Isabelle, in order to get into touch with Valère and enlighten him as to her kindly disposition, sends the young stranger a message to the effect that he must cease the importunities of which he has hitherto been modestly innocent. The Boccaccian episode had only recently been revived and exploited in *La Femme Industrieuse* of Dorimond, the heroine of whose play secures for herself a lover by the same artifice. Boisrobert in *La Folle Gageure*, a play produced by Molière himself since his return to Paris, contributes the moral of the comedy:

Qu'une femme qu'on garde, eût-elle cent Argus,
Si son cœur y consent, peut avoir des nouvelles
De l'amant qui la sert, malgré ses sentinelles.

In other words, a woman guarded is a woman won. Boisrobert adapted his play from *El Mayor Impossible* of Lope de Vega, who had, in yet another comedy, used the device of Boccaccio. Finally, there is a comedy entitled *El Marido Hace Mujer* or *It's the Husband Makes the Wife* of Antonio

Hurtado de Mendoza (1643). Here we have the essential substance of the play of Molière. Two brothers are married to two sisters. The one is generous and confiding; the other is brutal and suspicious. The first gains the love and esteem of his young wife; the other suffers the fate which husbands so frequently deserve. The suspicious husband, surprising his wife with her lover, is under the impression that he is witnessing the infidelities of his sister-in-law and makes merry at the expense of his brother in terms which crushingly rebound upon himself. This is Act III of the play of Molière. No better text for the charge of plagiary could, in fact, be found than *L'Ecole des Maris*. Situation, subject, moral, incidents, even the names of the heroines are borrowed, and Molière plainly advertises his sources, calling his more fortunate heroine Léonor after the happy wife of Mendoza and her more subtle companion Isabelle after the resourceful lady of Dorimond.

The contemporaries of Molière were, nevertheless, curiously silent in respect of these derivations. Hitherto extremely prompt to accuse him of thievery and imitation they allowed him in this case the benefit of his own proud formula: *Je prends mon bien où je le trouve*. Perhaps they realized that it was impossible to attack him on inconsistent grounds, and in this case they preferred a more insidious indictment, which was shortly to assume fantastic proportions. So original an author could never be severely hurt by any suggestion such as Greene had in a fit of passion brought against our own Shakespeare. Here was no "jay-in-peacock's feathers" or "shakescene," but the most individual author of his race. The author, accused of plagiary, serenely unmoved, had replied to his critics in the joyous preface to

Les Précieuses Ridicules. Now began the cruel hunt after the man. His plays were coverts to be drawn. His enemies reached after the intimacies of his private life, with perfidious allusions to the characters, incidents and ideas which they found in his works, and they were intelligent enough to realize that they could not have him both ways. They could not accuse a man of re-writing the *Adelphi* of Terence or *El Marido Hace Mujer* of Mendoza and at the same time suggest that he was dramatizing his own domestic interior.

The new line of attack was to prove vastly more effective. Molière, who had contemptuously ignored the charge of plagiarism, was soon to protest with vehemence against the charge that he was slavishly a realist, imitating this or that particular person or circumstance either at his own fireside or in the society about him. He was more indignant at the charge of imitating nature than of imitating his dramatic rivals or predecessors, being good enough critic to realize that the accusation was even more derogatory to his art. A comedian in the school of Terence, perhaps—he smiled at the charge; but not, he protested, the author of comedies with a key.

The key in the present instance seemed obvious enough. Here was a man of forty about to marry a girl of eighteen who, according to the gossips, had been brought up more or less under his supervision. What more natural than that he should write a play in defence of his personal adventure, exhibiting himself as the gentle guardian, beloved and trusted by his ward; expressing all the sentiments proper to the occasion; offering his future wife an example which he hoped would not be lost upon her; incidentally persuading himself, perhaps, of the wisdom of the step he was proposing to take; brilliantly justifying the experiment in advance by showing how, in fiction at any rate, the problems of feeling and conduct implicit in such a situation might be successfully solved with a little goodwill on both sides. The analogy was obvious—so obvious, indeed, that it has misled quite a number of shrewd and careful biographers.

For the analogy was far from being as simple as it seemed. The characters of the play bore no real resemblance to the characters in the private history of Molière. Molière was in love with Armande. Ariste had for Léonor no more than a moderate affection. Molière was a sensitive man of genius, bound to suffer for the step he was about to take. Ariste was an equable man of sense, who would obviously make a success of his experiment. No one, moreover, could be less like the headlong and capricious Armande than the docile and considerate Léonor. *L'Ecole des Maris* in essentials much more closely resembled the theatrical models from which it was derived than the personal comedy in which Molière was himself to be shortly involved. In this as, in all the plays of Molière in which he draws upon his private experience, the personal issues were transposed. The plays of Molière can never be read as a direct personal record. His art represented, on the contrary, the triumph of genius over experience. Those who have found in Ariste and Léonor a forecast in the optative mood of the relations of Molière and Armande profoundly misconceive his method of work. If we are to seek Molière in his play, we shall find him, not in the wise and gentle Ariste, who so persuasively voices the considered views of the dramatist on the upbringing of youth and the reasonable freedoms of the married state, but in Sganarelle. Sganarelle is the re-

venge of the artist upon the man. Molière was about to
marry a girl of eighteen whom he knew already as a spoiled
child, impatient of any form of correction or restraint. He
knew himself equally well as a man who would be hurt,
who had perhaps already suffered, owing to their essential
incompatibility. Sganarelle was an imaginative outlet for
the instinctive prophetic jealousy of the husband-to-be of
forty summers. He exposed the hidden creature to the
wonder of himself and posterity. The artist, far from
idealizing himself in the sagacious Ariste, instinctively derided his own possible defeat in the ignoble Sganarelle. This
was not the sublimated portrait of a domestic interior; it
was a *catharsis*. Critics have found it strange that Molière,
producing the play, assigned to himself, not the part of
Ariste, the interpreter of his views, but Sganarelle who was
their negation. Some seek an explanation in the fact that
Sganarelle was obviously the better part for a comedian;
others contend, with strange perversity, that he did not wish
too strongly to emphasize the personal analogy by taking
a part of which he was himself the original. The latter
explanation is directly opposed to the psychology of his
creative method. The whole question of the relation of
the man to his art will arise again and be progressively ex-
amined as other and more striking instances come up for discussion. Suffice it for the moment that, so far as Molière
draws upon his own experience for his comedies, the main-
spring of his inspiration is an effort to escape and to deride
his personal limitations. He views the progress of Sganarelle with his melancholy eyes and comic smile, and it is
a look which may be interpreted: there, but for the grace of
God, go I.

The success of the play was as immediate and as complete as that of his previous comedies. Loret celebrated it as being "fine" and "gay," and "the delight of Paris." It was played by request before the sister of Turenne; before Fouquet at Vaux; three times before the King at Fontainebleau; before Monsieur, the brother of the King. The author, in view of its popularity, took immediate steps to secure his copyright. The play, produced on 24th June, 1661, was licensed for publication on 9th July, and published on 20th August with a short preface addressed to Monsieur, official protector of the troop. Molière introduced his comedy as the first work published on his own initiative. The preface was written in the customary language of the period: nothing so fine as the name which stands at the head of his work and nothing so insignificant as the work itself; he is placing a crown of diamonds and pearls upon a figure of clay, conducting his readers, through magnificent portals and triumphal arches, to a lowly cabin; he has no choice, however, in following so discrepant a procedure; he makes no offering but performs a duty. A sensitive reader will find in these lines hints of a proud, indifferent irony which is to appear more strikingly on later occasions. It was the fashionable preface—with a difference; and its distinguished recipient was, perhaps, sufficiently intelligent to suspect that the daring fellow was pulling the princely leg. Posterity may be sure of it; for the author of this preface, in whom was no touch of servility before God or man, will shortly be found chaffing the King himself to his royal face.

L'Ecole des Maris completely obliterated the failure of *Don Garcie*. The Italianate author of the early farces, who

207

with *Les Précieuses Ridicules* had begun to discover the true
comedy in a satire upon contemporary manners, was now
revealed as a dramatist with definite views, who could deal
wisely and finely with problems of conduct and character.
He had passed from the brilliant sketching of an external
fashion to a serious study of social behaviour. He had thus
entered upon that perilous enterprise of dealing with the
accepted moral conventions of his day in the light of his
own individual ideas and temperament which was to in-
volve him in bitter and continuous controversy to the day
of his death.

XII

PORTRAITS

MONG the places visited by Molière and his company with *L'Ecole des Maris* in 1661 was the castle of Vaux where Fouquet, in the fulness of his power, with all France for his vineyard, was beginning to regard himself as a master to whom no pleasure or distraction might be denied. There, on the 12th July, Molière had played in the presence of Monsieur, the King's brother, and his bride, Henrietta of England. Fouquet now desired a more splendid festival. The shadow of Mazarin had passed in death. The King was supreme; Fouquet was his friend and manager; and the new Mæcenas was resolved that his risen sun should extinguish all previous lights. Le Notre was designing his gardens; Le Brun was decorating his palace; La Fontaine was his laureate; Molière should be his diversion. For company he invited the King, the Queen mother, all the princes and notables of the realm. He walked with his guests among the beds, fountains and falls of the park; in the great hall he served a banquet worthy of Amphitryon; thence to the well-trod stage, built at the end of a great avenue of fir-trees, where, amid twenty jets of water, came a giant oyster, a theme for contemporary gossips, disclosing a goddess, no less, who delivered the prologue:

209

Peut on voir nymphe plus gentille
Qu'était Béjart l'autre jour?
Lorsqu'on vit ouvrir sa coquille
Tout le monde disait à l'entour,
  Lorsqu'on vit ouvrir sa coquille:
Voici la mère d'Amour.

Fireworks, a brilliant ball, with a supper fit for a King, brought the evening to a close.

Within a few days Fouquet who had commanded the festival and Pellisson, who had written the prologue, were under arrest. The King when he came to Vaux in 1661 had already decided upon the disgrace of his favourite. It is the cause, it is the cause, my soul. Fouquet had committed so insolent a treason that he was lost from the moment it was revealed. Among the ladies of Madame, Henrietta of England, was the gentle, but as yet obscure, Mademoiselle de la Vallière. Nothing must please the magnificently promiscuous Fouquet but to wear also this modest feather in his cap. He had, however, found the lady strangely distant. In vain had he taken the usual steps. He had even induced a great lady to plead for him, and authorized her to pay the price. She might go as high, even, as 200,000 *livres*. But the damsel was not to be moved. Here was a pretty mystery, almost without precedent. What could be the reason? Fouquet was not for nothing *surintendant*, and his secret agents were shortly able to inform him that the modest and inconspicuous Mademoiselle de la Vallière, wonderful to relate, was secretly the mistress of the King himself, to whom she had revealed the unusual pleasure of being loved for his own sake. Fouquet very naturally decided to abandon his suit, but success had turned his head and he could not forego the satisfaction of letting the lady know that he had read the riddle of her astounding indifference. Meeting her one day in an antechamber he mockingly whispered his congratulations upon a conquest apparently dearer to her inclinations and perhaps more kindly to her interests. Mademoiselle de la Vallière, indignant at receiving such a compliment from such a man, went straight to the King, and the ruin of Fouquet was thenceforth merely a matter of time and occasion.

Walking with his gentlemen through the gardens, seeing everywhere the magnificence of his creature, enjoying the splendid hospitality which had been almost forced upon him, the most Christian King, gracious and smiling, boiled inwardly and when, on entering the study of his favourite, he found a portrait of Mademoiselle de la Vallière confronting him from the wall he boiled very nearly over. With difficulty could he be restrained from arresting the culprit then and there. But *noblesse oblige.* Louis was the guest of Fouquet, and the whole court was in train for feasting and play. "*Quoi,*" exclaimed the Queen mother, "*au milieu d'une fête qu'il vous donne!*"

Fouquet was warned during the festival by a friend of what had occurred and, as he played the host and applauded the comedy of Molière, knew that his disgrace was imminent. But these were gentlemen of France. Both Fouquet and his royal master were to all seeming enchanted with one another and with the occasion. Each of them had praise and attention to spare for a good comedian, and the King, as we shall see, even went so far as to suggest a new character for the play, which afterwards enabled Molière publicly to claim him as a collaborator.

Les Fâcheux encouraged the tendency, which had already
declared itself in connection with *Les Précieuses Ridicules,* to
find in the plays of Molière portraits and allusions to living
models, and it is certainly the best text on which to found the
charge of a photographic realism in portraiture which the
author himself, in other instances, so strongly resented. The
extent to which he drew his characters after the men and
women about him, taking this particular marquis or that
particular prude for a model, was a question that passionately exercised his contemporaries. The comedy-ballet of
Les Fâcheux is a special case. It is a play without a subject, almost without a plot—a series of sketches or cari-
catures, a gallery of bores, in which the author performs the
difficult feat of amusing us upon the stage with people who
in real life exist only to be tedious. The hero of the play
is no more than the victim of their importunities. Anxious
to keep an appointment with his lady, he is at every turn
waylaid and interrupted. The play accordingly stands or
falls by its portraiture. Its success hung on the fact that
every member of the audience had suffered in just that way
from just that sort of person; and, to emphasize the realism
and encourage the search for originals, there was the circumstance, proudly recorded by the author in his preface,
that the King himself had suggested a living model. "I
owe this success," the author affirms, "not only to the distinguished approval with which Your Majesty has honoured
my play and which so conspicuously stimulated the approval
of the world at large, but still more to the command which
you laid upon me to add to my comedy a bore whose picture
Your Majesty outlined, and who has proved to be best of
the bunch." The original in this case was no less a person

than the Marquis de Soyecourt, at that time the Grand Master of the Wardrobe and afterwards the King's Master of the Chase: tradition affirms that the King pointed him out as a fit subject after the first performance of the play and that Molière added him to the collection with the assistance of the victim himself, who supplied him with the necessary terms of venery. This Soyecourt was an entertaining person, given to abstraction, of a sweet simplicity of mind, and Madame de Sévigné is often amusing at his expense. One of his sayings is famous. Sleeping one night with friends he began to talk to one of them. The other who desired to sleep protested: *Eh, morbleu! tais-toi; tu m'empêches de dormir.* Soyecourt turned mildly upon him. *Est-ce que je te parle, à toi?* he ingeniously asked.

The author has cleverly contrived that virtually every character in the play should be a bore or the victim of a bore. The list is imposing. Even the hero's valet, with his untimely anxiety to serve and please his master on all occasions, is one of them. We find here the marquis who comes late to the theatre, takes his place on the stage, effusively greets his acquaintances and comments aloud on the play to the annoyance of all decent spectators and the embarrassment of the actors; the amateur musician who insists upon singing his airs and illustrating his intentions in and out of season; the gentleman who forces his courtesies upon those who desire only to avoid them; the man who talks continually of possible affairs of honour and roams in constant search of seconds for prospective encounters; the man who insists upon detailing the cards he held and the way he played them in his last game of piquet; the person who loves an argument and insists on the first comer being the arbiter

213

of some fine point of conduct or feeling; the sportsman (Soyecourt) who recounts minutely to all his friends his fortunes by field, forest and river; the man with a bee in his bonnet who desires, for example, to reform the writing of signs and inscriptions upon the inns and houses of Paris; the man with a brilliant idea which he wishes to put before the Government for the reform of the revenue and public services; the man who insists on offering to serve his friend in a quarrel that does not yet exist. Here, subject to changes of fashion, are, among others, the same people who are to-day the terror of clubs, the spoilers of parties, the enemies everywhere of polite intercourse. The author enhances our sense of their importunity and lack of all discretion by putting his hero in such a position that even the society of his best friends would at that particular moment have been unwelcome. Anxious only to be rid of their company, he fumes and frets, while one after another the bores serenely abound in their own impertinence.

The form of the play was novel and important. It was the first of the comedy-ballets written expressly for the Court which was to include such masterpieces as *Le Bourgeois Gentilhomme* and *Le Malade Imaginaire*. The King had a passion for the dance. His dancing master had been the most highly paid of his instructors, receiving 2,000 *livres* as compared with the 300 *livres* paid to the writing master under whom he had inscribed in his copybook the maxim that Kings might do as they pleased. He founded his *Académie Royale de Danse* in 1661—thirteen of the greatest experts in choreography—eight years before his *Académie de Musique*. The ballet, in public esteem, still ranked, with tragedy, high above the comic art. The King

214

himself was an excellent dancer and took the floor on all possible occasions until the increasing dignity of the royal estate forbade the indulgence of so promiscuous an exercise. Molière must conform to the royal passion, and, since the number of expert dancers at his disposal was limited, his problem was to write a comedy in which there should be, at intervals long enough for repose and a change of costume, a series of ballets or pantomimic interludes. *Les Fâcheux,* composed, learned and produced within fifteen days, was a first hasty experiment in this kind.

Molière, excusing himself for a lack of sequence and design in his comedy-ballet, refers to the fact that the entertainment was not under the control of a single head. Le Brun painted the decorations; Torelli was engineer; La Fontaine contributed some verses; Pellisson wrote the prologue; Le Notre designed the sylvan theatre; Lulli composed the music and probably rehearsed the ballets. There was presumably a plentiful lack of discipline in all these hurried activities, and in future the position of Molière as author and producer was to be more firmly recognized. He congratulates himself on the success of the experiment, but allows us to divine the haste and apprehension which attended it. He confesses that the ballets do not always enter as naturally into the comedy as they should and he adds that further experiments, more carefully considered, will perhaps be made. Incidentally, he discusses for the first time questions of form and construction and tantalizes us with a promise which he never had the leisure to fulfil— nothing less than a series of prefaces to his plays exposing his aims and method of work.

The experiment was strikingly successful. The Court

admired the skill and promptitude of a dramatic laureate. Loret, the gazetteer, emphasizes the impromptu nature of the entertainment and the ready response of the author. This was the first of the improvised diversions which Molière was harassed into organizing for imminent great occasions. The King's favour was of infinite value to the author of *Tartuffe,* but Molière must pay the price and he paid it frequently and in full. There will now and then be signs of impatience and fatigue, but he remained true to the concluding professions of his dedication. Those who were born to a high estate might have the honour to serve the King in great employments, but the sole glory to which he might aspire was to divert His Majesty. In that duty he would never fail for lack of zeal or study but only by such mischance as often defeated the best attentions.

Les Fâcheux was produced for the public at the Palais Royal on November 4th. Loret, celebrating its first public performance, dwelt upon the admirable nymph, Béjart, leaving her oystershell, la Brie with her conquering charms, the queenly du Parc, whose face and figure created havoc in a thousand breasts. Between November 4, 1661, and Easter, 1662, there were 44 performances at the Palais Royal, and seven further performances after the production of *L'Ecole des Femmes.* There were also numerous visits. Molière published the play as soon as its run was exhausted. There was no immediate malicious or hostile criticism. No interest or group was in any way attacked, and no one, of course, could admit to being a bore. The collaboration of the King tactfully indicated by the author made it, moreover, a bad text for a rival.

But though the play was allowed to pass without imme-

216

diate comment, it was subsequently quoted in support of the contention that the author slavishly drew his characters from living and particular models. The allegation that Molière was a mere recorder, with notebook ever ready in hand has, it is sad to say, received almost as much support from friendly as from hostile witnesses. Molière struck his contemporaries as a realist. For them he was "the painter," and they failed, some of them quite sincerely, and others because they wanted a stick to beat him with, to realize that his observation was the beginning and not the end of his art. Molière in his method of selection, which makes of his comic characters types as well as individuals, and in the moderation and balance of his general attitude to life, was a classic; in his disregard of established forms, his easy response to the pressure of his subject, and his refusal to be formally limited or hampered in the play of his mind or the running of his theme, he was a romantic; in his quick reaction to contemporary life and to the society about him and in the accuracy of his observation he was a realist. But these are labels which seldom fit even the groups for whom they were invented and fitting them to Molière is a barren diversion.

The charge of a slavish naturalism was first put by de Visé in his *Nouvelles Nouvelles* during the controversy which was shortly to break out over *L'Ecole des Femmes*. *Les Fâcheux* was the text. This play, says de Visé, is in no way either dramatic or creative; it is not in any sense a play; it is merely a collection of portraits for which the originals supplied the features. De Visé goes on to tell us that, after the success of *Les Précieuses Ridicules*, people of quality were in the habit of providing Molière with notes and sketches upon the foibles and faults of themselves and their friends in the hope that he would use this material and thus minister to their importance. The fine gentlemen of the period, says de Visé, felt that to be in the fashion it was essential to be ridiculed by Molière, and they would even, when attending one of his plays, model their deportment upon that of his actors, so that all the world might see for itself that they were in effect the originals upon which the author had drawn.

De Visé, in this passage, gives himself deliciously away and, with himself, all the critics who confuse the realism of the artist with that of the reporter. We bless him for that glimpse of the gentlemen of France trying to live up to a generalized and immortal presentation of themselves. Molière, the artist, was accused of merely imitating nature —which is incidentally an extremely difficult thing to do. But here was nature imitating the artist—a crushing retort. De Visé, who started the critics of Molière upon a false trail, himself records for our information a classic example of the fact that society is often more apt to follow the poet than to determine the shape and drift of the poet's work. Men and women, deeply moved, speak by the book; the conduct of people in a crisis instinctively falls into line with the sentimental or heroic creations of a fashionable author.

Molière himself replied to his critics upon this point in his contributions to the "comic war" (1663-1664), and his answer to the charge, so frequently made, that his characters were a slavish reproduction of individual models may here be conveniently anticipated. In *La Critique de l'Ecole des Femmes* (June, 1663), the wise Uranie explicitly defends Molière from this accusation. These satires, she maintains, fall directly upon the manners of the time and upon individuals only by reflection. A more striking and complete answer to the charge will be found in *L'Impromptu de Versailles* (October, 1663). Two marquises come upon the stage disputing which was the original of the marquis in *La Critique de l'Ecole des Femmes*. They receive a verdict which very clearly expresses the views of the author:

Vous êtes fous tous deux, de vouloir vous appliquer ces sortes de choses; et voilà de quoi j'ouïs l'autre jour se plaindre Molière, parlant à des personnes qui le chargeoient de même chose que vous. Il disoit que rien ne lui donnoit du déplaisir comme d'être accusé de regarder quelqu'un dans les portraits qu'il fait; que son dessein est de peindre les mœurs sans vouloir toucher aux personnes, et que tous les personnages qu'il représente sont des personnages en l'air, et des fantômes proprement, qu'il habille à sa fantaisie, pour réjouir les spectateurs . . . Comme l'affaire de la comédie est de représenter en général tous les défauts des hommes et principalement des hommes de notre siècle, il est impossible à Molière de faire aucun caractère qui ne rencontre quelqu'un dans le monde.

Molière was defending only the comedies in which he was most liable to the charge of painting individual likenesses, and we find him entirely aware of what he was doing. His portraits were general and not particular; and, being general, almost anyone might, if he so desired, find himself represented. Molière, though he insisted on the contemporary interest of his plays and proclaimed it his business to expose the faults and absurdities of the men of his own time, even more strongly emphasized that he was creating types; that his characters were the creatures of his fancy; that the business of comedy was to represent *en général* the features of men. English readers may find it unnecessary to emphasize the typical and representative nature of the characters of Molière. To us they are obviously less individual and more synthetic, less personal and more abstract, than the characters of almost any English dramatist. The nearest of kin to the characters of Molière are the characters of Ben Jonson, which were severe and logical generalizations, each personage being presented with a prevailing "humour" or temperament. For the French audiences of the seventeenth century, however, the plays of Molière, which brought the comic stage into intimate contact with the life of the time, were the last word in realistic portraiture and even his friends were not always aware of the extent to which his work was both formal and creative.

The production of *Les Fâcheux* marks an important step forward in the life of Molière and the progress of his art. It proclaimed his affiance with the King; it introduced a new form of theatrical composition, the comedy-ballet, with a definite promise of its future development; it elicited the charge of excessive realism in portraiture which the author himself took an early opportunity of refuting; it confirmed Molière in his conviction that with the royal support he might safely allow his comic genius to range the Court and allow no follies however exalted to be exempt from view; finally, it drew from La Fontaine the famous verses in which he first proclaimed Molière to be his man:

> C'est un ouvrage de Molière:
> Cet écrivain, par sa manière,
> Charme à présent toute la Cour.

. . . .

> J'en suis ravi, car c'est mon homme.
> Te, souvient-il bien qu'autre fois
> Nous avons conclu d'une voix
> Qu'il allait ramener en France
> Le bon goût et l'air de Terence?

Molière, continued La Fontaine, has fulfilled his promise. Plautus, beside him, is a stale buffoon. He is teaching men to laugh with a difference and the things which once were good enough in their day will no longer suffice. The whole method of comedy is changed:

> Et maintenant il ne faut pas
> Quitter la nature d'un pas.

XIII

The Marriage of Molière

ON the 23rd of January, 1662, at the house of Madeleine Béjart in the Place du Palais Royal, there assembled one of those family councils without which no event of any real importance in a French household may be permitted to occur. Jean Poquelin, fully reconciled to the fame and fortune of his eldest son, was present with André Baudet, merchant, who had married Marie-Madeleine, the sister of Molière. Of the Béjarts there attended Madeleine herself, now as always the leading figure in all that concerned the material and domestic fortunes of Molière, Louis Béjart and Marie Hervé, the mother of them all, who had followed the fortunes of her children through the length and breadth of France during the last twenty years. Joseph, alas, had scarce survived the return to Paris. He had been taken suddenly ill during a performance of *L'Etourdi* before the King at the Louvre in May, 1659, and had died within a fortnight of the performance. The purpose of the gathering in the Place du Palais Royal was the reading and signing of a contract of marriage between Jean Baptiste Poquelin de Molière and Armande-Grésinde-Claire-Elizabeth Béjart.

Who was Armande-Grésinde-Claire-Elizabeth Béjart? For over three hundred years she has inspired the malice, ingenuity, or chivalry of generations of critics and biographers. Let us begin with what Paris saw and believed in February, 1662.

First there was Madeleine, a handsome woman of forty-three, the lifelong companion of Molière, a striking figure of the time. Beside her was a girl, twenty-four years younger than herself, in whom she took a maternal interest, spoiled by the whole family, who had, it was said, been vaguely associated with the fortunes of the company from her earliest years, in whose favour Madeleine, the first companion of Molière, was now content to retire as an indulgent and affectionate witness of a somewhat hazardous experiment. Inconspicuously in the background hovered, rather uncertainly, an old lady who must be well over seventy, of whom nothing was known except that she had lived with, and presumably upon, her children for the last twenty years. What was the inference? All Paris looking at the group, assumed that this was a picture of three generations—that Marie Hervé was the mother of Madeleine, and that Madeleine was the mother of Armande. Armande, moreover, was in her twentieth year, and twenty years ago, so it was said, Madeleine had been the mistress of Molière.

Here was a pretty situation, and the enemies of the man who had just written *L'Ecole des Femmes* seized upon it without too nice an inquiry. The legend ran swiftly from mouth to mouth and in November, 1663, Montfleury, the fat tragedian of the Hôtel de Bourgogne, wrote to His Majesty accusing Molière, whom the King in the unreflecting candour of his royal heart had taken under his protection, *"d'avoir épousé la fille et d'autrefois avoir couché avec la mère."*

The King did not listen to Montfleury, and in February of the following year stood godfather to the first child of the marriage. But slander lives longer than its refutation. Seven years after the King had stood by proxy at the font with Molière and his young wife, Chalussay, the author of *Elomire Hypocondre,* was more explicit. Arnolphe of *L'Ecole des Femmes* had begun to mould his wife from infancy: Molière had been wiser than that:

> Arnolphe commença trop tard à la forger;
> C'est avant le berceau qu'il y devoit songer,
> Comme quelqu'un a fait. . . .

Molière obtained the instant suppression of this libel by royal injunction. Still, however, the legend grew. Six years after the suppression of *Elomire Hypocondre,* and four years after the death of Molière, a certain Guichard, a high official in the service of the King's brother, entered upon a lawsuit with the musician, Lulli, for which purpose he brought into court a wholesale indictment of the enemy and all his witnesses, among whom was Armande. Guichard wrote: "Everyone knows that the birth of *la Molière* was shameful and obscure, that it is uncertain who was her mother and only too certain who was her father; that she was the daughter of her husband and the wife of her sire." There was much more in a similar vein. The good Guichard was in such a passion that his indictment was somewhat confused, for if the mother of Armande was uncertain, it would seem to be difficult to establish very certainly who was the father. His assertions, however, deserved attention and they received it. He was condemned to make a public apology upon his knees and without a hat.

224

Our next witness is anonymous. There appeared, still later, dated for the first time in 1688, a life of Armande under the title of *La Fameuse Comédienne*. The author of this work affected a lighter vein than his predecessors, and his references to Madeleine Béjart are particularly engaging: "The deceased Béjart, an actress in the provinces, was contributing to the good fortune of a number of young gentlemen of Languedoc at about the time of her daughter's birth. It would be difficult, amid a gallantry so confused, to say who was the father of the child. All I can say is that her mother, in her promiscuous loves, could never endure any but persons of quality (Molière, of course, excepted), and that her daughter's blood was, therefore, in all probability true blue. . . . It has been alleged that she was the daughter of Molière, though she afterwards became his wife, but the truth of the matter is not at all clear."

The libels remained. Their punishment and suppression were forgotten. The tradition became firmly established that Armande was the daughter of Madeleine. Grimarest accepted it; Voltaire endorsed it; and four generations of biographers, starting with the assumption that Armande was the daughter of Madeleine, directed all their efforts to proving that she could not also be the daughter of Molière. The generous and unlearned were content to deny the imputation on grounds of decency. Molière, they pleaded, was not that sort of man, and so vile a calumny was on the face of it preposterous. The scholars, who desired to support their faith with evidence, skilfully manipulated dates that were usually incorrect and, following Grimarest, began a hunt after the real father which is still being continued by some of the best authorities.

225

The rapidity with which the tradition was established was not entirely due to the malice of the enemies of Molière. It was due even more to the backing of his friends. Racine, writing to one of his correspondents in 1663, and reporting the accusation of Montfleury, added with a cynical indifference, "but no one at Court listens to Montfleury." He expressed neither incredulity nor indignation. The Editors of 1682, make no reference to the matter at all, and La Grange, in his Register, noting the marriage of Molière, says nothing of the parentage or antecedents of his wife. Even more negligent was Boileau. Boileau was the Dr. Johnson of his time, and he had a Boswell in the person of Brossette. Brossette reports, or misreports, him as saying that Molière was first in love with Madeleine "whose daughter he subsequently married." Must we regard this declaration, if correctly reported, as justifying the tradition, or merely note that scandal, once it is loose, rarely fails to be acceptable even to those who might be expected most strongly to deny it? For the moment we will merely observe that none of the friends of Molière, during his lifetime, is recorded as having said a single word to invalidate the general belief that Armande was the daughter of Madeleine, and that one of them at least appears to have acquiesced in it without inquiry.

The sequel is the more amazing. A hundred and fifty-nine years after the event, in 1821, Beffara, an ex-commissioner of police, searching among the registers of Paris, discovered the marriage certificate of Molière in the parish of St. Germain l'Auxerrois. In this certificate Armande is given, not as the daughter, but as the sister of Madeleine, and the daughter of Joseph Béjart and Marie Hervé. All

226

the previous special pleadings, traditions, heartsearchings, manipulating of dates and evidence became in an instant superfluous. The discovery of Beffara seemed to dispose once for all of any doubt as to the parentage of Armande, and it was reinforced in 1863 by the publication of a legal document, dated March 10, 1643, in which Marie Hervé, the widow of Joeph Béjart, renounced for herself and her children an inheritance which, as we have seen, consisted mostly of liabilities. In this document reference is made to the four surviving children of Joseph and to an "infant not yet baptized," the infant, of course, being Armande, who was thus, in a legal document, signed and witnessed nineteen years before her marriage, stated to be the sister and not the daughter of Madeleine. Along with this act of renunciation a whole series of legal documents, which had come to light since the discovery of Beffara, were published by Soulié in 1863—all referring to Armande quite explicitly as the sister of Madeleine and extending over a period of thirty years.

It might be imagined that the scholars and critics would henceforth let the matter rest. The discovery of Beffara, however, far from terminating the controversy, only added to its complexity. Its astounding convolutions during the next hundred years are only explicable on the assumption that there is an unconscious human bias in favour of scandalous readings. The tradition must at all costs be saved; therefore the documents were false. There had been, it seems, a family conspiracy to conceal the facts; false declarations had been made to the authorities; Madeleine anxious to conceal her own maternity had induced Marie Hervé to pose as the mother of the child. No convincing explanation has ever been offered why this conspiracy should have been set on foot; there is no clear sign of its existence upon the documents themselves, and none of the motives ascribed to the various partners to the plot is at all in keeping with anything we know of their characters and dispositions. It is unnecessary to go into the details of the controversy. The literature on the subject constitutes a monument of perverted scholarship, and any attempt to add to it on one side or the other at this stage could only be regarded by any sane historian as an outrage on posterity. When we have eliminated the strained interpretations of commentators scrutinizing, with suspicions inflamed and in the firm grip of a false conclusion, every phase of the relevant documents and libels, and set aside all the hypotheses which since their invention have been destroyed by data subsequently discovered, it becomes possible to present the essential facts in a few brief paragraphs.

First, there is the apparent silence of Molière. The belief that Armande was the daughter of Madeleine was current during his life and almost universally believed within twenty years of his death. Why did he not publicly establish the facts and produce the necessary documents? Does not his failure to do so indicate that he desired to avoid a public inquiry, and must we not, therefore, assume that the documents were not such as would survive examination in a court of law? To this it may be answered, first, that far from acquiescing in the charges brought against him, Molière took the most effective and immediate steps to protect himself. He replied instantly to the libels published during his lifetime—to that of Montfleury by going to the King; to that of Chalussay by going to the magistrates. The King dismissed the libel of Montfleury in as public and conspicuous a manner as possible, and the magistrates suppressed the libel of Chalussay. Presumably neither the King nor the magistrates acted without going into the facts. The argument of silence is, in any case, of little worth. There remains of Molière's writing and conversation, apart from the plays, not above a dozen lines. Even his marriage certificate was lost to view for one hundred and thirty years. He may have protested a thousand times without leaving for posterity an echo of his refutation. All we know is that, so far as the charges were actionable and definite, he not only protested but protested with success, and that he very publicly and definitely announced what his own attitude would be in future to those who libelled him by caricature or insinuation. The passage will be found in *L'Impromptu de Versailles*.

La courtoisie doit avoir des bornes; et il y a des choses qui ne font rire ni les spectateurs, ni celui dont on parle. Je leur abandonne de bon cœur mes ouvrages, ma figure, mes gestes, mes paroles, mon ton de voix, et ma façon de réciter, pour en faire et dire tout ce qu'il leur plaira, s'ils en peuvent tirer quelque avantage. Je ne m'oppose point à toutes ces choses, et je serai ravi que cela puisse réjouir le monde; mais, en leur abandonnant tout cela, ils me doivent faire la grâce de me laisser le reste, et de ne point toucher à des matières de la nature de celles sur lesquelles on m'a dit qu'ils m'attaquoient dans leur comédies . . . et voilà toute la réponse qu'ils auront de moi.

The second group of arguments in favour of the tradition is its apparent acceptance by the friends of Molière. Why, it is asked, did they not denounce these errors? Boileau is reported as believing Armande to be the daughter of Madeleine. Racine mentioned the libel of Montfleury without contradicting it. La Grange made no reference to the matter either in his preface or in his Register. If Molière had in his possession documents which could have borne examination in a court of law, why is there no indication that his friends had ever seen them or heard of them? Why do they either avoid the subject or acquiesce in a tradition which these documents might at once have laid to rest?

The reported saying of Boileau—though it is a saying at second hand and not above suspicion—is the strongest of all the arguments for those who doubt the facts as recorded in the marriage certificate. Here was a man intimate with Molière. Did he accept a falsehood and never once give his friend an opportunity of setting him right on the subject? The supposition is difficult but not impossible. It is not always the habit even of close friends, whose bonds are mainly literary or social, to discuss their family affairs. Molière was not likely to introduce the subject, and Boileau, if he believed it to be delicate, would not himself be the first to do so. His saying, if correctly reported, admittedly shows that most people in Paris believed during the life of Molière that Armande was the daughter of Madeleine and that one at least of his intimate friends, accepting that belief, tactfully avoided any allusion to the subject in his conversation with the person most concerned.

The neutrality of Racine and the discretion of La Grange are of less account. Racine was at best indifferent and perhaps quite wilfully ambiguous, while La Grange merely followed his master. Molière had made it plain that he did not wish his family affairs to be discussed, and the Editors of 1682, in their short life of the dramatist, deliberately present the author rather than the man. It is not too much to suppose that Molière, who declared to the world in *L'Impromptu de Versailles* that he would make no further reply to his enemies regarding his private affairs, imposed a similar reticence upon his friends and colleagues.

The third group of arguments relates to the documents themselves, and especially to the act of renunciation of 1643. It is a significant feature of the controversy that in every case where the champions of tradition base their theories upon facts or dates the facts are ultimately disproved and the dates found to be erroneous. The most serious criticism of the document of 1643 is grounded on the fact that it describes all the children of Marie Hervé in March of that year as minors. Madeleine was born in January, 1618, and was, therefore, in her twenty-sixth year when the act was signed. Her father, however, very probably died in January, 1643, when Madeleine was not yet twenty-five, the legal majority, and an act of renunciation must date fictitiously from the moment of inheritance. Madeleine was thus for the purposes of the act, a minor, and, though her brother Joseph was named first as the eldest son, she was probably his senior. She is undoubtedly all through her life the effective chief of the family. There is, in fact, no evidence whatever that the document of 1643 is incorrect in describing all the children of Marie Hervé as minors or in any other particular.

The fourth group of arguments is obstetrical. Marie Hervé, in her death certificate given in the year 1670, is described as being eighty years of age. This would make her fifty-three at the time of the birth of Armande in 1643. What are the chances of a woman of fifty-three giving birth

231

to a daughter? Unusual but not impossible, say the doctors and statisticians. All these calculations were upset, however, by the discovery in 1883 of an epitaph in the archives of the cemetery of St. Paul composed for the tombstone erected by Madeleine to the memory of her mother. In that epitaph Marie Hervé is described as dying at the age of seventy-five. She would thus be in her forty-eighth year when Armande was born, and the obstetrical champions of tradition are thereby discomfited.

The fifth group of arguments is based on the marriage contract of 1662. Armande received, in addition to 4,000 *livres* from her future husband, a dowry of 10,000 *livres* from her mother, a third of which sum was to be held in common by husband and wife, and two-thirds to remain the property of the bride. It is urged that Marie Hervé had not 10,000 *livres* to her name, and it is consequentially inferred that the dowry received by Armande was really the maternal gift of Madeleine. The true mother is, in fact, presumed to have used the false mother as a screen for her generosity. There is, however, no evidence whatever that the money came from Madeleine. It might equally well have come from Molière himself who, in accordance with his known views on the position of women and his generous affection for Armande, might well have taken this indirect way of ensuring to his young wife a certain degree of financial independence. The act would have been entirely in keeping with everything we know or can intelligently divine of his temperament and character. The mysterious dowry, however, was too good an argument to lose, and for over a hundred years the critics have preferred to discuss it as evidence that Armande was the daughter of Madeleine rather than suggest that it might be evidence of Molière being in his marital dealings one of the first gentlemen of France.

There is no doubt that Madeleine, whether she did or did not provide Armande with a dowry, took a continuous and special interest in the youngest of her sisters. When Madeleine died in 1672 she constituted Armande her universal legatee, and even signed a special codicil on her deathbed in order to put her intentions beyond all doubt. Her sister Geneviève was to inherit her property only in the event of Molière and Armande dying without issue. This act of preference was, however, the natural climax of a lifelong predilection, and it is not without precedent that a woman, maternally disposed, with no surviving children of her own, should lavish upon a gifted and fascinating sister, young enough to be her daughter, an affection for which she had no other outlet or occasion. Madeleine lost her daughter Françoise shortly after the birth of Armande, and Armande had been the spoiled child of the company from her earliest years. She had married Molière, to whom Madeleine was utterly devoted, and all her hopes for his happiness were centred upon the marriage. These are intelligible and adequate motives, consistent with the documents and the proven facts. It seems hardly necessary to construct elaborate theories and invent wholly hypothetical reasons in order to explain a situation which was humanly normal and incidentally creditable to all the parties concerned.

This brings us to the human aspect of the problem. Madeleine, Molière and Armande, who have become ciphers in the course of this historic controversy, have somehow to be fitted into its equations as persons who behaved reasonably in the light of their business and desires. The account of Grimarest is humanly in contradiction with all we might reasonably expect of the persons concerned. Armande, according to Grimarest, was the daughter of Madeleine and the Comte de Modène with whom Madeleine had contracted a secret marriage. Armande, he tells us, was accustomed even as a child to address Molière as her husband to the general amusement of the company. Very soon, however, jest became earnest. Molière grew violently enamoured and resolved to make her his wife. He was terrified, however, of what Madeleine might have to say on the subject. He accordingly married Armande secretly, but dared not take her openly for wife under the jealous and constant observation of Madeleine who, even as it was, heckled him continually for his interest in her daughter. Finally, Armande, determined to end this ambiguous arrangement, brought the situation to a head by going to his room and refusing to leave it. Madeleine was furious and could only console herself with the reflection that her daughter could scarcely have done better for herself than marry Molière, and that Molière could scarcely have done worse than marry any woman.

This preposterous story presents the indulgent and sensible Madeleine as an amorous virago; Molière as a man without candour or courage, henpecked by his mistress into devious and undignified courses; Armande as a young girl romantically and resolutely in love with her husband. None of the portraits bears any resemblance to its original.

The story of Grimarest, moreover, is wholly inconsistent with the story, equally false in other respects, contained in the anonymous life of Armande published in 1886 under the title of *La Fameuse Comédienne*. A comparison of the two stories shows that within fifteen years of the death of Molière no one had any really accurate knowledge of his private life and disposition. Madeleine is still presented as the jealous mistress; but she is jealous not of her "daughter" Armande, but of the rival actresses of the troop. Molière, we are informed, rejected by the heartless "Marquise," Mademoiselle du Parc, fell back for consolation upon Mademoiselle de Brie, who received him so kindly that Madeleine began to fear for her supremacy. She accordingly decided that, as she could not keep Molière for herself, she would retain her hold upon him through her daughter, and used all her arts to bring about the very marriage which according to Grimarest she did her utmost to prevent.

Where shall we discover the truth of the courtship of Molière? There is, fortunately, a contemporary witness who at least puts us right on one or two essential points. It will be remembered that in the spring of 1659 Chapelle wrote to Molière from the country a letter which pointed already to a warm friendship between them. Molière had invited him to come to Paris and had told him of the trouble he was having at that time with certain members of his company. Chapelle, in reply, writes in praise of nature and repose. He cannot leave for another five or six days: "I would do my utmost to lighten your sorrows and you may be sure that you have in me a friend who would always try to banish or at least to share them." He then breaks into verse, in which he prettily refers to a young and tender plant which has not yet the strength to reach the summit of the willow tree whose arms are extended to receive it. Molière is to show these verses to Mademoiselle Menou.

235

There is no doubt as to the person intended. For the last six or seven years she had been the darling of the company. She had even been allowed at the age of nine —when the troop was at Lyon—to recite a few verses in the tragedy of *Andromède*. She was now seventeen and the friends of Molière quite candidly assumed that a marriage would shortly be arranged. The open allusions of Chapelle are a clear proof that the accounts are false which present Molière as hiding his inclinations and making a secret of his marriage.

The author of *La Fameuse Comédienne* has no special quarrel with Molière. His malice is all for Armande, and he slanders the dramatist only to strengthen the case against his wife. He has all the tricks of an able advocate, never lies until it becomes necessary to do so, and then with a peculiar deadliness. He mixes as much truth with his falsehood as his case will carry, is moderate, reasonable and good humoured. It is the more fortunate that his account of the married life of Armande begins with a libel so circumstantial that we are able to correct it in every detail. The fame of Molière, he tells us, attracted more lovers to his wife than her personal merits. Among the first of them was the Abbé de Richelieu, who was, he tells us, her lover several months previous to the production of *La Princesse d'Elide*. During the festivities of which this play was merely an incident, however, she fell violently enamoured of a handsome and popular nobleman, the Comte de Guiche. But alas! the Comte de Guiche was slow to respond, and in despite of him she fell back into the kindly arms of the Comte de Lauzan, who had in the meantime begun to sigh in vain and was waiting his opportunity. Meanwhile, the Abbé de Richelieu, jealously watching these manœuvres of his mistress, and in revenge for her disloyalty to himself, intimated to Molière that he would do well to look to his private affairs, for, while he was pleasing the whole world with his plays, the whole world was pleasing itself with his wife. Molière complained to Armande who burst into tears, confessed her love for the Comte de Guiche, and promised to amend her ways. Molière, wishing to believe her innocent, invented a thousand reasons to be kind, but pointed out that she should endeavour, for both their sakes, to be above suspicion, surrounded as they were by people who were only too anxious to believe the worst. The libellist takes care to be extremely well informed. Armande, he tells us, received for her favours from the Abbé de Richelieu, the sum of four *pistoles* a day, not including presents and fine clothes; he visited her every evening after dinner and sent his page with the money every morning. He even reproduces a letter written by Armande to the Comte de Guiche and intercepted by the Abbé.

The task of the biographer would be simple if it were always possible to deal with false witnesses as faithfully as in the present instance. *La Princesse d'Elide* was produced in May, 1664. The alleged intrigue with the Abbé de Richelieu was therefore in progress during the early months of that year. Armande was then nursing the second daughter of Molière, and the Abbé de Richelieu was fighting the Turks. The Comte de Guiche was in Poland and did not return to Paris until after the production of the play. The bad faith of the author is proven at the start. Four *pistoles* a day and an intercepted letter could not possibly be due to a careless acceptance of contemporary gossip. They are manifest inventions. This, in fact, was one of the occasions when the lie direct and circumstantial seemed best to serve the purpose of our anonymous author.

He continues. Armande, shortly after this episode, took as her adviser a creature of the name of Chateauneuf, who subsequently fulfilled the office of Dame Quickly, and undertook so to manage the affairs of her mistress that they should be a source of pleasure and profit to both of them. Armande accepted from Chateauneuf any lover who was willing to pay for her favours. Molière, warned of what was happening, threatened his wife in vain, for she was always able to win him with her tears and even put him in the wrong. Soon, however, she wearied of his submission, could no longer endure his presence and herself demanded a separation. It was agreed that, without any public or formal act, they should cease to be husband and wife. Armande remained in Paris, while Molière retired to live as a bachelor at Auteuil.

The author has chosen at this point to redeem his libel with a famous interview, wholly imaginary but of real significance, which he alleges to have taken place between Molière and Chapelle in the garden at Auteuil. Chapelle is described as finding his friend in a state of melancholy. Molière confessed that he was thinking of his wife. Chapelle rallied him and urged that the remedy for an affection so misplaced was contempt for the woman who inspired it. "I see," said Molière, "that you have never really loved." After touching upon various aspects of his marriage, Molière continues:

I took my wife so to speak from the cradle; I brought her up with the care which has given rise to the rumours

238

which you have doubtless heard; . . . Marriage did not in any way blunt my eagerness for her welfare, but I found her so indifferent that I began to realize that all my precautions had been in vain, and that what she felt for me was very far from what I would have wished for my happiness. . . . I accordingly . . . resolved to live with her as though she were not my wife. If, however, you knew what I suffer you would have pity on me. My love for her has reached such a point that it causes me to sympathize compassionately with her interests; and when I consider how impossible it is for me to suppress what I feel for her, I reflect at the same time that she has perhaps the same difficulty in overcoming her wayward inclinations, and I find myself more disposed to pity than to blame her. You will doubtless say that one must be a poet in order to love in this way. Personally, however, I believe that there is only one sort of love and that those who have never felt such scruples have never really loved at all. Everything in the world has some relation to her in my mind. I am so taken up with her that nothing in her absence can divert me, and, as soon as I behold her, feelings, which may be felt but cannot be expressed, deprive me of any capacity of reflection. I no longer have any eyes for her failings, and I must find her wholly lovable. Is not this the last degree of folly, and do you not wonder that all the wit I have serves only to acquaint me with my own weakness without enabling me to overcome it?

The passage has had a remarkable success. The entire libel, on the strength of so moving a diagnosis, has even been attributed to La Fontaine. But the enemies of genius are seldom fools. On the contrary, they are often found among the most successful and talented of its contemporaries. In many of the libels upon Molière there is much that is well observed and skilfully presented. The abilities of the author of *La Fameuse Comédienne* must not blind us to

239

his essential malice. These confidences between Chapelle and Molière are not evidence. They merely exhibit as attractively as possible what was likely to be believed by contemporaries. They present Molière as sensitive, indulgent and tormented.

Grimarest, telling the truth to the best of his ability, does not ascribe the difficulties which arose between husband and wife to the infidelities of Armande, but to a fundamental incompatibility of temper. He explains with an admirable justice how easy it was for a man of middle age married to a woman young enough to be his daughter to be mortified by her unfeeling disregard of his delicate position and of his extreme sensibility towards herself. He nowhere accuses Armande of being promiscuous in her loves and we may dismiss her flagrant and venal infidelities as wholly fictitious. On this point Grimarest is explicit:

An actress has only to show a noble lord the politeness due to him; the gossips are pitiless and give her to him for a mistress. Molière imagined that the whole Court and all the town coveted his wife. She did not trouble to undeceive him. On the contrary, the extraordinary care which she took with her adornment—as it seemed to him for the benefit of others, as he himself did not ask for any such attention—could only increase his suspicions and his jealousy. It was in vain that he urged upon his wife the way in which she should conduct herself if they were to live happily together. She paid no attention to his remonstrances, which seemed to her of too severe a character for a young person who had nothing with which to reproach herself. Molière accordingly, after having suffered many domestic estrangements and disputes, did his utmost to find refuge in his work and in his friends, without allowing himself to be grieved by her conduct.

240

Grimarest, not to be outdone by the libellist, likewise indites an imaginary conversation between Molière and his friends in the garden at Auteuil. He expressly denies, however, that Molière opened his heart to Chapelle, who was of too sanguine and frivolous a disposition to be a suitable confidant, but to his more serious companions, Mignard and Rohault. The passage is almost certainly intended as a deliberate correction of the corresponding pages of *La Fameuse Comédienne:*

I am the most unfortunate of men, Molière confessed, and I am only receiving my deserts. I did not realize that I was of too austere a character for domestic society. I imagined that my wife would behave in a manner suitable to her virtue and my expectations, though I am well aware that in her position she would have been still more unhappy than I am if she had tried to do so. She is full of vitality and nimble of mind. She likes to have her qualities recognized and to feel her power. All this mortifies me in spite of myself. I accordingly fall into reproaches and complaints. My wife, who is a hundred times more reasonable than I am, wishes to enjoy her life and to go her own way. Sure of her own innocence she disdains to observe the precautions which I urge upon her. I take her neglect of my advice for contempt. I must have some indication of affection to believe that it really exists, and more discretion in her conduct to set my mind at rest. My wife, however, always equable and free in her disposition, who would be exempt from any suspicion in the eyes of anyone of a less anxious turn of mind than I am, does nothing to ease my sufferings. She is possessed, like all women, with the wish to be generally pleasing, without having any particular affair in mind, and laughs at my weakness. . . .

M. Rohault urged upon Molière all the maxims of a sound philosophy, giving him to understand that he was wrong to abandon himself to such dejection. Ah! replied Molière, I could not be a philosopher with a wife as lovable as my own, and perhaps in my place you would suffer some uneasy moments.

Grimarest and the libellist each presents in his own way a picture of Molière which helps us to bring him a little nearer to ourselves. They differ as to motives and facts, but both describe a man of amiable disposition, with a curious faculty, in suffering, to view his woes with an almost contemplative detachment. The libellist, in despite of Armande, emphasizes his charity and its poor return, and, since he is presenting Armande as notoriously wanton, his Molière is of necessity the helpless victim of a passion which he knows to be unworthy. Grimarest, who presents Armande without rancour, contrives to be more subtle in his portrait of Molière. He shows us the comedian analyzing his griefs as if he were presenting the woes of Alceste or of Sganarelle. It is a flashing disclosure of the sadness that lies at the heart of the comic view of things, an intimate glimpse, to be always remembered, of a genius who was able to jump from his private and particular woe to a tranquil exposure of it which might be true for all men. Grimarest, inditing his imaginary scene, was presenting a view of the character of Molière in regard to which friends and enemies were alike unanimous. This is, in effect Molière *qui n'est pas rieur,* the *buffon trop sérieux* of whom Bayle was one day to write in his dictionary: *Médecin, guéris-toi toi-même: Molière, qui divertissez tout le public, divertissez-vous vous-même.*

Armande, plaguing Molière for a few brief years, became the immortal Celimène:

> Elle a l'art de me plaire;
> En dépit qu'on en ait, elle se fait aimer.
> J'ai beau voir ses défauts et j'ai beau l'en blâmer;

Exactly how grave were the faults thus idealized by the man who most intimately suffered them? All we know of Armande suggests rather a lack of comprehension than positive delinquency. She was greedy of pleasure, spoiled by flattery, vivacious of disposition, fond of company, rebellious to restraint, a woman of lively charm but little mind. She had small discretion, and was impatient of any demands that might be made on her for understanding or affection. She had almost no regard for her husband's position. Molière was surrounded by enemies who did not scruple to use his private troubles to discredit him, and Armande played continually into their hands. There was a fundamental incompatibility between them. Their relations were such as might have been expected to arise between a sensitive man of genius in middle life and a capricious girl whom everyone, including her own husband, had helped to spoil since she was a child of eight. Those who exaggerate her infidelities give us an entirely false idea of the real misfortune. Molière married a wife of a very real but superficial charm which promised more than it could ever possibly fulfil, and he loved her with a sincerity and a comprehension that has seldom been equalled. Everything we know of her subsequent history confirms this view. Molière left her all his property. She sold the *Festin de Pierre* to the younger Corneille to be versified at his discretion; she lost, bartered or destroyed every scrap of paper in her possession relating to her husband; and she married, four years after his death, a second-rate actor, Guerin d'Estriché, who ruled her firmly, and with whom she appears to have been entirely happy. It was her misfortune to have married a genius who treated her with every possible indulgence. She repaired that misfortune in later life by marrying a man of her own intellectual degree in whom she was able to recognize a master. In the words of a contemporary epigrammatist:

> Elle avait un mari d'esprit qu'elle aimait peu,
> Elle en a un de chair, qu'elle aime d'avantage.

The contemporaries of Armande all testify to her talent as an actress. Loret the gazetteer celebrated her pretty face, her sweet airs, her excellent playing. Robinet, the Court rhymester, rhetorically inquired who could forbear to love her, was lyrical upon her hairdressing, her clothes sewn with pearls and rubies, and her fair beauties. He admired her volubly in Celimène. It is a thousand pities, however, that these tributes, which might have been so illuminating on the subject of an actress who under the personal direction of Molière presented some of his best characters, are entirely commonplace and might apply to any pretty woman in almost any play. Fortunately there were other tributes which were more precise and creditable. Her playing with La Grange in Act II, Scene 5 of *Le Malade Imaginaire* was described by an anonymous author in 1681: "She plays as admirably listening or speaking; she is careful of her adornment before appearing and thinks of it no more once she is upon the stage. *La Molière* will sometimes touch her hair, adjust a ribbon, or play with a jewel, but her little tricks of deportment express a judicious and natural gift of satire and by these means she expresses what is ridiculous in the woman she presents. With all these advantages, however, she would be

244

scarcely so pleasing if her voice were less appealing." Clearly Molière had some excuse for his infatuation. She had an impish and delicate charm, a face that lived by impulse, a voice that stole away the hearts of men.

The only physical portrait which is said to be based on the description of an eye-witness describes her as of medium stature, of an engaging presence, with small eyes, with a mouth large but not full, graceful in all that she did down to the smallest particular and dressing always in a way that attracted attention, and deliberately regardless of the fashion. Tradition insists, and there is no reason to reject it, that Molière presented her likeness in Lucile of *Le Bourgeois Gentilhomme*.

Exactly how serious and how prolonged was the breach between husband and wife which culminated in the retreat of Molière to Auteuil? The dates of the various quarrels and reconciliations are difficult to determine with accuracy. There was, however, certainly a period of four years during which they were in effect separated. Molière began to be libelled as the husband of a faithless wife in 1664, and the author of *La Fameuse Comédienne* dated her alleged infidelities from the spring of that year. The festival at Versailles of which *La Princesse d'Elide* was an item, produced on 8th May, 1664, appears to have won for her the attentions of the gentlemen of the Court, and, though there is no good reason to believe that she yielded to their importunities, there is no evidence that they displeased her or that she wore her triumphs with discretion. She could, however, have had no serious disagreement with her husband during the first three years of her married life. The birth of a son in January, 1664, and of a daughter in August, 1665, indicates that a certain cordiality survived long after the libellists had assumed the worst, and we shall find Molière in *L'Impromptu de Versailles* lightheartedly chaffing his wife in public at the very moment when his enemies were attributing to him the fate which Arnolphe had so earnestly sought to avoid. Molière did not go to Auteuil until August, 1667. He was at that moment fatigued and discouraged by his long struggles on behalf of *Tartuffe*. He was in bad health, scandalously overworked, and living on a milk diet. He needed tranquillity, and was by no means good company for a young wife who was not obviously devoted. Even had there been no question of a separation between himself and Armande, his retirement to the country would at that moment have been natural and even necessary. During the previous twelve months, however, his relations with Armande had clearly taken a turn for the worse, and there is little doubt that they seized this occasion to discontinue their married life in the conviction that for the moment it was the best possible course.

One subject of dispute between Armande and Molière was his affection for the young Baron. Baron became the friend, almost the adopted son, of Molière. Molière died in his arms. It was from Baron that Grimarest obtained most of what was authentic in his chronicle. The manner of his adoption reveals a kindness of heart which shows in almost every recorded act of Molière. There was in Paris a company known as *"Comédiens de Monsieur le Dauphin,"* consisting mostly of the children of one Raisin, an organist of Troye, who achieved fame by constructing a spinet played, not by the devil as his audience imagined, but by his children imprisoned within it. Baron was introduced into the company of Raisin as a child of ten. Shortly afterward Raisin died and his widow, after a disastrous tour in the provinces, fell upon evil days. Returning to Paris, she begged Molière, of his charity, to lend her his theatre for three days so that she might restore the fortunes of her troop. Molière complied, and it was thus that Baron, now twelve years old, first appeared on the stage of the Palais Royal. On the third day Molière, hearing wonders of the young actor, went to see him perform. Struck with his talent, Molière sent for him to supper, and, indignant that the boy's genius should be exploited, subsequently obtained an order from the King that Baron should be removed from the custody of the woman Raisin. Whereupon she came to the house of Molière brandishing pistols, and, what was even more disturbing to his peace, breaking into tears and supplications. Molière was inflexible in his refusal to restore the child to her care, but allowed the boy to act on her behalf for a few days till she had made enough money to straighten her affairs. He then virtually adopted Baron as his son, cultivated his remarkable talents as an actor and encouraged his poetic inclinations. The pupil deserved well of his master and, after the death of Molière, became the most beloved and popular actor in France.

These facts were widely known; the adoption of Baron into the company of Molière had the approval of the King himself; his rescue and education of the child gave to France one of her finest actors; every incident in the story was to the credit of Molière; and the affection between master and pupil was one of the few happy circumstances of his final years. The relationship, however, did not escape calumny, and the anonymous author of *La Fameuse Comédienne* affirms that a jealous wife first maltreated the boy

247

who, it is suggested, was unnaturally usurping her place, and subsequently revenged herself by seducing him for her own vanity and pleasure. That such horrors could be suggested, even anonymously, strikingly indicates the ferocious hostility which Molière aroused among his contemporaries. The truth behind the calumny was innocent enough. Armande clearly resented the adoption of Baron. For years she had been the spoiled darling of the company. Here was a dangerous rival, and, as soon as the youth began to attend rehearsals, there was bound to be trouble. During the preparation of *Mélicerte*, produced at St. Germain in December, 1666, Baron was cast for the part of Myrtil. At one of the rehearsals Armande lost her temper and boxed his ears. To be cuffed by a woman was more than the boy's dignity would stand. He ran straight to the King, asked leave to withdraw from the performance, and, refusing to be pacified, returned to his old companions, apparently to wander with them for several years in the provinces. He returned to the Palais Royal in 1670, and the manner of his return, as recounted by Grimarest, reveals an affectionate and delicate disposition. It had come to the ears of Molière that the young man, in remorse for his behaviour, frequently spoke of his benefactor in the most admiring terms; openly regretted his withdrawal, but feared to return, feeling himself unworthy. Thereupon, Molière wrote a letter inviting the young man to come back and enclosing a royal order which sanctioned his re-admission to the company. Baron obeyed in such haste that he abandoned his purse on the way rather than lose time in its recovery. He arrived in Paris in clothes that must be covered with a cloak, and a speech upon his lips that he was too

248

moved to deliver. The allegation, brought by the author of *La Fameuse Comédienne,* that Baron after his return to the company in 1670 became the lover of Armande, has no better foundation than the fact that Baron played Love to the Psyche of Armande in the play of that name produced in January, 1671. Molière and Armande had come to their final reconciliation and the young Baron had only just returned. The past was forgotten. The libellists were determined, however, to have it both ways. When Armande and Molière quarrelled over Baron, they invented infamous reasons for the breach. Equally infamous were the implications now that Armande and Baron were seen acting together upon an amiable footing.

Grimarest, writing of the period of separation, tells us that at Auteuil Molière lived like a true philosopher. "He did not allow himself to be greatly disturbed by the humours of his wife whom he allowed to live according to her fancy, though he always had for her a true affection." This accords with an earlier declaration: "Molière, after having suffered keenly from his domestic quarrels and estrangements, devoted himself as much as possible to his work and to his friends without allowing himself to be distressed by the conduct of his wife." That Grimarest here exaggerates the philosophy of Molière is shown by his own account of the conversation between Molière and Rohault, but the general trend of his references clearly corresponds with a tradition which is reasonable and well supported. The retirement of Molière to Auteuil was obviously the result of a friendly agreement between husband and wife that it was better for both parties to live apart. There was no scandal, no legal act of separation, no admitted rupture. Molière saw his wife constantly at the theatre and socially their relations were entirely correct. But Armande, for her pleasure, lived in the town and Molière, for his peace, lived in the country. Throughout the period of separation he was writing for her a series of brilliant and sympathetic parts, instructing her how to play them, and himself playing beside her. Their relations were probably all the more friendly on the surface for being less intimate in substance, and what Molière suffered in secret was for himself alone. Grimarest himself comments on his unwillingness to discuss the matter. "Being," he says, "unhappy in his marriage, Molière would never speak of it except to his friends, and then only when he was absolutely compelled to do so."

This arrangement lasted from about August, 1667, to about the end of 1671. Some time during that year there was a reconciliation. Grimarest tells us that there was an intervention on the part of friends "who endeavoured to bring husband and wife together or, more accurately, to persuade them to live more in agreement." He goes on to inform us that Molière, "in order to render the union more complete, abandoned his milk diet, which he had not yet discontinued, and took to eating meat, a change which increased the severity of his cough and the trouble in his lungs." Grimarest misdates the reconciliation, placing it in April, 1672. The child of this event, the second son of Molière, was born on 15th September, 1672, so that the event itself must have occurred at latest in December, 1671. It was only appropriate that the godparents of the child should be a Boileau and a daughter of Pierre Mignard, the friends who had most probably brought about the reconciliation, and that the child himself received the christian names both

250

of Armande and Molière. The boy lived alas! for only three weeks.

Four months later Molière died in the arms of his friend Baron before his wife could reach the room where he was lying. We shall find her solacing as best she could his last days, petitioning the Archbishop of Paris and the King for his Christian burial, playing her part to the best of her ability in the confused events that attended the shuffling of his body into an unknown grave.

The marriage of Molière may be summarized in brief simplicity. Molière loved Armande as a child. She was in a sense his ward, the favourite sister of Madeleine, whom she had come to regard as a mother. Her feeling for Molière, as she grew to maturity, may be easily imagined —gratitude towards the man to whom she owed her education, pride in the man who was becoming so famous, pleasure in the man who undoubtedly charmed and spoiled her with his gifts. On the side of Molière was an indulgent affection for the child, which he never lost, to be gradually enlivened and intensified till it became the one serious passion of his life.

Madeleine in this story is the friend of Molière, and, in effect, the mother of Armande. She had lost her daughter Françoise, and her youngest sister had for years been the sole outlet for her strong maternal instinct. For her the marriage of Armande and Molière was a union of the two beings for whom she had cared most in her life. They were the children of her inclination. The experiment was in the sequel disastrous. Molière and his wife were unsuited in age, disposition and mind, and not even the comprehension which he brought to their relationship could

251

effect any real or lasting harmony. The man of genius understood his own misfortune and that of his wife; but the man of flesh and blood was sensitive and would not be reconciled to his defeat. There is no need, in default of any real evidence, to imagine Armande as grossly unfaithful. All the elements of the tragi-comedy were in the situation as between husband and wife. For five years the experiment survived. There was sufficient goodwill and affection on both sides to avoid an open breach. It then became obvious that a separation of the parties was necessary if they were to remain friends and colleagues. The separation lasted for over four years. Husband and wife continued to meet daily; their relations were outwardly friendly and for both of them the situation was so far eased that a reconciliation became more and more inevitable as the old intimate dissensions were forgotten. The reconciliation, when it came, was complete and not, so far as we know, again disturbed.

Such was the marriage of Molière, the origin of so many calumnies among those who feared or envied his genius. It was fatal to his happiness but the source of much that was profoundly and delicately expressed in his comedies.

It is a personal prelude to the most militant period of his career.

XIV

THE SCHOOL FOR WIVES

ON December 26, 1662, ten months after his marriage, Molière produced *L'Ecole des Femmes,* a companion comedy to *L'Ecole des Maris.* Hitherto he had excited only the jealousy of professional rivals and the resentment of a coterie. Henceforth he had to reckon with serious charges of licence and impiety. It is true that the attack made upon the play was for the most part delivered by authors and critics who desired for personal reasons to discredit or suppress the author, but it is equally true that the play in itself was profoundly disturbing to the orthodox and that the contemporary libels and criticisms represent a very solid and formidable opposition to its implications. Socially the play was more startling than a modern critic easily realizes. It anticipated the modern feminist attitude to male jealousy and the education of women by over two centuries, being, in effect, the first coherent and forcible challenge of modern times to the Miltonic conception of marriage.

L'Ecole des Femmes is a play with a thesis, but the thesis is a natural product of the interplay of its characters, who exist independently of anything the author may wish to prove. It is not any the less a comedy of character for being also a comedy of ideas. The people of the play move

253

freely and naturally within its limits. There is no forcing
of the characters to score a point of doctrine. *L'Ecole des
Femmes*, in other words, is a genuine comedy.

Arnolphe, the central figure of the play, is an embodiment
of man's sense of property in woman. It is the most complete dramatic indictment of sex jealousy, as rooted in a
sense of exclusive ownership, ever put upon the stage—
more human, various and equitable than any of the works
of the nineteenth century feminists.

> La femme est en effet le potage de l'homme;
> Et quand un homme voit d'autres hommes parfois
> Qui veulent dans sa soupe aller tremper leurs doigts,
> Il en montre aussitôt une colère extrême.

That is essentially the view which Molière stigmatizes in
many of his comedies, and his reaction against it is often
strong enough to render him liable to the charge of recommending an excessive indulgence on the part of husbands
to peccant wives. In Arnolphe every aspect of the offence
is presented and mocked. Arnolphe quintessentializes the
false point of honour. Like all the great characters of
Molière he is not only an individual but a generalization.
He is every husband that ever lived who underlines his
quality. He will marry a wife who has from the cradle
been taught to look only to him for her wisdom and pleasure.
He will marry a fool so that she shall not have the wit
to deceive him. She shall have no distractions, interests
or pursuits apart from himself. In vain does his friend
Chrysalde, as a good Aristotelian, insist that a fool cannot
be honest because she cannot know in what honesty consists;
that without knowledge there can be neither good nor evil;

254

that to live always with an ignoramus must in any case be
tedious. Arnolphe is neither to be laughed nor persuaded
out of his design. He has reared his Agnes apart from the
world in the care of servants as simple as herself. He
glories in the thought that she asks nothing of life but cream
tarts, and that she is ready to believe that children are born
by the ear. She will be as clay in the hands of the potter
and her husband will be able to mould her to his heart's
desire. We see him undertaking her social education. She
is to reflect upon her humble origin and admire the bounty
which has raised her to a high degree. She is to consider
how her husband, who might please so many women, has
selected her from all the rest for his embraces. She is to
be worthy of that distinction. Marriage is a serious estate,
and its duties are plain. Woman is the subordinate of man
as the soldier of his captain, or the monk of his abbot. She
should be flattered by the preference of her lord and seek no
other. For wives who trifle with their precious charge—
which is nothing less than the honour of their husbands—
there are boiling cauldrons in hell into which they will be
plunged to boil alive throughout eternity. Arnolphe pro-
duces a breviary of the maxims of marriage or the whole
duty of a wife; the man takes the woman for himself alone
—she must wish to be lovely only in his eyes, and the best
way to please a husband is to please no one else; she must
be content with household pleasures and avoid all parties
and excursions. With a wife thus instructed in her duties,
and profoundly ignorant in all else besides, Arnolphe antic-
ipates that he will be able securely to enjoy the misfortunes
of those who, being married to women of wit and enterprise,
must live in constant alarm and uncertainty. For Arnolphe,

255

like Sganarelle of *L'Ecole des Maris,* is obsessed with his
own crabbed reading of the point of honour, and, when not
anxious for himself, is complacently ready to enjoy the
misfortunes of his friends.

Agnes, the victim of this infamous experiment, is one of
the most attractive heroines of comedy. Well may Horace,
her young lover, bewail that the attempt to spoil so admirable a nature is not a punishable offence. She is a child
in knowledge but a woman in wit, and her wit is the more
original and effective for being the entirely candid expression
of a mind untouched by prejudice or fashion. Arnolphe,
informed of the wooing of Horace, bids her sternly to discourage it. Ingenuously she asks how one is to discourage
a thing which gives so much pleasure, and in perfect good
faith she assures Arnolphe—wormwood, wormwood!—that
to cure the young gallant of the ills of which he had complained she would have done anything that lay in her power.
When Arnolphe tells her it is a mortal sin to kiss hands
and allow herself to be moved by the vows of a lover, she
wonders innocently why such things should anger heaven:

> Courroucé! Mais pourquoi faut-il qu'il s'en courrouce?
> C'est une chose, hélas! si plaisante et si douce.

In pure naïveté she asks a question for which no convincing answer has yet been found. Her simplicity, which was
to have imprisoned her within the conventions on which
Arnolphe relies, become by an admirable turn of the tables
his torment and undoing; for, not having been instructed
in the social code, she follows her nature and cannot even
be aware of her transgressions. Love is her only master;
the affection she feels for Horace sharpens her wits and

256

L'ESCOLE
DES
MARIS

L'ESCOLE DES FEMMES.

L'Amour Medecin.

Le Misantrope.

FRONTISPIECES OF ORIGINAL EDITIONS

finally enables her to escape. The critics who urge that Agnes, being a simpleton, could never have had the ingenuity to conceive the plans whereby she circumvents her jealous warder have missed the point of the play as completely as those who argue that such a one must have been sly by nature and born to deceive. The freshness and perspicacity of her wit is due precisely to the fact that her mind is un-fuddled with instructions which are only too often inconsistent and artificial. Her resourcefulness, moreover, far from being that of a born intriguer, is forced upon her by a desperate situation. She is a helpless prisoner and she cozens her gaoler. That is the full extent of her offence and there is no inconsistency between her essential candour of disposition and the ingenuity with which she gets into correspondence with Horace and attains her end. Love laughs at locksmiths. Horace himself reads the riddle aright:

> Il le faut avouer, l'Amour est un grand maître:
> Ce qu'on ne fut jamais, il nous enseigne à l'être.

Still further astray are the moralists who find in the loves of Agnes and Horace a licentious disregard of orthodox morality. Molière is especially careful to present Horace as an amiable and honest youth, and no gallant in search of adventures. Horace is genuinely touched by the simplicity of Agnes, and never for a moment thinks of turning it to his advantage. Agnes leaves the house of her guardian and entrusts herself to his care. Horace, deeply moved by this proof of her uninstructed affection, trembles to think of what might have happened if she had chanced to meet any-one who loved her less. For Agnes the conventional problem has not begun to exist, but her instinctive rightness of

257

disposition is emphasized again and again, and never more clearly than in the famous letter in which she expresses her love for Horace:

Je veux vous écrire, et je suis bien en peine par où je m'y prendrai. J'ai des pensées que je désirerois que vous sussiez; mais je ne sais comment faire pour vous les dire, et je me défie de mes paroles. Comme je commence à connoître qu'on m'a toujours tenue dans l'ignorance, j'ai peur de mettre quelque chose qui ne soit pas bien, et d'en dire plus que je ne devrois. En vérité, je ne sais ce que vous m'avez fait, mais je sens que je suis fâchée à mourir de ce qu'on me fait faire contre vous, que j'aurai toutes les peines du monde à me passer de vous, et que je serois bien aise d'être à vous. Peut-être qu'il y a du mal à dire cela; mais enfin je ne puis m'empêcher de le dire.

It is astonishing that, in the face of this letter, in which the moral conscience comes shyly to life step by step with awakening knowledge, more than one distinguished moralist should have found the play socially dangerous and morally disconcerting. Brunetière discovered in Agnes a natural perversity against which Horace, as a married man, would do well to be on his guard. Bossuet anathematized the whole play as wicked and intolerable—a special pleading on behalf of a criminal indulgence. Rousseau censured its author for deriding the respectable and necessary rights of husbands over their wives, and thus threatening the very foundations of society. That, certainly, was the view of the strictly orthodox contemporaries of Molière and serious moralists of more than one generation have condemned the play in spite of the author's extreme discretion. Molière made it clear that for Horace and Agnes marriage was to be

258

the end of the adventure, and in Agnes he portrays nothing
that in the least resembles a minx. It is an exquisite portrait. A lesser dramatist would have used it to satirize the
conventional code. He would have allowed his Agnes to say
cleverly ingenuous things at the expense of an illogical
society. But Molière puts nothing into her mouth that is not
a natural expression of her character. The critics who find
her wilfully cynical and, marvellous to relate, unfeeling in
her attitude to Arnolphe, misread the play:

> *Arnolphe.* Mais il falloit chasser cet amoureux désir.
> *Agnes.* Le moyen de chasser ce qui fait du plaisir?
> *Arnolphe.* Et ne savez-vous pas que c'étoit me déplaire?
> *Agnes.* Moi? Point du tout. Quel mal cela vous peut-il

faire?

That is not cynicism but the commonsense of a young mind
which has been kept deliberately ignorant of the social
value of abstinence and the social importance of jealousy.
How am I to deny the pleasure that I feel in the company
of Horace, and what harm can it do to you? Arnolphe
is hoist with his own petard. He has infamously starved
this young mind of knowledge with the result that, when
he finds her slipping from his grasp, there is nothing to which
he can appeal. Agnes, being innocent of any prejudice,
answers him more aptly than the most accomplished woman
of the world:

> Voyez comme raisonne et répond la vilaine!
> Peste! une précieuse en diroit-elle plus?

he exclaims in torment. He cannot plead the orthodox pro-
hibitions because she has no knowledge of them, and he is
driven at the last, in helpless desperation, to the abject dec-

259

laration of a passion which is prepared to pay any price for
its satisfaction. Day and night he will love her; she shall
have anything she may desire; behave exactly as she pleases.
Agnes is very naturally unmoved, and the critics exclaim
against her "insensibility." But what did they expect?
These transports leave her entirely cold and very gently
but candidly she says so. How is she even to comprehend
Arnolphe in his despair. Nothing she has ever felt or known
has prepared her to appreciate the torments of his peculiar
gluttony. She is merely puzzled by the behaviour of an
elderly gentleman who at one moment cries out in his rage
that he would like to batter her with his fists and a moment
later falls at her feet in an agony of supplication. Her
"cruelty" to Arnolphe is no more than he deserves, and it
is really a little difficult to understand how anyone could
require from her a fuller measure of charity and submission.
She has every reason to detest the man who has deliberately
endeavoured to deform her spirit. Her attitude, however,
is one of frank, uncomprehending compassion:

> Du meilleur de mon cœur je voudrois vous complaire:
> Que me coûteroit-il si je le pouvois faire?

The censures passed by a solemn posterity upon the ingenuous love of Agnes for Horace and her successful deception of Arnolphe are mild in comparison with those which
have from time to time been provoked by the views of
Chrysalde who acts as a wise and elderly chorus to the play.
It is the part of Chrysalde to combat the obsession of his
friend, to condemn the wicked experiment upon the mind
and future of Agnes, to correct the pathological excesses of
Arnolphe. His speeches have been read as though he advo-

cated for husbands a complete indifference as to the conduct
of their wives. But Chrysalde merely points out that there
are other and possibly worse misfortunes than having a faithless wife. He even suggests that among such misfortunes
may be that of having a wife who considers that her possession of a single virtue enables her to dispense with all the
rest, assuming that, because she is chaste, she has a right
to be everything else that is disagreeable. That, at least,
is a point of view—not necessarily the author's, but a view
put wilfully at a maximum, in opposition to immoderate
contentions on the other side; and it is a point of view with
much to be said in its favour. It is a calamity to have a
faithless wife—

> . . . mais, à ne vous rien feindre,
> Dans le monde je vois cent choses plus à craindre
> Et dont je me ferois un bien plus grand malheur
> Que de cet accident qui vous fait tant de peur.
> Pensez-vous qu'à choisir de deux choses prescrites,
> Je n'aimasse pas mieux être ce que vous dites,
> Que de me voir mari de ces femmes de bien,
> Dont la mauvaise humeur fait un procès sur rien,
> Ces dragons de vertu, ces honnêtes diablesses,
> Se retranchant toujours sur leurs sages prouesses,
> Qui, pour un petit tort qu'elles ne nous font pas,
> Prennent droit de traiter les gens de haut en bas,
> Et veulent, sur le pied de nous être fidèles,
> Que nous soyons tenus à tout endurer d'elles?

The moral position so far as the husband is concerned is
rightly and vehemently urged. The assumption that a man
should forfeit respect because his wife is a wanton, is mercilessly satirized by Chrysalde, and who shall say that he is
wrong? Chrysalde very sensibly declares that a man shows

his mettle less in being deceived or not deceived, as the case may be, than in the way he meets the deception. As in all other contingencies wisdom consists in moderation: one should be neither too indulgent nor too severe:

> Car, pour se bien conduire en ces difficultés,
> Il y faut, comme en tout, fuir les extrémités.

The contemporary reaction to the play was immediate and prolonged. It had at the outset a public success which went far beyond any of its predecessors, perhaps the greatest success in the whole of its author's career. It was performed without interruption to full houses from December 26, 1662, to the Easter vacation of the following year. It was revived immediately after the holiday and remained in the bill until August. In March it was published with a dedication to Madame, Henrietta of England. It had the approbation of the King and the protection of a lady whose piety and decorum were above discussion.

Molière, however, despite the success of his play, needed all the support he could get. The crowds which flocked to his theatre came to be amused and, as they hoped, to be scandalized, but, through all the applause and appreciation of which we catch continual echoes, it is clear that from the production of *L'Ecole des Femmes* to the day of his death, Molière was fighting for the life and liberty of the comic art. It was the first of the plays which, within a few years, were to stimulate the orthodox into describing him, in the language of a certain Vicar of St. Barthélemy, as a "demon in the flesh and guise of a man."

To what extent is *L'Ecole des Femmes* to be read as a personal confession? For the second and not for the last

262

time Molière takes for a theme, to put it as generally as
possible, a prospective marriage between a man and woman
of unequal years. He satirizes in Arnolphe of *L'Ecole des
Femmes*, as in Sganarelle of *L'Ecole des Maris*, the jealous
instincts of an elderly male proprietor unredeemed. The
enemies of Molière were quick to seize the analogy and to
suggest that the agonies of Arnolphe were the expression
of a personal woe, and the critic must inevitably decide to
what extent the comedian was satirizing in himself a demon
which he could not wholly subdue. The question was raised
and implicitly answered in a previous chapter. We may
at once dismiss the grotesque supposition that Molière was
deliberately taking himself for a subject or writing in any
sense an autobiography. His genius was peculiarly a genius
of detachment, and no creature of imagination could be less
like Molière than Arnolphe. The theme and its possibilities, however, were indubitably suggested, even imposed, by
his private circumstances, and we have quite certainly in these
plays a generalization of ideas and feelings which were implicit in his relations with Armande. The man did undoubtedly brood and suffer, and his plays, though they were no
more a slavish record of his private adventure than his portraits were a slavish reproduction of living models, were a
projection into comic art of a personal experience. The projection, however, was not direct; but shown as it were in opposition. Molière, gentle as Ariste, wise as Chrysalde, blunders with Sganarelle and suffers with Arnolphe. Molière,
sick unto death, will one day write the comedy of a man sick
only in imagination and pass from the counterfeiting of
death upon the stage to death itself. So now, as the elderly
husband of a young wife, whose conduct will shortly cause

him a personal suffering for which his comic genius has no
compassion, he presents, *even before the event*—his creative
imagination running easily in advance of the facts—the comic
possibilities inherent in the situation. Molière was married
to Armande in January, 1662. *L'Ecole des Femmes* was
produced in December of the same year—before any very
real or definite estrangement had occurred. The situation
in fact is still only potential, but genius works out of time
and to the comic eye actual and potential verity are identical. In October, 1663, Molière, writing *L'Impromptu
de Versailles,* exhibited himself, naturally and carelessly,
as leader of his company, living upon terms of affectionate
raillery with his young wife, and the first child of the marriage was born in February, 1664. Not only, therefore, is
it needlessly derogatory to his genius—in its essence so universal and so disinterested—to imagine that *L'Ecole des
Femmes* is a merely personal outcry; it is demonstrably
unhistorical. The persistence of the legend in all its crudity
is only to be explained by the ineradicable habit in his coun-
trymen of exaggerating the importance of erotic influences
whenever they may plausibly be introduced. Molière, who
became an actor for love of Madeleine, was tormented by an
inconstant wife into becoming the greatest author of France.
Such is the tradition, and it is not the less profoundly childish for being in its superficial way so nearly correct.

XV

THE COMIC WAR

THE controversy provoked by the success of *L'Ecole des Femmes* came to be known as the comic war (*La Guerre Comique*) and it covered every aspect of the author's wit and practice. He was criticized for his manner of acting, his technique as a playwright, his characterization, his style of writing, his construction of plots, his moral and social doctrines, the impiety and licentiousness of his attitude to serious subjects, his lack of originality, his shameless pillage of other men, his slavish reproductions of living persons and the manners of the day. The comic war lasted for over two years, and it drew from Molière two statements in dramatic form of his personal and æsthetic views. On June 2, 1663, he produced *La Critique de l'Ecole des Femmes*, in which he turned upon his enemies and justified his own methods and intentions as a comic writer; while in October, 1663, he produced *L'Impromptu de Versailles*, in which, under dire provocation, he attacked the rival tragedians of the Hôtel de Bourgogne and made some extremely interesting observations on the general purposes of comedy and his own more particular conception of its scope and purpose.

L'Ecole des Femmes was produced on December 26th. On New Year's Day Molière received from Boileau a tribute in verse which was the beginning of a life-long friendship:

265

Laisse gronder les envieux;
Ils ont beau crier en tous lieux
Qu'en vain tu charmes le vulgaire,
Que tes vers n'ont rien de plaisant:
Si tu savois un peu moins plaire
Tu ne leur déplairois pas tant.

Boileau proclaimed the new comedy to be the author's finest
work and defended its "charming innocence" agai.ist the
censors. Loret, the gazetteer, writing of a performance
given on January 6, 1664, after telling us that their Majes-
ties were reduced to holding their sides with laughter, describes the comedy as a play "which was in certain circles
attacked." Loret himself, very prudently, remained ambiguous. The play was diverting and must be seen. He
refers to the pleasant simplicity of certain characters. He
is careful to assure us in the same breath, however, that,
though amused, he was not necessarily out of sympathy with
those who were distressed. Clearly, in spite of the King's
approval, the play from the outset aroused an opposition
sufficiently serious to worry a trimmer. The Comte du
Broussin, otherwise unknown to posterity, though an important leader of wit and fashion in his day, is said to have left
the theatre at the end of Act II, and the Comte de Plapisson
also earned a brief moment of distinction by rising from his
seat on the stage, shrugging his shoulders and crying to the
pit: "Laugh, silly groundlings, laugh!" Meanwhile the
pamphleteers and dramatists were busy. The success of the
piece and the feeling it aroused clearly made of it a valuable subject.

The first in the field was de Visé, a young man who had
recently come upon the town with a series of *Nouvelles*

266

Nouvelles. We are compelled to see Molière mainly through his detractors. We owe to the libels he inspired our most intimate glimpses of the man and his methods of work. We must therefore know something of the persons who attacked him. De Visé is a simple case. The young man is always with us—a clever, impressionable, unprincipled youth. He hovers to-day about the *sociétaires* of the Comédie Française, canvasses the publishers, frequents fashionable cafés, stands well with the critics and reviewers, and allows few editors to forget that he is ready to support or attack established reputations as impulse or opportunity may decide. De Visé had no personal or æsthetic quarrel with Molière, but his third volume of *Nouvelles Nouvelles* was in the press when the storm broke upon the audacious author of *L'Ecole des Femmes*. Paris would talk of nothing else but the new piece at the Palais Royal. The remedy was obvious. De Visé held back his book for a few days and inserted into it a discussion of the play. The comic war had begun.

De Visé, artful dodger of the muses, was careful not to burn his boats. He presents himself as cross-examining three expert witnesses on the merits of Molière and not as expressing his own opinions. Quite clearly he is reproducing the talk of the town—the best and worst of what was being said on the subject. The experts discuss the play in a ding-dong style. Molière is a great author and a great actor; his wit has made him famous; he is the Terence of the sixteenth century; he describes naturally and with truth the actions of men; he is an excellent producer—every actor knows exactly how many steps he must take and even his *œillades* are numbered. On the other hand, he is merely

an imitator of the Italian authors; he writes nothing which
is not based on plays already in existence or upon notes supplied to him for the purpose; he miserably fails in the serious
vein, witness *Don Garcie*; *L'Ecole des Femmes* is nothing
more than a misnamed repetition of *L'Ecole des Maris*;
everyone finds it wicked but everybody goes to see it; it is
packed with improbabilities and errors; it is a monster with
fine features; never were so many good and bad things
thrown together; there are inimitable passages; there is no
living author who could in a century do the business so
well; his portraits from nature might pass for originals and
seem to speak of themselves. Finally, de Visé sums up;
"All you have said to his glory bears the stamp of truth and
the shadows you have placed in the picture only brighten the
effect of your colours." This young man clearly wishes for
the moment to stand well with both sides. Apart from a
reference to Molière as a husband deceived, and, therefore, able to depict with fidelity a born cuckold, there is
nothing to which grave exception need be taken, and we may
be sure that the personal gibe was only included as a thing
which was passing freely among the gossips.

Molière, publishing his play on March 17th, declared in
his preface that many had attacked it, but had been unable
to spoil its success. He added that his friends were expecting him to defend himself and that he had already written
a dialogue discussing the merits of the play. The idea
had occurred to him, he says, after the first two or three
performances—a statement which again shows how immediate was the public reaction. He had mentioned his project
one evening at a party, and a person of quality, finding it
admirable, had incontinently gone home and written a dia-

logue himself. Molière was naturally embarrassed. When a person of quality submits in all good faith a dramatic exercise quite obviously unfit for production the position is a little difficult, especially when the producer himself happens to have a brilliant version of his own well on the way to completion. Molière found the proffered text, he says, too flattering, and at first decided to abandon his own rejoinder. His friends, however, continued to clamour for its production and six months later, on the 2nd June, he yielded to their importunities and produced *La Critique de l'Ecole des Femmes.*

Nothing on the subject had appeared in print since the *Nouvelles Nouvelles* of de Visé. The dispute, however, had obviously extended. Six months had elapsed since the production of *L'Ecole des Femmes,* but the Court and the public were still fiercely divided upon its merits. The King had felt it necessary to declare his own appreciation in no uncertain terms. To be publicly amused was not in this instance enough. The pension list for 1663, drawn up on the morrow of the production, was published in February. Molière "excellent comic poet" figured for 1,000 *livres* and improved the occasion with a *Remerciement au Roi* universally praised for its elegance and wit. It has a curious ironic, almost impertinent, familiarity—tactfully audacious, but without offence. The King might only accept such a tribute from a man who could safely assume that his homage was welcome. Molière bids his muse, disguised as a fashionable marquis, seek the royal presence with such flourishes as his quality may suggest. Let him, however, be brief, for great princes like short compliments, and the King of France is a busy man. A comparison of this daring sally with the stilted compliments traditional at the Louvre throws a vivid light upon the relations of the King and his comedians.

Molière in *La Critique de l'Ecole des Femmes* replied to his principal detractors, and the reply was light-hearted. The author, having the unreserved support of the King and the applause of the public, could still afford to be merry. His "apology" is in the form of a discussion of the merits of his comedy, which is severely rated by a marquis, by a representative of feminine gentility and by a rival author.

The Marquis is a significant apparition. He was henceforth to be a prominent feature of the comic theatre of Molière. There were evidently among the fine gentlemen of the Court many who were making common cause with the prudes, exquisites and rivals of Molière in the grand attack upon his work. This Molière was the son of a burgess and, with his commonsense and uncertain respect for persons of high degree, was clearly a man to be discouraged with a firm hand. He quite openly appealed to the pit over the heads of the arbiters of taste and fashion. He had held up to ridicule the accomplishments of the polite world. A gentleman could no longer compose a madrigal, pen a portrait, deliver a pun or venture an epigram without discomfortably wondering whether he were really as clever as he felt himself to be. The Marquis of the *Critique* contributes little to the discussion. He does not like the play. First, it had been difficult for him to find a seat and he had been jostled at the door. Secondly, the pit had laughed heartily and continually without awaiting the verdict of the balcony. Thirdly, the best actors in Paris had thought nothing of the performance. Fourthly, there had been a

270

reference to cream tarts. *Tarte à la crème, morbleu, tarte à la crème.* The fine lady is hardly more coherent. She has been to the play and expects in consequence to be indisposed for a fortnight. What is to be said of a man who recounts as evidence of the simplicity of his ward that she has inquired of him whether children are born by the ear? Or of a servant who illustrates the feelings of a husband for his wife by comparing her to a plate of soup? The play, moreover, is so full of obscenities that a modest woman cannot see it without shame. Take, for example, the scene in which Agnes, telling of her interview with Horace, confesses that he has taken from her the ribbon which Arnolphe had given her. What has he taken? The . . . ribbon. Why does she stay so long upon the definite article? That ambiguous pause is not there for nothing. It gives rise to strange thoughts. The play, moreover, is an outrageous satire upon the sex:

> Chose étrange d'aimer, et que, pour ces traîtresses
> Les hommes sont sujets à de telles foiblesses!
> Tout le monde connoit leur imperfection;
> Ce n'est qu'extravagance et qu'indiscrétion;
> Leur esprit est méchant et leur âme fragile;
> Il n'est rien de plus foible et de plus imbécile,
> Rien de plus infidèle: et, malgré tout cela,
> Dans le monde on fait tout pour ces animaux-là.

There's a way to talk of a lady. Animals, indeed.

The observations of the author, Lysidas, are more measured. He represents the views of the literary orthodox. He has arrived from a private reading of one of his own plays, and it is some time before he can turn his attention to less burning matters. At first he is cryptic. Authors do not, of course, condemn one another. The play is a good play. It is the finest play in the world. But it is not, of course, approved by those who really know what they are talking about, and it is not really, properly speaking, a play at all. Unfortunately, however, such trifles begin to be in the fashion. This particular play, moreover, offends against all the rules of art. There is neither protasis, epitasis, or peripeteia; there is no action; the play is no more than a series of narratives of what the characters have done or are about to do. The wit of it is poor—children by the ear, for example. The characterization is defective. Arnolphe gives money readily to Horace, though, being the absurd person of the play, he should not be shown performing a generous and commendable act. The sermon of Arnolphe on the duties of marriage is in itself ridiculous and wounds the respect which is due to the mysteries of religion. Arnolphe, declaring his passion for Agnes in the last Act, is outrageously extravagant.

The play is defended by Dorante, who speaks for the author, by Uranie, a woman of good sense, and Elise, who takes a malicious pleasure in provoking her opponents into declaring themselves as completely as possible and in affecting to admire their follies. This was the first part written by Molière for his young wife, and it enabled her to shine in just the mischievous and mutinous qualities that were at the same time his plague and his pleasure.

Most of the criticisms brought against the play answer themselves by the manner of their presentation. The Marquis is a simpleton who has not even listened to the play he criticizes and the prude-exquisite, by her false airs of modesty outraged, brings more discredit upon her-

self than upon the play. All this, however, is light skir-
mishing. Other criticisms, seriously presented and seriously
answered, give Molière an opportunity of explaining his
view of comedy and his method of writing. The test which
we find him constantly applying is that of fidelity to character. A line is to be judged not merely on its merits but
as appropriate to the character who utters it. Children by
the ear, for example, is not a witticism. Arnolphe, producing this instance of the simplicity of Agnes, is simply illustrating his own infatuation. Similarly the sermon with its
absurd maxims, the boiling cauldrons, the cream tarts, the
outburst of Arnolphe against women—all these things must
be read, not as jests of the author but as natural and appropriate to the persons of the play. It is true that Arnolphe
inveighs against women—*ces animaux-là*. But Arnolphe is
an imbecile and the whole comedy is a plea for the independence and dignity of women in their relations with men
and society. To those who urge that Arnolphe is too extravagant in his final passion, Dorante asks whether even
the worthiest and best do not at times suffer much extremity
for love; to those who argue that Arnolphe is too generous
with his purse he inquires whether a person cannot be absurd
in some things and estimable in others. He goes even further. Comedy, he suggests, which aims at a natural portraiture is perhaps a finer and a more difficult form of art
than tragedy, in which imagination may run riot and depict
a hero according to its will and pleasure. Nobody expects a
hero to resemble anything in nature and the poet may leave
truth behind him in his determination to achieve the marvellous. The comedian on the contrary must depict the
natural man and present him amusingly—*et c'est une étrange*

273

entreprise que celle de faire rire les honnêtes gens. This
is going a little far. Molière had failed in tragedy and
—with respect be it uttered—the grapes were sour. There
is, nevertheless, a kernel of truth in this special pleading.
Comedy is of all forms of art the most essentially civilized
—the latest to arrive and the most exacting.

Molière claims veracity in portraiture as the final test,
but, as we have already seen, he is careful to deny that the
comic poet is the slave of his models or that his art is in any
sense a mechanical reproduction. The comic truth at which
he aims is a general truth, though it be based on particular
instances. It has its own logic and remains true for all men
and every period. Molière, even when emphasizing his
realism, is always careful to qualify and limit its significance.
It is a classic realism. His portraits are not particular but
general.

He shows the same care, for all his lightness of touch,
in dealing with the question of the rules to be observed in
the construction of plays. He merrily disposes of Lysidas
with his protasis, epitasis and peripeteia. The first rule is
to please and all other rules are but a means to that end.
The spectator who laughs does not ask whether Aristotle
forbids him to do so. A comedy must be judged by its effect,
and it is useless asking the public to discover reasons why it
should or should not be diverted. This, however, does not
mean that the rules are of no account or can be disregarded
with impunity. It means, on the contrary, that they must
be intelligently interpreted and applied. They are not sacred
mysteries to be understood only by the few, but a straightforward application of common intelligence to a definite
purpose which no dramatist can afford to ignore. Dorante,

274

on behalf of Molière, denies that his author has in any
way offended against the rules thus reasonably interpreted.

La Critique de l'Ecole des Femmes is of interest, not only
for its discussion of the author's comic method, but as showing how he regarded his public. The Marquis expresses contempt for the pit. Molière replies with a satirical sketch of
the fine gentlemen who set up for arbiters of taste. The
Marquis will not allow that the commonalty have any
sense in such matters; he disdains to laugh with the crowd,
though the play be the best in the world; he listens to the
piece with a sad brow, frowns when the rest of the house
dissolves into laughter; finally he looks down upon the audience with compassion and rises to his feet: *ris donc, parterre,
ris donc*. Dorante, on behalf of Molière, declares that at
the theatre the difference between half-a-sovereign and six-
pence has little relation to the taste of the spectator; that a
man's judgment may be equally bad whether he be sitting
on the stage or standing in the pit; that, personally, he has
respect for the decisions of the pit, since it includes not only
persons who are quite capable of judging by the rules but
persons who come to the play without prejudice or affectation and are frankly ready to be amused or disappointed.
He is in favour of good sense wherever it may be found,
and he breaks out into a fine passion at the insolence of gentlemen who arrogate to themselves the right to express an
opinion on every subject under the sun without being in the
least qualified to do so; who smatter of art and its mysteries,
whether it be music or painting or literature, with a plentiful
lack of intelligence and reveal their ignorance with every
word they utter. These persons will, if they are wise, maintain a discreet silence, for only by saying nothing or as little

as possible can they hope to pass for knowing anything at all. This is, perhaps, the most vivacious protest in all the comedies of Molière. It has a personal ring. It has behind it all the indignation of the artist against the impertinent idlers who, in every age and country, are the most frequent and the loudest in their judgments.

The resentment of the marquises is recorded in stories apocryphal in form but true in substance. Critics have zealously tried to identify the gentleman, who, recognizing himself in the marquis of the play, revenged himself in so insolent a fashion that tradition affirms he was at least a duke and possibly a prince. This gentleman—various distinguished individuals of the Court compete not very successfully for the honour—meeting Molière one day at Court, so the story runs, made to embrace him. Molière bent forward, whereupon this avenger of all the marquises took him firmly by the head and exclaiming *"Tarte à la crème, Molière! tarte à la crème"* rubbed it violently against the buttons of his waistcoat. Gossip, to be satisfied, must exhibit the face of Molière running with blood, but history inclines to believe that the wig of the comedian was only slightly deranged. The affront was, in any case, sufficiently striking to call down upon its author a public reprimand from the King.

Molière, though he found it difficult to contain himself when satirizing the complacent futility of the marquises, was far from claiming a monopoly of wisdom for any class or rank of society. When Lysidas sneers at the judgment of the Court, Dorante, speaking still for Molière, turns upon him with no less swift a reprobation. The judgment of the Court, he maintains, is to be respected. There are

276

at Versailles and St. Germain men of learning who combine a native good sense with a knowledge of the world, and their intimate acquaintance with persons and events of the day is just what is needed to form a correct taste, particularly when it comes to judging between true wit and false. Not everyone at Court is above ridicule, but there are fools in every profession. Why not, for example, take the authors for a theme? Surely there is matter here for a comedy—their affectation of learning, their splitting of literary straws, their dogged pursuit of an audience, their insatiable appetite for flattery, the studious economy with which they contrive to make a few ideas go a very long way, their traffic in reputations, their leagues for offence and defence, their warfares of wits, their battles in prose and verse, their curious affection for works which are unpopular and no less curious distaste for those that succeed.

Molière was dealing with no imaginary foe. He attacked in Lysidas the small fry of letters who had been snapping at his heels from the moment of his arrival in Paris; and, just as there was more than one marquis ready to show how well the cap fitted, so there were authors only too prompt to take up this further challenge. Lysidas, naturally enough, found a champion in de Visé, who, having started the comic war with his *Nouvelles Nouvelles,* hastened to identify himself as the original of the poet of Molière and his avenger. The result was *Zélinde, Comédie, ou la Véritable Critique de l'Ecole des Femmes et Critique de la Critique.* The play was published on August 4, 1663, and is far from being the contemptible production which zealous biographers, with dignity after the event, have very righteously rebuked. De Visé was merely sailing before the wind—angling, incidentally, for a production at the Hôtel de Bourgogne. His play, we feel, is the work of a young man who would have honestly preferred to be the friend than the enemy of Molière; and, when the comic war was at an end, he made his peace and wrote two plays for the Palais Royal which Molière produced with success in 1665 and 1667. For the moment, however, opposition was the better policy. Here at least was a splendid advertisement. "I am Lysidas," he in effect proclaimed, "and Molière has written a play about me. Seconds, out of the ring." These are the normal tactics of ambitious young men in all ages resolutely in search of a reputation, and the criticism of de Visé is above rather than below the average of what a revolutionary genius may reasonably expect of his contemporaries.

The observations of de Visé vary considerably in justice and importance. Some are mistaken; some are trivial; others cannot be lightly ignored. Chrysalde, he urges, is a useless character who does not forward the play in any way; the action of the piece most improbably and inappropriately takes place in an open square, though it continually calls for privacy; Arnolphe desires above all to keep Agnes secluded from the world, but the audience sees her continually out of doors. Horace would not repeatedly have confided his adventures to Arnolphe or failed to notice the strange way in which his confidences were received; Agnes, who is introduced as a simpleton, excels at last every other character in cunning and resource; the scenes between Arnolphe and his servants are extravagantly farcical; the definite article, which modesty condemns, deliberately stimulates a licentious fancy; the famous maxims on marriage are religiously disrespectful and obviously bad instruction for a

278

young wife whose innocence her husband desires to keep intact; the conclusion of the piece is frankly detestable. Much of this criticism is technically reasonable and Molière himself could only have answered it by avoidance. He did not care very much about scenic realism or the liquidation of plots. The stage was for him a platform whereon his characters might meet, express themselves and thence depart. His test of good or bad craft was the immediate reaction of the audience and technically he was not prepared to quarrel with anything they would accept. De Visé cannot, of course, omit the charge of plagiarism. He suggests that a pleasant scene might be written of Molière in which all the actors from whom he has borrowed his tricks of deportment, all the authors whom he has laid under contribution, and all the gentlemen of quality who have provided him with material or posed for their characters should appear and claim their belongings. Molière would then be as naked as the crow who dressed himself in peacock's feathers. All this, however, is no more than a picturesque version of a common charge and it is not a view with which de Visé necessarily identifies himself. On the contrary, he would seem to justify Molière in borrowing to such good purpose; and, in conclusion, he handsomely declares: "The faults of Elomire are more to be pardoned than those of other men since he scarcely ever makes a mistake which he does not cover with some brilliant stroke that prevents us from detecting it."

This de Visé had quite obviously a sneaking admiration for his victim and we owe to him our first contemporary glimpse of Molière. The discussion upon the merits of *La Critique de l'Ecole des Femmes* takes place in the shop of

279

a lace merchant in the parish of St. Denis. The disputants hear that Elomire himself is below with a friend, and the merchant goes down to bring him, if possible, into the group. The merchant returns:

"I found him," he says, "leaning against the counter in the attitude of a man lost in reflection. His eyes were fixed on three or four persons of quality who were buying lace. He seemed to be following their conversation with attention, and it would be gathered from the expression in his eyes that he was looking into their souls and reading their unspoken thoughts. I even fancy that he had a tablet, and that, under cover of his cloak, he wrote down, without our perceiving it, their more characteristic sayings."

"Perhaps," suggests another, "he was using a pencil and sketching their portraits, so that he might present them according to nature on the stage."

"I have no doubt," says the merchant, "that he was imprinting them upon his imagination; he is a dangerous person; it may be said of him that he goes nowhere without his eyes and ears."

The merchant goes on to relate how, as he waited in the shop, a coach drove up to the door and its occupant called to Elomire bidding him come at once to dinner, since he was entertaining three or four *turlupins* (marquises) who could not fail to furnish him with more matter for his comedies. Whereupon Elomire drove off, leaving his friend behind him in the shop.

It is a vivid contemporary picture. The comic war takes shape and colour. De Visé shows us the fine gentlemen of the Court who in their vanity "love to see themselves in the living mirrors of Elomire," and laughingly address one

another as *turlupins* when they meet at Court; we hear
that all the world murmurs aloud that Molière, with his
ten maxims on marriage, has offended against the mysteries
of religion; we are told of the people who applaud his characters lest they should themselves be taken for the originals;
finally, we get a glimpse of the larger public which was
then being drawn to the theatre—a public of solid and respectable citizens who were rapidly becoming the real arbiters
of the stage. "I must confess to you," says our merchant of
lace, "that I have never known these worthy burgesses condemn a piece upon its production, but it fell flat, or praise
a piece which did not meet with a real success; the plays
that succeed with the pit succeed also with the balconies
and boxes."

Zélinde never came upon the stage. It was too genial
a picture for the bitter rivals of Molière at the Hôtel de
Bourgogne who had already a more savage rod in pickle.
Molière never, so far as we know, alluded explicitly to
the play of de Visé, but, three days after its publication—
on August 7, 1663—his own *La Critique de l'Ecole des
Femmes* was also put on sale; and it contained a reply, all
the more crushing as it was indirect, in the shape of a short
dedication to the Queen mother. The author rejoices that
he has had the honour to divert Her Majesty, since he can
take this for a signal proof that true devotion is in no way
incompatible with wholesome amusement. With a graceful
daring he is happy to know that Her Majesty does not disdain to laugh at his comedy "with the same mouth whereby
she prays to God." There could be no more crushing retort
upon those who murmured against his satire upon the sacred
mysteries of religion and the licence of his theme.

281

The comic war took now a more serious and a more personal turn. The tragedians of the Hôtel de Bourgogne were known to be busy and they had found an author in Edmé Boursault, a young dramatist whose first plays they had recently started to produce. Like de Visé he was only twenty-five years of age, and he, too, had a reputation to advertise. The title of his play was significant—*Le Portrait du Peintre ou la Contre Critique de l'Ecole des Femmes*. Boursault took the play of Molière, put it into verse and turned it inside out. In Boursault's comedy it is the fools who praise the work of Molière and the persons of discretion who incite them to the task. *Tarte à la crème,* no longer *détestable, du dernier détestable,* becomes *admirable, du dernier admirable.* The wit of Molière is turned against himself by a young author who had at least the sense to realize that he could find no better model. In the *Critique* of Molière it is the detractors who refuse to listen to reason; in the *Contre Critique* of Boursault it is the admirers who wilfully shut their ears. The *Contre Critique* was a looking-glass fugue upon the *Critique* of Molière.

Among the audience which witnessed this performance was Molière himself. His enemies refer later to his presence. He did his best, they say, to seem amused, but his laughter was forced. We may reasonably doubt whether he laughed very heartily, for there was little to laugh at in *Le Portrait du Peintre.* Reproached with his lack of merriment, he is said to have replied: "I am laughing as much as I can," which was interpreted by his enemies, rather clumsily, to signify that he was palpably hit, more particularly by certain perfidious allusions to the fact that he would naturally find it easy to play Arnolphe to the life—evidently one of the allusions to his private affairs which Boursault subsequently had the grace to expunge.

A later contributor to the comic war, Chevalier, an actor of the Théâtre du Marais, picturesquely refers in *Les Amours de Calotin* to the presence of Molière at the Hôtel de Bourgogne. It was pleasant, he tells us, to see the copy and the original side by side and he goes on to say that one of the spectators asked Molière, *whose honour was attacked,* what he thought of the comedy. Molière replied in his pleasant way, *Admirable, morbleu! du dernier admirable!* adding that his reply would be ready within eight days.

Such was the origin of *L'Impromptu de Versailles.* The retort was crushing both in itself and in the circumstances of its production. It was performed by special request of the King on October 18th or 19th. Molière was able to inform the public that the King had expressly commanded him to accept the challenge of his enemies and he skilfully shows himself to be on terms of affectionate familiarity with his royal protector. This appears in the design of the play itself, and in several audacious passages where he comments upon the foibles of majesty.

L'Impromptu de Versailles presents a rehearsal. Molière has been ordered to perform a comedy at Court in eight days. The company is far from ready, and the King is expected to arrive in a couple of hours. One of the players suggests that Molière shall respectfully present his excuses and plead for time. Molière replies:

Mon Dieu! mademoiselle, les rois n'aiment rien tant qu'une prompte obéissance, et ne se plaisent point du tout à trouver des obstacles. Les choses ne sont bonnes que dans le temps qu'ils les souhaitent . . . Nous ne sommes que pour leur plaire; et, lorsqu'ils nous ordonnent quelque chose, c'est à nous à profiter vite de l'envie où ils sont. Il vaut mieux s'acquitter mal de ce qu'ils nous demandent que de ne s'en acquitter pas assez tôt; et, si l'on a la honte de n'avoir pas bien réussi, on a toujours la gloire d'avoir obéi vite à leurs commandements.

The tone is light, but there is implicit a reproach to which time was to lend an increasing pertinence as the demands of Louis upon his favourite comedian became more frequent and exacting.

Molière deals first with his rivals at the Hôtel de Bourgogne. Urged by a member of his company to try his hand at their portraiture, he answers that he has neither the time nor the wish to do so. He has not seen them act more than three or four times, and can only reproduce their more obvious mannerisms. Nevertheless, he improvises then and there a rapid sketch, in which the styles of Montfleury, Beauchâteau, Hauteroche and the rest of them are imitated and contrasted with the more natural methods of the Palais Royal. Molière descends, for the first and last occasion in his life, to the personal method of attack. To play the King in his tragedy, he says, he needs a man of substance, a man who can fill a throne imposingly. This is a reference to the increasing girth of Montfleury. It is the only allusion to be found anywhere in his work which brings him down to the level of the men who throughout his career never ceased to taunt him with references to his physical defects and private misfortunes. Note, moreover, that the allusion is made in good humour and remember also that Montfleury, in his dealings with Molière, deserved the worst that anybody could ever say of him.

284

Molière, having dealt with the rival actors, turned next to the authors. His references show how universal was the confederacy against him—all the dramatists, *depuis le cèdre jusqu'à l'hysope*, are in it. The elder Corneille, though not actively a combatant, was clearly not sorry to behold his young rival with his back to the wall. Some pertinent questions are asked. Why do authors usually admire a play that fails with the public more than a play that succeeds? Why should Molière reply, in detail, to his enemies? Is it not obvious that his most damaging reply is to write another successful comedy? Henceforth let the critics rage. He will not allow himself to be drawn into a foolish controversy and thus be diverted from his work. He will say no more. Let them speak as ill as they please of his comedies. Let them take his plays, turn them as one turns a coat for use upon their stage and profit, if they can, from any agreeable or fortunate matter which they may find. He raises no objection. They have need of anything they can get, and he is quite content to contribute to their subsistence. He concludes with the passage, already quoted and discussed, in which he mentions the attacks made upon him in his private character and declares, once for all, that he will never again allude to them. He was faithful to that decision. This was his first and last word on the personal issue, and upon Boursault, a young and impressionable opponent, it took effect. The published version of *Le Portrait du Peintre*, as we know it, contains none of the personalities which provoked *L'Impromptu de Versailles*. Montfleury, as we shall see, was less amenable. Molière had dared to notice that he was fat.

L'Impromptu de Versailles is not merely, or even essentially, a reply to criticism. It shows us Molière at work as a producer. One by one he takes the members of his company, sketches for them the parts they are to play, and warns them against the faults to which they are liable. *Ah! les étranges animaux à conduire que des comédiens*—the saying has an international currency. All, however, passes in good humour, for this was the company which "so loved the Sieur de Molière . . . that they had sworn never to leave him whatever proposals might be made to them or whatever advantages they might be offered elsewhere." It gave him trouble enough and to spare, but the impression left by the *Impromptu* is that of a troop which was competent, familiar and devoted.

L'Impromptu de Versailles, first presented before the King, was played with success at the Palais Royal. The tragedians of the Hôtel de Bourgogne were furious, more particularly as their own *Portrait du Peintre* had failed to attract the public. Montfleury hastened to change his bill and produced, probably towards the end of October, *La Réponse à l'Impromptu de Versailles ou la Vengeance des Marquis*. The new play was by de Visé. The young man had at last forced his way upon the Burgundian stage, but at some cost both to his style and his convictions. The new play was inferior in tone and substance to *Zélinde*. De Visé is now obviously the hireling of an angry master. He renews all the ancient charges against Molière as actor and author, adds a few specific criticisms of the *Impromptu,* condemns the bad taste of Molière in referring to the girth of Montfleury, and then proceeds to mock the lameness of Louis Béjart, the portliness, oh, horrible! of Mademoiselle du Parc, the years, alas! of Madeleine Béjart, and the *hoquet*

286

of Molière. And once again he insinuates that Molière is damned in a fair wife.

Still the public was not amused. De Visé published his play on December 7 with a letter on the present state of the theatre, his last word against Molière, in which he boldly attempted to set the King against his favourite comedian. The nobility, he says, care little what Molière may write of them, but the honour of the State should move them to protest; to attack the nobility is to discredit the whole realm in foreign esteem and, by an attack upon the Court, the King himself may be prejudiced; it is not enough to show respect for the demi-god who is our ruler, but we should also spare those who have the privilege of standing near to his person. This was the first, but by no means the last, time that the critics of Molière presumed to warn His Majesty, in all respect, against the revolutionary whom he was so rashly cherishing. The King's attitude to those whose too much love and tender preservation of his person prompted them to such representations was sufficiently definite. Racine, writing to the Abbé Le Vasseur at the moment when de Visé was putting forth these mischievous suggestions, describes how Molière has just been admitted to the *lever du roi*, and there been praised to his face by Louis. Racine with the mild sneer that too often misbecomes him adds that Molière was pleased with the compliment and glad that he (Racine) should be there to hear it.

De Visé, blowing hot and cold, was now beginning to doubt whether he had better not change his livery. His hostility had been the result of pique rather than conviction. He had begun in the *Nouvelles Nouvelles* by praising Molière, but Molière had taken no notice. Hell knows no fury like an

author who has been ignored. He had since tried his luck
with the Burgundians and the play had failed. He now
affirms in his preface, almost with tears, that he never intended to attack Molière in person; that Molière is a gentleman; that he knows nothing of his private life, and would
never wish to refer to it even if he did; that all that has
ever been written against Molière has only served to increase
his fame. All this is difficult to reconcile with previous allusions. But when were the angry words of despited admirers
ever consistent? The pen of a young author easily runs
away. So Molière himself, in his generous comprehension
of human weakness, himself read the riddle. The author of
Zélinde was forgiven and, within two years, Molière had accepted him as one of the authors of the Palais Royal. He
ceased, in fact, to be the enemy of Molière when the comic
war of December, 1662, to March, 1664, gave place to the
more sinister and prolonged encounter of Molière with the
forces of orthodoxy which ended only with his death and
unchristian burial.

Meanwhile, the Hôtel de Bourgogne had found another
champion. Robinet, a friend of Boursault, in later years
a discreet admirer of Molière, came into the comic war
on November 30th with *La Panégyrique de l'Ecole des
Femmes*. It is difficult to decide whether this contribution
was the result of bad temper or a salaried scurrility.
Molière has the style of a lackey; he is a hater of women
and an advocate of their systemetic oppression; he amuses
the public at the expense of private individuals; he has driven
genuine comedy from the theatre; he has killed the taste for
fine feeling; he encourages licence and impiety; he offends
against all the rules of art; he is a destroyer of civilization

Four Prints of Brissart

Engraved by F. Sauvé for the edition of *Œuvres de Molière*
published in 1682 by Thierry-Rabouillet-Barbin.

and polite intercourse; he is an enemy of society and family life. Incidentally, Robinet, referring to *L'Ecole des Femmes* praises "the zeal shown by one of our wisest magistrates in endeavouring to secure the suppression of a thing so wicked and dangerous"—a statement which shows that the comic war was no laughing matter. Even at this early stage, Molière, but for the conspicuous favours of the King, might quite easily have been silenced.

For two months now Montfleury had been meditating his revenge, and his son, at the Hôtel de Bourgogne, was writing a play, to be produced early in December, 1663, and published in January, 1664. The play of Montfleury the younger was entitled *L'Impromptu de l'Hôtel de Condé*. Molière had secured the patronage of the King and the Queen mother. His rival flaunted the protection of a mighty prince. The result for Montfleury was socially disastrous. The Prince de Condé, great in mind and character, was one of the most constant and enthusiastic admirers of Molière. The Burgundians, however, had secured a friend in his son, the Duc d'Enghien, to whom Boursault had dedicated *Le Portrait du Peintre*, and Montfleury ventured to assume that the Prince would himself support the cabal against the author of *L'Ecole des Femmes*. Condé, realizing the implication of this manœuvre, took prompt and effective measures to correct any such impression. On December 11 the Duc d'Enghien married Anne of Bavaria. There was high festival at the Hôtel de Condé and the Prince invited Molière to contribute to the splendours of the occasion. Molière proposed *L'Impromptu de Versailles*, which was duly repeated in the presence of the King, the two Queens and an audience which included the whole of the royal family and court. Molière, in fact, accepted the social challenge imposed upon him by his enemies. With the Prince de Condé for ace, and King and Queen to follow, he held all the cards and he knew how to play them.

L'Impromptu de l'Hôtel de Condé is a painstaking repetition of previous criticisms with additions that are merely contradictious or inept. There are the usual references to Molière's misfortunes as a husband and, as a retort to *L'Impromptu de Versailles*, a parody of his acting. The author committed the supreme folly of denying, while Paris laughed, that *L'Impromptu de Versailles* was in any way amusing. The passage which redeems the play from oblivion is a spirited description of Molière as a tragic actor. These lines were quoted in a previous chapter.

It was then that Montfleury, raging at defeat, completely lost his head. His letter to the King on the marriage of Molière was written and despatched in December. The episode, so far as it relates to the private life of Molière, has been already described. Its significance in the comic war may be inferred from one or two facts which have not hitherto been sufficiently emphasized. It seems undoubtedly to have produced a reaction of public feeling even among the opposition. Montfleury had become intolerable even to his own supporters and the subsequent and final contributions to the comic war were on the side of Molière. De Visé, as we have seen, now desired peace with honour, and Boursault omitted from the published version of *Le Portrait du Peintre* the personal allusions to which Molière had referred in *L'Impromptu de Versailles*. It is one thing to suggest that your rival is equally liable with other men to the misfortune of having married a wife of whom he cannot always be sure.

290

It is another thing to insinuate, in an open letter to the King of France, that he has very probably married his own daughter. Montfleury probably believed his own libel. He would believe anything of the man who had commented on the loss of his figure. But that made it no better for his supporters. Montfleury, in November and December, 1663, can hardly have been sane on the subject of Molière, and even his friends were beginning to be bored, and even revolted, by his obsession. The letter to the King was the last straw. Thereafter no publisher or theatre would embark in the comic war against Molière, and Montfleury could find no dramatist to continue the campaign. The Théâtre du Marais declared for him in January, 1664, in a prologue to one of its plays, and Philippe de la Croix on March 7, 1664, published under the name of *La Guerre Comique ou la Défense de l'Ecole des Femmes,* a final review and apology which brought the controversy to a close.

Thus ended the comic war on a note of victory and appreciation. The enemies of Molière had attacked him in his work and in his person. They had endeavoured to mobilize against him the victims of his satire—the moralists, the prudes, the exquisites, the marquises. They had endeavoured to discredit him with the royal house. Molière struck back, and his enemies had decidedly the worst of the encounter, socially and upon the stage. Montfleury, in desperation, had appealed directly to the King. The King answered an infamous personal insinuation by standing godfather to the first child of a marriage publicly incriminated. But, though a victory had been won, the contest had been by no means an easy one. Molière had been insulted at court; his private life mishandled by the gossips; his plays seriously indicted before public authority. His enemies were only for a moment silenced and the irreconcilables would wait until he gave fresh and more serious matter for offence. The moment was not long in coming. The comic war ended in March, 1664. Three months later Molière had entered upon an infinitely more serious struggle in which he tested to the limits the influence and courage of his royal protector, and in which he was all but driven from the stage.

XVI

The Royal Diversions

MOLIÈRE was about to enter upon the most difficult period of his life. He would need the King
and he had every reason to believe that the King
was his friend. The royal protection was as yet unofficial,
but none the less it was adequate. The King had supported
him in the comic war; snubbed the insinuations of Montfleury; smiled upon *L'Impromptu de Versailles*, in which
the impatience and caprice of monarchs was amiably chaffed;
granted his "excellent comic poet" a pension of 1,000 *livres*,
and stood godfather to his child; called all his comedies to
court, held the royal sides with laughter, and even been
claimed as a collaborator in *Les Fâcheux*.

And now in January, 1664, the King was preparing to
adventure the royal person upon the stage. *Le Mariage
Forcé*, which has survived for posterity as a comedy in one
act was, on January 29, 1664, produced at the Louvre in the
apartments of the Queen mother as a diversion in three parts,
in which the comedy was reinforced with ballet, pantomime
and song. The King was cast for a gipsy. The great ladies
and masters of etiquette were, perhaps, on such occasions not
a little uneasy. Their royal master, be it whispered, had a
tendency to neglect the social degrees. Racine was soon
afterwards to give an indirect expression to this feeling,

293

which he was too good a courtier not to appreciate, in the famous passage of *Bérénice* in which Nero incurs the contempt of the Romans on account of his artistic proclivities. Old heads were in all probability shaken, and the young King may even have heard it whispered that the rôle of a gipsy in the troop of the Sieur de Molière was unlikely to increase respect for the King of France. But the King, in these early days, was obstinate in his pleasures. He was later to appear as a "ridiculous poet" in the *Ballet des Muses*. It was not until September, 1670, that he made his last appearance upon any stage.

Le Mariage Forcé, described by Loret as an "impromptu," has been dismissed as a merry trifle, but it was more than that. Sganarelle, fallen into the vale of years, debates whether he shall marry the young and beautiful Dorimène. His infatuation, while it provokes laughter, is depicted with a realism that would be bitter if it were not so gay. Sganarelle, thinking better of his project, foreseeing clearly the doom which it invites, but driven at last to his marriage by an angry brother at the point of the sword, is a figure of farce, adapted from sources easily identified. There are echoes from Lope de Vega and in Sganarelle, the spirit of Pantagruel lives again. But the comic genius of Molière— outwardly hilarious, inwardly contemplative—transforms this ancient material, and the cynicism of Dorimène, who marries for freedom, with a gallant already in attendance, points us forward to the merciless conclusions of *Tartuffe* and *George Dandin*. The play, slight as it is, also contains Pancrace and Marphurius, comic philosophers inherited from the *commedia dell' arte,* but revitalized by the young scholar of Clermont, the swift enemy of pedantry in all its forms.

294

Technically the play fulfils the promise made by the author in his preface to *Les Fâcheux*, in which he hinted at a possible development of the *comédie-ballet* as a coherent form of art. It may thus be regarded as the first of a brilliant series which culminated in *Le Bourgeois Gentilhomme* and *Le Malade Imaginaire*. *Le Mariage Forcé*, unlike *Les Fâcheux*, was created under a single direction. Molière came before the public as a producer whom the King was soon to recognize as the principal organizer of his splendid revels at Versailles and St. Germain. Lulli wrote the music, Beauchamp was choreographer and conductor, but the spectacle as a whole was under the control of Molière. The ballet was logically connected with the comedy, assisting its progress or embodying the fancies and distractions of the comic protagonist. It was the first essay of Molière in that union of the arts which has so often misled and tormented his successors.

The experiment from this point of view was an entire success. Henceforth, Molière contributed largely to all the great festivals at Versailles or St. Germain, and the first of them was already near at hand. *Les Plaisirs de l'Ile Enchantée* lasted from May 7 to May 13, 1664. It was organized in honour of the Queen mother and of the young Queen, Marie-Thérèse, though the gossips whispered that it was secretly dedicated to a lady who watched it from the crowd. Mademoiselle de la Vallière still held the affections of the King. "The entertainment," says Voltaire, "was for her alone." Thus is history written by the poets. Louis, though he might be morally reckless, was always socially discreet, and he was sufficiently a public man to realize that it was possible to indulge a private passion but fatal to parade it. The libel on the King calls for contradiction because it

295

has become, in effect, a libel upon Molière, who, in *La Princesse d'Elide*, urged the virtue and necessity of love:

> From fairest creatures we desire increase,
> That thereby beauty's rose might never die.

The insensibility of fair ladies to the tender passion was amiably chastised; it was, moreover, suggested that a great prince had need of a great passion to complete his education:

> Oui, cette passion, de toutes la plus belle,
> Traîne dans un esprit cent vertus après elle;
> Aux nobles actions elle pousse les cœurs,
> Et tous les grands héros ont senti ses ardeurs.

This has been read as a base flattery of the royal misdemeanours, but there is no proof or reason for taking it thus. Molière was composing an epithalamium in the fashion of the day, and the supposition that he was slyly complimenting the King upon his illicit ardours in the presence of the Queen is quite gratuitously offensive to everyone concerned.

Les Plaisirs de l'Ile Enchantée were long famous in the chronicles of a splendid reign. For six days at Versailles there was jousting, feasting and play-acting. The first three days passed as a fairy tale, in which legendary knights, mythical and allegorical figures, giants, dwarfs, the chariot of Apollo, Leviathan himself, to the music of Lulli, postured and declaimed. The honorary manager and librettist was the Duc de Saint Aignan, lyrically assisted by the courtly Benserade, the pioneer poet of the royal apotheosis, but the Sieur de Molière was his right and left hand. We behold with impatience the future author of *Le Festin de Pierre* and

Le Misanthrope, lavishly spending his wits upon this pageantry; but for Molière it meant success, a royal friend in need, and the promise of infinite scope for a man of the theatre, who, for all his genius, lived only for the rise and fall of the curtain upon a lighted stage. The stricken youth who twenty years before had been dunned by the proprietors of a tennis court and arrested at the suit of a tallow-chandler, had now at his disposal all the splendours of Versailles, and could look down from his high seat upon 4,000 candles of white wax burning in the alleys of the great park.

This was the mighty housewarming of Versailles. Nature, tamed into formality, and only then permitted to be gay, was the background. A small army of carpenters, engineers, builders and gardeners had in a few days transformed the park. At a crossing of wide alleys a large arena had been built, entered from its four approaches through lofty gates constructed of wood and gaily painted with the arms of the King. From one of the alleys rose tiers of seats to accommodate 200 persons. These were for the principal guests. The mere marquises and gentlemen must lean circlewise upon the wooden barrier. From the trees surrounding the arena hung huge chandeliers which would blaze with a thousand lights at nightfall.

The enchanted island lay at some distance, to be approached only on the third day. It was constructed in the great pond from which now, in the summer twilight, the frogs sing monotonously in a green desert. Here rose the palace of Alcina, the enchantress, sung by Ariosto, in which Roger and his knights lay ensorceled and awaiting their delivery by the magic ring of Angelica. They must meanwhile obey the commands of their mistress, who had brought her island to the land of France and bidden them amuse the royal ladies.

Punctually at six o'clock on the first day of the festival the enchanted knights rode into the arena. Most magnificent of them all was the Paladin, Roger. The trappings of his horse were of the colour of flame, blazing with gold and jewels. He was dressed as a Greek warrior, with a cuirass of silver, covered with cloth of gold sewn with diamonds. From his helmet streamed feathers of flame. A cry of respectful admiration went up from the crowd. For this was the King himself.

The Paladin had led his company hither to divert the ladies and gentlemen of France with an imitation of the Pythian games, for so the enchantress had decreed. The knights took up their position and awaited their divinity. Soon he appeared—Apollo, riding upon a lofty car. At his feet were the four ages of man, gold, silver, bronze and iron. The car was driven by Time, complete with scythe, wings and venerable beard. He drove four magnificent horses with the hand of an expert—for this was Millet the King's coachman. De Marigny wrote a few days later to an absent friend:

Time drove his car three or four times round the arena. He did not seem in the least embarrassed by his task; for, driving every day with skill and good fortune the most precious car in all the world, he knew very well that, if this one should be overturned, the accident would at the worst be fatal only to the theatre of Molière and that the theatre of the Hôtel de Bourgogne would be easily consoled.

"Fatal" was perhaps an exaggeration, but riding in the car was La Grange (Apollo), Mademoiselle de Molière (the

298

age of gold), Mademoiselle de Brie (the age of bronze), Hubert (the age of silver), and du Croisy (the age of iron). Compliments flew on winged verses from the car to the young Queen and the games began.

But the theatre of Molière had more to do that day. At nightfall the candles about the arena were lit. Lulli entered with his troop of musicians. Then came the four seasons: spring, on a Spanish horse, Mademoiselle du Parc in a green habit embroidered with silver and flowers; summer, on an elephant richly decked, the Sieur du Parc; autumn, on a camel, the Sieur de la Thorillière; winter, on a bear, the Sieur de Béjart; finally, Pan, the Sieur de Molière himself, upon a moving mountain of rocks and trees, and with him Mademoiselle Béjart as Diana, offering to the Queen and her ladies in poetic numbers, the fruits and meats of a splendid collation, served in the lists. There for the first day we will leave these splendid folk, feasting to music, diverted, as they dine, with a ballet of Hours, served by the spirits of Abundance, Joy, Cleanliness and Good Cheer.

What were the thoughts of Molière as from his lofty "machine" he addressed the young Queen in the ducal verse of the Duc de Saint Aignan? The candles are blazing between the great trees of the alley. To right and left are the musicians of Lulli, still his friend. Clustered about his feet are pages to serve the feast. Beside him in the car is Madeleine, for twenty years already his dearest supporter. At forty-seven she can still present Diana. In the foreground are his good comrades upon their strange steeds, an elephant, a camel and a bear, led by the lovely du Parc upon her Spanish horse. Lining the barrier leans the nobility of France, in helmets and plumes, as when they had jousted that

299

afternoon, assembled to see their sovereign feed. The brilliant candlelight wavers above them, for there is a strong wind that rustles in the big trees and teases their feathers. But it is as light as day in the sheltered lists where 200 masked attendants stand with torches of wax, and the eyes of Molière fall upon the King as he takes his seat at the table to the music of thirty-six violins, "all very well dressed." No gentleman may sit with him, so that it is of necessity a ladies' feast. Among them Molière must perceive Mademoiselle de la Vallière; and perhaps, as he does so, the unreality of this splendid ceremony, of the verses which his comrades have been called upon to recite, of the compliments which he has himself in all good faith composed, to be spoken in the play to-morrow, can hardly fail to intrude. This is comedy in the grand manner.

The impatience we feel at seeing genius reduced to menial offices would have greatly surprised the contemporaries of Molière. The son of Jean Poquelin was still *valet-tapissier du roi*—that, indeed, was his only claim to respectability. The gentlemen who waited upon the table below were of the highest families in France. Not that he would be paying much attention to the feast. He had other things to think about. There was the play to-morrow, finished in scrambling haste for the occasion. But even more important was that other matter, on which he had already spoken to the King. He had brought with him to Versailles the MS. of a comedy in three acts, entitled *Tartuffe ou l'Imposteur*, and he had asked leave to perform it as a sequel to *Les Plaisirs de l'Ile Enchantée*. The King had looked at the play and had found no offence in it. The news, however, had got about, and it seemed, rather surprisingly, that there might be trouble. The Archbishop of Paris had come mysteriously to Versailles and there had been a good deal of whispering in corners. The King, however, had promised to see the play and, if it pleased his most Christian Majesty, it should be good enough for the Archbishop—who, despite his office, was also a Christian. The King would see him through; and the royal licence for *Tartuffe* would be a just reward for all the trouble he had taken over these, be it secretly confessed, rather tedious proceedings.

Or was Molière, perhaps, thinking at that moment, not of *Tartuffe* and his debt to the King, which would always be loyally acknowledged, but of Armande his wife, who that afternoon, as the Age of Gold, had drawn all eyes, and was not, it was too evident, displeased by the attentions of the splendid gentlemen who lined the barrier below? This festival was the price he paid, and gladly paid, for the King's favour. Was it to be higher than he had imagined? For Armande this was an occasion to shine in a setting that became her well, and she did not seem to realize how easily slander might come the way of the wife of Molière. Yet, who could blame her upon such a night? She was still only twenty-three years old. He was himself already forty-four. What remained? All his masterpieces—as yet unwritten, though *Tartuffe,* in three Acts, had the makings of an excellent comedy. His life had been always dramatic and the stage was being set for a bigger scene. Meanwhile, he had been warned only a few months before that he was not physically as strong as he had been. Sickness, failure in marriage, and a bitter fight for the freedom and dignity of his art—coming events were casting already the shadows that so soon would lengthen about him.

Punctually at eight o'clock on the following evening, in a theatre constructed between palisades and covered with tapestry, the curtain went up upon *La Princesse d'Elide*. The play is of little consequence. Molière began it as a pastoral in verse, but had to finish it hastily as a comedy in prose, so that his muse, in the picturesque phrase of de Marigny, had come in a flutter to perform her duty with one shoe off and one shoe on. It may be read as a proof of the extraordinary versatility of Molière. He was writing in haste, and contrary to his genius, an heroic pastoral, but, even so, he leaves upon it the mark of the comedian. It is the kind of play in which Quinault was to rank as a master, but it is better than the best of Quinault. The theme of the play—a young prince amorous of a disdainful lady and winning her by an affected indifference—is gracefully handled and serves for an appropriate background to the six ballets for which Lulli supplied the music. Moron, fool to the Princess, played by Molière, is one of his happiest creations —trailing with him echoes of the immortal Falstaff.

> J'aime mieux qu'on dise:
> C'est ici qu'en fuyant, sans se faire prier,
> Moron sauva ses jours des fureurs d'un sanglier,
> Que si l'on y disoit: Voilà l'illustre place
> Où le brave Moron, d'une héroïque audace,
> Affrontant d'un sanglier l'impétueux effort,
> Par un coup de ses dents vit terminer son sort.

It is, moreover, singularly bracing to find Molière, amid the loud chorus of formal compliment, strike his inevitable note of independence. Moron, addressing Euryale, distrusts the anger and caprice of princes, who can, he affirms, be at times uncommonly troublesome and disconcerting. It should also

302

be noted, as Molière has been accused in this play of flattering his erotic master, that the warmest speeches are those of the Princess who scorns the poor weakness of love. If we are to read the play as an address to the King upon the tender passion there is no reason why its complacencies should be underlined and its censures ignored.

La Princesse d'Elide filled the second day. The third day passed upon the island itself where the Palace of Alcina, following upon a battle of giants and pigmies and compliments to the Queen mother, went up in a blaze of fireworks. Molière contributed a marine monster of prodigious size ridden by Mademoiselle du Parc, and a brace of whales ridden by Mademoiselle de Brie and Mademoiselle de Molière, concerning which the Court made merry after its fashion, some contending that the whales were from Biscay and others that they were small fish thrown into the King's pond and grown fat upon the royal bounty.

So ended *Les Plaisirs de l'Ile Enchantée* and Molière might be himself again. In the salon at Versailles performances were given of *Les Fâcheux* and *Le Mariage Forcé* on two separate evenings, while upon an evening between, the King "had performed a comedy, named *Tartuffe*, which the Sieur de Molière had made against the hypocrites." A single paragraph in the official account of the festival was devoted to this event, which reads like a protocol and suggests the hand of Louis. He, at any rate, realized before the festival had closed what a whirlwind his comedian was raising. Paris talked for a week of the pleasures of the enchanted island. *Tartuffe* was its theme for the next five years.

Molière left Versailles on May 13, 1666, but was called

303

to St. Germain-en-Laye in December of the same year. There he remained until February 19th of the year following. One royal festival is very like another. *Le Ballet des Muses* was composed of thirteen numbers. The general plan, the lyrics and compliments were by Benserade. The divinities of Parnassus, wishing to express their satisfaction that the King should be so solicitous for the arts, decided to make appearances in his favour. Among the actors were the King, the King's daughter, Madame and her ladies, and a rout of marquises. The King impersonated a shepherd, Cyrus the Great, and a ridiculous poet. Molière contributed three plays: *Mélicerte,* an heroic pastoral, "composed," according to the programme, "by the poet of all others who in this style can most justly be compared with the ancients"; a *Pastorale Comique* which was substituted for *Mélicerte* on the closing days of the festival; and *Le Sicilien ou l'Amour Peintre,* a comedy in one act.

Molière had been unable for lack of time to finish *La Princesse d'Elide* in verse; he was unable to finish *Mélicerte* at all, and the King had to be content with only two acts. They contain some agreeable verse; an amusing situation, which has since done considerable duty in the theatre, subject to a transposition of the sexes, in which a father imagines himself to be the subject of gallant addresses intended for his son; and a compliment to the King redeemed from a merely formal obedience by the concluding lines upon his courtiers:

> Ce sont autour de lui confusions plaisantes;
> Et l'on diroit d'un tas de mouches reluisantes
> Qui suivent en tous lieux un doux rayon de miel.

Flies about a honey-pot—Molière, even in compliment, could never wholly put off the comedian.

The reason of the substitution for *Mélicerte* of a comic pastoral, which survives only in fragments, during the last days of the festival, was probably domestic. Molière wrote *Mélicerte* partly for the young Baron, now his adopted son and the darling of the company. The boy was to play Myrtil, the young Adonis for whom at least two ladies, but happily not a third, languish in vain. The King's festivals were privately unfortunate for Molière. *Les Plaisirs de l'Ile Enchantée* had stimulated in Armande a taste for fine gallantry which was shortly to drive him to Auteuil, and *Le Ballet des Muses* was now to deprive him for a time of the young actor whose genius he was so carefully nursing. It was during the rehearsal, or one of the earlier performances of *Mélicerte*, that Armande, exasperated by the young interloper, administered to him the box on the ears which drove him temporarily from his benefactor. There is no occasion to dwell again upon the incident, but it serves to explain why Molière withdrew *Mélicerte* in full festival, and replaced it in *Le Ballet des Muses* with a comic pastoral which was little more than a scenario. *Mélicerte*, left disdainfully unfinished by its author, was completed after his death by Nicolas Guerin, the second husband of Armande, maritally more successful than Molière. His completion of the play was a tribute to the contemporary appeal of Molière's least considered work and a proof that the second husband of Armande was fatuous enough to imagine that he could follow his predecessor in the spirit as in the flesh.

L'Amour Sicilien, which figured also in the programme of *Le Ballet des Muses*, is one of the most charming and successful of the comedy-ballets of Molière. It has provoked comparisons with Shakespeare. The subject is ordinary

enough; a lover to gain access to his mistress offers to paint
her portrait.   It is a situation continually repeated in the
renaissance theatre, and possibly taken by Molière direct from
Calderon.   The prose in which the play is written is chec-
quered with hidden lines of verse, and more than one critic
has assumed that this is no accident.   Molière, it is suggested,
was experimenting with a style of writing midway between
verse and prose, a style which would correspond as nearly
as possible with that of the classical comedies written in ir-
regular metres, the *numeri innumeri* of Plautus.   He was to
carry this experiment further in *Amphitryon,* the later play
being a decided attempt to find a comic mean between his
voluble prose and the alexandrine, which, despite the variety
and elasticity with which he was able to employ it, must often
have hampered the eager freedom of his thought.   Such
experiments, needless to say, were to the contemporaries of
Molière abhorrent.   They heartily agreed, as most French-
men tend to agree, with the preceptor of M. Jourdain: *tout
ce qui n'est point prose est vers et tout ce qui n'est point vers
est prose.*   Here, however, was Molière writing something
which was neither one nor the other.   Ménage criticized the
prose of Molière in general and of *Le Sicilien* in particular
for just that poetic warmth and variety which commended it
in years to come to the romantics.   *Le Sicilien* has always
been a touchstone.   Victor Hugo was fond of reciting the
opening lines, written in prose, but declaimed by him as
verse:

> Il fait noir comme dans un four.
> Le Ciel s'est habillé ce soir en Scaramouche,
> Et je ne vois pas une étoile
> Qui montre le bout de son nez.

306

There is throughout the little play a sweet levity which was to reserve for it a special place in the affections of posterity. Even the cynical Voltaire acknowledged its charm, declaring it to be the only one-act play of Molière in which there was gallantry and grace. It stands somewhere between Horace, *molle atque facetum*, and de Musset. The comedian walks for a moment under the moon, coming very near to that wood near Athens which was only another name for Arden. Even so, he cannot altogether lose himself either in fancy or repose. The comedian looks through the poet and will suddenly deliver himself of a phrase which would suffice an Irishman of genius, three hundred years later, for a whole play: *Si j'aimois quelqu'un je n'aurois point de plus grand plaisir que de le voir aimé de tout le monde. Y a-t-il rien qui marque d'avantage la beauté du choix que l'on fait? Et n'est-ce pas pour s'applaudir, que ce que nous aimons soit trouvé fort aimable?* There, in one of the many nutshells to be cracked by his successors, is *How She Lied to Her Husband* by Mr. Bernard Shaw. Nor can the author of *Le Sicilien*, even under the moon, forget the author of *L'Ecole des Femmes*. The same moral attends the action of the play and again we are asked to believe that a woman guarded is a woman won.

Molière left St. Germain on February 20, 1665. He received from the King for his services 6,000 *livres* in addition to the pension of 6,000 *livres* which he had received since 1665. *Le Sicilien* was given to the town on June 10th, when it was produced with the *Attila* of Corneille. In the interval Molière had again been seriously ill and was now permanently on a milk diet. Robinet celebrates his return to the stage with *Le Sicilien:*

> Et lui tout rajeuni du lait
> S'y remontre enfin à nos yeux
> Plus que jamais facetieux;

and a few days later, writing to Madame on June 19, 1667, this faithful echo of the fashion describes it as a masterpiece:

> Je vis à mon aise et très bien,
> Dimanche, *le Sicilien*
> C'est un chef-d'œuvre, je vous jure.

The play was performed twenty times during the life of its author, seventy-four times during the subsequent years of the reign of Louis XIV, and ninety-eight times under Louis XV.

George Dandin, a *comédie-ballet* produced before the King, the Queen, the Dauphin, Monsieur and Madame at Versailles in July, 1668, must as a matter of form be included among the royal diversions. The comedy, dismissed by the Court chroniclers in a few lines, will be discussed in a later chapter, and only the occasion will be noted here.

France victoriously at peace, flushed with the conquest of Franche Comté and proud in possession of Flanders, was celebrating her achievements. The details may be read in the *Relation de la Fête de Versailles* of Félibien, usually printed among the works of Molière, and in the programme, considerably more interesting, which was distributed to the royal guests. The programme was, perhaps, dictated by Molière himself. It contains a reference which only he, or a most sedulous imitator of his pleasantry, could have written concerning the nicety of French audiences for whom a ribbon out of place, a syllable misdelivered, a wig awry or a clumsy gesture spoils the effect of the finest scene. These observations were offered in friendly excuse for the musicians who were called upon to sing and act with the players, and might find themselves not at home upon the stage. They give the writer an opportunity—which, if he were Molière, was afterwards ill rewarded—to pay a generous tribute to Lulli who, in music and dance, "shines with invention." The programme deals only with the play. It embalms the incidental verses, which linked the comedy, with the pastoral exercises and scenic wonders which for Félibien and the chroniclers— perhaps for the King himself—were more truly marvellous and diverting. Félibien tells of great alleys transformed for feasting; classical charades; costly and ingenious displays of flowers and fruits; improvised architecture and statuary. The trees of the forest were trimmed and plaited. Supper was served in a vast pentagonal arbour, approached by five alleys each of which held its appropriate surprises. One of the tables represented a mountain within whose caverns were disclosed an infinity of cold meats. Others—but why should the mouth of posterity be made to water? Molière was waiting to ring up his curtain in a theatre whose walls were a living foliage without and rich tapestries within. Thirty-two chandeliers of crystal, each containing ten candles of white wax hung from the roof. Near the door, between Ionic columns, stood Victory and Peace. There was much here to be admired before the play began, and it is all minutely described. Molière had for his stage an entire garden complete with Satyrs, busts, fountains, terraces and a navigable waterway. Félibien briefly commends the play— it is worth, to him, some fifteen lines in a thousand; tells at length of the shepherds and their songs; overflows in admiration of Lulli and his hundred voices and then returns to the real business of the day. The King went to supper in a gigantic arbour that beggared all previous descriptions. Its decorations included an artificial mountain with Pegasus atop, from between whose feet fell a cascade which formed, after much intermediate playfulness, four rivers, frequent with falls and losing themselves in small brooks upon lawns of moss. The nine muses were naturally present with Apollo and his lyre. The evening ended with dancing, illuminations, promenades and other diversions, which included a display of fireworks so impressive that some of the guests flung themselves upon the ground in terror. Molière, meanwhile, was perfecting himself in the arts of the showman to which he would be required to devote an increasing amount of his time. This festival, in which *George Dandin* was lost to view rather than displayed, was an allegoric foreshadowing of what in another twenty years would happen to the comedy of France, eclipsed by the opera-ballets of the tolerable Quinault and his intolerable apes.

In the year following *La Fête de Versailles*, the King called Molière to Chambord where for over a month he was retained to organize another of the royal festivals. There, in collaboration with Lulli, he produced, on October 6, 1669, the *comédie-ballet* of *Monsieur de Pourceaugnac*. This was the play, a farce in form and substance, of which Voltaire generously wrote that in all the farces of Molière there were "scenes upon the level of high comedy." Notably there is a passage in which the unfortunate Monsieur de Pourceaugnac falls into the hands of the medical faculty. Even more interesting, because more rare in the plays of Molière, is the fact that his hero is from the provinces. Monsieur de

310

Pourceaugnac is unkindly treated. He is deceived by a heart-less rascal, delivered up to the doctors without mercy, saddled with offences which he has never committed, and claimed simultaneously for a husband by a brace of baggages. The laugh is pushed against him and against Limoges, the city of his birth, almost beyond decent limits. Hence the legend, begun by Grimarest and ingeniously developed by his successors, that the author was paying off a personal score. Grimarest affirms that a gentleman from Limoges, quarrelling with the actors, made an offensive and ridiculous scene upon the stage of the Palais Royal; others that Molière, during his provincial wanderings, was hooted by the people of that city. Robinet, in a letter to Madame of November 23, 1669, reports, but only on hearsay and with considerable reserve, that the original of Monsieur de Pourceaugnac was in Paris, and swearing to be most horribly revenged. These stories merely show how easily a legend grows. The gentleman from the country, falling among sharpers of the town, was an immemorial comic theme, and in France the good city of Limoges did duty, like Bœotia in Hellas, as a cradle of bumpkins. It was a Limousine who in Rabelais murdered his mother-tongue and aspired to be taken for a gentleman of Paris. In the late seventeenth century protests were frequently raised against what was evidently a well-rooted tradition. La Fontaine in 1663, in a letter home to his wife, tells her, as in surprise, that the people of Limoges are "as refined and as polite as any in France," and, writing in praise of the Bishop's table, warns her not to believe that my lord has any reason to be ashamed of his diocese "as is commonly imagined in the provinces." La Fontaine, at the same time, finds a certain justification for the popular belief: *Beaucoup d'ail et peu de jasmin* is his malicious summary.

Thus, Molière, taking a Limousine for his hero, was merely accepting a literary tradition in dealing with a classic subject. There are obvious echoes from Plautus. The Neapolitan Sbrigani, leading the intrigue, is the traditional valet of infinite resource and sagacity, and Nerine is the near cousin of a dozen intriguing maids who live in farce merely to forward the action and utter their minds out of season. Harsh things have been said of the play which is, nevertheless, gay and ingenious. Molière is accused of sacrificing his fine wit to the gross tastes of the multitude. But how shall we censure the multitude? It loved Monsieur de Pourceaugnac, as shown by the fact that the play was performed forty-nine times during the life of its author. The piece, however, was written for the King, and Robinet announced on behalf of the Court: *C'est un vrai plaisir du roi*. Tradition confirms the announcement. Lulli who wrote the music for the ballets was an excellent mimic actor. In the original performance he played an apothecary and sang the exhortation against melancholy. It is recorded by Cizeron Rival in his memoirs that after the death of Molière Lulli, in order to recover the favour of the King, which he had temporarily lost, himself played the part of Pourceaugnac and that he went so far on that occasion in his efforts to avoid the apothecaries in pursuit of him with their syringes as to jump from the stage into the orchestra, alighting upon a clavecin which fell to pieces under the shock. The King must laugh and Lulli was pardoned. If a King laugh, how shall we blame the multitude?

For the biographer of Molière the interest of the play

312

lies pregnantly elsewhere. Monsieur de Pourceaugnac falls
into the hands of the doctors. Molière, playing the part,
was himself an invalid. An enemy was within a few months
to publish a satire in which *Elomire Hypocondre* was to be
painted with haggard eyes, a ravaged frame, a face on which
sickness had set its seal and a habit of settled melancholy.
It is precisely thus that one of the doctors in the play describes his patient: *Vous n'avez qu'à considerer . . . cette
tristesse . . . ces yeux rouges et hagards . . . cette habi-
tude du corps.* There is, again, no limit to the detachment
of Molière, the comedian. He was mocking his physical
condition to bright music and fantastic pantomime.

On February 4, 1670, during a festival at St. Germain,
the royal person was for the last time hazarded upon the
stage in the comedy-ballet of *Les Amants Magnifiques.*
The subject of the play was suggested by the King himself,
who in a ballet of tritons and marine deities appeared first
as Neptune and subsequently as Apollo. Molière discreetly
indicated the royal participation in a short preface. The
play itself points us forward to the polite and subtle art of
Marivaux. The Princess of the story, decorously playing
with the passion of the humble Sostrate, is a foretaste of the
marivaudage which became one of the most fertile developments of French social comedy. Molière also added in this
play to his gallery of impostors. Astrology is now his theme.

> Charlatans, faiseurs d'horoscope,
> Quittez les cours des princes de l'Europe,

La Fontaine had recently urged in one of his fables. Less
than four years previously astrologers had shared with the
doctors the sickroom of Pope Alexander VII, and a member

of the fraternity had, with the *accoucheurs,* been in at the birth of the King himself. Morin, who then held the chair of mathematics at the Collège de France, a passionate devotee of the art, was consulted by Richelieu and Mazarin; and Fénélon, a little later, described the astrologers as a "pest in every court." Molière's astrologer is a rogue, but the observations made in the course of the play upon a profession which still ranked with the respectable sciences are moderate and reasonable. Once again Molière rejects one of the most imposing superstitions of his time in the light of commonsense.

Molière, who in *Mélicerte* had played Moron, the fool, played in *Les Amants Magnifiques* Clitidas, the jester. Clitidas was comic chorus and general manager of the intrigue; he was free to say what he pleased, but used his liberty with discretion. There is an attractive personal note in the character. *Vous vous émancipez trop,* he tells himself, *et vous prenez de certaines libertés qui vous joueront un mauvais tour, je vous en avertis . . . Taisez-vous, si vous êtes sage.* The advice was excellent, but, fortunately for posterity, Clitidas-Molière seldom remembered it.

Molière, working for the King, had been gradually perfecting the *comédie-ballet,* to which he had first pointed the way in *Les Fâcheux.* Already he had produced a gem in that kind in *Le Sicilien.* He was now to produce within this hybrid and artificial form a play which not only met the ephemeral occasion but was accepted by posterity as a masterpiece. On October 3, 1670, he was summoned to Chambord, as in the previous year, to amuse the Court in the intervals of the chase. The King had again suggested a subject. The story goes that an envoy from the Grand Turk

314

upon a recent visit to Paris had failed to be impressed by
the royal splendour and had even been heard to say that his
master's horse was more richly caparisoned than the King
of France. Turks were, at any rate, in fashion. The King
demanded a *turquerie;* Molière accepted the commission;
the result was *Le Bourgeois Gentilhomme.*

It has been maintained that the King, with his *turquerie,*
spoiled a great comedy of character already planned. Such
an assumption is hardly compatible with the normal progress
and habit of Molière. Admittedly *Le Bourgeois Gentilhomme* is a comedy with a farcical appendix. The author
was so well aware of this that he carefully arranged that
Monsieur Jourdain, ere he was transformed from a comic
figure into a hero of burlesque, should have dined sufficiently
well to fit him for the occasion. *J'étois en humeur de dire
de jolies choses, et jamais je ne m'étois senti tant d'esprit.*
The symptoms are clear. Even so, Molière still felt that
the *turquerie* exceeded the limits of the comedy he was writing. *Avec lui on peut hazarder toute chose,* says the chief
conspirator of M. Jourdain. This is almost an apology.
There is not, however, any good reason to believe that the
King, demanding a *turquerie,* spoiled a comic masterpiece.
Rather he provoked the creation of a masterpiece by asking
for an occasional entertainment. Molière had perforce been
compelled to work to a formula so often that he was now
hardly conscious of constraint, and he was already sufficiently
a master of craft to blend farce, interlude and comic characterization in a coherent work of art, pleasing at the same
time his simplest and his most exacting auditors. He was
now able to construct the hybrid musical-dramatic-choreo-
graphic entertainment which had become the fashion of the

hour without serious detriment to his comedy. We may deplore the *turquerie* which delighted Versailles in 1670. But would M. Jourdain have reached the fantastical stature which has rendered him immortal if Molière had not found it necessary to make him capable of anything? Monsieur Jourdain, at bottom, is a shrewd and honest fellow—upright, simple and no weak lover of the sex. He has all the virtues of an excellent burgess. But in the grip of his major passion he is prepared to make love to a fine lady, lend his money upon no security, and marry his daughter to the son of the Grand Turk. The burlesque at the end of the play is the climax of an extravagance that grows inevitably from one scene to another.

Grimarest tells us that no play of Molière ever had a worse reception; that the King was at first taciturn; that the courtiers tore it to tatters; that Molière hid himself from sheer mortification for five days in his chamber; and that the piece was only saved by His Majesty, who, breaking silence at last declared it, on a second performance, to be excellent. Grimarest would appear to be more than usually careless in his facts. The play was performed four times at Chambord before the Court in eight days, and its subsequent success in the town at the Palais Royal can still be read in the receipts, which at the third performance amounted to 1,634 *livres*. There were twenty-eight public performances in 1671. The spectacle was given in full at the Palais Royal—ballets, music, interludes and *turquerie*. Grimarest mentions an anonymous Duke who was scandalized by the play, and possibly there is some ground for the tradition that it was misliked by the nobility. Molière, satirizing in Monsieur Jourdain the burgess with a passion for high living and gallant accomplishment, indirectly damages even more severely the fine gentlemen who exploit him. Monsieur Jourdain is absurd—even pitiful; but the Comte Dorante is odious.

This Monsieur Jourdain is something of a paradox. Snobbery is always mocked but never to be rooted out. It obsesses the moralist and secretly or openly stimulates ninety per cent of the normal desires and ambitions of men and women. Vast industries are founded upon it. Half of what is said or written in the civilized world is devoted to it. Inevitably Molière must deal with this universal theme, and we might reasonably have expected that he would do so with a far from gentle hand. Yet, strange to relate, this Monsieur Jourdain is fundamentally likeable. His passion for self-improvement, his innocent delight in the acquisition of new knowledge, his respect for the accomplishments he so earnestly desires to obtain, his fanatical strength of purpose—all these things are ridiculous only in their excess and thoroughly estimable in themselves. The profound humanity of Molière is here most strikingly exhibited. Where the superficial satirist would have extended least mercy we find him oddly charitable. Why, he seems to ask, this loud and universal derision of the man who would be above his station? The young scholar who had abandoned a respectable office for a socially disreputable profession could ask the question quite disinterestedly. *His* withers were unwrung, and he had no need to save his face by laughing too unkindly at a vice from which he was conspicuously immune. M. Jourdain is proof illustrious that a snob may yet be a good fellow, and it would be a poor look-out for society if this were not so. He inspires affection despite his ignoble failing. There

is such zest, such innocence, in the pleasure he takes in his
fine clothes, his lacqueys, his scraps of knowledge eagerly
acquired and, no sooner learned, than they must be shared
with all the world. The lesson in orthography endears him
to every heart. *Ah, les belles choses, les belles choses,* he
exclaims continually. His faith in education and his delight
in his ability at last to give a name to things are oddly engaging. Almost it is the miracle of the dumb man who at
last can speak. How unexpectedly he touches us with his
sudden sense of time lost in ignorance and of youth neglected: *Ah, mon père et ma mère que je vous veux de mal!*
Madame Jourdain is commonsense in person, and yet, when
Monsieur Jourdain stubbornly maintains against her his
faith in the humanities, who is not rather with than against
him? Note, also, that Monsieur Jourdain, apart from the
bee in his bonnet, is not a fool. He has even a shrewd eye
upon his own excesses. Had the tailor's apprentice addressed
him as Highness he would have given him all that was in
his purse, but the man stops short at Monseigneur. *Il a
bien fait,* says Monsieur Jourdain, *je lui allois tout donner.*
There you have a man who has a momentary glimpse of his
own comedy and such men are rare. His comments upon
the proposals of his master in philosophy are not those of a
simpleton, still less of a disagreeable simpleton, and his delicious answer to the question whether he understands Latin
is the honest expression of what most of us, if truth were
told, would wish to say on such occasions. He does not wish
to confess his ignorance, but neither does he desire to lose
any possible information. *Vous savez le latin, sans doute?*
says the philosopher. *Oui,* replies Monsieur Jourdain, *mais
faites comme si je ne le savois,*

318

Fundamentally the aspirations of Monsieur Jourdain are not ignoble. For him the condition of a gentleman is worthy of emulation; he desires something better than the virtues of a plain citizen. But while the virtues of the citizen are admirably portrayed in the family of Monsieur Jourdain, those of the nobility, which he so much admires, are sadly to seek. Dorante is a parasite and a sharper, who abuses the trust and hospitality of Monsieur Jourdain, and the Marquise Dorimène is partly his dupe and partly his accomplice. The folly of Monsieur Jourdain, indeed, consists in undervaluing the virtues of his own station, and finding virtues in a station above him which in the particular instance are illusory. *Le Bourgeois Gentilhomme,* far from being a satire upon the middle classes, is rather a satire upon the aristocracy. Where will you find in literature a prouder definition of the middle state than in the speech of Cléonte? Are you a gentleman? asks M. Jourdain. The fate of the young man depends upon his answer, but the answer, when it comes, embodies all the pride of a class which was later to change the face of the modern world:

Monsieur, la plupart des gens sur cette question n'hésitent pas beaucoup; on tranche le mot aisément. Ce nom ne fait aucun scrupule à prendre, et l'usage aujourd'hui semble en autoriser le vol. Pour moi, je vous l'avoue, j'ai les sentiments sur cette matière un peu plus délicats. . . . Je suis né de parents, sans doute, qui ont tenu des charges honorables; je me suis acquis dans les armes l'honneur de six ans de services, et je me trouve assez de bien pour tenir dans le monde un rang assez passable; mais, avec tout cela, je ne veux point me donner un nom où d'autres, en ma place, croiroient pouvoir prétendre, et je vous dirai franchement que je ne suis point gentilhomme.

This was a hero who had no wish to be a gentleman—a sentiment which smacked already of Beaumarchais and the revolution. Had the King, preoccupied with other matters, failed to be visibly amused at the first performance of *Le Bourgeois Gentilhomme*, the nobility might well have expressed some distaste for a play in which the honours so clearly lay with the plain citizens of Paris. The King, however, not only smiled but openly complimented the author, and thereafter the aristocracy must applaud its own undoing. The alliance between the King and his comedian upon a question of status was only natural. There were, perhaps, at Chambord only two persons who were above all considerations of rank—Louis Dieudonné and the Sieur de Molière.

Le Bourgeois Gentilhomme, like all the plays of Molière, is full of reminiscences. Aristophanes, Rotrou and Cervantes can be more or less clearly identified. Of the tide of gossip that has ebbed and flowed about it for the last three hundred years the most authentic is that which recognizes in Lucile, the daughter of Monsieur Jourdain, a portrait of Armande and the silliest is an allegation that Molière in his *turquerie* intended to mock by implication the Christian mysteries.

Three months later the King again had need of Molière. Tradition maliciously asserts that the *tragédie-ballet* of *Psyché* was imposed upon him in order that a fine set of properties representing Hell should not continue to lie idle in the King's repository. The assertion has a symbolic significance. Great art under the great King was frequently born of small occasions; and in the present instance we are asked to believe that four men of genius were put to the task of finding employment for an otherwise useless piece

320

of royal furniture. Molière planned the diversion and wrote some part of it; Lulli composed the music; Quinault contributed the lyrics; and a yet more illustrious partner, the great Corneille, invited to assist, ended by writing the bulk of it.

The preface to the first edition of the play is attributed to Molière:

M. Molière a dressé le plan de la pièce, et réglé la disposition . . . Le carnaval approchoit, et les ordres pressants du roi, qui se vouloit donner ce magnifique divertissement plusieurs fois avant le carême, l'ont mis dans la nécessité de souffrir un peu de secours. Ainsi, il n'y a que le prologue, le premier acte, la première scène du second, et la première du troisième dont les vers soient de lui. M. Corneille a employé une quinzaine au reste; et, par ce moyen, Sa Majesté s'est trouvée servie dans le temps qu'elle l'avoit ordonnée.

Note the phrase: *la nécessité de souffrir un peu de secours* —a friendly irony so much more eloquent than the usual flatteries. Note also the dry conclusion: *Sa Majesté s'est trouvée servie dans le temps qu'elle l'avoit ordonnée.* That, after all, was the main thing. This famous collaboration remains one of the freaks of literature. Molière and Corneille, profoundly dissimilar, remain themselves and yet chime with an astonishing grace and precision. This happy event is to the credit of both parties. Molière, bitterly disappointed in his own ambitions as a tragic author, acknowledges his master in that kind and the veteran of *Nicomède* and *Attila,* who had for years beheld his rival increasing in public and royal favour, responds with dignity and grace to the invitation of the younger man. Each, moreover, gives of his best. Molière, though writing out of his vein, is witty and felicitous in the free rhymed verse in which he was beginning to find a more appropriate and natural medium than the classic alexandrine. Corneille, amazingly supple for a veteran of sixty summers, writes easily and elegantly within the limits assigned him. This successful collaboration of the two authors is especially gratifying when we remember that Molière had good reason to suspect Corneille of supporting his enemies in the comic war.

But *Psyché*, which was a proof that great men are sometimes great, was equally a proof that small men are always small. The production was a triumph for two of the players. Baron, recovered from his fit of sulks, had returned to his benefactor and won the first conspicuous triumph of a long life by playing Love to the *Psyché* of Mademoiselle de Molière. The combination was, as we have seen, irresistible to the scandalmongers. Here was a charming youth publicly proclaiming a lively passion for the wife of his benefactor. The chance was too good to lose, and the author of *La Fameuse Comédienne* subsequently perpetuated a slander for which there was no historic evidence whatever. To present Baron as the lover of Armande is an extravagant libel upon all three people concerned. It supposes in Baron a monstrous ingratitude; in Armande an abnormal indecency; in Molière a blind infatuation—all this on the strength of the fact that Baron played Love in a pantomime. But scandal was not yet exhausted. The words of Love addressed to Armande were uttered by Baron, but written by Corneille, and not even his white hairs could save him. Armande received two additional lovers in one day—a boy of eighteen and an old gentleman of sixty-seven. It is

322

only fair to add that not even the gossips credit the old gentleman with any success in his hypothetical passion. He pined, if he pined, in vain. For the biographer of Molière that is sufficient.

Psyché has a more practical interest than as a basis for malicious fables. It shows us Molière at the height of his career as a manager of spectacle. The public of the town, infected by the Court, were beginning to ask for an equal elaboration and magnificence in their entertainments, and Molière was at this time reconstructing his theatre with a view to satisfying these demands. From March 18th to April 15th at a cost of 1,989 *livres,* the entire stage of the Palais Royal was rebuilt to accommodate the "machines" and an adequate orchestra. *Psyché* was the first play produced under the new conditions. The production cost 4,359 *livres,* and included all the effects which had drawn the applause of the nobility. Robinet, writing to Monsieur in July, 1671, made an inventory of these pleasures:

> Illec, ainsi qu'aux Tuileries,
> Il a les mêmes ornements,
> Même éclat, mêmes agréments;
> Les divers changements de scène, . . .
> Les mers, les jardins, les déserts,
> Les palais, les Cieux, les Enfers,
> Les mêmes Dieux, même Déesses . . .
>   On y voit aussi tous les vols,
>   Les aériens caracols,
>   Les machines et les entrées,
>   Qui furent là tant admirées.

Molière, as producer, lived through three epochs in the subsidiary arts of the stage. Hardy, Rotrou and the prede-

323

cessors of Corneille, with Corneille himself, inherited the stagecraft of the mediæval mystery. The typical mystery had many mansions. The stage was open and would show simultaneously the house of the Virgin at Nazareth, the palace of Pilate, the hill of Calvary, Paradise and the Entrance into Hell. The dramas of Hardy and his contemporaries were constructed for a multiple stage of this pattern. Hardy in *La Belle Egyptienne* showed simultaneously a palace, a prison, a temple and a sea-coast. A multiple scene in one of the plays of Durval disclosed a room which could be opened and closed, with a superb bed in it; an ancient fortress; a cave in which a small boat could be moored; a cemetery with three tombs and a seat; a window through which could be seen the shop of a painter; a garden or wood with an orchard and windmill. Another of his plays exhibited, at once and altogether, hell, two heavens, the mountain of Sisyphus, the garden of the Hesperides, a ship at sea, the palace of Circe, and the Styx with Charon and his boat. This multiple system, in which the stage was regarded as alternately an extension of one of several "sets" simultaneously exposed, remained in force during the first thirty or forty years of the seventeenth century. The action of the play might move easily and without a break from scene to scene. The system encouraged variety and bustle; the construction was go-as-you-please; the audience was ready to step without a pause from heaven to hell, from a palace to a ship on the ocean, from a street with its shops to a cemetery with its tombs.

There still exists at the Bibliothèque Nationale in Paris a list of plays performed at the Hôtel de Bourgogne, compiled by one Mahelot, a sceneshifter, with brief notes as to the sets and properties required. The list dates from about the year 1633 and the most famous of the entries refers to the *Illusion Comique* of Corneille. The scene is described as follows: In the middle of the stage, one saw a palace well appointed; on the side of the stage, a cave for a magician; above the cave, rose a mountain; on the other side of the stage, there was a park. The properties of this scene include a moon which rises and sets, a nightingale which sings, an enchanted mirror, a wand for the magician and a magic hat. The plays which Molière saw as a boy and helped to produce as a young man were upon this pattern.

By the middle of the century, however, the method of production had entirely changed, and the change was to affect the principles of dramatic construction, not only in France but in all the countries which in the seventeenth century came under French influence—including our own. The unities became suddenly sacred, including the unity of place, which condemned the characters in a play to remain for all dramatic purposes in the same spot from the rise to the fall of the curtain. This momentous revolution in stage-craft, though it was primarily due to a natural bent of the French genius in favour of coherence and simplicity, was greatly assisted by an accidental fashion. The theatre no sooner became of interest to the nobility than they perceived that it was uncomfortable and inconvenient. The galleries were awkwardly placed in a house ill-lighted and built without reference to its acoustics. Moreover, there were not always seats to be had in the gallery, and when *Le Cid* was produced in 1637 the fashionable crowd was so large and clamorous that seats were placed provisionally upon the

325

stage. A precedent was thus established and within a few years no man of fashion would consent to sit anywhere else. Tallemant de Réaux writes in 1657: "A practice began to intrude about this time which was disastrously inconvenient to the play. The sides of the stage were wholly occupied by young people sitting upon cane chairs. They would not go into the pit. The boxes were expensive and must be retained well in advance, whereas for a crown or half a *louis* one might sit upon the stage itself; this spoiled everything and one inconsiderate spectator might throw the whole performance into disorder." Molière himself frequently referred to the insolence of the gentlemen upon the stage and their lack of consideration for the rest of the audience. They entered late, called lustily for chairs, came to be observed, loudly greeted their more distinguished friends, commented frequently upon the play and took upon themselves to lead in censure or applause. Chappuzeau, who admired everything that related to the fashionable world, wrote in his history of the theatre: "The actors often find it difficult to take up an appropriate position upon the stage, the wings being so crowded with persons of quality, *who cannot fail to add to its adornment.*" The custom was finally so inconsiderately abused that the actors in self-defence had to rail off a minimum space for their manœuvres, and the climax came when women of fashion also claimed a privilege which had for long been enjoyed by the men alone. Le Sage describes the production of *Judith* by the Abbé Boyer, rival of Racine and master of the lachrymose. Two hundred ladies sat upon benches on the stage, holding their handkerchiefs upon their knees, and there was a scene in the fourth Act in which they so unanimously mourned that it became known as the scene of the handkerchiefs. The ladies wept; the pit was merry to behold them; and the good Abbé, overwhelmed with compliments, shaking his fist playfully at his illustrious rival, exclaimed in his Gascon accent: *Je leur eng donnerai bieng d'autres! Je tiengs le public, a préseng que je sais song gout. Ah! Mossieur de Racine!*

The dramatic art of France was thus obliged to conform itself to a practice which reduced the stage to a small open space with a backcloth, in which the actors could do little more than deliver their lines. Marmontel, writing in the *Mercure*, in 1759, insisted that the classic drama of France must be judged almost entirely in the light of this practice. No real action or movement was possible to actors speaking between two serried rows of spectators. The stage, he points out, had become a "parlour to which all the players must be brought." The immobility of the classic drama of France and its sole reliance upon the uttered word were due to the fact that in the days of its supremacy no effect could be obtained from scenery or movement.

Only a fashion more distinguished could drive out one that had become a test of social degree. Formal unity was imposed upon Racine, whose plays were written at the height of this disastrous fashion. But Louis XIV had always loved a spectacle; the ballet was his darling, and Molière owed his success at Court to the skill with which he contrived to satisfy the royal craving and at the same time amuse the King with comic characters and situations. A habit which respect for the comic and tragic muses was powerless to reform yielded to respect for the royal inclination and a desire to be in a fashion more novel, and, therefore, more deserving of allegiance, than the last. The chattering mar-

quises and weeping women must now give way to flying
Mercuries and Apollo in his car. There was a swift reaction
against the immobile classicism of the sixties and Molière,
reconstructing his theatre for the production of *Psyché* in
1671, was going with the times.

All three periods in this development left their impression upon the stagecraft of Molière, and he uses all three
conventions quite indifferently. The mediæval system persisted in so late a play as *Le Médecin Malgré Lui* where
three distinct sets were presented simultaneously: in the
centre of the stage was the forest where the woodcutter was
discovered at work; to one side was the house of Geronte,
and to the other side was the house of M. Robert. The
stage belonged indifferently to the three scenes as the
action required. Modern editors and producers have felt
it necessary to correct this arrangement and to change the
sets—a proceeding which is both unhistorical and unnecessary. A frequent practice of Molière was to place his scene
in a street or square round which were grouped the houses
of the various characters necessary to the action. To get
his man upon the stage it was only necessary to knock at
the appropriate door. This was a survival of the mediæval
system of mansions.

The craft of Molière was, however, essentially classic in
his greater comedies of the middle period. Scenery and
movement count for little in his plays. All is in the dialogue, gesture and business of the actor; and the author is
sometimes, as we saw in *L'Ecole des Femmes*, indifferent
to propriety of place. Arnolphe lectures Agnes in the public
street, though he is at pains to keep her secluded from the
world. Such anomalies, which strike the modern realist,

328

were of small account in a theatre where the actor was in
effect standing in a narrow rectangle with an audience literally at his elbow. In the later plays, however, written after
the spectator has been driven from the stage, an increasing
attention is paid to scenic fitness, and there is allowance for
scenic effects. The legend that *Psyché* was written to make
use of a set in the royal repository thus represents an essential truth. Molière, yielding to the fashion, was henceforth obliged to compete with the Hôtel de Bourgogne,
and especially with the Marais, in giving the public the
pièce à machines which the Court had brought into favour. *Le Festin de Pierre* was technically a *pièce à
machines,* and its scenery, complete with tomb and trap-
door, was advertised and acclaimed as a production in the
latest style.

There were many who deplored this further revolution.
Molière died before its excesses had substituted for the classic
drama of Racine the dreary mythologies of French opera
and the childish pantomimes before which the King in his
later years would sit for hours contemplating an apotheosis
of his royal person. The public grew weary of the new
fashion long before the Court was permitted to do so. La
Fontaine, writing eighteen years after the death of Molière,
is our witness. He describes how, at first, the public was
enchanted and how, very soon, it was bored and inclined to
make merry over the small accidents that so often happened
on these occasions:

> Quand j'entends le sifflet, je ne trouve jamais
> Le changement si prompt que je me le promets.
> Souvent au plus beau char le contre-poids résiste;
> Un Dieu pend à la corde et crie au machiniste;

329

Un reste de forêt demeure dans la mer,
Ou la moitié du ciel au milieu de l'enfer.

We may be sure that, if Molière had lived even a few years longer, he would have mocked the excesses of the new fashion as roundly as he had satirized its predecessor. But alas! he lived only to see the marquises driven from the stage and never beheld the desert which his successors made of the wider spaces and finer opportunities thus placed at their disposal.

There were during the life of Molière eighty-two performances of *Psyché*, earning a total of 77,119 *livres*. As author and actor Molière had won his laurels. This was a tribute to the producer. He had written only a small portion of the play, and he himself played the minor part, when he played at all, of Zephyre. For the production, however, he was entirely responsible, and the contemporary records are unanimous in celebrating the success of the play as a spectacle. Molière, actor and author of genius, was also a great showman.

Meanwhile, on November 21, 1671, Monsieur had married the Princess Palatine, and the occasion must be suitably honoured. Molière was called to St. Germain on November 27th, where he remained till December 27th. The King suggested a selection from the ballets that had found most favour on previous occasions, and asked Molière to provide a sketch to hold them together. *La Comtesse d'Escarbagnas*, the result of this invitation, was produced at St. Germain on December 2, 1671, and was repeated four times during the festival. Molière thought lightly of his Countess, for he did not publish the play. The public, however, was more appreciative. The comedy was played 254

330

times under Louis XIV; 271 times under Louis XV; 36 times between 1774 and 1789, and 19 times under the Revolution.

The Countess of the play is from Angoulême, a provincial lady who affects the manners and graces of the fashionable dames of Paris and the piece is perhaps adapted from one of the provincial farces. It is merry and shrewd. It obviously cost its author little pains in the writing, but it earned the commendation of Boileau and La Harpe. The characters include a Monsieur le Conseiller Tibaudier and a Monsieur Harpin, *le Receveur des Tailles,* who, if Molière had lived longer, would have led him further afield and who pointed a way for his successors in the comic field. In *Princesse d'Elide* Molière looked forward to Marivaux, in *Le Sicilien* to de Musset, in *Le Bourgeois Gentilhomme* to Beaumarchais; in *La Comtesse d'Escarbagnas* to the modern realist comedy of provincial and middle class life. M. Tibaudier is the prototype of the family solicitor of the modern stage, precise but human at the red ripe o' the heart, while M. Harpin is the first of the city men, hard, insolent, possessive, uncouth, without respect of persons, who were to come crowding upon the stages of a later generation. Le Sage undoubtedly found in him a model for his *Turcaret,* the first of the big stage financiers, the hero of the play in which he scourged the speculators and middlemen.

Molière was to write one other *comédie-ballet,* but it was a work so intimately his own and so poignant in its associations that it must be discussed in a more appropriate place. There are limits to the respect which is due to princes, and we may reasonably refuse to include *Le Malade Imaginaire* among the King's diversions.

XVII

Tartuffe

WHEN Molière came to Versailles in May, 1664, to assist in organizing *Les Plaisirs de l'Ile Enchantée,* bringing with him the first version of a comedy entitled *Tartuffe ou l'Imposteur,* the subject and tenor of the play were already known and a powerful opposition to its public presentation was being rapidly organized. Five years previously the author had challenged the literary exquisites. He was challenging now a more formidable sect and his ultimate victory was to cost him five long years of continuous effort and provoke a rancour which followed him beyond the grave.

The exquisites of the Hôtel de Rambouillet had come together as a protest against the hooligan pleasures of the Fronde. Their code of social and amative behaviour had begun as a salutary corrective of an illiterate and brutal society. Parallel with this æsthetic movement there had been a moral and religious reaction against the cynicism and impiety of a generation which had taken for its device the royal conviction that a kingdom was worth a mass. In May, 1627, a devout gentleman, Henri de Levis, Duc de Vendatour and peer of France, had founded a pious association to promote the Catholic religion. It was to be composed of persons living in society, devoted to good works, meeting constantly

332

for their own edification and ready to defend the interests of the church against impiety, heresy and indifference. The association, known as the Compagnie du Saint Sacrement, became a secret religious freemasonry, with an elaborate system of rules, ready to intervene unobtrusively in any question which affected the prestige of sacred subjects and institutions. Every care was taken to preserve the secrecy of its activities, but now and then the zeal of its members revealed the hidden hand and exposed it to the jealousy and suspicion of the regular authorities. The bishops, parliament and Mazarin himself, aware of its existence, but unable to suppress it or even discover exactly who were its members, conducted an occasional enquiry and issued an occasional decree against unlawful assemblies and congregations; but these measures merely had the effect of driving the pious conspirators farther underground. The aims of the association were both social and religious. They interested themselves in prisoners and the sick, organized works of charity, founded foreign missions, conducted discreet campaigns against the licence and debauchery of the time. Among its more notable achievements was the official suppression of the duel by royal edict, which Louis, at his coronation in 1654, swore to enforce. The Queen mother was privy to its activities and the Prince de Conti, reformed, was one of its most active members.

The historian of this curious masonic association, the Comte d'Argenson, tells of a secret meeting, held on April 17, 1664, at which the members of the group who were present solemnly undertook to procure the suppression of the "wicked comedy of *Tartuffe*." Each of them promised to speak on the subject to such of his friends as had any in-

333

fluence at Court. Observe that Molière had not yet gone to Versailles and that there is no record of his comedy having yet been anywhere read or discussed. The pious fraternity was well posted. It had advance information and was acting upon it with admirable promptitude.

Molière went to Versailles on April 30th, where he remained until May 22nd. He read his play to the King, who admired it, spoke well of it and had it performed, as an item of the festival then in progress, on May 12th. But the cabal had meantime been hard at work and had won to their cause no less a person than the Archbishop of Paris, formerly the King's tutor, M. de Péréfixe. The archbishop appears to have been both voluble and disconcerting; and the King would seem to have taken Molière into his confidence, urging that it would be unwise to provoke the devotees who belonged to a species that was implacable. Privately admiring the play, he felt himself bound officially to prohibit its performance in public, and he soon found himself, to his embarrassment, the subject of some quaint and misguided eulogies for the step which had been forced upon him. The *Gazette* of May 21st praised him for prohibiting a "piece entitled *The Hypocrite*, which His Majesty, enlightened in all things, has judged to be injurious to religion and likely to exercise a very harmful influence." Simple souls among the minor clergy went considerably further. Among them was a certain Pierre Roullé, vicar of St. Barthélemy, who published in August, 1664, a tribute to the Most Glorious King in all the World, celebrating among other things, his piety. As an "heroic act worthy of his greatness of heart and his respect for God and the church," the vicar relates what he conceives to be the true history of *Tartuffe*.

334

"A man, or rather a demon in flesh and habited as a man, the most notably impious creature and libertine who ever lived throughout the centuries, has had the impiety and abomination to bring forth from his devilish mind a play ready to be rendered public, and has had this play performed on the stage, to the derision of the whole church. . . . He deserves for this sacrilegious and impious act the severest exemplary and public punishment; he should be burned at the stake as a foretaste of the fires of hell in expiation of a crime which is a treason against heaven and calculated to ruin the Catholic religion by censuring and counterfeiting its most religious and holy practice, which is the conduct and direction of souls and families by means of wise guides and pious conductors. His Majesty, having severely reproached him, though moved by a strong indignation, has, in the exercise of his ordinary clemency, in which he imitates the essential gentleness of God . . . pardoned the devilish hardihood of this creature in order to give him time to devote the rest of his life to a public and solemn penitence; but, to keep this licentious and wicked composition from public sight and view, His Majesty has ordered the author, on pain of death, to suppress, tear up, stifle and burn all that he has set down, and to do nothing in the future so infamous and so unworthy, or to produce anything to the light of day so insulting to God and so outrageous to the church, religion, and the holy sacraments."

The worthy vicar wrote in simplicity rather than in malice and he must have been sorely puzzled and distressed by the royal reprimand which was undoubtedly conveyed to him. In a subsequent pamphlet he informs the world that, though he may in the past have erred in ignorance and affection,

335

in none of his works has he ever written anything except in love and respect for the royal house or with any desire to injure anyone in the world. In other words the reference to a demon in flesh and blood was inspired, as is usual with such expressions, by a pure love of humanity.

The public attitude of the King was carefully defined in the official protocol to the festival at Versailles:

This evening His Majesty had a comedy entitled *Tartuffe* performed which the Sieur de Molière had written against the hypocrites. Although His Majesty found it extremely diverting, he felt that there was so great a resemblance between those whom a sincere devotion put in the way of heaven and those whom a vain ostentation of good works did not prevent from achieving bad ones, that in his extreme care for matters pertaining to religion he could not permit this resemblance between vice and virtue, which might be mistaken one for the other; and although he did not doubt the good intentions of the author, he prohibited the public performance of the play and deprived himself of this pleasure in order that it should not be abused by others who might be less capable of a just discrimination.

The passage has an official ring. It justifies the prohibition but apologizes for the act.

For Molière the prohibition was financially and morally a disaster. He had been relying on *Tartuffe* for his season at the Palais Royal, having nothing in hand but *La Princesse d'Elide*, which needed time and money for its production, and *La Thébaïde*, the tragedy of a young author, Racine by name, whose work so far had been appreciated by no one save Molière himself. The moral damage was even worse. Molière was henceforth a suspect. He had every reason, apart from the indignation of affronted genius and a man un-

336

justly accused, to do his utmost to obtain a public performance. Only the King could help him now—if he dared; and Loret records how Molière, after the festival, went back and forth between Paris and Versailles in vain efforts to obtain a reprieve for his play. Night and day, says the gazetteer, the critics abused it, the Court admired it and the author pleaded its cause.

The King was steadfast in his original policy. He did not feel it possible to sanction a public performance, but privately took every possible occasion to show his esteem for the author and to dissociate himself as pointedly as possible from the zealots. In July an admirable opportunity occurred. Cardinal Chigi came, as papal legate, to Fontainebleau and Molière was summoned to assist in his entertainment. A scene of high comedy was staged by arrangement between the King and his master of the revels, His Eminence being induced to hear a reading of the play in the presence of all the prelates of his suite. The Italian church dignatories have seldom found it difficult to reconcile a generous humanism with their more austere professions and the play, which the King must consider unfit to be seen by the citizens of Paris, was received at Fontainebleau with edification by the envoy of Christ's vicar upon earth.

Meanwhile Molière took pen in hand. His first *placet* to the King would seem to have been written in July or August, 1664. First he was careful to interpret, firmly and tactfully, the attitude of his royal master. The vicar of St. Barthélemy had just published his conviction that the author of *Tartuffe* was a demon in human flesh and congratulated the King on his decision to suppress, destroy, stifle and burn the offending work. Molière not only corrected the vicar in his facts, but quoted the pamphlet as a proof how necessary it was for him to be justified by a public performance of his play. Until he could let the public see how harmless it was and satisfy itself once for all that he was satirizing a false and not a genuine devotion, he would necessarily be exposed to insult and persecution. This was an obvious plea. More skilful were his references to the King himself. His Majesty, he suggested, had allowed himself to be manœuvred into a false position. He had approved the play, and the violent attacks upon it were therefore implicitly a criticism of the royal judgment. All this was conveyed with apparent innocence by a mere recital of the facts, which included a lively and telling reference to the reading of the play in the presence of Cardinal Chigi. He intimated in conclusion that Kings as enlightened as His Majesty had no need to be instructed in the desires of their subjects and that he would accordingly await with respect what it might please His Majesty to decide.

Molière waited for over four years. The King was prepared to do anything but authorize a public production. He rebuked the vicar of St. Barthélemy, conspicuously favoured the author, and took no exception to private readings or performances. Ambitious hosts of the period enticed the quality to their functions with hints that Molière might perhaps be induced to read them the reprobated work after supper. Boileau remembered thirty years later how, when *Tartuffe* was forbidden fruit, everyone tried to secure Molière to give a reading of the play. Among those who heard the comedy read in this way were Ménage, Chapelain, the Abbé de Marolles and Ninon de l'Enclos. Of the private performances, subsequent to the original production

338

at Versailles, the most conspicuous was one given in July
in the house of Monsieur, the official protector of the troop.
This was an event of real importance in the controversy.
The opposition had from the first endeavoured to enlist upon
their side the Queen mother. They enquired among themselves, in terms that were meant to be overheard, how
Molière could for shame abuse the patience of a great lady
who could not fail to desire the suppression of a work so
shocking to a pious mind. Molière was accordingly determined that the whole royal family should be conspicuously
implicated and, at the private performance of the play
given at the house of his official protector, he secured the
presence of the King, the Queen and the Queen mother.
Further private performances were given at Raincy, the
country home of the Princess Palatine, where, in November,
1664, and November, 1665, by order of the Prince de
Condé, a new version of the play in five acts was presented.

At the height of the controversy, Molière committed a
further act of audacious provocation, plainly showing that
he had no intention of retreating or compromising with the
moralists, but intended to attack them quite definitely on their
own ground. In February, 1665, he produced *Le Festin de
Pierre*. The further uproar it created will be noted in due
course. Suffice it for the moment that in the fifth act Molière
challenged directly the moralists who were trying to suppress
Tartuffe. The cynicism and impiety of Don Juan culmi-
nate in a famous scene in which he pretends to see the error
of his ways, promises amendment and asks his father to find
him a director, to guide him in the paths of truth. This is
his final infamy—to add hypocrisy to his other vices, and he
shamelessly confesses that his conduct is dictated by pure

policy and the examples whereby he is surrounded. He has resorted to a useful stratagem, a necessary grimace, to shelter himself from the inconveniences to which a more candid villainy exposes him. This was adding fuel to the fire and, lest there should be any doubt of the persons to whom the passage was addressed, Don Juan explicitly referred to the cabals of the moralists and the secret censorship which they were presuming to exercise.

Meanwhile the King was clearly determined that his interdict should not be misunderstood. Molière, as we have seen, was called to Versailles in October, 1664, and in June, 1665. In June, 1665, he was facing the further clamour which had been aroused in the previous February by the production of *Le Festin de Pierre*, and the King, though in the public interest he still prohibited *Tartuffe* and urged amendments to *Le Festin de Pierre*, proclaimed his private conviction by asking his brother to surrender to him the protectorship of the company. Henceforth the players of Molière are the *Troupe du Roi*. The King chose precisely this difficult moment for a public manifestation of his increasing regard for an author whose work was anathema.

Boileau, of high reputation and a familiar at the Court, ranged himself openly on the side of his friend. In 1665 he wrote a spirited attack in verse upon those who felt it necessary to censure those who dared to laugh:

> Leur cœur, qui se connait et qui fuit la lumière,
>   S'il se moque de Dieu, craint Tartuffe et Molière.

Meanwhile *Tartuffe* had already begun to arouse interest abroad. The librarian of the Queen Christina of Sweden wrote from Rome in February, 1666, to the French Secretary

340

of State for Foreign Affairs asking whether he could obtain
for Her Majesty a copy of the play so that it might be performed for her pleasure. The French Minister replied on
February 26th that he could not possibly comply with the request. The play, he said, was still in the private possession
of Molière, who dared not let it out of his hands until he
had himself been allowed to present it. Had Molière released his play for performance elsewhere it would have
fallen into the common stock, and his ownership would thereby have been destroyed. The Minister informed his correspondent that Molière expected to make for his company at
least 20,000 crowns from the play if he should ever get permission to produce it, adding that the King obviously could
not urge Molière to release the play for production abroad
after having prohibited the production in Paris.

From December 1, 1666, to February 25, 1667, Molière
spent nearly three months in the special service of the King
at St. Germain. He took with him to the palace the new
version of the play in five acts and the King must hear
continually of *Tartuffe*. His Majesty was first entreated by
Madame explicitly to authorize a private performance of the
completed work. He was next begged to withdraw his prohibition altogether. Molière had skilfully prepared the
ground. The King had justified his prohibition on the
ground that a comedy which aimed at hypocrisy might easily
be construed as an attack upon a genuine piety. Molière in
the new version of his play carefully met this objection. The
first two Acts were in fact mainly devoted to ensuring that
there should be no mistake, and the author's desire to distinguish between a true and a false devotion was repeatedly
emphasized.

341

He had made even more striking concessions. The name of *Tartuffe* had already an ill sound in pious ears. It was passing into the language. Molière, as an act of conciliation, changed the title of his play, which for this occasion was announced as *L'Imposteur*. Tartuffe, a name provoking to the pious, became Panulphe, who, instead of wearing the semi-clerical garb of his predecessor, appeared as a man of the world with hat, wig, sword and fine laces. Molière had, however, in several places softened his text; and removed everything "which might give the shadow of a pretext to the celebrated originals of the portrait" (Second Placet).

The King was moved. Madame, a cordial champion of the play, was urging him to license it publicly, and the moment was propitious. The King had just been lectured by an archbishop upon his mistress, and the Jansenists, who might, if one chose, be identified as objects of the satire, were in his bad books. He was shortly to start upon a campaign in Flanders but, before leaving Paris he quietly authorized Molière to produce the new version of the play at the Palais Royal.

The battle seemed at last to be won, but the sequel only showed how formidable and bitter was the opposition.

The play was performed on Friday, August 5, 1667. The public fought for admission, and the receipts amounted to 1,890 *livres*. Molière announced a further performance for the following Sunday. On Saturday morning, however, came a messenger from M. de Lamoignan, Président du Parlement, who ordinarily fulfilled the office of Mr. Speaker, and was acting as Home Secretary in the absence of the King: the play, so ran the order, was not again to be performed. Guards were placed at the doors of the theatre, and the posters were torn down. Posterity has learned from the secret records of the Compagnie du Saint-Sacrement that Monsieur de Lamoignan was a member of that mysterious fraternity. The devotees, in the King's absence, were prepared to go any lengths. They even dared to prohibit the play which the King had authorized.

Molière complained first to Madame, who sent one of her gentlemen to remonstrate with Monsieur de Lamoignan. Mr. Speaker very firmly replied that he knew his business, but would be delighted to wait upon her—as, indeed, he did some three or four days later; but Madame by that time was so appalled by the storm she had raised that she did not even dare to mention the subject. Meanwhile, Molière went himself to see Monsieur de Lamoignan, asking Boileau to present him. Monsieur de Lamoignan was polite. He overflowed in compliments to Molière, but refused bluntly to authorize a performance. "I am persuaded," he said, "that the play is a fine and instructive piece of work, but it is not the duty of comedians to instruct people in matters concerning Christian morality and religion; the theatre is no place for preaching the gospel." Molière for the first and last recorded time in his life was struck speechless—presumably with indignation—and found himself dismissed before he had recovered sufficient control of himself to make a reply. Mr. Speaker, moreover, was not prepared to argue the matter. "Sir," he said, when at last Molière began to struggle for utterance, "you will perceive that it is nearly twelve o'clock. I fear I shall be late for mass if we stay to discuss this matter further."

Molière realized that the King was his only remedy. The play was prohibited on Saturday. On Monday two members

343

of his company, one of them his editor and first biographer, La Grange, left Paris for the royal camp. They carried with them a letter which was subsequently published with the play as the second *placet:*

Molière excuses himself for coming to importune a great King in the midst of his glorious conquests. Against an abuse of power, however, there is no remedy but an appeal to the source of all authority. The author summarizes the concessions which he has made in the presentation of his comedy. His enemies, however, remain implacable, and he can only wait with respect the decision which His Majesty may be pleased to take in the matter. He concludes with a celebrated statement: *mais il est très assuré, Sire, qu'il ne faut plus que je songe à faire des comédies, si les Tartuffes ont l'avantage.* He hopes that the King will protect him against the rage of his adversaries, and that he may be able to divert His Majesty on his return from victory, thus affording him innocent pleasure after his noble achievements. He has only one ambition—*faire rire le monarque qui fait trembler toute l'Europe.*

Molière in this letter claimed the royal support with the candour of expression and the familiar respect which characterize all his addresses to the King and his envoys were well received. The King promised to look into the matter on his return and intimated that the play, subject to a further examination, would be produced. The journey, La Grange woefully concludes, cost the company a thousand pounds.

The King, however, did not return to Paris until September 7th, and the enemies of *Tartuffe* had by that time manœuvred into the front line a champion who could not be ignored, no less a person than the Archbishop of Paris.

344

On August 11th, there issued from the archiepiscopal palace a decree prohibiting anyone within his diocese from representing, reading or hearing the comedy of *Tartuffe* either in public or in private, under any name or pretext whatever, on pain of excommunication.

Here was a pretty pickle! The King himself, a diocesan of Paris, had repeatedly been guilty of the very offences which were thus publicly stigmatized. The Archbishop had, in fact, retrospectively excommunicated a monarch who ruled by divine right. The King was in the same case as his comedian, and he seems to have been seriously worried, for he apparently took the opinion of canonical counsel on the validity of the archiepiscopal decree, finally deciding that the production of the play was for the moment impossible.

Molière was profoundly discouraged. *Tartuffe* had become for him a symbol of the freedom and dignity of his profession, and it looked as though he were fighting a lost cause. For the first time in twenty-eight years his theatre remained closed for seven weeks: *il est très assuré, Sire, qu'il ne faut plus que je songe à faire des comédies, si les Tartuffes ont l'avantage.* Molière was to all appearances driven from the stage, and Paris no longer laughed. But it takes a good deal to extinguish the candles of a born actor, and the King was determined not to lose his favourite comedian. The Palais Royal was re-opened on September 25th, and Loret on October 4th wrote, for a gazetteer, in terms of reckless jubilation:

> Molière, reprenant courage,
> Malgré la bourrasque et l'orage,
> Sur la scène se fait revoir.
> Au nom des dieux, qu'on l'aille voir!

345

The hand of the King is visible in this event, for a few days later, on November 6th, we find Molière with his company at Versailles, and, though the ban rested on *Tartuffe* all through the following year, the King was prodigal of his esteem. Molière was called to Versailles in April and July, and to St. Germain-en-Laye in November, while in September the Prince de Condé witnessed a private performance of the proscribed comedy at Chantilly. The heavens omitted to fall and the King, then busily composing his quarrels with the Vatican, seized the occasion, when pious minds were bent upon peace with honour, to authorize at last the public performance for which Molière had struggled continuously for over four years. The royal licence was issued on February 5, 1669. The play, in a third version, was produced on February 9 and was played for twenty-eight consecutive performances.

Its success with the public was immediate and sensational. Robinet, in a letter written on the day of the first performance, gives a lively description of the people fighting for admission, a struggle in which the desire to see the celebrated Monsieur Tartuffe exposed many members of the crowd to a risk of death by suffocation. There were twenty further performances in 1669; eighteen performances in 1670; nine performances in 1671, and five performances in 1672. The first edition of the play, published at the expense of the author on March 23rd, was exhausted in a few days at a crown a volume. It contained, in addition to the text of the play, the first *placet* and second *placet* to the King, to which allusion has already been made, together with a third *placet* written on the day of the "great resurrection of *Tartuffe*, living again by royal favour." The book of the play included also a preface in which the author briefly reviewed the controversy.

It is a fighting preface. Molière had no intention of creeping to his victory. He presents his comedy to the public as a work that has for a long while been unjustly persecuted and defamed. The persons at whom it is aimed, he says, have shown abundantly that they are the most powerful people in France. The fine gentlemen, the exquisites, the doctors, the fashionable poets—he has taken them all for a theme, and they have made haste to laugh with the rest of the world. The hypocrites alone have clamoured and protested. He has in vain submitted his play to the criticism of his friends and the public; in vain amended it and obtained for it the approval of the King and some of the most distinguished judges in the land. The zealots have not yielded an inch. Their voices are still raised against the play and its author. Piously they continue to insult and damn him out of pure charity. To those who have inspired the opposition to his comedy he owes no apology or justification. But they have unfortunately attracted to their cause men of sincere piety and honest convictions. To them the author addresses himself.

Much of the argument that follows is special pleading. In the battle of the exquisites Molière had urged that he was satirizing not the true but the false exquisites. This, as we saw, was simple courtesy to an enemy who had acknowledged himself defeated. In his dispute with the actors, critics and dramatists, who had attacked his social comedies upon literary and technical grounds, he had replied that the end of comedy was to please, and that his plays were justified by their success. In the present controversy he was called to account

347

on moral grounds, and he realized that in the circumstances his answer must be pertinent. It would literally have been as much as his life, and certainly the life of his comedy, was worth, to take the high æsthetic line; to declare that the dramatist was less concerned with morality than with the expression and delineation of character and to claim the right as an imaginative artist to portray life as he saw it without continual reference to orthodox ways of feeling and thinking. Such a defence would have ruined his cause, and not even the King could have saved him from a wilful martyrdom. The zealots, when they raised the moral issue, obliged Molière to figure as a moralist. The real significance of the controversy over *Tartuffe* lies in the extent to which Molière, not only in his preface, which is a small matter, but, as we shall see, in the successive versions of the play itself, was driven to present what was originally a pure comedy of character, written to amuse the public, as a comedy with a definite moral aim. No one could have been more astonished than Molière, to whom the moral implications of his comedy were not at the outset of obvious importance, by the pious uproar which it immediately aroused. The intervention of an Archbishop within a few days of its first reading at Versailles was a bolt from the blue. The adroit tactician, who had successively defeated the exquisites, quizzed the marquises and beaten the critics in their own line of business, realized at once, however, that, having been challenged on the moral issue, he must meet his enemies upon that issue or be driven from the field. He had, in policy, no choice in the matter, and his policy was in the sequel justified. In writing the first version of *Tartuffe* he had not been primarily interested in the moral issue; but, once his attention had been called to that issue, he could claim with justice that, if the public chose to apply the moral test, his comedy triumphantly supported it. He had every right to plead that he was morally unassailable and he had no choice but to emphasize the moral issue in his subsequent versions of the play.

To that issue the preface is wholly devoted. Molière emphasizes his distinction between a false and a genuine piety, then passes almost at once to the argument of Mr. Speaker. It has, he says, been declared that the theatre is no place for the discussion of moral and religious questions. On the contrary, urges Molière, the theatre had its origin in religion, and it is still the principal end of comedy to correct the vices of men, who are more likely to be laughed than scolded out of their sins. Men may desire to be wicked, but no one desires to be ridiculous. Either, he argues, you must approve of *Tartuffe*, which chastises a vice which is of all vices the most dangerous to society, or you must condemn comedies altogether—and that, he infers, is really the intention of the zealots. It is the theatre itself which is in danger. Never was so intense a campaign ever conducted against an institution whose utility and excellence was admitted by all the wise men of antiquity and many fathers of the church.

In conclusion he deals firmly with the extreme position of the saints who are at least logical and worthy of all respect. He is aware that there are men whose delicacy cannot endure any form of comedy, and who declare that the most deserving plays are the most dangerous, since they are the most likely to touch the souls of men. He maintains, however, that this high degree of insensibility represents a remote condition of virtue to which few can successfully aspire. He doubts

349

whether so austere a perfection is really compatible with ordinary human nature, and inquires whether it is not better to aim at correcting and softening the passions of men than at suppressing them altogether. He confesses that there are places which it may be better to frequent than the theatre, and admits that, if one is to censure everything which does not directly concern God and the salvation of man, comedy must needs be included. If, however, occasional intervals may be permitted in the practice of piety, and if it be granted that men have need of diversion, he contends that no more innocent form of amusement can be found than the performance of comedies.

The preface is an admirable document; but it must be read in connection with the play and with other pleadings of its author. Molière would never have claimed to reform the world if his enemies had not charged him with corrupting the world. He wrote *Tartuffe*, as he had written *Le Cocu Imaginaire*, to amuse the public, and as he had written *L'Ecole des Femmes* to express the life of his time in the light of his own ideas and temperament. The point is of cardinal importance to an understanding of Molière and the whole practice of dramatic art and it is, therefore, all the more fortunate that, with the exercise of a little ingenuity, we are able in this instance, to compare the original comic intention of Molière, in writing the first version of his play, with the subsequent moral intention which was thrust upon him in writing the later versions. The two versions were quite clearly poles asunder in effect and in intention. The preface to the final version of the play could not possibly have stood as a preface to the version of 1664.

There exists a whole literature on the revisions of *Tartuffe*

350

and their relation to one another. We have for our guidance only the final text, some contemporary references to the early versions, and the statements of Molière himself concerning the concessions or *adoucissements* which he made to avoid unnecessary offence. A discussion in detail of the evidence and a close analytical examination of the text of the play would fill a volume as long again as the present biography. Only the results can here be presented. Every critic has his own views on the subject, and the reconstruction here submitted, like most of its predecessors, is personal conjecture.

The first two Acts in the final version of the play—the only version we possess—are devoted to emphasizing the credulity of Organ—his blind belief in the impostor—and to exhibiting the lamentable effects of that credulity upon his household. In Act III Tartuffe makes love to the wife of his protector, is detected and denounced, but successfully outfaces his accuser. In Act IV Tartuffe falls into the trap laid for him by his enemies. Organ is undeceived, but it is now too late. He has surrendered everything to the impostor, and is to be driven from his house. In Act V, Organ is saved by a sensational intervention of the King's justice.

The version performed at Versailles in 1664 was in three Acts. It was received by the King and his Court as a diversion. It was a play written, like its predecessors, *pour faire rire les honnêtes gens* and the principal comic character, a figure of fun from start to finish, was Organ, enacted by Molière himself. The theme of the play, the source of its laughter, the excess which Molière according to his habit derided, was, in fact, less the hypocrisy of Tartuffe than the credulity of Organ. There is every reason to conclude that

351

there was in this first version of the play no unmasking of Tartuffe, no sinister triumph of the impostor, and certainly no intervention of the King as *deus ex machina*. All these incidents are a later development imposed upon the author when the play, which had begun as a diverting comedy, became, as a result of the controversy, a serious morality. The climax of the original version was, in effect, the position which obtains at the end of the third Act of the final version. Tartuffe has made his attempt upon the virtue of Elmire. He is denounced. Organ refuses to believe in his guilt, and the play closes with the infatuated husband insisting that Tartuffe shall continue to frequent the company of his wife and promising to endow the impostor with all his worldly goods. The first version of the play would thus close in a shout of laughter at the expense of Organ, and not, like the final version, in a salutary exhibition of the royal justice. The earlier conclusion is admittedly cynical. The impostor triumphs, and we laugh at his dupe, on whom no sympathy is wasted. If you seek a moral to such a play, it can only be found in the inference that hypocrisy pays. Such an end, however—drily comic, a dispassionate presentation of human weakness as a subject for salutary laughter—was more in the spirit of Molière than the dramatic thesis in five Acts on the ethics of imposture which the play ultimately became. Such an end, moreover, was in keeping with his other plays of the same date and spirit. The comic characters of Molière invariably remain comic to the end. He leaves them in the pillory. There is no mitigation for their excesses or any compunction for their misfortunes. So should it be with Organ.

Tartuffe, in three Acts, concluding with the triumph of

352

Seconde Journée.

Theatre fait dans la mesme, allée, sur lequel la Comedie, et le Ballet
de la Princesse d'Elide furent representez.

SCENE FROM THE "PRINCESSE D'ELIDE"

After the original engraving by Israel Silvestre.

the impostor and the besotted persistence of Organ in his delusion is in the normal tradition.

But the unexpected happened. Molière, intent upon his characters, seeking to divert his audience with the comic presentation of an impostor and his dupe, suddenly found himself charged with impious disrespect of religion. He had depicted a villain who had all the semblances of a devotee. The bewilderment of the artist, suddenly confronted with the moral test, looks occasionally through his defence. How, he exclaims, am I to present a hypocrite on the stage without making him perform outwardly the gestures of an honest man? He realized at once, however, that it was no use arguing the matter on the basis of dramatic creation or propriety. The moral gauntlet had been flung and he must take it up, especially as the King felt bound to prohibit the play on the ground that it might offend or mislead those who did not realize that a false and not a true devotion was indicated. Molière could not ignore a charge which had thus been to some extent officially endorsed. He was forced to fight upon the moral issue and, first of all, the play itself must be revised. A comic satire in three Acts became a comic morality in five. The distinction between a true and a false devotion was in the new version emphasized repeatedly in passages superfluous to the action or to a prompt understanding of the play, and quite obviously grafted upon the previous text. There shall be no mistake about it this time:

> Et comme je ne vois nul genre de héros
> Qui soient plus à priser que les parfaits dévots,
> Aucune chose au monde et plus noble et plus belle
> Que la sainte ferveur d'un veritable zèle,
> Aussi ne vois-je rien qui soit plus odieux
> Que le dehors plâtré d'un zèle spécieux. . . .

353

It scarcely needs the author's confession in his first *placet* to the King that he has removed everything which might risk a confusion between good and evil to realize that such lines as these were not an original product of his comic inspiration. The objection that the comedy confounded a true with a false devotion could obviously not have been urged against the version of the play which has come down to us. Molière fully met that count in the indictment, and his more intelligent critics, like Monsieur de Lamoignan, Président du Parlement, were driven to take up quite a different position. Charged with writing an immoral play, the author had retorted by presenting a revised version and showing that it was triumphantly and consistently moral. Mr. Speaker's retort was inconsistent with the previous charge, but it was crushing. The play may be moral, he said, but the theatre has no right to meddle with morality. The opposition of Mr. Speaker to the comedy of 1667 was a protest against any interference of the theatre with spiritual concerns; and Molière, in his final preface, was thus driven still further into the ethical wilderness. Not only does he claim defiantly that the theatre may indirectly be a school of virtue, he even insists that the "use of comedy is to correct the vices of men." Such a plea would never have occurred to the author of the first version of *Tartuffe*, but it is highly relevant to the play as subsequently revised.

The second version of the play in five Acts was performed privately at Raincy in November, 1664. Molière had lost no time in the work of revision. The addition of the fourth and fifth Acts must necessarily have entailed a recasting of the Acts already in existence, but the general disposition of the material can hardly have been seriously disturbed. To a first version in three Acts, whose principal comic theme was the credulity of Organ, ending in a triumphant exhibition of the virtuosity of Tartuffe and the abject folly of his dupe, were appended two additional Acts in which the impostor, after exhibiting his villainy in darker colours and attaining a stature in wickedness that almost removed him from the sphere of comedy, was finally brought to justice. The comedy of Organ has sunk into the background, and the play ends after the fashion of an old morality with an unexpected intervention of Olympian power in the person of the King's messenger. Moreover, lest the moral of this edifying conclusion should be overlooked, it is emphasized in advance by ethical interpolations in the first three Acts, distinguishing between pure devotion and false hypocrisy, and by a careful preparation of the audience to recognize in Tartuffe the villain of the piece long before he appears on the stage. No sensitive reader can fail to be struck in the first three Acts by an obvious contrast between the passages in which the author is distinguishing between saints and hypocrites and preparing us to feel for Tartuffe an edifying moral reprobation and the original vital staff of the comedy. The work of revision has been well done. There are no protruding inconsistencies and the joints are well covered. But for a reader with his sense of comedy in tune the interpolations will be heard in a different key. The author is revising in moral indignation scenes which he originally wrote in a spirit of smiling detachment. Note also that the concrete illustrations given of Tartuffe's piety, obviously original to the first version of the play, are purely comic—such as his outburst of indignation at finding a lady's handkerchief between the pages of the *Fleur des Saints* or his remorse for having, when in prayer, caught a flea and killed it in anger—whereas the moral arguments and distinctions, subsequently interpolated, are severely didactic. The difference of tone between the interpolated passages and the original text are, indeed, as marked as the difference between the beginning and end of the comedy. In the fourth Act, written when the moral issue had become predominant, Tartuffe almost ceases to be a comic figure. He pushes his villainy to so dark an extreme that either we laugh unseasonably—and that is not the sort of laughter for which Molière normally asks—or we are appalled. Tartuffe was to be a comic character and not a terrifying monster of iniquity. He only became a monster when Molière, driven from the true purpose of his comedy, was provoked into writing a morality with Tartuffe in the part of the devil.

The fifth Act, with its intervention of the King, is a mere postscript to the controversy. Molière, saved by the King, takes the King for his *deus ex machina*. Louis XIV is celebrated as an enemy of fraud whom no impostor can deceive, who sees things as they are and distributes justice with an even hand. The incident is an excrescence upon the comedy —a politic proclamation of the King's favour and support— and it completely transforms the original design.

Herein lies the fascination of *Tartuffe*. It is a study in the procedure of genius. The comedy is not only in itself a masterpiece, it enables the critic to catch the author in the process of its composition, adapting his original plan to fit intentions which were subsequently forced upon him by external considerations. Tartuffe himself is transformed from a purely comic character, designed for our diversion, into a sinister and implacable figure, who finally arouses, even as

356

we laugh, an indignation and abhorrence that carries us beyond the limits of comic detachment. The play must be read in the light of the controversy which it aroused. We may then discern from internal evidence how the original comedy in three Acts was necessarily modified to meet a wholly different purpose and occasion.

Many of the problems surrounding *Tartuffe* which have exercised posterity have been dealt with by implication. Most of them, indeed, are as hypothetical as the questions which vexed the mediæval schoolmen: how many angels can be accommodated on the point of a needle. Was Molière, in satirizing the devout, aiming at the Jesuits or the Jansenists? Was his play a revenge upon the clerical profession for their attitude to his own? Was *Tartuffe* a defence of liberty and pleasure menaced by the puritans or by the mystics? Was it part of a systematic exposition of a philosophy of nature? Was it an attack upon Christianity masquerading as an attack upon hypocrisy or an attack upon hypocrisy which was falsely construed as an attack upon Christianity? Had Molière a secret knowledge of the Compagnie du Saint-Sacrement and was the play aimed directly at the masonic brotherhood which in the event became his most active opponent? All that can usefully be said of these questions is that they need never have been asked. It is true that the play is packed with hidden references to the social and religious views, practices and habits of thought of the time, but these references were natural and inevitable in a man who read and observed everything that came his way. To tear them from their context, wrest from them a doctrine and employ them to prove that Molière was attacking the Jesuits, or undermining the faith of Christendom, or pursuing either a personal or professional

357

vendetta, is utterly to mistake the man and his method.
Molière was driven to take up the moral issue, but he wrote
his comedy in the first instance with a disinterestedness as
complete as that in which he wrote *George Dandin* or *Le
Bourgeois Gentilhomme.* *Tartuffe* is equally the product
of a comic imagination nourished upon reading and observation. Equally, it perpetuates and enlivens a theme that had
been used by his predecessors, bringing a traditional figure of
play and story into touch with contemporary life. Tartuffe is
not the exponent of a new and original heresy. He is the
heir of impostors already famous in comedy whom the curious hunters after coincidence or plagiary will find in the
works of Scarron, Lope de Vega and Régnier.

To what extent the fear and fury of the devout enemies
of *Tartuffe* was justified is another question. Molière wrote
in innocence, but innocence may in its effects be more destructive than deliberate malice. The pious seventeenth century
reader, confronted with the first version of *Tartuffe,* might
with justice feel a little uneasy. Molière alludes in his
preface to those whose sensibilities are wounded by the comic
art, and he admires the high estate of virtue in which they
live. He doubts, however, whether such an attitude is compatible with ordinary human nature, or whether the normal
man can confine himself to heavenly things. This challenge
to a mystical view of life, with its implicit suggestion that
there are week-days as well as Sundays, is as natural in a
comedian as it would be unnatural in a saint, and it is precisely this challenge which, in the last resort, is the basic
inspiration of the first version of the comedy. Organ, the
original comic hero, puts the mystical view at a maximum
and in a light which makes it inevitably ridiculous. He has

found the ultimate peace. Tartuffe has taught him to despise
all the things of this world:

> Qui suit bien ses leçons goûte une paix profonde,
> Et comme du fumier regarde tout le monde.
> Oui, je deviens tout autre avec son entretien;
> Il m'enseigne à n'avoir affection pour rien;
> De toutes amitiés il détache mon âme;
> Et je verrois mourir frère, enfants, mère, et femme,
> Que je m'en soucierois autant que de cela.

Therein lies the real offence of the play to a devoutly religious mind—not in the exposure of Tartuffe, the impostor,
but in the author's insistence—instinctive in a comedian—
that the things of Cæsar must be rendered unto Cæsar and
that a man who systematically neglects this world owing to
an excessive preoccupation with the next becomes to the comic
eye as liable to chastisement as the man who ignores altogether the things of heaven. Molière was, to that degree
and in that sense, irreligious; and the fears of the devout
were to that extent justified. Unfortunately, none of them
had the wit to see it. They felt vaguely uneasy—as well
they might—at the author's innocent application of common
sense to things of the spirit, but, failing to diagnose his
offence correctly, they wasted their comminations upon the
impostor when they should have challenged the assumption
which underlay the author's satire upon the other-worldli-
ness of Organ. Molière, with his usual quick leap at the
essentials of a situation, understood the real nature of his
crime better than his accusers, and his final word in defence
of his comedy went straight to the heart of the matter. His
substantial offence consisted in his having put forward the
infamous suggestion that man should permit himself no

359

holiday from holiness: *mais supposé, comme il est vrai, que les exercices de la piété souffrent des intervalles et que les hommes aient besoin de divertissement je soutiens qu'on ne leur en peut trouver un qui soit plus innocent que la comédie.*

With that proud and incisive declaration we may leave *Tartuffe* and pass to a consideration of a play which presented a similar problem from the opposite angle. Organ, the victim of excessive credulity, must now give place to Don Juan, the victim of excessive doubt.

XVIII

The Wicked Marquis

NO great play has been more severely criticized than
Don Juan or *Le Festin de Pierre*. What, indeed, are we to say of a composition which
ranges from farce, through the whole range of comedy, to
scenes of terror; in which the ludicrous and the supernatural
meet and elbow for a place upon the stage; in which we are
confronted with the mysteries of life and death so that a
comic man-servant may tremble like a clown at the circus;
in which scenes that wring every gentle and sacred sentiment
are subjected to a swift, surprising ribaldry; in which the
final catastrophe is shared by a ghost from the grave and a
valet crying for his wages. No wonder many an excellent
critic has found the play incoherent, out of time and tune, a
thing of shreds and patches.

There is a whole literature of extenuation on the subject
—in the course of which Molière has been extolled as a
philosopher, hailed as a precursor of the romantic literature
of revolt, or discussed as the originator of a revolutionary
technique. None of this elaborate justification is really
necessary. *Don Juan,* which has so often puzzled the moralists, and which to the artisans of comedy has seemed so
lacking in unity, becomes immediately coherent if it is read in
the light of what has been already inferred about the dra-

361

matic methods and purposes of the author. Molière is chiefly
concerned in all his plays, from first to last, with the portrayal of character. He will borrow his plots from any available source, but his characters are always his own. He will
write a farce in which incident predominates to meet the taste
of a public formed upon Italian and Spanish models, but even
in these plays character comes breaking in, so that we find
such solid human figures as M. Jourdain and Argan living
in a fantastic world of ballet and burlesque. The supreme
interest of Molière in character makes him comparatively indifferent to other matters. Unity of mood or plot or doctrine
is often sacrificed or overlooked by an author who is in swift
pursuit of his creatures. He will take any means, seize any
occasion, which reveals them to himself or to his audience.
He hurries after them through scenes of highest comedy or
lowest farce, from incidents entirely natural to episodes
wholly fantastic, from scenes that are a conventional inheritance from an older theatre to scenes that anticipate the
modern comedy of manners. Finally, when the character has
been thoroughly exposed, the author hurriedly bids him farewell and presents us with one of those fifth Act conclusions
which justly scandalized his contemporaries and still crave
the indulgence of posterity. There is scarcely a comedy of
Molière which does not descend to farce and scarcely a farce
that does not rise to comedy. The characters are pursued by
their author through a world where they may run from the
streets of Paris into a transformation scene, where harlequin
waits for them with his wand or the clown meets them to
receive a smacking. The result is often a lack of unity in
temper and design, but this is more than offset by the author's
concentration upon his characters, and the prompt under-

362

standing which he contrives to establish with his audience.
The spectator who follows the characters of Molière from
scene to scene does not notice the change of air.   Those who
read *Don Juan* for a philosophy will be distracted; those
who view it as a formal work of dramatic art will be disconcerted, though there is philosophy and beauty to spare in
the play as it runs; those, however, who read it, as the plays
of Molière must be read, as the dramatic presentation of a
character, will have little time or inclination to observe its
nonconformities; and, far from complaining of any lack of
coherence, they will find it almost too ruthlessly persistent.
There is not a moment of relaxation from the main business
of the play, which is to present us with a very complete picture of a credibly and impressively wicked nobleman.   It is
merely an incidental feature of this modest undertaking that,
in the course of it, we catch glimpses, as we are hurried along,
of issues and suggestions that go far beyond the immediate
purpose and gesture of the scene.   Therein lies the virtue of
genius.   It holds up a light that enables us to peer beyond
the circle which it effectively illuminates.   We run in this
play upon a mountain crest in pursuit of a figure whom we
must keep continually in sight.   We come up with him at
last and see him for an instant clear against the sky before
he drops headlong into the abyss.   Only then, in looking
back, do we realize how strange and perilous a path we have
so lightly followed; and, finding ourselves alone with shapes
of pride and evil, with thin, metaphysical shadows and problems that hung over the cradle of man, we are appalled to
find ourselves upon this pinnacle of laughter.

*Mais un grand seigneur, méchant homme, est une terrible
chose*—a fine gentleman, deliberately wicked, is a terrible

thing. Thus speaks Sganarelle on behalf of all those who,
like himself, are wicked only in compliance or surrender to
the temptations of their kind. He feels that the proud,
active, conscious wickedness of his master is extraordinary
and unnatural—that it calls for condign and remarkable
punishment in order to redress the normal balance of things.
Sganarelle thus speaks the prologue to the play, and gives
us the key to its intention. The author announces at once
that he is setting out to portray a man who is bad, not because he has fallen under the dominion of any particular passion or habit, but because he delights in badness for its own
sake. Let me tell you, as between ourselves, says Sganarelle,
that you see in Don Juan, my master, the greatest villain that
ever trod the earth, an enthusiastic villain who believes in
nothing—neither in heaven nor any sacred thing, nor God,
nor devil; who shuts his ears to all Christian warnings that
may be addressed to him, and treats with contempt everything in which we put our trust. Don Juan is wicked, out of
sheer contempt for common humanity—contempt for its
faith, its good intentions, its feeble compromises with evil,
its humility in the face of heaven. We are warned at once
not to take him for an ordinary hedonist on pleasure bent;
and, lest we should do so, Don Juan himself describes for us,
upon his first appearance, the precise nature of the satisfaction
which he derives from his seductive arts. He has no delight
in a woman won. All his pleasure comes from the slow defeat of her scruples. He is quite explicit on the subject. His
escapades are not prompted by absolute lust. Still less are
they the transports of a fickle nature that believes each new
love to be eternal and an ultimate solution of the passionate
riddle. His pleasure lies in the deliberate corruption of

innocence, which ministers to his sense of intellectual power. The speech in which he first reveals himself expresses the insolence of a virtuoso, confident that he can argue God out of heaven. He looks his wickedness in the face, viewing it with admiration, and, when Sganarelle ventures to deprecate his mockery of the sacred mystery of marriage, he instantly replies that this is a matter between him and heaven; they will settle it together in their own good time and way.

All this was new to the legend. Neither the Italian nor French models from which the play was drawn, nor even the Spanish original of Molina, contained anything in the least degree comparable with this preliminary exposition. The emphasis laid by Molière on the intellectual arrogance of his hero, as distinguished from the commonplace sensuality of his predecessors, not only puts the comedy in a different rank, but completely changes its character. This is not to be the story of a seducer brought to justice for an offence against ordinary human standards of kindness and decency. It is the story of an insolent spirit, who dares to be emancipated from the faith and practice of his kind, and who takes delight in the mischievous exercise of a bold intelligence. This is not to be the comedy of a man of pleasure but the comedy of a man whose wits must be continuously exercised at the expense of his fellows and in contempt and defiance of all traditional limits. He will acknowledge no impediment to his will, and is thus, in a sense far transcending the ordinary narrow acceptance of the term, a libertine. His licentiousness and cruelty are only incidental—a species of moral sadism nourished upon intellectual pretensions which can most exquisitely be realized in the deliberate infliction of suffering and humiliation.

The introductory exposition of Sganarelle is followed by a scene which dramatically emphasizes the predominant motive of the play. Don Juan, reproached by Elvire for deserting her, refers this proud lady for explanations to his valet. He alleges, in justification of his flight, a scruple of conscience; he cannot continue his relations with her. He has snatched her from the convent. She is the bride of heaven. Shall he venture to draw upon himself celestial wrath? This is not hypocrisy. He neither deceives nor intends to deceive. He seduced Elvire in mockery of her human weakness and now he excuses himself for his desertion by deliberately mocking her faith. She is the bride of heaven. Her marriage with himself is, in effect, an adultery. He feels that he must give her an opportunity of returning to her first allegiance and she, of course, will be the last to oppose so exemplary a resolution.

The scene with Elvire is preceded by a short dialogue with Sganarelle. Don Juan is planning to abduct a young girl on the eve of her marriage. Tranquilly he explains the motive of his act—not a physical attraction, still less anything in the least amiable or romantic. He has seen the young couple together, and he has never beheld two persons so happy in one another. Such delight is a challenge to his sense of power. The demon of mischief is awakened. He was, he tells us, struck to the heart; he could not endure to see them together. Envy had awakened his desire, and he felt it would be a rare pleasure to break an attachment which was an affront to his own more delicate perceptions. This is the first enterprise on which we see him embark. It reveals him as a deliberate, perverse, insolent and heartless villain, and at once we are in pursuit of him, through a suc-

366

cession of scenes, varying in mood and gesture, but all enriching the character, making it more credible and leading us inevitably to the final catastrophe in which a supernatural intervention becomes the dramatically appropriate doom for a man who has obstinately set himself above humanity.

The second Act has been severely censured, and may be regarded as a test of our appreciation. Don Juan, rescued from drowning by the rustic Pierrot, amuses himself by stealing Charlotte, the sweetheart of his saviour, and maltreating the man himself. The whole Act could be cut from the play without in any way affecting its subsequent progress. It is even, from the point of view of construction, a non-sequitur. Don Juan, shown in pursuit of one victim in the first Act, has in the interval been diverted to the pursuit of another. The whole Act is an episode unrelated to the other four, and it contains a scene of pure farce in which Don Juan lies symmetrically to the two maidens whom he has simultaneously promised to marry. The Act, in brief, cannot be defended against those who insist upon a strict sequence in action and evenness of texture in a play.

For those, however, who are following the author in headlong pursuit of his character, the Act is so extremely pertinent that the looseness of construction is unperceived. Don Juan is further illustrating the characteristics which were indicated at the outset. His seduction of Charlotte is a holiday exercise. He derives his pleasure from playing successfully upon the vanity and credulity of his victim, which he at once perceives and flatters. The motives which would have given pause to another man—the fact that his life has been saved by Pierrot and that the simple Charlotte was obviously unfair game for so accomplished a tactician—adds perversely to the attraction of the enterprise. There is a puckish malevolence in his conduct of the scene. Lord, what fools these mortals be! Incidentally, we see beneath the elegant and fine exterior of the man to his essential brutality and contempt of fair dealing. He assumes that every licence is permitted him in dealing with God's simple creatures. He praises the beauties of Charlotte to her face as though she were a beast at a show, and, knowing she has not the art to resist his promises, delights in her silly acquiescence. The farce with which the Act concludes is extravagant, but its extravagance is pertinent to the author's design, and, therefore, justified. It exceeds the ordinary limits of nature, but so does the character of Don Juan. This is not the customary farce of the man caught between two women; it is a flamboyant expression of a mischievous spirit, exercising his faculties to the top of their bent. Don Juan is drunk with the sense of his own resource.

Molière was censured by envious contemporaries, and has been dubiously regarded by a delicate posterity, for his habit of dropping from comedy into farce. Critics have deplored that comedies like *L'Ecole des Femmes* or *Le Bourgeois Gentilhomme* should contain scenes that pass from realism into extravagance. This is to deplore that Molière was Molière. His genius was a compound of accurate observation and lively fancy, of a passion for veracity and a desire to follow an assumption to its extreme, of classic sobriety and Gallic exuberance. No one has more finely smiled or more broadly laughed than Molière, and the two sides of his genius were equally necessary—each correcting or enlivening the other. There is, moreover, a profound psycho-

368

logical justification for his habit of passing from comedy to farce. His comic characters are comic in proportion as they fall out of touch with their normal companions and become increasingly insensitive to their environment. In the grip of a ruling idea or passion, they depart ever more widely from the mean of good sense, and the author must follow them to their extreme till at last they stand isolated from their kind in a peerless extravagance. The farce in Molière is always an extreme logical development of his comedy, and in the case of *Don Juan* it is fundamentally justified. The scene with the two women in Act II is humanly absurd. It exceeds the normal. But so does the insolence of which it is a dramatic expression. That, precisely, is the fault of Don Juan and the cause of his supernatural doom—that he claims to stand outside and above the humanity of his victims. The quality in his character that makes him terrible is the quality which makes him also absurd, and for that reason his doom, while it is terrible, is also grotesque. There is a sense in which farce stands nearer to tragedy than to comedy, and Molière, writing a comedy with awful implications, instinctively introduced the farcical element to emphasize and accompany his dreadful conclusion.

The second Act reveals the insolence of Don Juan towards his fellows. The third Act emphasizes his insolence towards heaven. I believe that two and two are four, Sganarelle, and that four and four are eight—such is his profession of faith. He believes neither in heaven nor in earth, nor in another life, nor in the devil, nor in the bogeyman. Sganarelle dilates upon the wonders of nature. Who made the trees and the rocks? The earth did not grow like a mushroom in the night. And consider the miracle of man. Is

it not amazing that he should have thoughts in his head
and that he should be able to do as he pleases with his body
—clap his hands, raise his eyes to heaven, go to right or
left and wheel about. Sganarelle, wheeling about to illustrate his thesis, overbalances himself and falls down. "Capital," says his master, "there lies your argument with a
broken nose."

To the contemporaries of Molière this scene was particularly scandalous. Molière, they said, has entrusted the
defence of the mysteries of religion to a buffoon who concludes his argument by falling down like a clown at the
fair. He might at least, they urge, have provided heaven
with a more respectable champion. An author, they contend,
who sets out to write a philosophic play should be fair to
both sides, but here the dice are loaded in the devil's favour.

Molière, however, was not setting out to write a philosophic play. He was setting out to present a wicked marquis, and the scene with Sganarelle is one of many which
illustrate the peculiar nature of his master's wickedness.
The insolence of two-and-two-are-four needed just the blun-
dering simplicity of Sganarelle to throw it into relief. The
comic figure of the scene is not, as the criticism implies,
Sganarelle earnestly attempting to prove the existence of
God, but the sceptic who mocks his innocence. Our sympa-
thies are with the poor clown struggling to express his faith
and his sense of the wonder of life, not with the master who
waits to trip him with a sneer. Molière was not thinking of
the philosophic issue, but emphasizing a heartless impiety
which shows up darker against the pathetic and impotent
conclusions of Sganarelle than it could possibly have done
against the pleadings of a whole synod of divines.

370

This brings us to the notorious episode of the beggar.
A beggar solicits alms of Don Juan, and will pray God to
bless his benefactor for the charity. Pray God to give you
a new coat, replies Don Juan and proceeds to mock the
pious man for being so ill-rewarded by heaven for all his
prayers. Don Juan offers the beggar a coin on condition
that the man shall swear an oath. The beggar recoils from
an act which he considers to be impious and refuses the
alms. He would rather die of hunger. Don Juan finally
thrusts the alms upon him, insisting that he shall take it *for
the love of humanity.*

This scene so shocked the contemporaries of Molière
that it was omitted from the earlier editions of the play,
while posterity has found it not only impious but inconsistent.
Why, it is asked, should Don Juan heartlessly tempt the
beggar and immediately afterwards generously assist him?
Was this a genuine act of grace? Was the wicked marquis
moved by the stubborn loyalty of the beggar to his creed?
All these difficulties vanish if we follow, once more, the
author in a logical pursuit of his character. The scene with
the beggar is a natural sequel to the argument with Sganarelle. Here is another simple soul to be confounded and,
perhaps, seduced. But Don Juan has met his match. This
is no Sganarelle, whom he can destroy in argument and
bend to his wicked will, no Charlotte to be flustered out of
her virtue, but one of the incorruptibles. Don Juan finds
himself on the brink of defeat. Observe his mortification.
Note how he presses his alms on the beggar with a growing
insistence. *Prends, voilà, prends, te dis-je; mais jure donc.*
Still the man stubbornly refuses. Don Juan is discomfited,
and instinctively, somehow, he must save his face. The ges-

ture whereby he finally thrusts his alms upon the beggar
for the love of humanity is inspired by no charitable relenting, but by an imperious need to have the last and best
word of the encounter. He will not admit his defeat. The
beggar, accepting the coin, shall at least be made to realize
that the love of humanity is as good a phrase to conjure
with as the love of God. Commentators have asked whether
the author intended here to present his hero as a prototype
of the romantic atheists of the nineteenth century, while
others are merely puzzled to find Don Juan yielding to
the prick of charity. All this merely means that they are
losing the dramatist in quest of a philosopher. The motive
of the act is clear. Don Juan has no real love of humanity
—unless it be a humanity that ministers to his own conceit.
He forces his coin on the beggar in no spirit of charity, but
in a contemptuous effort to belittle the beggar's faith. "I
am an infidel," he says in effect. "I care nothing for this
God to whom you so constantly pray in vain; but take this
coin. You have no need to thank God for it. God is neither
here nor there. I give it you for the love of humanity."

Don Juan, charitable from conceit, is for the same reason
courageous. Don Carlos is attacked by robbers in the forest.
Don Juan, sword in hand, runs swiftly to the rescue. Here,
again, is a generous act. But note how carefully the author
defines its motive. "I have done nothing, Sir," he says in
reply to the grateful Don Carlos, "which you would not
have done yourself in my place. Our honour is concerned
in such adventures." His rescue of a gentleman set upon by
ruffians is the reflex of his caste. He owes it to himself not
to fail in such matters, and Don Juan instinctively pays the
debts that are due to Don Juan. His wickedness is rooted

372

in pride and he naturally has the qualities of his defects. His rescue of Don Carlos is as natural to the character as the mystification and mockery in which he at once indulges when he realizes the identity of the man he has saved. Moreover, he is at once ready to prosecute the feud. He has saved Don Carlos by accident, but he is quite prepared to kill him by design.

The character is now humanly complete. It only remains to apply to it the supreme test imposed by the legend. How will this man, who sets himself above the ordinary human standards of faith and conduct, behave when his challenge is apparently accepted. He has stated the sum of his philosophy; two and two are four. How will he respond when confronted with something that lies apparently quite outside a strictly arithmetical universe. The answer of the dramatist to that question is given in the last two Acts of the play, and it is an answer which, going beyond the individual case, constitutes a profound and lasting contribution to the problem of faith.

The first reaction of Don Juan is one of indignant protest. Two and two are four, but here is a marble statue nodding its head in acceptance of an invitation to supper. The thing is entirely preposterous. He withdraws, a little shaken, to think it over, but no amount of thinking can alter his conviction. Belief is not a matter of intelligence or even of will. It is a matter of taste and habit. In men of an independent turn of mind it flows from the hidden springs of disposition. They first believe and afterwards find a reason. The faith of such is the expression of a private and original taste. Taste, however, is with most men largely a matter of fashion, and their faith is merely epidemic.

They believe in machinery, ghosts, Moses or Michael Angelo according to their period and environment.

Don Juan does not believe in the supernatural, and not a whole avenue of statues nodding their marble heads, though they might startle or even terrify him, could seriously affect his unbelief. The statue has nodded. It is a miracle. But Don Juan is not the man to believe in miracles—at least, not in that sort of miracle. The incident must be ignored. He will not hear of it. He will thrash Sganarelle within an inch of his life if he ever dares to mention it again.

The scene between Don Juan and his tailor, occurring shortly after the incident of the statue, in which he overwhelms the good man with his civilities so that he cannot press for the payment of his dues, has been condemned as a merry impertinence. But it is diverting in the right way and at the right moment. Don Juan, secretly affected by the incident of the statue but resolved to ignore it, resumes his comic progress. Don Juan has seen a ghost. No matter. He will be one too many for his creditors. He owes that, once again, to his pride.

Molière, however, is too profound a dramatist to leave his hero quite stubbornly unconcerned. Don Juan cannot believe in the statue. Courage and honour would forbid him to surrender even if he did. But the bottom has been knocked out of his universe. There is something here that passes his understanding. His insolence is troubled. He is no longer the cool miscreant of the earlier scenes. There is a touch of bravado, now, in all that he does. The man is a bundle of nerves, and he exaggerates all his previous attitudes and proceedings. Where he formerly listened to the remonstrances of Sganarelle with an indulgent irony he now flies into a passion and in the more serious scenes with his father we realize the full effect of his recent shattering adventure. He controls himself sufficiently at first to conduct the interview with an odious affectation of respect; but the strain is too great, and at the end of the scene—his calm collapses and he breaks out with a violence to which he would never have been moved but for a secret defiance of the warning he has received: *Eh! mourez le plus tôt que vous pourrez, c'est le mieux que vous puissiez faire.* On that he flings himself into a chair. But almost instantly he is on his feet again, menacing the wretched Sganarelle who ventures to disapprove of such strikingly unfilial sentiments. Molière is usually sparing with his stage directions, and the few indications which here and there he has inserted are, therefore, of capital significance. He does not cause his hero to sit down and rise immediately afterwards without a reason. The wicked marquis, for all his airs, has been thoroughly upset by the breach in his philosophy. Two and two are four; but he has invited a dead man to supper. Defiantly he goes from bad to worse. He listens in stubborn silence during the scene with Elvire, now taking the veil, when she pleads for his salvation in terms that move even Sganarelle to tears. But, when she has finished, he pulls himself together, remembers he is Don Juan, begs her to stay and informs Sganarelle when she has left that the sight of her in that pious habit, expressing such novel sentiments, has stirred again in him the ashes of a passion which he had thought extinct. When Sganarelle, staggered by these observations, protests: *C'est-à-dire que ses paroles n'ont fait aucun effet sur vous,* he merely replies:

375

Vite à souper. It is the third time in the same Act that he has called for supper and asked for it quickly.

Supper is served, and the scene is pure farce. Don Juan jests with his valet in a spirit of sheer buffoonery. What, say the critics, is this? The solemn moment approaches but the comedy drops to the level of a harlequinade. The dramatist, however, is right—as right as Shakespeare when Hamlet seizes the recorders. There is in farce an extravagance which makes it equally an outlet for comic and tragic expression when driven to the limit. Farce is, above all, the language of hysteria. The statue arrives. Don Juan is boisterous and effusive; he will have a toast and a song. The statue invites him for the following evening. *En aurez-vous le courage?* he asks. It is a challenge which Don Juan, as we have come to know him, could not possibly refuse. With a supreme effort of the will he accepts and bids Sganarelle in a defiant gesture of courtesy to light his awful guest from the room.

Sganarelle is amazed. What a man, what a man! is all he can say. Don Juan has seen with his own eyes a statue that moves and speaks and yet he will not amend. *Il y a bien quelque chose là-dedans que je ne comprends pas*— the admission for Don Juan is handsome and substantial— *mais, quoique ce puisse être, cela n'est pas capable ni de convaincre mon esprit, ni d'ébranler mon âme.* He goes on to explain, in a scene to which reference has been made, that henceforth he intends to ape the virtues so that he may more securely enjoy the pleasures of life. Observe that Sganarelle is still to be in his confidence: *Je suis bien aisé d'avoir un témoin du fond de mon âme et des véritables motives qui m'obligent à faire des choses.* There, to the

376

end, speaks a stubborn vanity. There can be little satisfaction in a defiance that remains unseen. Don Juan is striking his final attitude, and it is no use striking an attitude unless there is to be a spectator.

In the second scene with Don Carlos, Don Juan pleads penitence and heaven is so odiously mocked that Sganarelle declares that, though formerly he had hopes of his master's salvation, he is now convinced that God, who has hitherto tolerated him, will be unable to suffer this last indignity. Heaven quickly arrives in the form of a veiled spectre. Don Juan is unshaken. *Spectre, fantôme, ou diable, je veux voir ce que c'est,* he exclaims, and he still persists when the spectre changes its form: *Non, non, rien n'est capable de m'imprimer de la terreur et je veux éprouver avec mon épée si c'est un corps ou un esprit . . . il ne sera pas dit, quoi qu'il arrive, que je sois capable de me repentir.* The statue enters. In final proof of his courage Don Juan gives his hand and in the last agony there is no whisper of surrender or regret.

The comedy of *Don Juan* is a companion to the comedy of Organ and it was not, as in the case of *Tartuffe,* revised to become a morality. Molière ridiculed an excessive credulity in Organ; in Don Juan he chastises an excessive scepticism. Organ believes too easily and too much. Don Juan believes nothing at all. The real moral of the play—if a moral must be sought—is the constant and inevitable lesson of the comic muse, which slips almost unawares into every comedy the author wrote—to avoid extremes and keep to the middle way. The crime of Don Juan was that he insolently claimed to be above and beyond his kind. His wickedness was rooted in this insolence—taking that word

377

in its classic and original sense, and this insolence was necessarily comic since it distorted all his normal sentiments and relationships. It is a sad commentary on the literature of criticism that nine-tenths of it in this particular case has been devoted to irrelevant discussions whether Molière was an atheist attempting to undermine our belief in heaven and hell, a moralist intent upon chastising a libertine, or a pioneer of romantic rebellion anticipating, in terms of comedy, the glories of *Prometheus Unbound*. There are illustrious advocates for many such readings of the play and the worst offenders are not so much the devout who denounce the author's heresy as the enthusiasts who have acclaimed his philosophic freedom. Theodore de Banville went so far as to find in Don Juan a religion of the future. He celebrated the hero as a magnificent incarnation of the renaissance, bravely claiming for man his place in the sun, an intrepid champion of free thought and unfettered self-expression. All such interpretations are essentially mistaken. They begin by ignoring that Molière was a dramatist. Was Molière with Don Juan, the brilliant libertine, with Sganarelle, the representative of simple faith and the ordinary human sentiments, with the compassionate Elvire, the avenging Carlos, or the statue as an instrument of wrath? The answer has already been suggested. He was presenting the complete picture of a wicked marquis, and, for his comic purpose, he must contrast the abnormal characteristics of his hero with the normal virtues and weaknesses of other types and classes. The sympathetic characters of the play are foils to the qualities which set Don Juan apart and bring upon him an exceptional doom. Normal human virtue and dignity are flouted in the persons of Elvire, Don Carlos,

Don Louis and the beggar who refuses to swear; while, for a continual comic chorus to the play, there is always Sganarelle to emphasize at every turn that his master is not as other men. Molière is with all or none of these characters. They exist. He depicts with an equal vivacity the chivalrous Don Carlos, the sturdy beggar, the sentimental Sganarelle with the vices and virtues of the man predestined to serve his betters. Note, however, that the wicked marquis, challenging the sympathetic characters of the play one by one, comes off worst in every single instance. He is brought to the test of the comic norm and found wanting.

Why was Don Juan so profoundly disconcerting to his contemporaries? A false identification of the author with his hero is not reason enough, and it would be an insult to the intelligence of a host of distinguished commentators to attribute to them at every turn so obvious a fallacy. The reason lies deeper. Essentially it is to be sought in the fact that Don Juan, for all his wickedness, and for all the care Molière has taken to exhibit him in his true light, is, nevertheless, a popular character. The author shows him no mercy, exposes him, turns his wit the seamy side without on all occasions. But there is a secret disposition in most of us to admire the man who has the courage of his wickedness. There is an unacknowledged and unregenerate prejudice in favour of the fearless and illustrious rebels of legend and romance. Lucifer, when he fell from heaven, became the morning star. Prometheus, when he challenged Zeus, became the hero of mankind. The sinister prestige of a spirit damned in his pride invests each of his many incarnations, and the devil remains the most popular character in history or fiction. There is no one, theology apart,

379

who does not secretly lament the fallen angels. Don Juan is the hero of *Le Festin de Pierre* in the sense that Satan is the hero of *Paradise Lost*. The Adversary who dared to challenge heaven has our admiration, unconfessed but ineradicable. Don Juan may be odious and not to be forgiven in his conduct towards Elvire, Don Carlos and the rest, but he is secretly redeemed by his conduct towards the statue. In the final scene he trails with him the glory of the Fiends and Titans. His vices drop into oblivion. We behold only his courage. He is faithful unto damnation.

The contemporary critics who started the long outcry against *Le Festin de Pierre* were uneasily aware of this. They felt that the doom of the wicked marquis was in effect his triumph. The play was produced on February 15th, and on April 18th appeared *Observations sur une Comédie de Molière intitulée le Festin de Pierre* by a certain Sieur de Rochemont, *avocat en Parlement*. "The work of Molière," so runs the indictment, "is truly devilish, and truly devilish is his brain; nothing more impious has ever appeared even in pagan times." The pamphlet is skilfully written by an author who is determined to be moderate if only he can keep his temper, and his observations upon Don Juan are interesting because they point straight at the real motive of the outcry. He censures the play on two main grounds: first, that the cause of true religion is entrusted to Sganarelle, who covers it with ridicule, and, secondly, that the retribution which falls upon Don Juan takes the form of a little stage thunder and red fire unlikely to frighten a mouse. Don Juan, in other words, is technically doomed, but substantially he has the best of it. He remains undefeated in argument, lords it wickedly from

380

scene to scene and cuts rather a fine figure at the close, while the spectator can have no respect whatever for the rather childish exhibition of omnipotence to which heaven is finally reduced. The Sieur de Rochemont feels that the sympathy of the audience, however it may have been shocked and estranged by the heartlessness and impiety of Don Juan, is with him in the moment of his punishment. The wicked marquis is by no means a sympathetic character, but at least he is more sympathetic than the statue. Hence the peril of the play. This, in fact, is the old ecclesiastical grievance against the devil that somehow or other he usually contrives to get the best tunes. It is unfair, however, to blame the dramatist. If his audience insists upon indulging a sneaking sympathy for the most completely wicked man in the whole range of literature—that is its own affair, and must be taken as a proof of the profoundly unregenerate character of the human race. The complaint that the heavenly thunder at the close is ineffectual is æsthetically justified, though this is a strange complaint in the mouth of a critic who almost in the same breath charges Molière with impiety for having ventured to make merry in *L'Ecole des Femmes* with the boiling cauldrons of hell. Molière uses the traditional machinery of a Christian legend to enforce a Christian moral, and it is not his fault if the machinery fails to impress a seventeenth century audience. Still less can he be blamed because the devil is a more popular figure than he imagined.

The true offence of the play is further revealed if we compare it with previous versions of the legend. Don Juan, beginning rather solemnly with Tirso de Molina in the Spanish theatre, had passed merrily by way of Italian comedy into the French theatre, and Molière wrote his own play with

381

at least three versions in mind. Whether he actually used the Spanish original of Molina is extremely doubtful, but he was certainly familiar with the version of Giacinto Andrea Cicognini and the French versions of Dorimond and Villiers, which had all been quite recently acted in France. No one had quarrelled with these previous versions of the play. Why was the comedy of Molière passionately denounced as impious while the French versions of Dorimond and Villiers went untaxed?

Don Juan in the earlier plays was the conventional libertine. His vices had hitherto consisted in the prompt satisfaction of his desires regardless of consequences. He would, like the ordinary human sinner, repent if he could. He was, in fact, no more than a spoiled sprig of nobility, whose rebellion against all authority, human and divine, was inspired by the impatient cravings of a man of pleasure. His celebrated thousand-and-three conquests merely witnessed to an insatiable appetite. He was exceptional in nothing except in the scale of his performances and his resolution to be satisfied. His attitude towards heaven—when he must think of it—was that of the small boy loose in the larder. Probably he would be punished, but perhaps it was worth it. There was nothing in the heroes of Dorimond and Villiers in the least resembling the insolent and defiant wickedness of the hero of Molière; there was no challenge in their attitude, either moral or intellectual, unless the escapades of an unlicked profligate be regarded as a challenge. There was no suggestion of Lucifer or the Titan.

Molière changed the whole spirit and purpose of the legend. Equally in the episodes which he adapted from his models and in those which he invented or amplified, the

traditional libertine was transformed from an embodiment
of human weakness condignly punished into an embodiment
of superhuman pride erect in defiance to the limit of damnation; and nowhere is the contrast more striking than in his
treatment of the statue. In the earlier plays the statue was
the divine advocate. He reasoned with his victim and justified the heavenly doom. He had the last word and the
story closed upon a note of edification. The conclusion of
Molière is of another mettle. The pleadings are finished
and the case is complete when the statue comes at last to
claim his victim. Here is no preacher to point the moral
of the tale but a laconic figure of doom. There is no arguing with destiny, but an heroic attitude is still possible, and
Don Juan, in striking it, affirms, to the instinctive indignation of the orthodox and the secret admiration of the unregenerate, that impiety also has its martyrs.

Molière, presenting the wicked Marquis and conducting
him inexorably to the doom reserved for him by a pious
tradition, had no idea of the storm he was raising. He desired at this moment not a further controversy but a play
with which to fill his theatre. He was still fighting for
Tartuffe, and that was scandal enough. The play, so far
as the public was concerned, fulfilled his expectations.
During the first nine performances the receipts did not fall
below a thousand, and for four of them they amounted to
over two thousand, *livres.* He sold the play, moreover,
to a publisher who at once applied for a licence. All, indeed,
appeared to be going well. Loret, the gazetteer, referred
to the awful legend as likely to touch even hearts of bronze
or marble and further prophesied that its scenic transforma-
tions would surprise the world. With Loret so dulcet, we

must conclude that the barometer at the outset showed no indication of bad weather. Then the storm broke. The play ran smoothly into Passion Week, but after the Easter recess it was not revived. Something had happened. The opponents of *Tartuffe* had been mobilized. The play was not revived during the lifetime of its author, while the publisher to whom he had sold it hesitated for over two months to register his privilege and finally decided not to make use of it. Molière, who fought tooth and nail for five years on behalf of *Tartuffe*, did nothing, so far as we know, on behalf of *Le Festin de Pierre*, and there can be no reasonable doubt that he was acting under the advice of the King, who, having been obliged to prohibit *Tartuffe* against his better judgment, had now to face this further embarrassment.

The Sieur de Rochemont in his *Observations sur une Comédie intitulée le Festin de Pierre*, denounced the work of its author root and branch and appealed directly to the King for its suppression:

While this noble prince devotes all his care to maintaining religion, Molière is working to destroy it. The King throws down the temples of heresy while Molière raises altars to impiety, and, in proportion as the virtue of the prince endeavours, by his example, to establish in the hearts of his subjects a worship of the true God, the licentious spirit of Molière endeavours to undermine their faith by the licence of his works. . . .

I maintain that his comedy is pernicious. . . . Augustus put to death a buffoon who mocked at Jupiter, and prohibited women from attending comedies that were more modest than those of Molière. . . . I do not think I am rash in maintaining that there is no man so little enlightened

SCENE FROM THE "MALADE IMAGINAIRE"

Played on the third day of the Versailles entertainments, which were given by the King to celebrate the conquest of Franche-Comté in 1674. After an engraving by Le Pautre.

in the doctrines of the faith who, having seen this play, or realizing what it contains, can affirm that Molière, so long as he persists in presenting it, is worthy to participate in the sacraments or to be received into penitence without a public reparation. . . .

We have every reason to hope that the same power which is the support of our religion will strike down this monster and for ever confound his insolence. Insults paid to God rebound upon the faces of kings, who are his lieutenants and embodiments.

Only one of the royal observations has come down to us in answer to the critics who condemned the impieties of Don Juan. "He is not rewarded," said His Majesty. The royal actions were more significant. The Sieur de Rochemont published his exhortation in April, and the outcry against the author of *Tartuffe* and *Le Festin de Pierre* was at its height throughout the summer of 1665. In August, as has been recorded in another chapter, Louis XIV summoned Molière to St. Germain, granted him a pension of 6,000 *livres*, and took over the company from his brother. The devil in human form was henceforth the director of the King's players. It is not surprising that the fashionable Robinet, writing on August 9, 1665, is, in despite of all things, friendly to the recipient of these royal favours. He alludes to the Sieur de Rochemont as a "bilious doctor," and commends a brace of pamphleteers who have appeared in defence of Molière. Incidentally, one of these same pamphleteers, in an admirable letter upon the observations of the Sieur de Rochemont, corrected him very explicitly upon the royal attitude, affirming that His Majesty "knew very well what he was about in allowing *Le Festin de Pierre* to be performed," that His Majesty "had no desire that the

Tartuffes should have more power in the realm than himself," and "was well aware that, if Molière had not written *Tartuffe,* there would have been less said about *Don Juan.*" The position is accordingly pretty clear. The King, embarrassed but sympathetic, supported Molière, but advised him to be prudent.

The prejudice against the play persisted for long after the death of its author. When in 1677 *Don Juan* returned to the theatre, the company of Molière, with the approval of his widow, presented, not the masterpiece of their vanished leader, but a version prepared for the occasion by Thomas Corneille. The play of Molière was "purged" and presented in verse. The work was as well done as could be expected of a man of talent adapting the play of a man of genius; it was presented in a modest preface as the "same piece which M. de Molière had presented in prose shortly before his death," and for many generations it was performed with admiration and respect at the *Comédie Française.* The original play of Molière was all but lost, for La Grange and Vinot in 1682 did not dare to include it, as originally written, in his collected works. Passages which Molière himself had been obliged to omit after the first performance, like the passage of the beggar soliciting an alms, were suppressed; and the police, intervening at the last moment, insisted on further excisions. Two sheets had to be changed in the press, and fourteen pages in the sheets that remained. It was only by a fortunate accident that the original version was preserved. We owe the *Don Juan* of Molière to certain piratical publishers who in 1683 and 1694, in Amsterdam and Brussels respectively, printed the original text. The play was thus restored to literature, but

not for nearly two hundred years was it restored to the
theatre. Up to 1841 the version of Thomas Corneille was
alone performed in the house of Molière.

Don Juan has had the misfortune to be seldom read as
Molière intended. His contemporaries censured it, and posterity at long last commended it, for intentions of which
the author was entirely innocent. *Don Juan,* from being a
glorification of profligacy and unbelief, became the champion of free thought and adventurous living. He comes
down to us, like so many of the great characters of fiction,
invested with traditions that obscure the original figure, and
his prestige, splendid or sinister, makes it difficult for us
justly to appreciate the play in which he figures. It is not
a play with a thesis. The author is not presenting a case
for free thought or a material philosophy. He is writing
a comedy of character and his hero falls naturally into line
with his other comic figures.

He is ridiculous in his excessive unbelief as Organ in
his excessive credulity or Harpagon in his excessive avarice.
The nature of his excess, rooted in pride of place and
intellect, gives him, however, a stature above the normal
comic level. Molière was obliged to be faithful to the
legend. Don Juan must needs be damned and miraculously
exposed, and the author took the only form of excess that
could adequately meet the case—the sin by which the
angels fell. He created a consistent character to fit the
ancient legend and thereby achieved a masterpiece. Comic
genius can go no further. It has led us in laughter to the
threshold of the supernatural, brought us in laughter to the
edge of doom.

387

XIX

The Golden Mean

<hr>

A DRAMATIC author, though he does not necessarily speak his opinions through his characters, or write a comedy to illustrate a conviction, must, in surveying the world, be standing somewhere. He has a temperament and an attitude. He identifies himself in turn with the creatures of his theatre, but there must, nevertheless, be in his work a coherence and a tendency, something which persists and reveals a mind which for all its variety of expression, works upon lines which are deliberately or instinctively consistent. There is, moreover, a special need in the work of a comedian, for a standpoint or criterion. All absurdity is relative; there is no such thing as an absolute joke. People are ridiculous because they fail to be like the people who are considered to be just right. The man who gets flustered with his forks is a joke in Wimbledon, but not in Whitechapel; the man who locks up his wife is a joke in Mayfair, but not in Arabia. The writer of comedies must have a norm or none of his characters will be funny.

The criterion in all the comedies of Molière is invariable:

> La parfaite raison fuit toute extrémité,
> Et veut que l'on soit sage avec sobriété.

Ridicule lies in wait for the man who runs to an extreme. Wisdom consists in a perpetual adaptation of the man to his environment. Virtue is social. The reasonable man is before all things conformable. He becomes absurd in proportion as he becomes unaware of his fellows or insensitive to his surroundings. Anything in the nature of a fixed idea; the exaggeration of any quality that disturbs the balance of the rest; obstinate fidelity to a preconception; all forms of obsession, professional, social or merely individual; any mechanical sacrifice of normal sentiments and ideas to some predominant passion or foible; the condition of mind which can perceive only one thing at a time and most of the time —this was the origin and substance of comedy as Molière understood and practised it. The example might vary in quality and degree. His comic range embraced at one end the absurd pedant dragged from the stage feet foremost still maintaining his thesis to the man who ruined himself for love of an impostor or went defiantly to his damnation from sheer persistence in an attitude which not even heaven itself could shake. *Don Juan* was so outrageously unsocial that the very nature of things turned against him, and he suffered at the end a supernatural doom.

Le Festin de Pierre was an extreme instance, and it might be imagined that Molière could take no further his doctrine of the golden mean. There still remained, however, the case of the man who suffered from an excess of virtue; for even virtue, carried to extremes and unseasonably practised, might be unsocial and ridiculous. Alceste in moderation and good sense falls as far short of Aristotelian perfection as his wicked cousin. The heroes of both comedies were professed enemies of mankind, and it is significant that Molière was working upon *Le Misanthrope* concurrently with *Le Festin de Pierre*. He began the play in 1664, but finished it at

389

leisure—such leisure as he was ever able to secure—and it was not produced until June, 1666.

Le Misanthrope is not a popular play, and its implications are not immediately perceptible. The comedy of Alceste seems at times to be no more than a study in social deportment. That, however, is a false impression. The origin of his misanthropy and the quality that renders him a comic figure is an egocentricity, profoundly unsocial, which, with amiable reservations, is exhibited as essentially ridiculous. The comic suggestions of the play are so finely conveyed that we must marvel at the author who, filling a boisterous stage, could set the whole theatre upon a roar, and yet write a play of so delicate a texture. The man who shook the sides of his generation with Sganarelle could yet raise in its finer spirits a smile which almost justifies the ineffable contention of Lord Chesterfield that mere laughter is derogatory and that in the polite world an audible amusement is barbarous.

The success of the play was such as might be expected from its quality. It was applauded by the finer spirits, but its success was only moderate. The appropriate setting for a comedy of social values was Versailles, but the Queen mother had just died (30th January, 1666), and the Court was in mourning. Molière, however, was now in such repute that, if he could not go to Versailles, Versailles must come to him. De Visé informs us that the people of the Court who attended the play, coming especially to the Palais Royal to see it, were loud in applause and found it a fine comedy. Grimarest adds that Madame asked him, but in vain, to suppress the famous Count of Flanders who passed his time spitting into a pool to make circles. The story is almost certainly false. Molière was unlikely to refuse the Princess so small a concession, and the Princess was unlikely to request it. At a time when gentlemen might spit in the drawing-room, a lady was not likely to be shocked by his spitting into a pool.

More important are the emphatic and circumstantial assertions of Grimarest concerning the play's reception. He declares that it pleased only the lettered public, and that Molière, returning from its first performance, confronted with failure, shut himself up at once in his study to write *Le Médecin Malgré Lui*, which was given at the fourth performance in support of its predecessor. The two pieces together, he tells us, drew the town; those who came to laugh at the farce remained to admire the comedy, and at the end of about the tenth performance *Le Misanthrope* was by this means firmly established. Molière, we are to infer, smiled at the success of his tactics, but the smile was bitter on the mouth. The public must be persuaded to endure his finest comedy, written at such pains, by means of a piece improvised in three days from one of his provincial sketches.

The story has all the literary persuasiveness of Grimarest, but it is entirely false to the facts. *Le Médecin Malgré Lui* was not written to support *Le Misanthrope* but to be performed with a later comedy of de Visé. The first performances of *Le Misanthrope* were moderately successful, and the comedy, far from being established after the tenth performance, began precisely at that moment to decline. Grimarest, moreover, alleges that the comparative failure of the piece was due to the fact that Alceste was regarded by several noblemen as a libel upon themselves. This is sheer invention. The gentleman who, according to a doubtful tradition, sat for Alceste, and in an apocryphal anecdote declared that he was proud of the allegation, was the Marquis de Montausier, who was extravagant in its praise. *Le Misanthrope*, indeed, was the first of the comic masterpieces of Molière which was never attacked either upon social, literary or moral grounds by his contemporaries. It was left to a later generation, and more especially to Jean Jacques Rousseau, to stigmatize it as an insidious attack upon the social virtues and the work of a profoundly immoral genius. The impression of failure left upon contemporary critics was merely the result of comparing it with the phenomenal successes to which Molière was accustomed. The receipts for the first and second performances were 1,447 *livres* and 1,617 *livres* respectively. The play was presented 21 times up to August 1st consecutively and without accompaniment. It was revived in September, probably with *Le Médecin Malgré Lui*, and performed 34 times. It was played on 19 other occasions during the author's lifetime. All the contemporary references to the play were favourable. The Court rhymsters, echoing the general verdict of Versailles, celebrated it as a masterpiece, and exclaimed that Molière had surpassed himself.

Of the many traditions relating to the play there is one that has the double advantage of being probably true and certainly characteristic of all concerned. Molière, taking steps to publish his play, obtained a privilege on 21st June, which he handed to the publisher Jean Ribou. De Visé, once the critic, but now the friend of Molière, went privately to the publisher, and, wishing to show the same zeal in his conversion as in his unregeneracy, offered him a *Lettre écrite sur la Comédie du Misanthrope*, which Ribou agreed to place at the head of the first edition of the play. De Visé was no longer the young man whose road to fame lay in lampooning the author of *L'Ecole des Femmes*. He had made his peace, and Molière had one of his comedies in rehearsal. The letter in defence of *Le Misanthrope* was to be a pleasant surprise for his friend, and a public amends for the offences which his protector had so conveniently agreed to forget. The first edition of the play duly appeared with the letter of de Visé for a preface. Molière, to the amazement of all concerned, was furious. He called for his publisher, denounced the pleasant conspiracy as an outrage, and ordered him to destroy the whole edition. His stupefied apologist discovered that to praise Molière was even more dangerous than to blame him. The story has been rejected or modified for the very reasons that make it so entirely acceptable. To account for the indignation of Molière, Brossette in his memoirs of Boileau, accused Ribou, in alliance with de Visé, of trying to pirate the play as he had pirated *Les Précieuses Ridicules*. Brossette is here quite obviously wrong. De Visé certainly would not try to rob the man who was about to become his producer. What, moreover, could be more natural than this zeal of a convert, this readiness of a wicked publisher to make amends to a distinguished client and this fury of the unconscious victim of these amiable manœuvres? Is it so amazing that the author of *Le Misanthrope* should resent an apology for his work by the author of *La Mère Coquette?* The letter of de Visé was worse than impertinent; it must raise a smile at the expense of everyone concerned.

It is odd that the first thing to establish in approaching *Le Misanthrope* is that Alceste is a comic character. A romantic and rebellious generation subsequently found in him, as in Don Juan, an embodiment of virtues and ideals which would have considerably astonished his creator. Alceste, the noble, sensitive, refined and contemplative spirit, for whom the worldly Philinte is merely a foil to display his virtues the more conspicuously, was the invention of a period for whom the edge of comedy had been blunted by romantic excess. The Alceste of Molière has many virtues and much right upon his side. But from start to finish he is ludicrous. Often he is in the wrong, and, even when he is in the right, he spoils his case with overstatement and by being completely insensitive to the reasonable views and feelings of others.

The transfiguration of Alceste into the embodiment of a delicate virtue rejecting compromise with folly or fraud has driven another school of critics to the opposite extreme. Alceste, according to them, is an embodiment of all that is least desirable in a member of society. He is bilious, disagreeable and unjust—a perfect type of the man who would make human society impossible if he were not on all occasions promptly discouraged and suppressed. Alceste, accorded divine honours by his admirers, is by his detractors turned out to grass with Nebuchadnezzar. The variations upon these two extremes have been many and complicated. Alceste is a political and social malcontent. Alceste is a precursor of the Jacobins. Alceste is the champion of the individualist against the herd. Alceste is virtue personified, for whom there is no refuge in a wicked world. Alceste is the first of the romantics. Alceste is the last of the Stilites. Alceste is pathetic. Alceste is absurd. Alceste is a survival of the austere virtues of the pagan. Alceste is a prototype

394

of ultimate Christian perfection. Molière, in Alceste, pillories the unsocial vices. Molière, in Alceste, portrays the virtues which can alone redeem and ennoble human society.

All this merely means that Alceste, like all the great characters of Molière, is not as simple as he seems. The characters of Molière are usually complex, and Alceste is the most complex of them all. Even his virtues are not always what they seem. He is now noble and then ridiculous, now intolerable and then pathetic. He is often all these things together, and it is small wonder that he has been all things to all men. There is only one mistake about him that should never have been made. Whatever else he may be at any moment, he never ceases to be comic.

Follow him quickly through the play. His first words in themselves must raise a smile: *Moi, je veux me fâcher et ne veux point entendre.* Alceste is in a passion—I *will* be angry and I won't listen to a word you have to say. His friend Philinte has been guilty of an unpardonable offence. Philinte is infamous and cowardly; he has sinned against the light; his soul is corrupt; he is invited to die of pure shame or to hang himself. What act is this that roars so loud and thunders in the index? He has met a man in the street whom he can scarcely remember, but whose friendly greeting he has returned with the customary oaths and embraces. The fashion is a little fulsome by modern standards, but normal and general at that epoch. So might one, walking with a friend, meet a man to-day in Piccadilly. He stops to greet you. You cannot remember his name, but you do not wish to hurt his feelings. You accordingly shake hands and continue on your way. That is the crime of Philinte—the crime for which he is invited to die of shame and to hang him-

395

self. The contention of Alceste that men should be honest in their relations and shake hands only when they mean it—that he has no use for these false shows of friendship and that in all his social encounters he requires a revelation of heart and soul—may be fine in theory and a credit to his noble disposition. But not only is his particular protest ridiculous; his whole case is put with an exaggeration that must raise a smile at his expense.

Such is the professed attitude of Alceste to the social conventions, and the author passes at once to a concrete example. Oronte, like most fine gentlemen of the time, has written a sonnet. He reads it to Alceste and Philinte, requesting an opinion. Philinte pays him the usual compliments, but Alceste must tell him the whole truth and nothing but the truth. The sonnet is pure affectation; it sins against nature; and the author hasn't even the excuse that he writes for a living. Why should a gentleman expose himself unnecessarily to criticism by writing bad verse? Oronte is naturally offended and Alceste soon has an affair of honour upon his hands in which both parties are equally ridiculous. It is true that Alceste in the course of his dispute says some excellent things. One of them has even become a proverb: *On peut être honnête homme et faire mal les vers.* Alceste is substantially right about the sonnet, but his conduct of the quarrel is absurd. His honesty is a virtue, but his complete disregard of other views and feelings than his own and his fire and fury in a small cause are ludicrous. Even Eliante, who is in love with him, admits that he is a strange fellow and can excuse him only on the score that there is "an heroical quality in the sincerity on which he prides himself." The attitude of most men of goodwill would be the

396

attitude of Philinte. He remonstrates with his friend, appreciates his absurdity and does his best to retrieve him from a false position. He describes the affair of honour with Oronte in terms undeniably comic, and the solemn search for a formula satisfactory to both parties is a delicious parody of the diplomatic protocol which was once necessary as between testy individuals but which is now only practised as between sovereign States.

The comic note in the character of Alceste, thus struck at the outset, is consistently maintained. He becomes the more comic in the expression of his misanthropy as his indignation grows. He has a lawsuit, but he will not conform with the ordinary procedure. He refuses, in other words, to call upon the judge who has the case in hand. He will rely on the justice of his cause. His enemy is a scoundrel, and the whole world, if it is a just world, must be aware of it. Illustrious critics, including La Bruyère and Rousseau, have approved Alceste in this particular. Here, they exclaim, is a noble fellow who refuses to corrupt his judge or walk in the shady byways of the law. There is no ground in the comedy, however, for such a reading. Alceste, in the conduct of his lawsuit, is merely absurd. To call upon the judge in charge of a case was in the seventeenth century equivalent to briefing counsel. Alceste refuses, in fact, to take the most elementary precautions. Reason and right are upon his side. He will see whether men can be sufficiently wicked as to commit an injustice *in sight of the universe,* and on losing his case he exclaims that there is no justice upon earth. This is the litigant who assumes that the whole world must be interested in his affair. The stars in their courses must be with him. It is a comic assumption and

397

it is comically presented. His subsequent conduct is even more unreasonable. He will not appeal against the sentence. Let it remain on record as a sign to posterity of the wickedness of his time and race. He has lost 20,000 *livres*, but has thereby purchased the right to curse mankind and nourish an immortal hatred of its iniquity.

Alceste, in his social encounters and the conduct of his interests, is thus revealed as extravagant and uncompromising —essentially absurd. He is now to be shown in his more intimate dealings. Alceste is in love with Celimène, and Celimène is everything that by profession he abhors. She is frivolous and loves company. She will fool a man to the top of his bent. There is nothing she dislikes so much as the plain answer to a plain question. How shall we interpret the relationship between them? Those who read the play in the light of Molière's domestic afflictions discover here a man of delicate integrity hopelessly enamoured, a man to be pitied for his weakness in loving a foolish woman, but admired in the conduct of his passion. There is no ground for such a reading. It is true that in the speeches of Alceste there are passages which might have been written with less feeling if Molière had never had an uneasy moment with Armande:

> Je confesse mon foible; elle a l'art de me plaire:
> J'ai beau voir ses défauts et j'ai beau l'en blâmer,
> En dépit qu'on en ait, elle se fait aimer.

But Molière never allowed his private woes to trouble his comic vision. *Le Misanthrope* is not the tragedy of a man mismated in affection; it is the comedy of a man who, from an inflamed sense of virtue, is ridiculous in all his relation-

398

ships. The conduct of Alceste towards Celimène is no exception. On the contrary, it is a supreme example of his absurdity.

Consider his first references to Celimène. He loves her, but he is not blind to her defects. He will continue to love her, he tells us, because he hopes that his love will redeem her from the faults of the age:

> . . . et sans doute ma flamme
> De ces vices du temps pourra purger son âme.

There is here, not only complacency, but a complete misunderstanding of the woman with whom he is dealing—a misunderstanding which culminates at the end of the play in his preposterous suggestion that she should abandon the world and retire with him into a desert—Celimène in a desert! Philinte can only smile: cure Celimène of her worldliness, if you can, but it will be no small achievement; and he goes on very pertinently to ask Alceste whether he thinks Celimène really loves him. The reply of Alceste throws a swift gleam into the depths of his character. I should not love her, he says, if I did not think that she loved me. It is the voice of Sir Willoughby Patterne.

Alceste, in his scene with Philinte, scolds his friend for extending to others marks of esteem and affection which he should reserve for his intimates. Similarly, in his first scene with Celimène, he upbraids her for allowing herself to be too readily accessible. She has too many admirers and he cannot pretend to like it. He is indignant that the friendly assurances which he receives from Celimène should be lavished equally upon others. In a word he is jealous. This, however, is not the jealousy of an ardent lover but of a nature that must invariably claim an exclusive consideration. He ascribes to sincerity a delicacy which springs in reality from conceit.

The critical scene of the comedy, however, is that in which Alceste, having as he thinks clear proof that Celimène is playing him false, first upbraids her and then begs for a proof of her innocence. Here, if anywhere, is the opportunity for Alceste to show that he is, in effect, a noble lover pathetically wronged in his affection. Observe, however, that Molière has most carefully avoided any such suggestion, not only in the scene itself, but in the scene, curiously neglected by the critics, which immediately precedes it. Alceste, full of fire and fury, is looking for Celimène; but he meets Eliante instead and the two scenes must be read together. The whole character of Eliante is designed, almost too obviously designed, to throw into relief the master passion of Alceste. Eliante is generous and compassionate, ready always to appreciate the feelings of others and to efface herself. It is Eliante who delivers the famous passage, rescued from the vanished translation of Lucretius, on the blindness of lovers. It is put into her mouth in sweet opposition to the contention of Alceste that it is a lover's duty to chasten his mistress and correct in her the vices of the time:

> La pâle est aux jasmins en blancheur comparable;
> La noire à faire peur, une brune adorable;
> La maigre a de la taille et de la liberté;
> La grasse est, dans son port, pleine de majesté;
> La malpropre sur soi, de peu d'attraits chargée,
> Est mise sous le nom de beauté négligée;
> La géante paroît une déesse aux yeux;
> La naine, un abrégé des merveilles des cieux;

L'orgueilleuse a le cœur digne d'une couronne;
La fourbe a de l'esprit; la sotte est toute bonne;
La trop grande parleuse est d'agréable humeur;
Et la muette garde une honnête pudeur—
C'est ainsi qu'un amant dont l'ardeur est extrême
Aime jusqu'aux défauts des personnes qu'il aime.

Eliante has for Alceste a genuine affection. She admires his sincerity. She honestly confesses to Philinte that she is ready to marry Alceste should he realize, as in the end he must, the incompatibility of Celimène. Alceste finds in her a refuge for his wounded complacency and is ready to exploit for his consolation her generous affection. He will punish Celimène by offering to Eliante his trampled heart. Here is balm for a bruised spirit and a wounded dignity. The scene between them is unexampled in the comedy of unconscious egoism. Alceste asks Eliante to accept his addresses merely in order that he may revenge himself upon her rival and he calmly assumes that Eliante, equally horrified by the indifference of Celimène to himself, will jump at this opportunity of setting right so obvious an injustice.

The ensuing scene with Celimène, in the light of this previous revelation, can only be read as a scene of pure comedy. Alceste, odiously complacent in his interview with Eliante, is helplessly absurd in his encounter with Celimène. First he upbraids her for the letter which, as he considers, establishes that she is intriguing with Oronte. He expects her to be confused, ashamed and overwhelmed. He finds her cool, rebellious and hinting at a possible explanation. Instantly he feels that his dignity is in peril. He is getting the worst of the interview. He had thought he had a safe text for a really fine declamation and that Celimène would

401

at last be humbled. But the ground is slipping from under him. In a panic he veers, and he who came to scold remains to pray. He begs her to prove her innocence. Make an effort to prove it, and I will try to believe you, he implores. Now or never is the moment for Alceste to awaken our sympathy and compassion. Here, if anywhere, is your noble fellow basely betrayed but helplessly loving. Deceive, deceive me once again, he entreats—deploring, as he does so, that he is incapable of the generous scorn with which he should meet the unworthy object of his affection. Undoubtedly Alceste here is pitiful, but he is not heroically pitiful. We must still smile upon his discomfiture. Our compassion is less for his wounded love than for his wounded pride. His last words reveal again the master passion of his comedy. Nothing, he says, can be compared with his love for Celimène. He would even wish to see her destitute and abandoned so that she might owe everything to him:

> Ah! rien n'est comparable à mon amour extrême;
> Et dans l'ardeur qu'il a de se montrer à tous,
> Il va jusqu'à former des souhaits contre vous.
> Oui, je voudrois qu'aucun ne vous trouvât aimable,
> Que vous fussiez réduite en un sort misérable;
> Que le ciel, en naissant, ne vous eût donné rien,
> Que vous n'eussiez ni rang, ni naissance, ni bien,
> Afin que de mon cœur l'éclatant sacrifice
> Vous pût d'un pareil sort réparer l'injustice,
> Et que j'eusse la joie et la gloire, en ce jour,
> De vous voir tenir tout des mains de mon amour.

This is not the lover who speaks but still the incorrigible egoist, who only a moment before had shown himself ready to exploit for his consolation the generous affection of Eliante.

402

Alceste, on the heroic plane, or anywhere near it, is impossible. He fails in the critical scene with Celimène and he remains to the end a figure of fun. His final suggestion that Celimène should retire with him into the desert is not only ridiculous in itself but still further reveals the unsleeping egoist. A noble heart, he says, abhors your insincerity, but will yet make shift to love you if you can afford it this proof of a genuine repentance. Celimène offers him marriage, but that will not suffice. It is an *outrage*, he affirms, that she should not be prepared to find all that she needs in him, and he will seek his wilderness alone, where a man of honour may still be free. Observe, however, that nobody takes this declaration seriously. He will fly to the desert. He has sworn it. But Philinte, who knows him, is profoundly unimpressed. He has heard all this before and the curtain falls on a couplet that raises a last smile at the expense of the departed eremite:

> Allons, Madame, allons employer toute chose,
> Pour rompre le dessein que son cœur se propose.

It is the final strophe of the comic chorus and we can have no doubt that Alceste will continue to live in a world unworthy of his presence, and that some day, perhaps, he will meet and marry a woman who will take a Miltonic view of her position and responsibilities:

> He for God only, she for God in him.

Le Misanthrope has always been regarded, and rightly regarded, as the most personal of the plays of Molière. It must not, however, be assumed that in Alceste he was unpacking his private sorrows, that Celimène is a portrait of his

wife, that the play embodies his domestic griefs or expresses
a temporary fit of hatred for the world. That Molière
sometimes rebuked Armande and protested against her in-
sincerities is more than probable; that he was deeply in love
with her and profoundly unhappy in his love is certain;
that he was sensitive, melancholy and seclusive is shown by
all we see and hear of him. *Le Misanthrope,* however, is
in no sense a cry from the heart. Alceste, as we have seen,
is a comic character. Molière, as in his earlier plays, stands
aside and sees himself along with the rest of the world, as
part of the universal comedy. "There, but for the grace of
God, go I," would again be his feeling as he stepped back
to look upon the portrait of Alceste. To assume that in the
speeches of Alceste he expresses a noble sorrow or plays for
sympathy is to invert the personal significance of the play.
Rather he laughs in Alceste at what he might conceivably
have become—as he had already done in Sganarelle of
L'Ecole des Maris and Arnolphe of *L'Ecole des Femmes.*
He stigmatizes the man he might have been if Molière, who
created Alceste, Sganarelle and Arnolphe, had not also been
able to create Philinte, Chrysalde and Ariste. Deprive me,
he says in effect, of my sense of humour, remove the re-
straints of commonsense, blunt me to the views and make
me obtuse to the feelings of those who surround me, give
full play to this or that impulse to which I might perhaps
have yielded yesterday, and there you have the origin of
my Alceste. I do not, however, admire the fellow. Compare him, for example, with the admirable Eliante or the
wise Philinte. Here are characters who stand secure in their
temperate virtues. Who would not choose to be Philinte
if he could mix the elements to his liking? Philinte is an

embodiment of social virtue. He conforms without losing his integrity and smiles at the extravagances of his friend without prejudice to his affection. He is a foil to the absurdities of Alceste, but equally a witness to his merits. Therein lies the essential fineness of the comedy. Alceste, though always ridiculous, does not forfeit the respect or affection of his friends. Even Celimène is ready to marry him—though heaven pity her if she did! Philinte appreciates his stubborn virtue, but deplores his excess. Philinte sees men and things as they are, equably, without rancour and he gives striking expression to the immense toleration of the comic spirit:

> Oui, je vois ces défauts, dont votre âme murmure,
> Comme vices unis à l'humaine nature;
> Et mon esprit enfin n'est pas plus offensé
> De voir un homme fourbe, injuste, intéressé,
> Que de voir des vautours affamés de carnage,
> Des singes malfaisants, et des loups pleins de rage.

Le Misanthrope, then, is a personal play, but not in the sense too often accepted. Molière is not here exposing his married woes, weeping with noble rage, or crying for the wings of a dove. He creates in Philinte the man he would choose to be in an instinctive reaction against his own impulsive nature. The impetuous and sensitive comedian, taking up his pen, becomes instantly wise, moderate and cool. That is the first of his personal reactions, to be found in all his serious plays. Molière sometimes lived, but he never wrote, in a passion, and Philinte is the most complete presentation of his reasoned attitude to life. This is Molière in the Olympian mood. The second reaction is more intimate and

405

peculiar to this special play. In Alceste he was correcting a fault to which he was himself naturally liable. Exaggerate his love of sincerity, carry to excess his hatred of imposture, increase unreasonably and to the point of malady the melancholy detachment which made him the perfect comedian but might have made him the perfect fool—and from a distortion of what was Molière we should obtain Alceste. Alceste is Molière, but with a difference—not the presentation of an idealized portrait but a caricature. And the author has made his intention plain not only in every scene of the play but even in the sub-title. Do not forget that *Le Misanthrope* has another name which is usually omitted, though Molière himself indited it. If the play had always been printed with its full description, *Le Misanthrope ou l'Atrabiliaire Amoureux,* the legend of Alceste as an embodiment of philosophic virtue would have had less chance of survival.

How did the legend arise? When did Alceste, created as a comic character, take upon him the sad airs of nobility? The answer is fortunately clear. The Alceste of Molière survived his creator for just one week. Seven days after the death of Molière *Le Misanthrope* was revived at the Palais Royal with Baron in the part. Baron was then just twenty years of age, but already a public darling. His speaking of verse or prose was a delight to the ear; his presence and gesture were full of charm and grace. He could say or do nothing to which he did not lend distinction. It is easy to divine what happened to Alceste and fortunately we have a witness. There appeared in the *Nouveau Spectateur* of June 15, 1776, a letter from an anonymous correspondent who claimed to have seen Baron in the part—not, of course,

406

the young Baron of 1674, but the veteran of seventy summers who was still playing Alceste at the end of half a century. "I will tell you," says our correspondent, "how Baron played Alceste. Not only did he invest the part with nobility and dignity, but added to it a delicate courtesy and an essential humanity which made us love the misanthrope. He permitted himself an occasional display of impatience and humour, but it was always redeemed by his tone and manner. He was never discourteous or uncouth. Baron rightly thought that it was essential for the actor to adopt the tone of the polite world. He accordingly softened the part instead of carrying it to extremes." The writer goes on to say that, in criticizing the verses of Oronte, the Alceste of Baron was a model of forbearance and tact; that he played most feelingly the scenes with Celimène and never forgot the courtesy due to a lady.

Here was a pretty revolution. With Molière scarcely cold in his grave, Alceste had, if you please, already become a model of courtesy—sorry to offend, invariably tactful and, above all, dignified. Small wonder that the romantic critics of a later generation were led away and that Alceste ultimately found himself in the company of Hamlet and Fantasio. Nor is it surprising that the biographers, following the critics, were soon tempted to identify this noble, solitary understanding and sympathetic figure with Molière himself and to find in Celimène the plague of his existence.

There is no such figure in *Le Misanthrope.* You may catch Molière laughing at the man he might have been if he had lacked the toleration and good sense to avoid such a destiny; you may find him admiring the secure and reason-

able man he would like to have been if he had not been the
generous and impulsive man that he was; but you will never
for one moment find him admiring or justifying himself in
the presentation of a hero after his own heart. The one
weakness of which Molière as man or artist was naturally
quite incapable was the weakness of Narcissus.

XX

IMPIOUS IN MEDICINE

TOUT leur art est pure grimace—thus Don Juan speaking of the doctors to Sganarelle, who discovered to his consternation that his master was also impious in medicine. Why did Molière mock continually at the medical profession? What was the motive which prompted him in play after play to gird at the disciples of Hippocrates and to destroy them in a final masterpiece. That Molière believed or did not believe overmuch in doctors is a small matter. Nine-tenths of the practice of medicine in the seventeenth century was, as Don Juan declared, pure grimace. The incredulity of Molière was natural—almost inevitable. He had a keen eye for the charlatan in art, science or religion, and could not fail, as he came to know them better, to add the doctors to his gallery of impostors. But there are wider questions at issue and, for an understanding of the method of work of Molière, it is essential to deal with them.

Ingenious biographers have invented private reasons for his unremitting persecution of the Faculty. Grimarest relates that Armande took lodgings with a doctor's wife, who raised the rent and evicted Armande when she refused to pay the extra sum, taking as a lodger in her place Mademoiselle du Parc. Mademoiselle du Parc, desiring to be in the

409

good graces of her landlady, gave her a ticket for the theatre, whereupon Armande sent two stout fellows to throw the woman out. Words ran high, and Molière, taking up his wife's quarrel, wrote the comedy of *L'Amour Médecin.*

This silly fable has no basis in fact, and is contrary to everything we know or can reasonably infer of our author's relations with the medical profession. We may, in fact, at once eliminate any personal grounds of rancour. There is fortunately a document which textually disproves a theory which commonsense itself sufficiently disclaims. The personal physician of Molière in 1669 was a certain Monsieur de Mauvillain and his relations with Molière were of the friendliest description. Molière would even chaff him on occasion as when, in his presence and in the presence of the King, he said: "We reason with one another; he prescribes me remedies; I omit to take them and I recover." The man who dared to poke fun at his doctor must needs have been upon excellent terms with him, and there is fortunately proof positive of this very legitimate inference in the third *placet* to *Tartuffe* where Molière begs the King to bestow upon the son of Monsieur de Mauvillain a canonry in the royal chapel of Vincennes. His doctor, he assures the King, has sworn to prolong his life for another thirty years if the petition is granted: "I told him, on receiving this promise, that I was not asking him for as much as that and that I should be quite content if he would be so good as to refrain from killing me."

Molière, then, had no personal grievance. He had a doctor whom he esteemed and with whom he could safely jest even on the subject of his notorious mockery of the profession. We must look elsewhere for the beginning and subsequent development of his satire; and the inquiry will throw considerable light upon the origin and progress of the comedy of Molière in general. Molière's treatment of the Faculty is a particular instance of his general procedure.

Molière began as a disciple of the classic and Italian authors. *L'Etourdi, Le Dépit Amoureux* and the sketch with which he caught the attention of Louis XIV at the Louvre in 1659, owed more, in form and method, to theatrical convention than to personal observation. One of the stock figures of fun in all previous theatres was the doctor or pedant. He was not necessarily a doctor of medicine. He was essentially the pedant or man of learning as distinguished from the man in the street. The man in the street had need of him, must trust him up to a point, but always delighted in his discomfiture. Molière inherited the pedant. He made immortal fun of him whether he be a physician, grammarian or philosopher. He did not in his early plays insist on the peculiar misdemeanours of the medical doctor. On the contrary, his first authentic study in that kind was Metaphraste of *Le Dépit Amoureux*, and that is a grammarian's funeral. If we look to the provincial sketches the doctor in *La Jalousie de Barbouillé*, who is a philosopher, takes precedence of the doctor in *Le Médecin Volant*, who is a physician. The same order is to be observed in the later plays. The best scenes in *Le Mariage Forcé* are those in which Sganarelle seeks the advice of Pancrace the Aristotelian and of Marphurius the Pyrrhonien, philosophers both and *Le Mariage Forcé* was written before and not after *L'Amour Médecin*, in which the doctor of medicine takes his turn at the whipping post. Molière, satirizing the

pedant in accordance with a tradition inherited from his
Italian predecessors, accords priority to the philosophers.

From 1665, however, the medical Faculty becomes increasingly his theme. The first serious declaration of war
was the passage in *Don Juan* already quoted. Don Juan
is a villain who believes in nothing, but he is the most intelligent man in the play and he declares the so-called science
of medicine to be one of the great errors of mankind. To
the dismay of Sganarelle he believes neither in senna nor
in emetic wine. *Don Juan,* produced in February, 1665, was
followed by *L'Amour Médecin* produced in September of
the same year. The impiety which looked between the lines
of *Don Juan* is now openly confessed. The Faculty is represented by four doctors who discuss their mysteries to the
scandal of the profession and the delight of the profane.
These four doctors, moreover, were no fantastic figures of
farce but drawn from the life, being modelled upon the four
physicians of the Court then in attendance upon the royal
family. Guy Patin, himself a doctor, wrote in high delight
to a friend on September 22nd: "A comedy has recently been
acted at Versailles upon the doctors of the Court, in which
they are most ridiculously entreated—before the King, too,
who was heartily amused"; and he added three days later:
"All Paris is crowding to see the doctors of the Court upon
the stage."

What is the precise significance of this sudden onslaught?
Why has the traditional pedant of the *Commedia dell' Arte*
become a contemporary figure?

First let us beware of exaggeration. *L'Amour Médecin*
was hastily written to meet a special request of the King.
It was planned, completed, learned and produced in five

days. Molière had no time to be particular. His dialogue is full of echoes, mainly of himself, and his incidents are lifted from dramatists who range from Plautus to Cyrano de Bergerac.

The play cannot, therefore, be read as a considered project and Molière even apologized for its publication: *Ce n'est qu'un simple crayon, un petit impromptu dont le roi a voulu faire un divertissement.* But the mere fact that Molière was in a hurry, though it discounts a serious intention, makes his choice of theme in some ways the more significant. The author in a hurry naturally takes the subject which comes uppermost. Molière in 1665 had begun to be an invalid who was shortly to be put permanently upon a milk diet. He was already the patient of Monsieur de Mauvillain. He was taking a personal interest in medicine, and we may be sure that a man of such lively curiosity could not fail to have had some interesting conversations with his doctor. The gossip of the Faculty was beginning to come his way. Molière, falling sick, turned his predicament to comic account, just as Molière, the man of forty about to marry a girl of eighteen, had turned to account his potential relations with Armande. His treatment of the doctors illuminates his general progress. He began with an inherited puppet, but the pupppet could not satisfy him always and for ever. Enter the comic genius, the observer of men, the satirist who detested fraud and scourged excess. He had in *Tartuffe* exposed the victim of religious credulity. He was now preparing to expose, in Argan, a victim of scientific credulity.

It was high time. Montaigne, it is true, had ventured, in his universal scepticism, to hesitate a doubt as to the

413

therapeutics of his day, but things had gone from bad to worse and it is probably true to say that medicine was never so dangerous to human life as in the early seventeenth century. A credulous public was impressed with its ceremony, intimidated with its bonnet and gown, cowed with Latin and a big wig, while those who were beginning to feel a dawning reverence for science did not dare to question its remedies. It had one foot in divinity, so that a man who presumed to doubt his doctor might find himself accused of heresy, and the other in right reason, so that a man who questioned its precepts might find himself suspected of insanity. The credulity of the public had behind it the most powerful of all motives—the fear of sickness and death. Faith in medicine has the basic inspiration of all true faith—the will to believe. Hence the implicit trust of King and peasant. Happily for mankind, however, experts seldom agree; and Paris had in 1666 been recently shaken by a series of notorious bedside disputations. Much medical linen had been publicly laundered, and there were even doctors who took a malicious pleasure in the misfortunes of their rivals. Guy Patin was one of them—a witty, malicious fellow who wrote of the court physicians in a way that more than justified the satire of Molière. Certain doctors of Rouen and Marseilles had in 1664 come before the courts complaining that the local apothecaries were infringing upon their rights. Manifestoes were issued on both sides, whence it was abundantly clear that, if a patient had much to fear from his apothecary, he had more to fear from his doctor. Guy Patin described Daquin, the personal physician of *Madame*, one of the victims of Molière, "as a poisonous fellow . . . a great charlatan . . . poor in science but rich in chemical mystifications." Desfougerais, another victim, physician to the King, equally execrated by Patin, was openly accused by Bussy Rabutin of practising abortion by means of violent emetics. Guénot, the third of the famous quartet, with a craze for antimony, was charged with having killed his wife, daughter, nephew, a brace of sons-in-law and a host of patients with his panacea. Guénot attended Mazarin in his last hours. Shortly afterwards he was held up in a press of traffic and a carter, recognizing him, shouted gaily to the crowd: "Way, there, for his honour! It's the good doctor who killed the cardinal." The consultation in *L'Amour Médecin*, which reads to-day like an impossible burlesque, was not even a caricature. It was a comic transcription, faithful in form and substance, of an authentic dispute upon the last sickness of Mazarin, in which four physicians severally declared that the seat of the malady was the liver, the abdomen, the spleen and the lungs respectively. One of these men, Vallot, was a few years later to be publicly credited with the death of Queen Henrietta of England. The truth or falsehood of these particular instances is of small importance. Suffice it that they were believed, and were subjects for social gossip or popular ballad. Such, however, was the prestige of the Faculty and the need of its patients that the profession was not seriously shaken. Public opinion as to the value of medicine wavered between blind faith and nervous mockery. Louis XIV might laugh at a travesty of his physicians in ordinary, but he was obliged to entrust his life into their hands, and they got him at last. The King, who hated bleeding, must open his veins with the meanest of his subjects, and the greatest monarch in Christendom, who shrank from the purge, was on one occasion so soundly dealt with by his physicians that he went to stool nine times in a single day.

Louis XIV was tortured and misused by a succession of doctors whose proceedings would have been incredible to posterity—had they not left a minute record of their grotesque proceedings. The curious may still read the *Journal de la Santé du Roi* in which Vallot, Daquin and Fagon in turn exhibit with a dreadful complacency the wonders of their science. It is clear from the *Journal* that the King, apart from the fact that he suffered from worms—a circumstance which made the royal appetite the wonder and envy of the realm—had a magnificent constitution, and could only with the greatest difficulty be reduced and kept by his doctors in the condition of a chronic invalid. He should never have needed a doctor, but he was seldom out of their hands. Finally, they contrived by a course of purging, bleeding, blistering and sweating which would have killed any ordinary man in his prime, to remove him from the world in the seventy-second year of his reign with all his organs still sound as a bell but naturally a little fatigued from the constant "refreshment"—it is the favourite word of Daquin —which had been lavished upon them for over forty years. The royal dentists had by this time removed his teeth and perforated his palate so that he could no longer masticate or even taste his food. Nothing in the comedies of Molière concerning the doctors of the period exceeds the fantastical reality as disclosed in this professional record and in none of his attacks upon contemporary prejudices does he keep more strictly to the sober facts of the case.

The dress and habit of the physician was still that of the sorcerer. He never stirred abroad without his wig and his gown. He wore a conical hat and rode to his patients upon a mule. He talked in a barbaric mixture of Greek and Latin. His discourse was stuffed with technical terms and allusions to theories which had misled his historic predecessors for over two hundred years. It was thus that he emphasized the hieratic nature of his profession. Public opinion would have been as shocked to see a doctor attending a patient without a wig as to see a priest officiating without a cassock. The first doctor to abandon the wig was Corvisat, and as one of the founders of a rational system of medicine he made it a question of principle. Quite early in his career he was recommended to Madame Necker as the best possible candidate for a hospital which she had recently founded. Corvisat duly presented himself, but without a wig, whereupon Madame Necker roundly informed him that a doctor with so little respect for his mystery could not possibly be appointed. He must choose between his hair and his hospital. Corvisat preferred to keep his hair.

Such was the profession with which Molière in 1666, entering upon the sick-period of his life, had recently come into personal contact. He had inherited a traditional figure of fun from an older theatre and used it to excellent effect in his early farces. But now, once again, he discovered that fact is better comedy than the wildest fiction and the doctor of ancient farce became a contemporary comic figure—such a man as you might see riding to the Louvre upon his mule at any hour of the busy day. It is true that you will find in *L'Amour Médecin* quips from his earlier farces and transcriptions from other sources; but the picture as a whole is, in a vital sense, contemporary and some of its best episodes reflect the professional gossip and public scandal of the day.

417

There is one passage, in particular, which rings a clear echo to controversies and discontents which were troubling the profession itself. Monsieur Filerin, alarmed by the disputes of his four colleagues counsels moderation. Let them beware lest their differences should reveal the uncertainty of their knowledge; for, when experts disagree, men of sense may come by their own. Heaven, he urges, has allowed men to believe for centuries in the Faculty. Do not undeceive them, but, just as the alchemist profits from the desire for riches, so let the doctors profit from the love of life. The public venerates the medical profession made credulous by the fear of death. The doctors have only to take credit for all their patients who recover and blame nature for all their patients who die and their position will remain impregnable.

The passage is typical and the doctors are from nature. We must not be misled by the farcical framework. Molière, even when he goes to life for his comedy, cannot forget the theatre in which he was bred, and farce is ever the skeleton or bonework of his plays. He can forget nothing, moreover, that may serve his turn in the literature that has come his way: *Que voulez-vous, Monsieur, de quatre médecins? N'est-ce-pas assez d'un pour tuer une personne. . . . Il vaut mieux mourir selon les règles que de réchapper contre les règles*—there is chapter and verse for such witticisms as these in a literature that ranges from Pliny the Elder to Montaigne. Such reminiscences, however, do not, any more than the farcical framework, detract from the contemporary comic interest. Therein lies its significance. Here, again, is a specific instance of Molière's normal development from formal farce to natural comedy. He changes under our eyes from the professional young man of the theatre to the independent comic observer.

L'Amour Médecin was produced in December, 1666. In January, Molière fell ill, and for fifty-five days there was no performance at the Palais Royal. He returned to the theatre on February 27th and resumed at once the interrupted performances. The comedian, barely escaped from his sick-bed, returned to the stage to mock his own misfortunes, an astonishing example of that mental trick of creation whereby he detached himself from his private woes, and used them for his art. Molière, provoking the laughter of Paris with *L'Amour Médecin* in February, 1667, helps us to understand Molière who in *L'Ecole des Femmes* did, in the sense we have considered, take his own personal temperament and domestic projects for a theme.

The critics of the day were not slow to seize upon this circumstance. Most important of them was Chalussay who, three years later, published *Elomire Hypocondre*. Of the theatrical libels upon Molière it is the most circumstantial and malign. It is impossible to discover a motive for this sudden attack. The comic war was forgotten, and the battle for *Tartuffe* was won. *Elomire Hypocondre* was written on behalf of no particular coterie or sect. This was either the play of a man with a private grudge or of one who perhaps believed that a possible opening to fame and distinction lay in thus conspicuously affronting a man with many enemies. The play has a sub-title, *Les Médecins Vengés;* but it presents no systematic defence or apology for the doctors. Its chief interest lies in its emphasis upon the paradox with which we are dealing. That a sick man should make a comedy of his sickness had evidently struck the

419

public imagination. Chalussay, incapable of understanding such a paradox, made it serve the turn of his malice. He shows us Molière, as his title implies, sick in imagination, secretly terrified of the profession he has mocked, and consulting it under a disguise. Chalussay would have us believe that for *L'Amour Médecin* Molière was soundly hated by the whole profession. There is no proof of this, however, in contemporary medical literature, and the evidence of Guy Patin is to the contrary.

More interesting are the passages which purport to show Molière at work. Chalussay describes how Elomire, after having written *L'Amour Médecin*, falls sick. His wife sends for the doctors and Molière in a panic suffers their disputes and ministrations. He is cured, however, not so much by their remedies as by the interest he takes in confirming from their proceedings the truth of his comedy:

> A la fin je guéris; mais, s'il faut avouer,
> Ce fut par le plaisir que j'eus de voir jouer
> Mon *Amour Médecin* par mes médecins mêmes;
> Car malgré mes chagrins et mes douleurs extrêmes,
> J'admirai ma copie en ces originaux.

This is, perhaps, the greatest tribute ever paid to Molière, the observer of men. It is drawn reluctantly from a malignant enemy, and it is false in fact. But it shows the extent to which Molière was regarded by his contemporaries as incorrigibly the "painter." Even more striking is the tribute to his detachment. Chalussay describes for us a Molière who is no sooner released from the immediate fear of death than his comic spirit is instantly alert and alive. He watches his doctors at work, delights in their activities, carefully notes

420

the more amusing episodes and on his return to the theatre revises his play in the light of his experience. There could hardly be a better example of falsehood in the letter and truth in the spirit. It was true that Molière was ill for several weeks during the run of *L'Amour Médecin*. He was undoubtedly capable of the detachment, and he was certainly the incorrigible observer of men, depicted by the libellist. The bedside consultations described by Chalussay are, however, purely fictitious. Molière had his own personal physician whom he esteemed and the alleged revision of the play is a pure invention.

Le Médecin Malgré Lui written in 1666 immediately after the production of *Le Misanthrope* does not add appreciably to our present theme. It is, perhaps, the most popular of the farces of Molière; but, be it whispered, far from being his best in that kind, and the indignation of Voltaire that it should have been used as a decoy to attract a dwindling public to the later performances of *Le Misanthrope* is easily understood. Almost more than any other farce of Molière, it depends on what he described as *jeux de théâtre,* and what the modern producer describes as "business." Bottle, bastinado and kisses wrongly bestowed count for much and all the most amusing turns of the plot are lifted, with the effrontery of genius, from other sources. It is distinguished, above other plays, less by comic insight or satirical purpose, than by its astonishing gaiety—frank, sane, vital, blowing through it like a spring wind. To this neither analysis nor quotation—though the play is full of quotations—can do justice. The strictly medical passages are inferior to those of *L'Amour Médecin*. Note, however, that many of the witticisms at the expense of the profession which might be taken for exaggerations of the satirist are a record of sober fact. *Comme on boit pour la soif à venir*, says Sganarelle, *il faut se faire aussi saigner pour la maladie à venir.* The doctors of Louis XIV physicked him soundly *pour la maladie à venir* at least once a month, while the *purgation ou saignée de précaution* was as much in favour as the preventive medicine of to-day.

The popular and professional feeling about the two plays is shown in the short titles by which they came to be known. *L'Amour Médecin* was usually referred to quite simply as *Les Médecins* whereas *Le Médecin Malgré Lui* often reverted to its original title of *Le Fagotier.*

In *Monsieur de Pourceaugnac,* the doctors into whose custody the good citizen of Limoges was committed fill the better part of a full act of joyous satire, in which new jests are added and a new turn given to old ones. We again find it laid down as an axiom that it is better to die by the rules than be cured by unlicensed remedies—which is no more than a candid statement of the professional view from Galen to Lord Dawson of Penn. We have again the comic diagnosis and the indignation of the doctor whose patient escapes him: *Il est lié et engagé à mes remèdes et je veux le faire saisir où je le trouverai, comme déserteur de la médecine et infracteur à mes ordonnances . . . Sa maladie, qu'on m'a donnée à guérir, est un meuble qui m'appartient et que je compte entre mes effets.*

There remains *Le Malade Imaginaire.* It is the last of the medical satires, but it is also the story of the death of Molière. The final word must, therefore, be reserved. Here, however, it may be noted, in passing, that the whole balance of the comedy is changed. Not the doctors but

422

the patient is now in the centre of the picture. This is the comedy of Argan, the robust, imaginary invalid prepared to ruin himself and his family in deference to the false professions of the Faculty. Argan of *Le Malade Imaginaire,* credulous in medicine, is the companion portrait to Organ of *Tartuffe,* credulous in piety. Molière, sick unto death, writes the comedy of the man sick only in imagination, an act of courage and detachment unequalled in the history of genius, passing from the stage where he counterfeited death to death itself, a supreme gesture of the comic spirit which illuminates and explains every significant act of his life. This comedy of Argan, however, is a climax which should not be taken before its time and place. For the moment we are concerned with the doctors.

Note that the satire has taken a more serious and general turn. Molière mocks less at the specific absurdities of the profession, and more at the academic spirit which renders them possible. Thomas Diafoirus, horrid little monster of learning, with his elaborate speeches conned by rote, his classical tropes, his idiotic insensibility, his invitation to the lady of his choice: *Je vous invite à venir voir un de ces jours, pour vous divertir, la dissection d'une femme, sur quoi je dois raisonner*—all this epitomizes the pedant in every subject and clime. His father's pride in this little conservative born and bred—*jamais il n'a voulu comprendre ni écouter les raisons et les expériences des prétendus découvertes de notre siècle*—presents a general indictment of orthodoxy in all its forms and phases. Even more significant, however, is the serious discussion between Argan and his brother Béralde on the true value of medicine. Here Molière seriously justified his scepticism. Béralde regards

423

it as an impertinence to meddle overmuch with nature; belief in medicine has in it a considerable element of superstition, to which the doctors who believe in their remedies, who think it a crime to doubt their efficacy and will help you into the next world in absolute good faith, are the first to fall a victim. There is in this discussion a faith in nature which goes beyond what is reasonable in the light of modern science, but which was more than justified in 1669 when, in nine out of ten cases, it was clearly more dangerous for a sick man to consult a doctor than trust to his constitution. This is the final *apologia* of Molière *impie en médecine,* and, as though to emphasize that for once he has permitted himself to intrude his personal views, Béralde, at the end of his discourse, offers to take his brother to the Palais Royal:

Béralde. . . . j'aurois souhaité de pouvoir un peu vous tirer de l'erreur où vous êtes et, pour vous divertir, vous mener voir, sur ce chapitre, quelqu'une des comédies de Molière.

Argan. C'est un bon impertinent que votre Molière avec ses comédies, et je le trouve bien plaisant d'aller jouer d'honnêtes gens comme les médecins . . .

. . . Si j'étois que des médecins, je me vengerois de son impertinence; et quand il sera malade, je le laisserois mourir sans secours. Il auroit beau faire et beau dire, je ne lui ordonnerois pas la moindre petite saignée, le moindre petit lavement; et je lui dirois: Crève, crève; cela t'apprendra une autre fois à te jouer à la Faculté.

Three days after these words had been first delivered from the stage Molière died without benefit of medicine.

We note in this play not only a more considered treatment of the medical theme, but a certain severe justice to the profession. Dr. Purgon is a fanatic but, unlike Tar-

424

tuffe, who plays on the credulity of Argan, he is an honest man.   Argan is his best patient, an exhaustible source of revenue, and his nephew, Thomas Diafoirus, is to marry the daughter of Argan with a handsome dowry.   But the good doctor does not hesitate to forego all these advantages when his professional advice is questioned.   He falls promptly into a passion.   He will not hear a word of explanation.   This is an affront to the profession, treason to the Faculty.   He breaks the marriage, tears up the marriage settlement, and excommunicates his patient: *Je vous abandonne à votre mauvaise constitution, à l'intempérie de vos entrailles, à la corruption de votre sang, à l'âcreté de votre bileet à la féculence de vos humeurs.*   He is deaf to the appeals of his frenzied and profitable client.

The final ballet takes the form of a burlesque ceremony, showing the induction of a doctor into his profession.   It must not be imagined that this was a purely fantastical invention.   Molière was following closely a consecrated ritual. In 1776, three years after the death of Molière, Thomas Locke visited Montpellier and was present at just such a commemoration.   He describes for us a procession of doctors with red robes and black caps; ten violins play airs from Lulli; the president rises, bids the music cease, makes a long speech in praise of his colleagues and in denunciation of impious innovations such as the circulation of the blood and other such absurdities; finally the candidate, to the sound of more music, is received into the profession, the president investing him with the cap of office, a ring and a chain of gold.

All these details, with the oath of office, imitated by Molière, are to be found in the statutes of the Faculty.

425

Tradition says that Boileau assisted Molière with the grotesque Latin of his parody one evening when they were dining with Ninon de L'Enclos and Madame de la Sablière. It is a pleasant picture, but may be safely doubted. The late scholar of Clermont was fully equal to the task.

XXI

Auteuil

I T was in the summer of 1667 that Molière went to
live in the house at Auteuil round which most of the
legends of his later years revolve. The time he spent
there as joint tenant with Chapelle is rightly regarded as
more truly characteristic of the man than the brilliant and
combative years which preceded it. There were several
reasons for the change. A serious illness had two years
previously interrupted the performances of *L'Amour
Médecin,* while in the spring of 1667 he had been obliged to
postpone the production of *Le Sicilien* at the Palais Royal
on account of an even more serious relapse. In April the
rumour, even, was abroad that Molière was dying. He
had returned, however, to the theatre in June saved by the
milk diet to which he remained faithful for the next few
years. Clearly he had need of as much tranquillity as was
compatible with his busy life. The house at Auteuil had
a small garden, and was then sufficiently remote from Paris
to protect him from needless importunities.

Secondly, there were his relations with Armande. She
was now in the first flush of her young success, and enjoying it to the full. The years at Auteuil indicate, as we have
seen, a partial but necessary separation between husband and
wife. Armande in the pride of life was no fit companion

427

for a man of forty-five upon a milk diet; and, though her conduct was far from being as bad as the libellists affirmed, she, at least, made no serious effort to discredit their accusations. There is no proof that she was making anyone particularly happy, but she was certainly making her husband profoundly wretched.

Thirdly, this was professionally a period of fatigue and discouragement. The enemies of Molière had for the moment prevailed. The King, returning from his campaign in Flanders, had been unable to sanction the performance of *Tartuffe*, and from the 6th August to 25th September, 1667, the theatre of Molière was closed.

Auteuil, however, was far from being the idle solitude to which Alceste had threatened to withdraw. Molière, on a milk diet, wrote during this "retirement" three of his best plays, *Amphitryon, George Dandin* and *L'Avare*. He was in daily touch with his theatre and with his wife. He issued periodically from his hermitage to organize the splendid series of festivals at Chambord, St. Germain and the Tuileries. His retreat was, nevertheless, a reality. It left its mark upon his work, and brings us to a more intimate appreciation of the man.

The housemate of Molière during this period was Chapelle. Baron also was frequently at hand and among the more familiar visitors were Boileau and La Fontaine. This chapter in the life of Molière is traditionally devoted to his friendships. There was one missing from the circle who should undoubtedly have been there. Racine, who a few years before had been in close attendance upon Molière, was no longer his friend, and it is for the biographer of Racine to apologize. Racine, at twenty-one, already a dramatic author, had, in 1660, the year after Molière came to Paris, tried, but in vain, to get his plays performed at the Théâtre du Marais and the Hôtel de Bourgogne. Three years later, he was still unacted, but the friend of Molière. In a letter dated November 3, 1663, Racine described how he was present with Molière at the *lever du roi*. Molière received some royal compliments. Racine was glad for his friend's sake, and Molière, says Racine, was glad that I was there to hear him praised. There is in the conclusion a malice, faintly sour, which we find too often in the sayings of Racine. Some days later Racine wrote again to the effect that he had not seen Molière for eight days, a statement which points to a considerable familiarity. This letter contains the notorious passage in which Racine refers, without comment or indignation, to the libel of Montfleury. Was this indifferent backing of his friend disdain for a slander too infamous for words or was it sheer indifference? Racine, as always, remains ambiguous. Suffice it that in 1663, still the friend of Molière, he reported an atrocious calumny with astonishing calm. Meanwhile he had failed to interest the royal tragedians in his plays and it was Molière who finally brought him to the stage. On 20th June, 1664, *La Thébaïde*, which the royal tragedians had been hesitating for months to produce, was presented by Molière at the Palais Royal.

But alas! this promising association was shortlived. *La Thébaïde*, produced in June, 1664, was followed by *Alexandre le Grand*, produced also at the Palais Royal in December, 1665. People were beginning to talk of the young Racine and this was something of an occasion. Monsieur, Madame, the great Condé and the Princess Palatine were

429

present, and Molière had not spared himself either in expense or deference to the wishes of the author. Robinet commented on the magnificent attire of the actresses. Molière did not act himself—a concession, probably, to an author who admired Montfleury, and could not, therefore, admire Molière, as a tragic actor. The leading part was given to Mademoiselle du Parc, who certainly looked it, and not to Madeleine, who might have acted it. Here, too, the young Racine had his way. Already he was passionately in love with the most beautiful but least intelligent of the actresses of Molière.

Molière had done his best, but Racine was dissatisfied and his friends were not slow to urge the superior merits of the royal tragedians. On December 14th, ten days after the production of *Alexandre le Grand* at the Palais Royal and the day after its fourth performance by the company of Molière, the guests of the Countess d'Armagnac—including the King, Monsieur and Madame—were invited, after dinner, to witness a private performance of the tragedy by the company of the Hôtel de Bourgogne. Racine preferred this production, and, without a word of warning to Molière, authorized the tragedians to present the play for a public run. Thus we read in the Register of La Grange that on December 18th "the troop was surprised to discover that the same tragedy was being played at the Théâtre de l'Hôtel de Bourgogne. As the new arrangement had been made with the connivance of Monsieur Racine, the company did not feel bound to pay him his share as author, since he had used them so ill as to give his play to another theatre."

At that time the rights of authors and managers were simply a matter of current practice and fair dealing, but the

430

recognized habit of the profession was in this case clearly violated. A manager was normally regarded as having an exclusive right to perform a play which he had produced at his own risk and expense until it had been published and the first run of it exhausted. The legal and professional merits of the case were, however, a small matter in comparison with the personal issue. Even if Racine had been acting within the law and custom of the profession, and his dissatisfaction with the production at the Palais Royal was justified, there could be no excuse, except such as might be urged on behalf of a young man indecently anxious to arrive, for his failure to warn Molière of his intention. Clearly he was blind to any consideration, save that of exploiting his success to the limit. "The thing was arranged by collusion with Monsieur Racine"—the phrase of La Grange is not too severe. Here was the friend of Molière, who for the moment owed everything to his first producer, in secret correspondence with a rival company with a view to an arrangement which, if successful, must necessarily humiliate Molière as an artist and materially prejudice his interests. It is, perhaps, asking too much of genius to forego any opportunity of coming before the world with a maximum of brilliance and effect. It was asking too much, at any rate, of the young Racine. To get what he considered to be an adequate performance of *Alexandre* he was prepared to sacrifice his friend. He was not, however, prepared to lose his mistress. Mademoiselle du Parc, a little later, followed him to the rival establishment, where he had the pleasure of showing her how to play *Andromaque*—a tedious business even for a lover. Boileau tells us that he had to teach her the part word for word like a schoolgirl.

431

There were here the grounds for a pretty quarrel. But Molière was too generous, and Racine was too prudent, to make much of it. Molière staged a poor but unmalicious skit upon *Andromaque* six months after its production, but this was advertisement rather than revenge. The piece was by Subligny. Racine retorted, wittily enough, by wilfully mistaking it for one of the best works of Molière. Thereafter the relations of the two men were merely polite. It is recorded of Molière that he defended *Les Plaideurs* against the ill judgment of the town, and it is recorded of Racine that he snubbed a detractor of *Le Misanthrope* by declaring that it was impossible for Molière to write a bad play.

So much for the friend who was absent from the intimate circle that gathered about Molière in his retreat at Auteuil. The other three most constantly named, Boileau, La Fontaine and Chapelle, remained to the end of the story. Their association had been constant from the early days of the comic war. La Fontaine had been one of the first to proclaim Molière to be "his man," and Boileau was the first of the critics to appreciate his genius correctly. Upon the outbreak of the comic war Molière had found Boileau by his side, first and most generous of his supporters in the controversy over *L'Ecole des Femmes:*

> En vain mille jaloux esprits,
> Molière, osent avec mépris
> Censurer ton plus bel ouvrage;
> Sa charmante naïveté
> S'en va pour jamais d'âge en âge
> Divertir la postérité.

. . . . .

> Ta muse, avec utilité,
> Dit plaisamment la vérité;
> Chacun profite à ton Ecole;
> Tout en est beau, tout en es bon;
> Et ta plus burlesque parole
> Vaut souvent un docte sermon.

Boileau's declaration to the King that he considered Molière to be the rarest genius of his reign has been already noted. The King's surprise was not unreasonable in its time and place. Few critics would then have placed Molière seriously upon a level with Corneille, Racine or Bossuet. It is infinitely to the credit of Boileau, the severest classic of them all, that he was able to realize that his friend was big enough to break and exceed the rules of formal art:

> Quelque fois dans sa course un esprit vigoureux,
> Trop resserré par l'art, sort des règles prescrites,
> Et de l'art même apprend à franchir les limites.

This whole question of form and freedom was a frequent subject of argument between the friends and Molière invariably argued on these occasions that formal regularity of expression must be sacrificed to aptness. "One should sacrifice everything to the right word," he is reported to have said in the discussion of an epigram; "it is the business of art to teach us how to dispense with the rules of art." Louis Racine had this saying of Molière from his father.

The earlier meetings of the group—for these were friends before Molière went to Auteuil—took place in a flat in the rue du Vieux Colombier where Boileau would receive his intimates two or three times a week. The nature of the gatherings is described by La Fontaine in his *Psyché:*

433

Four friends, whose acquaintance had begun upon Parnassus came together in a species of society which I would call an academy if the number of its members had been greater, and if they had shown as much regard for the muses as for their diversion. The first thing they did was to banish any conversations conducted by the rules and anything which suggested an academic conference. When they were met together, if by chance they happened, in recounting their experiences, upon any point of literature or science, they profited by the occasion, without, however, dwelling too long upon the same matter, but proceeding lightly from one subject to another in the manner of bees who happen upon various kinds of flowers. Nothing malicious or envious or in the nature of scandal was ever heard among them. They adored the works of the ancients, and did not refuse a tribute to those of modern authors to whom praise was due. They spoke of their own works with modesty, and they exchanged their views in all sincerity when by chance any one of them happened to contract the malady of the age and produced a book. But that was a disaster which but rarely occurred.

Chapelain, dispenser of the King's bounties, who as the "greatest French poet who ever lived" had voted himself a royal pension of 3,000 *livres*—Molière in the same list received a thousand and Racine 800 *livres*—was, for these free spirits, an embodiment of successful mediocrity. His *Pucelle* remained always opened on the table of Boileau and any guest who committed an error of speech was condemned to read ten or fifteen lines. To read an entire page was equivalent to the death penalty.

In addition to these meetings at the flat of Boileau there were literary and other diversions at the celebrated cabarets Au Mouton Blanc and La Croix de Lorraine, where Molière reserved for himself a contemplative corner. We do not

434

imagine him to have been an active performer in the gay
disputes of the tavern, the competitions in fierce paradox
over the wine, the livelier pleasures of the table, the escapades of Chapelle and his rout of merry companions. The
stories which have come down to us, apocryphal in themselves, perpetuate a contemporary impression, and all agree
in showing that, if Molière was necessary to these assemblies,
it was owing to no brilliant assertion of himself but to a
quiet understanding which included all moods and persons.
He was the born moderator, arbiter of the discussions, a court
of appeal in jest and earnest. The story of the supper party
at Auteuil, recounted by Grimarest, and included by Louis
Racine in his memoirs, suspect in its extravagance, is, nevertheless, an embellishment of essential truth. The party included Boileau, Chapelle and Lulli. Molière that evening
drank his milk apart, while Chapelle so successfully plied
his guests with wine that even the wise Boileau went the
way of all convivial flesh. Chapelle, ex-pupil of Gassendi,
ran to philosophy in his cups, and his guests had soon reached
the stage when profound reflections upon life and death must
be exchanged. There was a solemn conclusion in support
of the antique view that no man could be called happy until
he was dead. Most fortunate of all was never to be born;
second best was promptly to pass away. It was accordingly
proposed that the party should adjourn to the river and
there unanimously perish. Molière, warned of what was
happening by one more sober than the rest, came from his
room and realized that his friends were unlikely to listen to
reason. Diplomacy, in fact, was indicated. "What have I
done, gentlemen," he said, "that you should conceive so
excellent a project without allowing me to share it? Would

435

you drown yourselves without me? I took you for my friends." Chapelle agreed. This was a palpable injustice. "Come, therefore, and drown yourself with us," he very handsomely offered. "One moment," said Molière, "this is not an affair to be lightly undertaken. It will be the last act of our lives, and it must not fail to shine at its true worth. People will be malicious enough to discredit our enterprise if we drown ourselves here and now. It will be said that we committed this deed in the dead of night like desperate men. It might even be suggested that we were drunk. Let us choose a moment which will do us greater honour and place our conduct in a proper light. To-morrow at eight or nine o'clock in the morning, fasting and publicly before all the world, we will throw ourselves into the river."

Here we find Molière, as we expect, aloof from the merry circle, but ready to intervene effectively at a critical moment. Molière, referring to himself as Damon in *La Critique de l'Ecole des Femmes*, makes pleasant fun of his "natural idleness in sustaining a conversation." He describes the disappointment of those who invited him to parties as a man of wit and hung desperately upon the lips of a silent oracle; and it was Boileau, who loved his company, that named him *Le Contemplateur*. He must, nevertheless, have life all about him.

It seems strange at first sight to find him with Chapelle for a housemate, for Chapelle was becoming more frequent in disorder as the years increased. But Boileau, too, who was not a man to lose his head to the firstcomer, found Chapelle impossible to resist, a fact which sufficiently justifies the attachment of Molière. Chapelle, however, was scarcely a fit companion for a man who needed peace, and Molière

436

was certainly not insensible to his shortcomings. Molière especially deplored his drunkenness, a vice he detested above all things as spoiling good fellowship and confidence between friends. "I know of no passion more unworthy of a good companion," Grimarest reports him as saying to Baron. "Chapelle is my friend, but his unfortunate weakness deprives me of the advantages of friendship. I dare not tell him anything without incurring the risk of finding myself committed with all the world." Incidentally he also warned his young pupil against sacrificing his best friends for the sake of a jest, as Chapelle was too often inclined to do. Nevertheless Molière had for Chapelle a real affection. The vital gaiety and rude spirits of his friend were a corrective to his own contemplative disposition. He was melancholy but sociable. We cannot think of him as loud in company, but neither can we think of him as liking to be alone. His silence was that of a listener and not of a recluse. With Chapelle for a companion he was unlikely to want for distraction when he needed it, and these were friends who knew him too well to be importunate. His esteem for Boileau and La Fontaine remained unshaken to the end. In Boileau he found a scholar and a fine intelligence after his own heart, and in La Fontaine a natural truant who could not fail to be dear to Jean-Baptiste Poquelin who had chosen to be Molière. His admiration is well attested. La Fontaine was apparently the butt of the company and his simplicity and good humour fitted him well for the part. On one occasion the laugh against him was carried too far; and Molière, on leaving the table, pushing Descoteaux, the flute-player, into a window, declared in lively indignation: *Nos beaux esprits ont beau se tremousser. Ils n'effaceront pas le bon-*

437

homme. This must have been one of the parties in the Rue du Vieux Colombier, for Racine was present and the anecdote is recorded by his son.

Was the great Corneille a member of the circle? He had never made any secret of his conviction that comedy was an inferior form of art to tragedy, but any jealousy or mis- understanding which might have existed between the two men before or during the comic war could hardly have sur- vived the generous admiration of Molière and his lifelong fidelity to the Cornelian theatre. Corneille, however, was a recluse. His taciturnity was notorious, and he had no love of company. A friend of the Abbé de Bellegarde dined at the same table with him for six months without discovering his identity. His friendships were mainly professional and such as could not be avoided. It is therefore not surprising that there should be no record of any personal relations until in 1666 Corneille began to entrust Molière with the produc- tion of his plays. Racine in 1665 had gone over to the Burgundians and Corneille then came to the Palais Royal. Molière produced *Agésilas* in 1666, *Attila* in 1667, *Tite et Bérénice* in 1671, while shortly afterwards, as we have seen, the two authors collaborated in *Psyché.* Cizeron Rival tells a story from which it would appear that Corneille was at least on visiting terms with Molière. Baron, studying his lines as Domitien in *Tite et Bérénice* came to Molière with a passage he could not clearly understand. Molière also was baffled, but Corneille was coming to supper and would solve the difficulty. Corneille duly arrived, considered the lines and found them equally incomprehensible. "Never mind," he said, "deliver them as they are written and those who do not understand them will admire them all the better." It is pleasant to think that Molière and Corneille may have spent many hours together in a silent respect of one another; but there was no real affinity between them and the admiration on both sides could hardly fail to be qualified. A saying of Molière, which comes to us indirectly through Boileau, is perhaps authentic. Molière was referring to the genius of his friend. "There is a fairy," he said, "who whispers in his ear from time to time the most admirable verses, but every now and then the fairy will desert him, saying: Let us see how he will manage by himself. Then the poor fellow can do nothing of consequence and the fairy is merry at his expense."

He lived like a true philosopher—such is the impression which the contemporary gossips, as reported and embellished by Grimarest, almost unanimously emphasize in their references to Molière at Auteuil; and, since a philosopher must needs be absent-minded, and a comedian must needs be humorous, the appropriate anecdotes are abundant. Molière, in haste to reach the theatre, hired a conveyance. The man driving him was slow, and Molière, impatient to arrive, jumped from the vehicle and helped to push it along. Molière, returning to Auteuil by water with Chapelle, challenged by his friend, entered upon one of their frequent philosophic discussions—Descartes versus Gassendi. In the boat was a learned friar, and the friends, each in turn, appealed to him as an arbiter. The friar, caught between two fires, encouraged them with inarticulate noises which each of the disputants interpreted as being corroboratory. The argument ranged far and wide; tempers rose; the friar found himself a judge upon Olympus, and prodigies of learning were performed to win from him a final verdict.

439

The boat duly reached its destination. The friar bent to
recover his effects from under the seat. They included a
besace, sign of the lay brother, who had obviously not understood a word of the discussion. *Solvitur ridendo*, for
Molière was delighted to find himself ridiculous. Such
anecdotes, true or false, are final touches to the portrait of
a contemplative comedian.

On February 25, 1669, died the father of Molière.
The *tapissier* whose limited but worthy ambitions had been
so rudely disappointed must, during the last ten years, have
watched with amazement and with alarm his son's career.
Was he ever at Court during the magnificent festivals of
which Molière was the chief artificer? Was he often to be
found at the Palais Royal when Molière was tempting fortune with a masterpiece? What did he think or say of the
men who applauded or reviled the author of *L'Ecole des
Femmes* or *Tartuffe*? Did he understand his own achievement in having successfully been the father of Molière?
How often did Jean Poquelin and his son foregather in that
house under the pillars of the market? There is not a word
that helps us to answer these questions in all the vast literature that surrounds the life of Molière. We know only
that Molière, all through his career, had business dealings
with his father, in which both parties were equally accom-
modating, and, in family fashion, very particular about
having their transactions recorded in black and white.
Molière had long been out of his father's debt, and his
father at the last appears to have fallen on evil days. The
house under the pillars of the market had of late been badly
in need of repair, and only a year before Molière had, as

we have noted, lent him under cover of a third party the sum of 10,000 *livres* for its restoration. Had Jean Poquelin, father of a famous son, been tempted into extravagant living? Nothing can be definitely said.

It would seem that Molière, invited by Mademoiselle to play *Tartuffe* at the Luxembourg, did not ask to be excused, though his father was at that moment either dead or dying. La Grange briefly records on February 21st: This same day died the father of M. de Molière. The death actually occurred on February 25th, but La Grange, if he is wrong about the date, is probably right about the coincidence. Here, then, was a son play-acting while his father was on his deathbed, and much has been made of it. We know nothing, however, of the circumstances. His father might have been weeks a-dying, and Molière could not be expected to close his theatre indefinitely. Further, let it be remembered that Molière, if he acted upon the day of his father's death, acted also on the day of his own, and that he paid for his father in August of the following year a debt of 1,062 *livres* and five sous—an act in effect more dutiful than a momentary suspension of his professional activities.

The friends of Molière, Boileau in particular, frequently protested against his merciless devotion to the stage. Boileau was not only solicitous for the health of his friend but jealous for the genius which he of all men most truly appreciated. It was towards the end of the residence at Auteuil that he begged Molière to leave acting and devote himself entirely to authorship. Molière replied: "It is a point of honour with me not to abandon the stage." "A queer point of honour," is the comment of Boileau, "to blacken the face

441

every day with the moustache of Sganarelle and to devote one's back to all the thwackings of comedy. This man, the most apt of his time for the disposition and intelligence of a true philosopher, this ingenious satirist of human follies, had himself a weakness more extraordinary than any of those which he mocked." Boileau was right and wrong. Everyone would prefer Molière to have devoted himself to writing another *Misanthrope* than to organizing the King's diversions or providing the public at the Palais Royal with farce and spectacle. Boileau, however, did not realize that to Molière, man of the theatre, living contact with the public and the problems of the stage was the breath of life; he had no comprehension of that passion and fellowship of the stage which possesses the born actor, and it was with a profound and generous indignation that he saw Molière lavishing his precious energies upon tasks of the showman and the clown, instead of putting them to better use in creative work. He could not perceive that the comic genius of his friend, which included the finer values of Alceste, needed for its refreshment a continuous contact with earthen simplicities. The farce from which the comedy of Molière had sprung was something which Boileau must necessarily deplore; he could only feel that comedy, having climbed to *Le Misanthrope*, might henceforth scorn the base degrees of its ascent, and he could not understand how Molière could so easily relapse. Molière (he mourns in his *Art Poétique*):

> Peut-être de son art eût remporté le prix,
> Si, moins ami du peuple en ses doctes peintures,
> I'l n'eût point fait souvent grimacer ses figures,

Quilté pour le buffon l'agréable et le fin,
Et sans honte à Térence allié Tabarin.
Dans ce sac ridicule où Scapin s'enveloppe,
Je ne reconnois plus l'auteur du *Misanthrope*.

Here was a fertile theme on which the two friends must
often have disagreed. It could never have occurred to
Boileau that the genius of Molière was perhaps the more
liberal and the more profound owing precisely to that instinct which sent him continually for refreshment to the
original springs of laughter. Still less likely was he to
realize that for Molière the traffic of the stage, the conduct
of his actors, the gesture and delivery of the written work
as a living play, supremely mattered.

Boileau did not apparently confine himself to personal
persuasion. It is recorded by Louis Racine that the Academy,
stimulated by Boileau, offered to receive Molière on condition that he abandoned the stage and devoted himself entirely to authorship; and the negotiations that ensued appear
to have been serious, for more than one contemporary
memoirist alludes to them. La Motte even refers to an
agreement between Molière and the Academy under which
Molière, as a prospective Academician, promised to appear
henceforth only in high comedy. The possibility was almost
undoubtedly discussed. But it was hardly likely to lead to
a definite arrangement and there could never have been any
serious agreement of the kind suggested. Actors and comic
poets were deliberately excluded from the Academy for
many years to come, and neither Le Sage nor Beaumarchais
were allowed to enter. It was not till 1778 that even the
bust of Molière was admitted. The amends, when they
came, were honourable. "Nothing is lacking to his glory

but he was lacking to our own," ran the inscription, sanctioned by a more liberal generation of Academicians. The hypothetical agreement is equally improbable on both sides. Molière was unlikely to yield upon the point of honour, and the Academy was in any case unlikely to receive him. With Molière indeed the point of honour was inflexible. All that he did in the service of the theatre was gladly done and in no spirit of concession or compromise. For him there was no meanness or shame in the grimaces and hazards of the stage. He wrote for the people as a friend, never in condescension. He rejoiced in the thwackings which his friend Boileau so nicely deplored. Gorgibus in the sack was as much a part of his theatre as Alceste in the alcove. Grimarest tells a story which must be read with care or it may leave a wrong impression of the attitude of Molière to his profession in later life. He records an imaginary conversation in which Molière, speaking to a young man who desired to be an actor and had come to him for advice, dissuades the youth from his purpose by recounting the woes and disabilities which he must inevitably encounter. It is one thing, however, to dissuade an impetuous youth, drawn by the glitter and fallacious liberties of the stage and entirely unaware of its hardships, from embarking upon a career for which he may not have had either the talent or conviction, and quite another to feel doubts as to his own vocation. Molière knew that only those can live happily by the stage who have a passion for the stage. That Molière was at times distracted and discouraged is clear, but that he ever repented his decision to become an actor is impossible of belief.

The Palais Royal gave only three performances a week, so

that Molière, except for the brief periods when he was at court, would have more leisure than the modern actor and manager. Every day he would drive into Paris. There was always some call for his presence, though his comrades, especially the responsible La Grange and the careful Madeleine, would relieve him of a good deal of the work. On free evenings he might read his authors, entertain his friends or write. Three plays in addition to those which he wrote at command for the royal festivals were the product of his retirement, and the mood of semi-seclusion is upon them all. Molière, tranquil at Auteuil, returned to his classical models or to the traditional theatre as he had known it before troubling its innocence with contemporary themes and extending its bounds to include so many new aspects of the human comedy. *Amphitryon* is a Greco-Roman fantasy, transformed to express the Gallic spirit. *L'Avare* is Plautus translated in form and substance, but entirely individual and peculiarly national in its exposure of the vice into which French thrift so easily degenerates. *Les Fourberies de Scapin* is the last of the plays after the Italian theatre—a masterpiece which fittingly concludes the series which *L'Etourdi* so triumphantly began at Lyon some sixteen years previously.

Amphitryon is an author's holiday. Molière, reading again his Plautus, lets his fancy play about the ancient theme. The gaiety of the comedy is that of a spirit loosened. The formal alexandrine breaks into free verse where aptness and felicity of expression are untrammelled. The comedy, human in its essentials, takes wings. Plautus supplies the model; but, while Molière darts and hovers in the upper air, Plautus plods far below.

445

The theme was at the moment in fashion. Rotrou with *Les Sosies,* recently produced at the *Marais,* had won success with an excellent version of the legend, and Molière, writing his own play, sufficiently respected his predecessor to read him with attention and remember some of his more successful episodes. No play, however, is more intimately characteristic of its author than *Amphitryon.* The scholar, the poet, the man of dreams and fancies, the shrewd comedian, the skilful artificer, the virtuoso in metre and phrase—all meet in a composition which, in tone and spirit, was without a precedent.

Amphitryon, first produced at the Palais Royal on January 13, 1668, was presented before the Court at the Tuileries three days later and repeated at Versailles in April. Molière was accused in this play, not for the first time, of basely flattering the vices of the King. Jupiter, wooing Alcmene in the guise of her husband, Amphitryon, is alleged to be Louis XIV, winning the favours of Mme. de Montespan, and much learning has been wasted on the malicious parallel.

> Un partage avec Jupiter
> N'a rien du tout qui déshonore.

The couplet has been quoted as indicating a complacent servility, and Michelet, in his hatred of Louis XIV, has constructed a fantastic conspiracy between the King and his comedian to deify his vices and incidentally to deliver up his mistress to derision on the public stage. The insinuation is not worth a tenth of the learning that has been wasted upon its refutation, and it is sometimes difficult to believe that those who solemnly defend or attack the hypothesis can have read the play. In none of his comedies has Molière

446

more finely dared to criticize by irony, implication and straightforward mockery exactly that zealous servility of which he is accused and which after his death was, in the same Court of a monarchy grown hyperbolical, to degrade the conclusion of a great reign. The couplet quoted against Molière itself refutes the accusation. It is Jupiter himself who speaks the lines, and his Olympian fatuity is more calculated to provoke laughter than respect. *Le Seigneur Jupiter sait dorer la pilule* is the comment of Sosie, and it is Sosie, comic chorus to the play, enacted by Molière himself, who concludes:

> Messieurs, voulez-vous bien suivre mon sentiment?
> Ne vous embarquez nullement
> Dans ces douceurs congratulantes:
> C'est un mauvais embarquement,
> Et d'une et d'autre part, pour un tel compliment,
> Les phrases sont embarrassantes.
>
> .   .   .   .
>
> Sur telles affaires, toujours
> Le meilleur est de ne rien dire.

Irony is often misunderstood, but there is no room for misunderstanding in the prologue, where Mercury, celestial pandar, and Night, bidden by the King of heaven to smooth his way to the embraces of Alcmene, express themselves in terms that could hardly fail to tweak a conscience here and there among the distinguished auditors of the play, whose services to His Majesty more often increased the royal pleasure than their noble credit:

> Voilà sans doute un bel emploi
> Que le Grand Jupiter m'apprête;
> Et l'on donne un nom fort honnête
> Au service qu'il veut de moi;

447

while to the protest of Night, an honest creature, Mercury
replies with a stroke as audacious as any that Molière ever
allowed himself:

> Un tel emploi n'est bassesse
> Que chez les petits gens.
> Lorsque dans un haut rang on a l'heur de paraître,
> Tout ce qu'on fait est toujours bel et bon,
> Et, suivant ce qu'on peut être,
> Les choses changent de nom.

Amphitryon was clearly written without any respect of
persons, a comedy which its author enjoyed as a dramatist
who was for the moment free to follow his inclinations.
He throws the reins loose upon the neck of Pegasus, writing
in the easy numbers towards which he had been feeling his
way in *L'Amour Sicilien.* They are a perfect instrument—
strong, flexible, voluble, moving easily from mood to mood,
by turns ironical, sententious, formal or familiar. The comedian was never in better vein and never more diverse and
comprehensive. He looks back to the antique theatre of
Plautus and forward to a comedy which is still with us and
still to be explored. Molière could take nothing into his theatre, however fantastical, without suggesting a human significance; translating it from the realm of incident to the world
of character. In Plautus Jupiter borrows the form of
Amphitryon to win Alcmene, an incident rich in comic situation and comic surprise. But in Molière, to use a word not
yet in fashion, the substitution assumes a psychological
significance which is exploited seriously in the scenes between
Jupiter and Alcmene and comically in the scenes, original
to Molière, between Sosie and Cleanthis. The human implications become perceptible. We feel that in another

448

moment we shall be confronted, perceptibly, with the whole enigma of personal identity. Sosie, playing upon the double personality forced upon him by the mischievous Mercury and Jupiter distinguishing between himself as lover and husband point us forward to the modern Italian theatre of Pirandello and Antonelli.

The vitality and freshness of the play and its immediate appeal to the modern mind is thrown into high relief by its antique form and fashion. Mercury is a god, but this only gives an added piquancy to his human observations. Wooing Cleanthis in the guise of Sosie, he expresses himself as any husband to any wife:

> Ne sois point si femme de bien,
> Et me romps un peu moins la tête.

These gods exist only to reveal the humanity of their victims and are divine only in being more human than the men whose shapes they borrow. This is equally true of the perplexities arising from the confusion of identities. Some touch of character or commonsense strikes suddenly through the fantasy and appeals to us all the more for being unexpected. Sosie issues from his perplexity to declare:

> Le véritable Amphitryon
> Est l'Amphitryon où l'on dîne.

Cleanthis, torn between a stubborn virtue and her natural disposition to be kind. exclaims:

> Ah! que dans cette occasion,
> J'enrage d'être honnête femme!

Amphitryon, faced with the innocent infidelity of his wife, confesses:

449

De semblables erreurs, quelque jour qu'on leur donne,
Touchent des endroits délicats;
Et la raison bien souvent les pardonne,
Que l'honneur et l'amour ne les pardonnent pas.

Such touches are among the surest and most humanly comic
in the theatre of Molière. Voltaire, often astray in his
judgments, was as right in claiming this play for a masterpiece, as Boileau was wrong in decrying it as an unsuccessful imitation of Plautus. Voltaire finds the *Amphitryon* of
Molière superior to that of the Latin author both in spirit
and construction, affirming that it succeeds beyond dispute,
being a play that must please the simple, vulgar and refined.
Boileau, on the other hand, if his Boswell is to be trusted,
could not endure the enigmatic loves of Alcmene and Jupiter.
He preferred his Plautus and even in places the version of
Rotrou. A good critic was for the moment out of his depth.
This free blend of fact and fantasy in which wisdom and
truth break suddenly into a smile, broad as ten thousand
beeves at pasture, was not within his range.

George Dandin ou Le Mari Confondu, produced at Versailles in 1668, was, as we have seen, an item in a royal
festival. The *comédie-ballet* of which it formed a part,
however, was conspicuously a hybrid and the pastoral interludes have mercifully dropped from the final text and left
the comedy intact. Molière, in writing it, borrowed largely
from himself, transposing scenes and incidents from *La
Jalousie de Barbouillé* which he had written for the provinces and revised for production in Paris as *La Jalousie de
Gros-René* or *Gros-René jaloux*. He borrowed also from
Boccaccio and from the French and Italian authors who
carried on the decameronian tradition. The sources, how-

450

ever, whether to be found either in his own plays or in the
works of another, are immaterial. The spirit of the comedy
is not only individual to Molière but peculiar to the play,
a curious blend of gaiety and cynicism in which the two
main facets of his genius boldly relieve each other and
sharpen the general effect. *George Dandin* is the story, incorrigibly Gallic, of a husband outwitted and perhaps deceived. The play is not however merely merry. For all
its high spirits and loose humours, it is a logical and cool
exposure of the consequences of a social blunder. "The
subject," runs the programme which in a previous chapter
we attributed to Molière, "is a peasant who has married the
daughter of a gentleman and who throughout the comedy
is punished for his ambition." The merry tale of Boccaccio
is thus transformed into the comic study of a misalliance.
George Dandin has married into the de Sottenvilles, and
Angelique, his wife, overwhelmed with her condescension,
feels that her husband should be grateful to her for anything it may please her to do. Molière has placed his de
Sottenvilles neither too high nor too low. Snobbery is of
the middle state, so that Angelique can both despise her
husband and be highly flattered with the attentions of a
gentleman of the Court. She remains throughout ambiguous and disagreeable. It has been pointed out by those who
feel Molière to be in need of a moral apology that this is the
only play he ever wrote with adultery for a theme. It
would, however, take a pertinacious and most ungentlemanly
lawyer to prove misconduct; and the offence, even though it
be imminent, is not the subject of the play. The theme is
stated by Angelique herself, and for Dandin it becomes almost a refrain. Dandin has married out of his station with-

451

out even consulting his future wife. He has made the arrangements with her parents. "You are, in effect, married to them," says Angelique, "and if you have any complaints to make, you know where to go." Angelique, though a definitely unsympathetic character, is allowed, as is usual with Molière, to say some extremely pertinent and plausible things, and she is prompt with her own wanton reading of doctrines worthy of a better cause. "I will not be buried alive in a husband," she protests; she will see something of the world and have her pleasure; her husband must take his punishment like a man and thank heaven she is not capable of worse. The critic wonders of what exactly she was or might be capable. George Dandin believes her capable of anything, and the loving promises of amendment which she lavishes upon him in a tight corner leave him unmoved. "Crocodile," is his comment, and he desires only to expose her perfidious treatment of himself and be rid of his bond. Was Dandin justified in his suspicions? Essentially right, but technically wrong, would probably be the answer of Molière. Angelique in a panic would promise anything; there is no proof that the worst had happened but every likelihood that it would not be very long delayed.

The poignancy of the comedy is enhanced by the fact that Dandin clearly appreciates his own misfortune; he knows exactly how uncomfortable is this bed which he has made and at the close he can think of no remedy but to drown himself. Dandin is his own comic chorus, aware at every turn of his predicament, pitiless in his reading of every situation, shrewd in every crisis. The comic characters of Molière are usually blind to themselves and their environment, and it is precisely this blindness that renders

452

them ridiculous. Dandin, on the contrary, is aware of his folly and unerring in his diagnosis; and the comedy consists in his efforts to get the other people of the play to realize the facts. The comic method of Molière is turned inside out. Dandin, instead of being the only mad person in a sane world, is in this case the only right person in a world at fault. He knows Angelique to be a minx, but he cannot prove it. That is the essence of his comedy, and it is not unnatural that Molière failed to be very precise concerning the exact degree of her infidelity. This is not the comedy of the husband deceived but of the husband confounded.

The reprobation of the moralists, for whom *George Dandin* has been a rock of offence for generations, was loud in the land within ten years of the death of Molière. Bourdaloue, preaching before the King in 1682, quoted it as a climax of disorder—the good husband sensible of his misfortune is mocked and the wanton triumphs; such a play must corrupt more souls than the gospel is likely to convert. Rousseau wondered which was the more criminal—a peasant who was silly enough to marry a lady or a woman who sought to dishonour her lord. What, he asks, are we to say of a piece in which the pit applauds the infidelity, deceit and impudence of a wife and laughs at the stupidity of the poor fool who is her victim? Marmontel answered him roundly. This, he urged, was a lash laid to the vanity of the social climber, and not one of the characters, presented for laughter, is in the least likely to seduce our affection or respect. Thus proceed the moralists—ding-dong down the generations, arguing, as moralists will, altogether aside from the comedy itself. Molière, the comedian, took a merry tale

453

and converted it into a comedy unusual in method, profoundly disconcerting in its singleness of spirit and fearless in its consequences. Both elements of the play are distasteful to those for whom the world is a moral gymnasium: the merry tale which survives in its episodes and the comic diagnosis which lives in its characters.

Among the more perverse suggestions which have been made concerning George Dandin is an allegation that Molière, in his portrait of Angelique, intended to pillory his wife. Angelique, it is urged, was his revenge upon Armande for her infidelities and he took malicious pleasure in publicly exhibiting her in the rôle of a wanton. It seems hardly necessary to affirm that there is no ground whatever for this assumption and there is certainly no need to consider it as a serious contribution to the biography of Molière.

The King at Versailles in 1668 had no misgivings as to the morality of the play. It was produced in July, repeated in November, and Robinet records that the royal spectators laughed and to spare. It was presented at the Palais Royal on November 9th. It was publicly played 39 times during the life of Molière, and 315 times during the reign of Louis XIV. It may accordingly be reckoned among the successes of Molière.

Meanwhile, on September 9, 1668, *Amphitryon* at the Palais Royal had been followed by *L'Avare*. Here again was Plautus transformed and, in this instance, all unprejudiced critics are agreed. Boileau, Voltaire and La Harpe all find the comedy of Molière more delicate, veracious and profound. In no play has Molière more successfully lived up to his confession: *Je prends mon bien où je le trouve.* Plautus, Boisrobert, Ariosto and a host of minor authors,

454

French, Spanish and Italian, are here remembered. **But**
the result is Molière pure and undefiled.

The play was not conspicuously successful during its first
run. The receipts fell from over 10,000 *livres* at its first
performance, attended by the King and the Court, to less
than 500 *livres* at the second and less than 150 *livres* at
the eighth. Several distinguished authorities, following a
confused and clearly inaccurate passage in Grimarest have
attributed the comparatively cold reception of the play to
the fact that it was written in prose. Voltaire, with his
pleasant habit of improving a falsehood, stated that Molière
sketched his comedy in prose with the intention of transcrib-
ing it into verse, but that his actors found the prose so excellent that they insisted on playing it in the provisional
version. All this is quite unfounded. Nor is it possible to
admit as an explanation the contention that extreme avarice
has ceased to be a sufficiently comprehensible vice to form
a suitable subject of comedy in modern times. These are ingenious explanations invented to account for facts which are
to a large extent imaginary. *L'Avare*, though it was not immediately popular, was as successful as the other great comedies of Molière which had no immediate advertisement. All
Paris crowded to his farces, to his satires of contemporary
life, or to a play like *Tartuffe* which had been a public
scandal for five years previous to its production. *L'Avare*,
however, like *Le Festin de Pierre* and *Le Misanthrope*, had
to stand upon merits not obvious to the average spectator
upon a first production. It is clearly not likely to provoke a
boisterous response. The laughter of the spectators was
rather an internal gesture than a public demonstration. A
famous passage of arms between Boileau and Racine is in

this connection significant. "I saw you recently," said Racine, "at the play (he is referring to *L'Avare*), "and you were laughing all alone." To which Boileau replied, "I think too highly of you to believe you were not also laughing—*at least inwardly*." This was a play that grew upon the attention of the public. It was played forty-seven times during the first four years of its existence to audiences that steadily increased and from the first it was admired by the Court. Robinet, faithfully echoing the best people, not only praised the play but commended the prose, *si théâtrale*, in which it was written.

L'Avare was one of the plays quoted by Rousseau as illustrating the wicked and anti-social spirit of its author. The son of Harpagon, says Rousseau, is prepared to rob his father and makes light of his father's curse—a nice school of manners, indeed, in which a young man, capable of such enormities, is allowed to bid for our sympathy. To accuse Molière of being unsocial for showing the son of Harpagon lacking in regard for his father is sheer perversity. Harpagon, in the grip of his passion, forfeits, it is true, the respect of his children, but this only means that Molière does not flinch from the true consequences of his theme. In satirizing an excess he not only reveals the fatal havoc which it wreaks upon the individual who suffers it; but shows also its effects upon the persons surrounding him. The avarice of Harpagon, like the egoism of Arnolphe and the credulity of Organ, spoils not only himself but corrupts all his domestic relations. Molière, if we need a moral, is merely emphasizing that an unsocial vice must have consequences ruinous to society, an axiom which hardly needed the support of his comic genius or deserved the illustrious censure of

456

his critic. He was perfectly aware of the moral enormities which Rousseau so vehemently stigmatized. It is, if you please, monstrous and unedifying that two children should be in rebellion against their father, but Valère, the lover of Elise, overcomes her reluctance by justifying in advance her unfilial behaviour. The whole of the first scene between the two children is expressly designed to show that their conduct is a natural and human consequence. *"A-t-on jamais vu une fille parler de la sorte à son père?"* exclaims Harpagon, enraged at the resistance of his daughter. *"Mais a-t-on jamais vu un père marier sa fille de la sorte?"* counters Elise. *"Voilà où les jeunes gens sont réduits par la maudite avarice des pères,"* exclaims Cléante, *"et on s'étonne, après cela, que les fils souhaitent qu'ils meurent!"*

Avarice is an ugly text, and it would seem difficult to draw laughter from so dark a source. Molière, however, cuts and polishes his theme till it sparkles from a thousand facets. The vice being itself fundamentally unnatural lends itself to an extravagant presentation. Harpagon is a marionette whose jerking upon the strings of his passion strikes our sense of the ludicrous like the stiff inevitable movements of a clockwork figure. There is an absurd logic in all he does and says: *Donner est un mot pour qu'il a tant d'aversion qu'il ne dit jamais: je vous donne, mais: je vous prête le bonjour.* To vary and strengthen the comedy, Molière, as in his other plays, shows the vice with which he is dealing at issue with motives which are essentially incompatible. Harpagon, the miser, organizes a banquet. Harpagon, who loves only his treasure, is planning to marry a young wife. Observe that it is precisely in these scenes that Harpagon, aping the gestures of hospitality or courtship, is most su-

premely comic in his avarice. Molière is invariably at his
best in exhibiting his characters thus at issue with themselves;
from Arnolphe who abandons all his theories upon the
schooling of wives in abject doting upon Agnes, to Alceste
who yields against his philosophy and disposition to the fas-
cinations of Célimène.

Molière at Auteuil returned for his release to the classics.
Plautus served him well. Terence followed, earliest and
dearest of his masters. *Les Fourberies de Scapin,* based upon
Phormio, with echoes from Plautus, a paraphrase from *La
Soeur* of Rotrou and a famous scene lifted from Cyrano de
Bergerac, is the last of the farces of Molière. Twelve years
had elapsed since he had come before the town with his first
example in that kind, and between *L'Etourdi* and *Les Fourberies de Scapin* the public had learned to appreciate a finer
product. It was played to moderate houses for only eighteen
times during the life of its author. The play is frank farce,
more robust but admittedly less refined, than the antique
model from which it was derived. Molière was probably
using one of his early sketches. There are references in the
Register of La Grange to a piece entitled *Gorgibus dans
le Sac* performed in 1661, 1662 and 1663. *Gorgibus dans
le Sac* almost certainly contained an earlier version of the
most notorious of the *fourberies,* so feelingly deplored by
Boileau, in which Scapin lured his victim into the famous
bag. Molière wrote this play as much to amuse himself as
to amuse the crowd. The simple gaiety of his farces is as
natural to him as the sad inspection of his finer work. We
have seen that Boileau, with his aquiline taste, was unable to
appreciate this aspect of his friend. He regarded Scapin as
the deplorable lapse of a great comedian; the fine smile of

Terence is distorted and the author of *Le Misanthrope,* entering the sack in which Geronte suffers *toutes les bastonnades de la comédie* is profaning his art and wasting his talents. For the delicate Boileau, Scapin is a bitter pill. His sack and cudgel are an ancient inheritance whose plenty will only be exhausted when children cease to laugh at a man who falls upstairs or sits upon his hat. The use of these properties in a play derived from Terence was to Boileau simply shocking; they belonged to Tabarin and had no place in a civilized theatre.

Molière writing *Les Fourberies de Scapin* borrowed a scene from Cyrano de Bergerac—the scene, no less, than that in which we find the classic refrain: *qu'est ce qu'il allait faire dans cette galère.* The traditional reply of Molière to the apocryphal remonstrance of a critic against this particular larceny has been often quoted, or perhaps misquoted, in these pages: *Je prends mon bien où je le trouve.* Some authorities, reading *"reprends,"* insist that Molière was the original author of the scene, or more ingeniously, that he collaborated with Cyrano, hypothetically the friend of his youth, in writing *Le Pédant Joué,* and that in *Les Fourberies de Scapin* he was merely resuming possession of his own literary property. This is to rob an excellent, if apocryphal, utterance of its value as a general statement of policy. The saying attributed to Molière, accused of having robbed Cyrano of his galley, is an appropriate device for an author sure of his right to take all life and literature for his province. Molière was too modest a man to have so insolently claimed that right for himself, but the unknown gossip, who invented the tale, has provided posterity with an apt retort upon all the critics, contemporary or otherwise, who find in him an echo of other men.

459

XXII

The Death of Molière

M OLIÈRE lived apart from his wife at Auteuil
from the summer of 1667 to the autumn of
1671. Well before December of that year, however, he returned to Paris, abandoned a milk diet and resumed the married state.

He resumed also his militant career as a satirist of contemporary life. *Les Femmes Savantes,* last but one of his
plays, brought him back to the field which he had entered
thirteen years previously with *Les Précieuses Ridicules.* It
killed an Academician, glanced disrespectfully at a duchess,
and dealt firmly with a social problem which was then beginning to be urgent and has not yet ceased to be troublesome. The contemporaries of Molière found in the play
two striking portraits drawn from the life. Trissotin and
Vadius, the rival wits of the comedy, were identified as the
Abbé Cotin and the poet Ménage. Molière in a harangue,
unfortunately lost, publicly denied the charge, but his denial
was more probably a confession ironically phrased. That he
did, in this case, wilfully point at living models is hardly
open to dispute. Voltaire rebuked him lightly for a practice
which he deplored in principle, but imitated in practice.

It may be urged in apology that Molière did not satirize
his victims unprovoked. The Abbé Cotin was a persistent,

460

though usually an anonymous, critic of Molière. He is accused with Ménage of having tried to set the Duc de Montausier against *Le Misanthrope* by suggesting that his Grace had seemed as a model for Alceste. The sequel was crushing, for the duke went to the play, was enchanted, thanked them cordially for so flattering a suggestion and invited Molière to dinner.

The interest of these personalities is to be sought, however, less in the greater or less provocation of Molière, than in their bearing upon his method of work. Trissotin and Vadius were recognized as contemporary portraits in 1671, but no one reading the play to-day and unacquainted with its history would suspect that these two characters were created less independently than the rest. The personal portrait is lost in the general character. The play may be read without a key, and should not be read in any other way. Trissotin is the universal pedant. He lives in the play without reference to any topical appeal; he is essential to the action and a necessary figure in the general composition. He in no way disturbs the comedy with suggestions or allusions to persons or events outside it. The comic world of the author is sufficient unto itself, and his characters, once they have entered it, live of their own vitality and logic. Molière took a living model, but he might claim in principle, here as always, that his play was not a slavish study from the life.

Tradition, not content with identifying the poet's characters, has insisted on improving the occasion out of all resemblance to the facts. It is variously recorded that the part of Trissotin was played in a mask resembling the features of the victim; that the actor was instructed to imitate his deportment and gestures; that the author even secured

461

and used for his production an old coat which had belonged to the unfortunate Abbé. These stories are, upon their evidence, suspect, and, in their substance, incredible. They have as little basis as the legend, perpetuated by Voltaire, that the Abbé Cotin, mortally wounded by the satire, fell into a decline and died as a result of it. Chronology indicates, at any rate, that the decline was extremely gradual. The Abbé Cotin, outliving Molière by nine years, passed away in December, 1681, at the ripe old age of seventy-eight. Ménage was more adroit than Cotin, whose mortification was notorious. He refused to see any likeness of himself in either of the poets, and admired the play on all occasions as conspicuously as possible.

Molière was cruel in his satire, but he was also bold. He attacked a fashionable pedantry from which few were exempt. The Abbé Cotin was an academician and almoner to the King. His verses, derided in the play, had been read to Mademoiselle, who had apparently had no fault to find with them, and had been accepted as a tribute by the duchesse de Nemours. Boileau affirms that the Abbé in his affliction ran to the King for comfort, hoping that so impertinent a libel would be instantly suppressed:

Et le roi, que dit-il?—Le Roi se prit à rire.

Satire is of necessity cruel, but it is shocking only when it is aimed at the weak or the defeated. Molière was challenging the great ones and would have been the first to suffer if his mockery had been esteemed inopportune or unjustified.

A comparison between *Les Précieuses Ridicules* and *Les Femmes Savantes* is inevitable. The first was aimed lightly at a fashion; it was gay, mischievous and destructive. It

462

indicted a contemporary affectation. *Les Femmes Savantes,* though it was also aimed at a contemporary form of pedantry, seriously raised a social problem of permanent interest. The species of learning affected by the blue-stockings of the period and their tame poets, a curious blend of literary conceit with premature smatterings of the new science which was to become the principal nourishment of a younger generation, is of small importance. The play strikes deeper than that. Within the limits of comedy, which does not permit of any tragic or emotional implications, Molière reveals in Bélise, who sees in every male a secret lover, and in Armande, who, subscribing to the doctrines of the prude, allows us, nevertheless, to see that nature is taking her revenge, a comprehension, in his day entirely precocious, of the consequences of an affected suppression of normal instincts. He further contrasts these prudes by affectation, who refine upon their emotions and deny their sex, with Philaminte, honestly a prude from militant conviction. In Belisé and Armande he presents the victims of feminism; in Philaminte he presents one of its leaders and he allows her all the virtues of leadership. Philaminte is absurd in her excessive pretensions, but she is sincere; and, in disaster or misfortune, she is undismayed. She has the courage of her creed and of her intellectual professions. She is a potential champion of nineteenth century feminism born two hundred years too soon. She embodies the principal issue of the play. What is the true wisdom of women? Is it of the hearth or the forum?

Molière ridicules false learning and a silly erudition. But he does not, as has often been alleged, in any way retract his liberal views upon the education of women which he had

463

suggested eight years previously in *L'École des Femmes*. Nowhere does he deny to women the right to higher knowledge; he merely asks that they shall wear it gracefully—avoid learning for the sake of learning, never parade their knowledge, be wise in all things without insistence. This is the feeling of the average man of sense. Pedantry is anti-social and, if women become pedantic, there is an end of society. Molière utters no word in this play against learning in either sex, but satirizes in both the erudition which fails of its purpose. Philaminte accuses the wise Clitandre of hating science and wit. No, he protests, I hate only the science and wit which spoil a man; in themselves they are excellent and lovely. He concludes with the definite challenge:

> . . . et je vous suis garant
> Qu'on sot savant est sot plus qu'un sot ignorant.

Clitandre speaks for the commonsense of the educated man. A more robust view of woman's duty to the home, which was to enrage the feminists of a later generation is put by Chrysale, the unfortunate husband of Philaminte. Chrysale speaks according to his character and situation. Molière is not to be censured for the views of his creature. The antipathy of Chrysale for book-learning in a woman is proper to his station and is justified by his experience. Any husband whose wife dismisses a good cook for bad grammar may be excused a point of view which is traditional rather than generous. Chrysale would have his wife burn all her books and leave all learning to the doctors. One volume only he would spare—a large Plutarch, useful for pressing his cravats. Is this, we wonder, the Plutarch

464

used by Jean Poquelin for a similar purpose in the house of the monkeys?

Chrysale is not a philosopher or an authority on social behaviour. He is an essentially comic character—one of the best in all the comedies of Molière. Especially is he absurd in his declarations of independence—the verbal courage of a weak man who will inevitably yield at the critical moment. He is a comic Hamlet, losing the capacity for action in the energy of resolve, ruled by his wife and affectionately pitied by his daughter, who sees through his professions of defiance but appreciates his soundness of heart. His creator allows him sense enough to put the common view shrewdly and forcibly; but there is nowhere any suggestion that Molière endorses his opinions on the education of women. There are more uses for a Plutarch than Chrysale allows, though he is obviously right on the subject of cooks:

J'aime bien mieux, pour moi, qu'en épluchant ses herbes,
Elle accomode mal les noms avec les verbes,
Et redise cent fois un bas ou méchant mot,
Que de brûler ma viande ou saler trop mon pot.
Je vis de bonne soupe, et non de beau langage.

To what extent is learning in a woman to be encouraged? The answer of Chrysale is contrasted with the answer of Clitandre. Chrysale urges kitchen and cupboard, while Clitandre expresses the view of the man who is liberal with discretion. Parallel with this question, to which Clitandre gives an answer which accords with the general attitude of Molière in all his comedies, is a deeper and more delicate issue. Here already, in the seventeenth century, was an intimation of that sex antagonism which was to be a recurrent theme of sociologists as yet unborn. Molière announces the

465

subject in the first lines of the comedy, plunging us at once into an ardent discussion between the sisters Armande and Henriette on the subject of marriage. Henriette defends the normal view. She is, perhaps, the most charming of all the heroines of Molière, candid, equable, nimble of mind and wit, warm in her affections, not asking too much of life, but gladly accepting what is offered. Armande, her mother's daughter, has, with affected prudery, rejected the addresses of Clitandre, loudly despising a love that will not be satisfied with spiritual fulfilments. These repressions have their revenges. The passion with which she stigmatizes the married state expresses a secret envy of her sister for accepting the lover whom she herself has refused. She can neither take nor leave a man. Her sex has, quite literally, gone to her head. She suffers the doom of the false prude, which is to be lascivious only in imagination. The very word marriage has become offensive in her ears. Cannot her sister realize how revolting are the ideas which it suggests, how unclean are the paths into which it decoys the imagination? Let her sister leave marriage to the vulgar, elevate her thoughts, cultivate pleasures more refined, despise matter and the senses, show herself to be the true daughter of her distinguished mother, devote herself to study and eschew the servitude of man.

Complexes and inhibitions had not yet been invented, but the genius of Molière had already found them out. The professions of Armande are themselves a revelation of her malady. The real woman, angry, jealous and sexually acquisitive, looks out at us from every scene in which she figures. From denouncing marriage and its consequences, she passes inconsequently, but how inevitably, to

466

scolding her sister for having deprived her of a potential husband, and she is finally reduced to throwing herself bodily at the head of the man she had previously disdained.

Mind or matter, spirit or flesh? Such is the fundamental issue of the play, and the answers are as various as the characters presented. Henriette answers for the normal woman. To the hot fancies of her sister she tranquilly replies that marriage has for her no terrors. It means a husband, children, a family—things at which she cannot honestly profess to be shocked. Chrysale, lectured by his wife on the grossness of matter in general and of his own body in particular, boldly upholds the flesh. It may, as Philaminte affirms, be merely a carcase that he owns, but the carcase is dear to him. Clitandre, as near as can be, answers for Molière. To Armande, who pleads on behalf of a union of hearts in which the body remains unconcerned, he replies with a candid declaration of his inability to follow her to the high regions where corporal love is regarded as an offence against the spirit. He has a body as well as a mind. He apologizes for mentioning the fact, but it refuses to be ignored. He has not the art to divide them, and they insist upon going together. Nothing, of course, could be finer than a union of hearts completely dissociated from any traffic of the senses, but such loves are for him too subtle. He loves with all his being, and wishes his love to be as extensively returned.

In a play of so varied an interest and so wide a scope Trissotin and Vadius, the comic poets, obviously do not deserve quite all the attention they have received from posterity. The scenes in which Molière lashes the learned affectations of his contemporaries show us only a portion of his design. His real theme is the disorder which arises

467

from a lack of balance between natural feeling and civilized intelligence. His method, as in all his plays, is to contrast the victims of excess with characters who represent the normal virtues. Philaminte, Armande and Bélise are tested by an enforced comparison with the plain commonsense of Chrysale, the frank normality of Henriette, the educated intelligence of Clitandre. Intellectual excess is chastised in Philaminte. Her pedantry is honest and untroubled with any emotional complications. She sticks to her guns and is not essentially disgraced. The case of Armande is different. Her intellectualism is forced, the result of morbid suppressions. She is thus compacted of contradictions. She wilfully denies her nature, dismisses the lover for whom she craves, reveals at every turn a temperament at war with itself. To the seventeenth century philosopher she would present the fashionable dichotomy—mind or matter. Clitandre is the happy man. Clitandre—a pupil, evidently, of Gassendi—refuses to make any such distinction, insisting that physically and mentally he is one and indivisible. Finally, there is Bélise, an acute case of the complaint from which Armande also suffers. She lives upon the far edge of the comedy and over the border lies the region, not of farce, but of tragic pathology.

It will be noted that in one significant point *Les Femmes Savantes* differs from *Le Bourgeois Gentilhomme,* so near to it in date. The sterling qualities of Monsieur Jourdain were in the previous play contrasted with the false glitter of the worthless Dorante. Molière, in Clitandre, now handsomely apologizes to the nobility. He was the first dramatist who dared to ridicule the vices and fashions of the Court, but he would be the last to suggest that no

468

gentleman was really a gentleman. Clitandre defends his class in fair and reasonable terms. It is by no means as stupid as certain clever ones profess to believe. The society of the Court is an excellent school, and the sense and wit of the great world are more worthy of respect than the decrees of an academy.

Molière, writing in praise of the Court, was about to suffer, and might have lived to suffer worse, from the intrigues of, perhaps, the most accomplished courtier of the day. The musical genius of Lulli was respectable, but his genius as a monopolist of favours such as can only be obtained by an unsleeping industry in antechambers was unique. Hitherto he had been the constant friend and partner of Molière in the King's diversions. He had written the music for the whole series of the comedy-ballets of Molière from *Les Plaisirs de l'Ile Enchantée* to *Le Bourgeois Gentilhomme*. He was now to enter upon a career of successful aggression which was shortly to make him a supreme dictator of the arts, and in which he would tolerate no colleague upon equal terms. Within ten years no one might publicly sing, dance or play any sort of musical instrument in France without his permission. Louis XIV had in 1669 created an "Academy of Opera or Musical Performances in the French Language," and he had granted to the Abbé Perrin an exclusive privilege for twelve years to present such performances in France. Lulli in 1672 succeeded in having this privilege transferred to himself by using his influence with Madame de Montespan, and avoided paying compensation to those whom he had dispossessed by using his influence with Colbert. Under this privilege he immediately claimed and enforced the right to forbid anybody

469

else to introduce song or music into a public spectacle. The subsequent career of Lulli as a monopolist is one of the scandals of theatrical history. He annexed the theatre of Molière after his death, and even went so far as to suppress a famous company of marionettes which had dared to break into song. This Lulli, hat in hand to minister or mistress, would live to be described by La Fontaine as an ogre who devoured everything before him: *C'est un mâtin . . . qui tout devore,* and to be stigmatized by Boileau as being, for all his genius, a tyrant in his profession and a clown in company.

His musical monopoly, so harshly exercised, was a severe blow to the theatre generally and to the Palais Royal in particular. Molière must look for another partner, and the Italian *maestro* was henceforth—but, alas, only on two occasions—replaced by Charpentier. Molière must have taken the defection of Lulli greatly to heart. This new development, moreover, had alarming implications. It was the first definite sign of deterioration in the royal taste which in another ten years would substitute insipid opera and pantomime for the comedy of Molière and the tragedy of Racine. It meant also that Lulli had won the ear of the King, and he was certainly not using it in the interests of his former colleague.

Molière was living no longer in the Rue St. Thomas but had moved with his wife to a house in the Rue de Richelieu. Already one familiar and beloved figure had passed from his intimate circle. In February, 1672, occurred the death of Madeleine Béjart, his friend and counsellor for thirty years. The day of her death is marked in the Register of La Grange with a black lozenge. On the

470

same day of the following year Molière himself was to die. She was spared that bereavement, and the pious horrors that attended it. Madeleine, moreover, who had initiated the young Poquelin into an infamous profession, was able herself to renounce it at the close in due and proper form. She received the sacraments and her body, with the permission of the Archbishop of Paris, was borne in sanctity to Saint-Paul and laid away in Christian burial.

Reference has already been made to another loss that occurred later in the year. On October 11, 1672, died the son who had been born to Molière less than a month before. His first child, godson of the King, had died in 1664 in his first year, and there now remained to him only his daughter, Esprit-Madeleine. To a man as sensitive as Molière the loss of this late child of his reconciliation with Armande must have been keenly felt:

> Et, lorsque pour toujours on perd ce que tu perds,
> La Sagesse, crois-moi, peut pleurer elle-même.

Eight years ago he had addressed these lines to La Mothe la Vayer, who had suffered a like bereavement, exhorting his friend, though a philosopher of the Stoic sect, to allow his grief to take the way of nature.

Meanwhile, his own health, abused with the worries and fatigues of his profession, was beginning to give his friends and colleagues the greatest anxiety. La Grange notes in his Register that in August he was absent for two days from the theatre which had, therefore, to be closed. Meanwhile, a characteristic incident had shown that playgoers in 1672 were still, in manners, as barbarous as in the days of Alexander Hardy. The contrast between the brutal conduct of

471

the time and its intellectual refinement is a striking paradox.
The spectators who appreciated with respect the plays of
Corneille, Molière and Racine could be as cruel and disorderly as a cock-fighting audience at a village fair. On
October 16, 1672, at a performance of *La Comtesse d'Escarbagnas,* two days after Molière had lost his son, occurred
one of the frequent play house riots of the period. A
spectator was beaten on the stage, swords were drawn, stones
thrown at the players and Molière just missed receiving
for himself the heavy end of a clay pipe. This was no
profession for a sick man. *Quantum mutatus ab illo.* Some
years earlier Molière had dealt firmly and promptly with
a more serious disturbance. It had been the privilege of
the members of the King's household to attend the theatre
free of charge. Molière, however, shortly after his re-
moval to the Palais Royal, had protested against a custom
which was abused by every lackey and musketeer in the
royal service and Louis XIV had very reasonably given
orders that the practice should cease. The result was a
riot in the theatre. The man in charge of the gate was
brutally killed, and the players found themselves in peril
of their lives. The situation was saved by the younger
Béjart, who, dressed to enact an old man, raised a laugh
by pleading to be spared on the ground that he had in any
case only a few days to live. Molière, coming forward, then
delivered one of his celebrated harangues.

Molière had stubbornly refused on that occasion to surrender the right he had won to admit or exclude whom he
pleased of his unpaying guests. His company, thoroughly
scared by the incident, begged him to ask for a revocation
of the royal order. Molière, however, was made of sterner

stuff. He defended his rights, and shamed his assailants, for, hearing that the King was making inquiries with a view to punishing the rioters, he went to the palace and himself confronted the assembled guards. His request to the King had not, he said, been aimed at them, but at the idlers who crowded daily to his theatre, filling the pit to the exclusion of the real public and thus depriving his comrades of their lawful gains. To enter the theatre without paying was not a prerogative which gentlemen of their quality were likely to value, still less to enforce at the point of the sword. It was a small privilege which might appropriately be left to authors and penniless persons who could only hope to see a play by charity.

This incident belonged to the days of militant confidence. Molière was now, in October, 1672, a sick man, tired, bereaved and beginning to feel that the odds were against him. His best and wisest friend was urging him to retire from the stage; he was losing touch with the King, whose taste and favour were changing; the melancholy which had always lain at the heart of his laughter was closing in upon his spirit. Baron, many years later, dictating to Grimarest, embodied his last impressions of Molière in an apocryphal speech delivered by the dramatist to his wife and friend on the eve of his death: "So long as my life was mingled joy and sorrow I esteemed myself a happy man; but, now that I am overwhelmed with troubles and can count upon no real satisfaction or release, I feel it is time to be going."

Such was the mood in which Molière sat down to write the gayest comedy upon the darkest theme to which a man may set his fancy. At the heart of his comedy of the credulous Argan, the *malade imaginaire,* is the fear of

473

death. Merrily the author, sick himself, mocks the pre-occupation of a healthy man with disease. He stands aside from his private destiny and laughs, on behalf of us all, in the face of the King of Terrors. Reality, which had all his life trodden so closely upon the heels of his art, was quick to take the offered cue. Molière, sitting in the chair of Argan, counterfeited death upon the stage, and death accepted the challenge. Within a few hours of that brave and pleasant mockery Molière had ceased to be.

For the details of an event which engraved itself upon the memory of its witnesses with a fidelity which time could not efface or any literary artifice embellish, we may without misgiving confide in Grimarest, who had the story from Baron, and in La Grange who tells us quite simply of what happened on the stage. *Le Malade Imaginaire* was performed for the first time on Friday, February 10, 1673. It was repeated on the following Sunday and Tuesday. On the following Friday came the scene of premonition: "I feel it is time to be going." Molière was entreated by Baron and by his wife not to play that evening. But Molière was deaf to their persuasion. This was the "point of honour," which Boileau had found so odd in so great a man. The curtain would be rising in an hour, and the actor must be in his place. His company would be assembled and he was their providence: "What am I to do? There are some fifty poor workers who have only their daily wage. What is to become of them if we do not play. I should reproach myself for having neglected to support them for a single day, being able to do so."

The curtain thus rises upon the final comedy. Molière, in the habit of Argan, yields himself to the grotesque ministrations of the Faculty; all about him is the solemn ritual of the profession which he had mocked through many years of intermittent sickness; Argan, in a whirlwind of laughter, is abandoned by his furious physicians to a terrible tale of imaginary ills, and at long last, to the delight of a crowded house, having simulated death in his chair, recovers to be ultimately sworn into the mysteries of medicine. It is the climax of the comedy. *Juro,* he declaims in the litany of his induction. The face of the actor changes. The hand of death has reached suddenly through the masquerade, and for an instant he feels the cold summons at his heart. Indomitably he rises to the supreme moment of his comic progress and hides with a forced laugh the convulsion which has shaken him.

La Grange marked in his Register with a black lozenge the death of Madeleine. To the death of Molière he devoted six lines, to be followed nine years later by a single paragraph in the Preface of 1682. Molière, he tells us in the preface, found it so difficult to play his part that the audience "might clearly perceive that he was nothing less in truth than what he feigned to be": he finished the performance however, and went immediately to bed where he died within half-an-hour of his last convulsion. The entry in the Register is scarcely more than a memorandum: "That same day, after the play, at ten o'clock in the evening, Monsieur de Molière died in his house, Rue de Richelieu, having played the part of the said *malade imaginaire,* much inconvenienced by a cold and a discharge from the lungs which caused him to cough violently, so that, in the efforts he made to be rid of the phlegm, he broke a blood vessel and lived afterwards for only three-quarters of an hour."

475

Grimarest, recording the memories of Baron, more than thirty years later, had tact enough to realize that any excursion into gossip or literature must spoil rather than heighten the impression of his account. He brings into the story in addition to Baron and the wife of Molière, La Forêt, the devoted servant of Molière, to whom, as posterity insisted, the dramatist would, as a test of their efficiency, read his plays, and two sisters of charity whom he was accustomed to lodge at his house when they came to Paris in Lent seeking alms:

Molière played that evening with much difficulty and many of the spectators noticed that in delivering the word *Juro* in the ceremony of the *malade imaginaire* he was seized with a convulsion. Realizing that the audience had perceived what had happened, he made an effort and covered his condition with a forced laugh.

When the play was ended he took his gown and, being in the dressing room of Baron, asked him what was the impression made on the public by his comedy. Baron replied that his works always gained from being closely followed, and that, the more often they were acted, the more they were enjoyed. 'But,' added Baron, 'you seem to be not so well as you were a moment ago.' 'True,' said Molière, 'I am cold, fit to die of it.' Baron touched his hands, which he found to be cold as ice, and, to warm them, put them in his muff. He then sent for porters to carry Molière to his house, and stayed by his chair for fear that some accident might happen to him on the way from the Palais Royal to the Rue de Richelieu, where he then lived.

When Molière reached his room, Baron wished to bring him some broth which his wife had always at hand, for no one could take more care of herself than she did. 'No,' said Molière, 'my wife's broth is fire-water for me; you

476

know what a deal of things she puts into it. Give me instead
a small piece of Parmesan cheese.' La Forêt brought him
the cheese and he ate it with a little bread, and had his bed
prepared. He had sent his wife a moment before to fetch
him a pillow stuffed with a herb which she had promised
him in order to make him sleep. 'I willingly take anything,' he said, 'which does not enter the body, but I am
afraid of remedies which must be taken. A mere nothing
would suffice to rob me of the little strength that remains.'

A moment afterwards he coughed violently, and, having
spit, called for a light. 'Here,' he said, 'is something different.' Baron, seeing the blood which he had spit, cried
out in alarm. 'There's no need to be frightened,' said
Molière, 'you've seen me spit more than that and to spare.
Nevertheless,' he added, 'go and ask my wife to come up
to me.'

He remained in his room helped by two sisters of charity
who belonged to a community whose members were accustomed to visit Paris to seek alms during Lent, and for whom
on such occasions he provided hospitality. They afforded
him during these last moments of his life all the comfort
which might be expected of their charity, and he expressed
to them the sentiments of a good Christian and all the resignation which he owed to God. Finally, he expired in the
arms of the two sisters choked by the blood which came
from his mouth in abundance. Thus, his wife and Baron,
on coming up to the room, found him dead.

Molière died in the arms of two sisters of charity, and
he died a professing Christian. "He turned all his thoughts
to heaven," says La Grange, thus confirming the statement
of Grimarest. How deep was the Christian orthodoxy of
this free spirit, read in the pagan philosophers and devoted
to an excommunicated profession, who had seemed to
acknowledge no sanctions, doctrines or standards but those

477

of moderation and good sense? The answer need go no further than saying that Molière, dying as a Christian and entreating, as we shall see, the sacraments of the Church, was, in his death as in his life, a representative of the normal man. Clearly he was not of a deeply religious temper; you will look vainly in his work for any immediate sense of spiritual mysteries or surrender to the ecstatic mood. Clearly, too, he was no helplessly orthodox subscriber to clerical views and pretensions; he had serenely faced his damnation by a priest. The heresy of Molière, however, went no further than a refusal to surrender his judgment in temporal things to the experts in eternity. To Cæsar the things that are Cæsar's—and Molière was Cæsar in the comic realm, but equally to God the things that are God's— and he never overstepped the boundary. There is not a syllable in his plays or an act of his life that is inconsistent with the professions of a catholic Christian, and nothing was further from his philosophy or his practice than a militant nonconformity. It may be whispered that he did not care sufficiently about matters of faith to be a heretic, but it cannot reasonably be urged that there was anything inconsistent in his dying as a professing member of the Church. The motive and passion of his life lay elsewhere. He was not the man to fight for a philosophy or a sect, but he had fought with a generous audacity for his right to see men and things as they were and to present them with candour and simplicity. He died, as most men die, with his thoughts turning hereafter, requesting in that moment the secular rites which had fortified the passing of so many souls. This was no gesture of recantation or hypocrisy. He had no wish, then or at any time, to be not as other men. He had been

478

baptized and married as a Christian. He wished to be confessed, shriven and buried as a Christian.

But Molière died without formally renouncing his profession and without benefit of clergy. Dying, he had sent urgently to St. Eustache for a priest. Two priests of the parish refused to come. A third was roused from his bed by Jean Aubry, son of the Léonard Aubry, who had befriended the Illustrious Theatre over thirty years previously, but nearly an hour had been lost and he arrived too late. When, therefore, the widow of Molière asked that her husband should receive Christian burial in the cemetery of the parish, the vicar was technically right—as he had taken good care to be—in refusing the request. The canonical law and practice in this matter has already been discussed, and we are concerned here only with the facts. Suffice it that the representatives of the Church were determined that there should be no joy in heaven over this particular sinner. Armande appealed to the Archbishop of Paris, no longer Hardouin de Péréfixe, the honest enemy of *Tartuffe,* but Harlay de Chanvallon, the handsomest man in Paris, whose proclivities were so notorious that Madame de Sévigné refused to invite him to her house on the ground that she had no daughters young enough for his entertainment. Armande stated the facts, and prayed him by a special act of grace to overrule the vicar of St. Eustache.

But this was the hour of Tartuffe. Armande was appealing on behalf of the Sieur de Molière, who had died in the arms of two sisters of charity whom he had piously sheltered, to the Sieur de Harlay, who some years later, at the age of seventy, was to die of apoplexy in the arms of his mistress, and history was determined to justify her great comedian.

479

The Archbishop piously referred the petition to one of his officers for an inquiry into the circumstances, and it was soon clear that he intended to do nothing. For four days Molière remained unburied, and Armande went to the King. Her contemporaries suggest that she did not grieve either long or overmuch for her husband; but she was certainly angry. "They refuse a tomb to the man who deserves an altar"— she was proud of the saying, and, according to Brossette, repeated it everywhere, perhaps to the King himself. Being ardent in the cause she was almost certainly tactless, roundly pleading, again according to Brossette, that, if her husband were a criminal, his crimes had been authorized by His Majesty. She took with her to the royal presence, moreover, the vicar of Auteuil, who was suspected of being a Jansenist. Jansenist or Jesuit was probably all one to the widow of Molière, but her failure to appreciate these fine distinctions was in the present case unfortunate, for the good man, instead of witnessing to the exemplary life of his late parishioner, seized the occasion to defend his orthodoxy. The interview was not successful.

The attitude of the King, difficult to determine in its finer implications, was broadly definite and clear. He would do what he decently could for his faithful servant, but there must be no undesirable incident. He would not formally offend clerical opinion or risk a public outcry. The importunate widow was referred back to the Archbishop, with whom, as the King insisted, the decision must lie, and the Sieur de Harlay received concurrently a message to the effect that he was to find a solution which would avoid any sort of incident or disturbance: "His Majesty intimated that his Grace must so arrange matters as to avoid any demonstration

480

or scandal. The Archbishop accordingly withdrew his prohibition on condition that the interment was conducted without ceremony or advertisement" (Brossette).

The problem for the authorities seemed simple enough:
here was a corpse unburied and it was essential to get it out
of the way as quietly as possible. The Archbishop was precise as to the conditions: "We authorize the vicar of St.
Eustache to give ecclesiastical burial to the body of the
deceased Molière in the cemetery of the parish on condition
that there shall be no ceremony, with two priests only, after
nightfall, and that there shall be no solemn service for him
either in the parish of St. Eustache or elsewhere, in any
church of the regular clergy." The rest is silence or confusion, and the truth is unlikely ever to be known. The
only clear circumstance that emerges from the riot and
rumour that attended the death and burial of Molière is
that the authorities failed to prevent the scandal which they
were trying to avoid.

The body was taken to the cemetery of St. Joseph, and
the Abbé Boyvin, a priest of the parish, received an account
of the matter from a correspondent who sealed but did not
sign his letter. The Abbé was informed that four priests
carried the body, and that three "ecclesiastics" officiated; the
bier was covered with the pall of the *tapissiers;* six children
in blue bore six wax candles in six candlesticks of silver;
lacqueys carried torches of white wax; a hundred of his
friends followed Molière to the grave with lighted tapers
and a huge crowd assembled for the ceremony. The interment took place on the 21st February, 1673, and the body
was buried, according to our anonymous witness, "at the foot
of the cross."

481

The instructions of the Archbishop were, therefore, disregarded. This unlicensed pomp was, moreover, accompanied by incidents whose exact significance cannot be determined, but which were obviously scandalous. A huge crowd, whether hostile or friendly, it is oddly impossible to discover, had assembled outside the house where the body rested, and was only appeased by a lavish distribution of money thrown by the terrified or grateful widow of Molière from the windows. It must suffice posterity to know that the death of Molière and the conduct of the authorities did not leave either his friends or the public indifferent. Whether the crowd which assembled on the night of February 21, 1673, had come to trouble the proceedings or to protest against their inadequacy is not at all clear. There seems, in any case, to have been a riot or the makings of one; and, if fancy be permitted to embellish fact, the incident may without great risk of error be reconstructed—the friends of Molière assembled in the street, loud murmur and low discussion, a fringe of inquisitive idlers prompt in comment and quick in dispute, a scene growing in animation, with words soon, perhaps, running high on the merits of the case. Here was enough to frighten a widow who had, during the last three days, had every opportunity of realizing the formidable opposition which she must be ready to encounter.

The scandal raised by Molière unburied was as nothing, however, compared with the scandal that grew upon his tomb. An obstinate tradition, supported by the memory of an aged sexton, affirms that Molière was not buried, as the correspondent of the Abbé Boyvin affirmed "at the foot of the cross," but in a more remote portion of the cemetery—in other words, in the portion reserved for suicides, stillbirths and other poor bodies who had lost or never found their souls. There is no means of ascertaining the truth. The grave of Molière, upon which legend gleams for a moment now and then, was lost to the view of history on the night of February 21, 1673. The Editors of 1682 are silent. Grimarest excuses himself for not having written at length on what passed after the death of Molière. He hints that a very curious volume might be printed on the subject; adds that he had found the matter so difficult and delicate that he dared not undertake it; and refers to facts "whose gravity impose silence upon everyone concerned." Clearly the scandal was immense, and the historian must at least pause a moment in contemplation of the possibility, almost incredible but, nevertheless, the only working hypothesis yet put forward, that the Archbishop of Paris did at the eleventh hour succeed in defrauding Molière of his patch of consecrated earth. Within a year of the event a libellous poet could at all events dare to write a *Sonnet on the Burial of Jean Baptiste Poquelin, known as Molière, an Actor, in the cemetery of the Stillborn in Paris:*

> Molière, baptisé, perd l'effet du baptême,
> Et dans sa sépulture il devient un mort-né.

The historic sequel to these obscure events justified the author who in his plays had so often found in farce a climax for his comedy. On July 6, 1792, a revolutionary Government decided that the section of Paris which had elected to call itself *La Section de Molière et de La Fontaine* should honour the mortal remains of their secular patrons. Two commissioners of the Section accordingly repaired to the cemetery of St. Joseph. By this time tradition had given to Molière for a ghostly companion in this enclosure the friend who had early proclaimed him to be "his man." The legend ran that they were buried, if not side by side, at least in the same cemetery, and the zealous commissioners, proceeding to St. Joseph, exhumed on two separate occasions the hypothetical bones of the fabulist and the comedian. Molière they sought, and naturally found—for the people must not be defrauded of its relics—in the cemetery of the stillborn. La Fontaine—who was in reality lying somewhere in the Cemetery of the Holy Innocents—they discovered "at the foot of the cross." Two monuments, constructed by Alexandre Lenoir, received these fragments of two persons unknown in 1799, and in 1817 they were transferred to Père-Lachaise, where they still remain as evidence of an admiration none the worse for being technically misdirected. The bones of Molière share with those of the major saints the privilege of being adored by substitution.

Upon the unknown grave of Molière fell a shower of observations and epitaphs. The King, to whom Baron brought the news at St. Germain, "was touched and deigned to show it." The Prince de Conde, to whom an officious poet showed, with pride the epitaph he had written upon Molière, said in genuine sorrow: "Would it had been his epitaph upon yourself." The lines of La Fontaine are deservedly the most familiar:

> Sous ce tombeau gisent Plaute et Térence,
> Et cependant le seul Molière y gît.
> Leurs trois talents ne formoient qu'un esprit,
> Dont le bel art réjouissoit la France.

> Ils sont partis! et j'ai peu d'espérance
> De les revoir. Malgré tous nos efforts,
> Pour un long temps, selon toute apparence,
> Térence et Plaute et Molière sont morts.

La Fontaine expressed the general view, and was, alas! only too quickly justified. With the death of Molière comedy went into temporary eclipse, and the friends who lived to see the triumph of the mythologies and operatic hybrids in which the classic movement lay so long adying in the closing years of the century had not the comfort of knowing that one day the Comédie Française would cherish its inheritance as the Maison de Molière. Boileau, like La Fontaine, mourned in the death of Molière an irreparable disaster:

> L'aimable comédie, avec lui terrassée,
> En vain d'un coup si rude espéra revenir,
> Et sur ses brodequins ne put plusse tenir.

The contemporary epitaphs and epigrams corroborate the opinions passed upon the living man. The public imagination was especially struck by the grim circumstance that Death so quickly avenged himself upon the comedian who had mocked and counterfeited him upon the stage. Molière, taking death as he had taken life for a model, so well succeeded that death, enchanted with the copy claimed it for an original . . . Was Molière really dead? With so excellent a pretender one could never be quite sure . . . Death, angry at being mocked, turned mockery into earnest . . . The epigrammatists ring a score of changes upon the theme —some in admiration, but many also in malice. Meanwhile, the anathema of Bossuet rolls down the years in an effort to drown the friendly poets, who mourned the passing of this

485

lord of laughter: "Posterity will, perhaps, remember the end of this comic poet who, playing his *Malade Imaginaire* or his *Médecin par Force*, felt the fatal onslaught of the malady from which he died a few hours afterwards, passing thus from the jests of the theatre, amid which he yielded almost his final breath, to the judgment seat of Him that said: Woe unto them that laugh, for they shall weep."

Of Molière it may be said with confidence that he was not only a great author but a great man. His life has a dramatic quality which makes it possible to think of it as perhaps the greatest of his plays. Apart from the many legends, to which very little credit has been allowed in this biography, the events and productions of his career speak for themselves. He not only represents the most vital and enduring qualities of his race, but his works are a protest and a correction of the defects to which the French genius is peculiarly liable. His mind was without prejudice; he rejected nothing till it threatened to limit the free exercise of a sane intelligence, or to distort a reasonable conduct. He was thus the natural scourge of academies and sects, the enemy of all excess. The logic of his race pushed to extremes often results in a rationalism and a formality which it was his peculiar mission to expose and to deride. To this enterprise he brought an unsleeping commonsense, an inexhaustible gaiety, an accurate perception and an obstinate survival, which no amount of sober scholarship or sad experience could destroy, of the old Gallic spirit, near to earth and the realities, which has often been the salvation of French literature when in danger of becoming too remote from ordinary human concerns. His comedies are a constant plea for sanity and the golden mean, and a challenge to bigotry,

486

imposture and exaggeration in every class and profession of society. The perfect balance of the mind and disposition of Molière was most clearly shown by the fact that he could take his own misfortunes and sorrows for a comic theme as sweetly and evenly as the vices or foibles of other men. There was never a trace of malignancy in his satire. It was always generous in inspiration and inexhaustively vivacious.

The Epicurean sanity of Molière, with its persistent correction of all extremes, has exposed him to criticism more formidable than that of the sectaries. Men of a generous habit have felt its limitations, complaining that Molière seems often to be no more than a champion of prudence and the middle way, and that there are whole tracts of human experience which lie beyond the scope of his art. But this is only to say that Molière was a comedian. He was not a mystical philosopher, or even a poet of passion. His subject was man in society. The answer to those who accuse him of an excessive moderation is to be found in the fact that the critics of his own age charged him with anarchism, atheism and impiety. To the people of his own time he was a splendid or an infamous revolutionary according to their creed and temper. To the critics who complain that he cared for no truth or principle sufficiently to be either a moral or a religious revolutionary, it may be objected that on behalf of the moderation which for him was the secret of social wisdom he fought a lifelong battle with a courage and persistence that has rarely been equalled. His lack of formal doctrine was due, not to any moral indifference, but to his sense of the unlimited energy and possibilities of life. The human spirit was for him too various to be limited by a formula or confined within a system.

487

The style of Molière, in verse and prose, was a reflection
of his free spirit and his candid intelligence. He wrote
with extreme facility, but he was never a sloven. He was
both voluble and precise. His prose dialogue is unequalled
outside the plays of Shakespeare, and his verse has an ease
and variety that makes it immediately tolerable even to the
foreign reader for whom the French alexandrine is a taste
to be painfully acquired. The most exacting authors of the
classical tradition, like Boileau, no less than their romantic
successors, like Victor Hugo, unite in praising the style of
Molière from opposite angles. Foreign readers, though
their appreciation of French felicities may be limited, rarely
fail to appreciate the lucidity and vivacity of his writing.

For Molière's personal appearance we have the portraits
of Mignard and the description of Mademoiselle Poisson,
who saw him in the flesh; he was "neither too stout nor too
thin, tall rather than short; he had a noble carriage, a good
leg, walked slowly, and had a very serious expression. His
nose was thick, his mouth large with thick lips, his complexion
brown, his eyebrows black and strongly marked, and it was
his way of moving these that gave him his comic expression
on the stage." He was of a grave and melancholy disposition
—a contemplative genius, given to fits of abstraction. But
he could speak well on occasion, and all his friends bear witness to the wit and charm of his conversation. In his private
dealings he was generous, sympathetic and candid, tolerant
for the faults he understood so well, delicate in his appreciation of the views and sentiments of others. He was free,
gentle and fearless. Exposed to a criticism and calumny such
as few men have had to sustain, we can find in him no trace
of envy or malice. This satirist of folly was a man of in-

488

finite charity. His indignation was always generous and his comic severity was an inevitable consequence of lucid and just perceptions to which he must needs be loyal. To confine such a man within the limits of any school or to summarize his achievements in the light of any single or even predominant aspect of his work has proved fatal to every critic and biographer who has attempted it. There can be no summing-up of the life and work of Molière. We can but show him at work, place him within his period and environment and leave men free to take for themselves such pieces of him as they may require. The elements were so mixed in him that Nature might stand up and say to all the world "This was the perfect comedian." She has not yet shown any disposition to repeat the performance and Molière shares with Shakespeare the privilege of winning for the theatre the two highest peaks in the whole range of imaginative literature.

BIBLIOGRAPHICAL NOTE

THE standard edition of the works of Molière is that contained in the collection of the *Grands Ecrivains de la France* edited by MM. Eugène Despois et Paul Mesnard (Paris, Hachette et Cie 1873-1927). It includes the best biography of Molière (Vol. X), and a bibliography which is complete up to 1893 (Vol. XI). The earliest life of Molière is the preface to the first edition of his works published in 1682 by La Grange and Vinot. This is included in the edition of MM. Despois et Mesnard. Grimarest, who obtained most of his information from Baron, a young actor who was for many years in the company of Molière, published a life of the dramatist in 1705; he is, however, untrustworthy, and his statements are not to be accepted without corroboration. The life of Molière by Voltaire (1882) throws more light upon the editor than upon his subject, and the excellent biography of Taschereau (1863) requires careful correction in the light of recent researches. The life prefixed by Ste. Beuve to the edition of 1825 is of more value as criticism than biography. Among later biographies are those of Jules Claretie (1873); J. J. Weiss (1900); Georges Lafenestre (1909); Maurice Donnay (1911). But their name is legion. The contemporary sources may be studied in the documents collected by Edouard Soulié, *Recherches sur Molière et sa Famille* (1863), and the *Collection Molièresque* of Paul Lacroix

493

(1867-1875). This last work contains the more important contemporary libels including *La Fameuse Comédienne*, *Elomire Hypocondre* and *Zélinde*. It was supplemented by a *Nouvelle Collection Molièresque*, begun by Paul Lacroix (1863-1884) and continued by Georges Monval (1884-1890). Georges Monval also edited a monthly review entitled *Le Molièriste*, which is an important source of information (1879-1889).

Among the authors who have dealt with the problems of the marriage and family relations of Molière are Jules Loiseleur in *Les Points Obscurs de la Vie de Molière* (1877) and Edouard Fournier in *Etudes sur la Vie de Molière* and *Le Roman de Molière* (1885).

The most searching and authoritative modern studies in the biography of Molière are those of Gustave Michaut, who critically reviews much of the previous evidence. The results of his investigations are given in *La Jeunesse de Molière* (1922), *Les Débuts de Molière à Paris* (1923), and *Les Luttes de Molière* (1925). These studies for the moment go no further than the production of *Le Misanthrope* in 1666.

Critical studies of Molière and his plays will be found in *Impressions de Théâtre* by Jules Lemaître (1888-1890), *Etudes et Portraits* by Paul Bourget (1889), *Epoques du Théâtre Français* (1892) and *Etudes Critiques sur l'Histoire de la Littérature Française* (1895-1908) by Brunetière.

494

INDEX

A

Académie de Musique, 214

Académie des Femmes, L' (Chappu-zeau), 151

Académie Française, L', and Molière, 443-44

Académie Royale de Danse, 214

Academy, see Académie Française, L'

Actor: ambiguous status of, in seventeenth century, 47-49; and playwright, 108

Adelphi (Terence), as source for L'Ecole des Maris, 202

Affectation: fostered by the salon of the Marquise de Rambouillet, 141 ff.; as theme for Molière, 145 ff.

Agen: visits of Molière to, 76, 83

Agésilas (Corneille), 438

Albi: visits of Molière to, 76, 82

Aleth, Bishop of, 94-95, 97

Alexandre le Grand (Racine), presented at Palais Royal, 429; private performance at Hôtel de Bourgogne, 430-31

Angennes, Charles d', Marquis de Rambouillet, 139

Anne of Bavaria, 289

Antonelli, Luigi, anticipated by Molière, 449

Ariosto, Ludovico: influence on L'Avare, 454

Aristophanes: influence on Le Bourgeois Gentilhomme, 320

Aristotle: Gassendi's criticism, of 30

Arrogance, intellectual, of Don Juan, 364-87 passim

Artaxerce, L' (Magnon), 63-64

Art Poétique, L' (Boileau): on Molière's theatrical career, 442-43

Assoucy, d': on his meeting with Molière, 85-87

Astrology, as theme of Les Amants Magnifiques, 313-14

Attila (Corneille), 307, 438

Aubijoux, Comte d', 82

Aubry, Jean, 479

Aubry, Léonard: paves roadway in front of Jeu de Paume des me-stayers, 62-63; assumes responsibility for debts of Molière's company, 67

Audience: Molière's attitude towards, as explained in La Critique de l'Ecole des Femmes, 275-77; intrusion of upon stage, 325 ff.

Au Mouton Blanc (cabaret), 434

Auteuil, vicar of, 480

Authors, rival: Molière's attitude to, 285

Autissier, Jean, 12

Avarice, as theme of comedy for Molière, 454-58

Avignon, visits of Molière to, 76, 86-87, 98

B

Ballet des Muses, Le, 294, 304

Ballets: presentation of, at college of Clermont, 24, 28-29

Banville, Theodore de: on *Don Juan ou Le Festin de Pierre,* 378

Barbieri, Niccolò, *see* Beltrame

Baron, Michel: Molière's interest in and affection for, 246-47; Armande's quarrel with, 248, 305; leaves Molière's company, 248; returns, 248-49; appears as Love in *Psyché,* 249; present at death of Molière, 251, 476-77; *Mélicerte* written for, 305; appears as Alceste in *Le Misanthrope,* 406-7; and incomprehensible passage in Corneille's *Tite et Bérénice,* 438-39; repeats apocryphal speech by Molière on eve of his death, 473

Baudet, André, 222

Baulot, Sieur: loan to Molière's company, 65

Bayle, Pierre: on Molière, 242

Beauchamp (choreographer), 295

Beauchâteau, François Mathieu, 284

Beaumarchais, Pierre Augustin Caron de, 331, 443

Béjart family, 35 ff.

Béjart, Armande-Grésinde-Claire-Elizabeth: Molière's expected marriage to, 195; marriage contract, 222; rumors concerning parentage of, 223-32; close relationship with Madeleine, 233; slandered in *La Fameuse Comédienne,* 234-50 *passim;* Grimarest's account of, 240-41; Molière's incompatibility with, 243-44; talent of, 244-45; personal appearance of, 245; children of, 245, 250; Molière's temporary sep-aration from, 246, 249-50, 251, 427-28; is jealous of Baron, 246-48; reconciliation with Molière, 250, 252; appears as Elise in *La Critique de l'Ecole des Femmes,* 272; Grimarest's account of quarrel with landlady, 409-10; attempts to secure Christian burial for Molière, 479-82; widowhood and remarriage, 243-44, 251; *see also* Molière, Mlle de

Béjart, Geneviève: joins company of Duc d'Epernon, 77; on tour with Molière, 87; in Madeleine's will, 233

Béjart, Joseph (senior), 35

Béjart, Joseph: leaves the Illustrious Theatre company, 66; joins company of Duc d'Epernon, 77; on tour with Molière, 87; *Recueil des Titres et Blazons,* 96-97; performance in *Nicomède,* 127; death of, 222

Béjart, Louis: on tour with Molière, 87; at signing of Molière's marriage contract, 222; at riot in theatre, 472

Béjart, Madeleine, 35-37; association with Molière, 37-38; provision concerning in contract of the Illustrious Theatre, 57-58; buys house in Rue de Thorigny, 59; probable attitude towards Molière at founding of Illustrious Theatre, 60-61; association with Duc d'Epernon, 76-77; on tour with Molière, 79, 87; legendary accounts of Molière's relations with, 88-89; friendship with Mignard, 99; negotiations for Paris theatre, 124; performance in *Nicomède,* 127; appears in *Scévole,* 136; appears in *La Mort de*

Chrispe, 137; plays nymph in *Les Fâcheux,* 216; at signing of Molière's marriage contract, 222; reputed to be mother of Armande Béjart, 223-35 *passim;* motherlike affection for Armande, 233, 251; appears in *Les Plaisirs de l'Ile Enchantée,* 299; death and burial, 470-71

Béjart, Marie Hervé, 35; house in Rue de la Perle as scene of signing of contract of Illustrious Theatre, 58; stands security for rent of *Jeu de Paume des Mestauers,* 62; stands security for money borrowed by Molière's company, 65; is guarantor for Molière and her daughters, 66; at signing of Molière's marriage contract, 222; and question of Armande's parentage, 223-32 *passim;* death of, 231-32

Belle Egyptienne, La (Hardy), 324

Bellerose, Pierre Le Messier, 44

Belleville, Sieur de, *see* Béjart, Joseph (senior)

Beltrame (Niccolò Barbieri): influence on *L'Etourdi,* 112

Benserade, Isaac de, 296, 304

Bérénice (Racine), 294

Bernier: friendship with Molière, 31; influence of Gassendi on, 32

Beys, Denis: signs contract of Illustrious Theatre, 58

Béziers, visits of Molière to, 76, 96-97

Biographical writings, contemporary, as sources of information on Molière, 22

Biographies, contemporary, of Molière, 21-22

Bocaccio, Giovanni: influence on *L'Ecole des Maris,* 202, on *George Dandin,* 450

Boileau-Despréaux, Nicolas: friendship with Chapelle, 31; on Molière's relations with Madeleine Béjart and Mlle de Brie, 89; on *Les Précieuses Ridicules,* 146; to Louis XIV, on genius of Molière, 165; verse tribute to Molière following production of *L'Ecole des Femmes,* 265-66; commends *La Comtesse d'Escarbagnas,* 331; on private readings of *Tartuffe,* 338; defense of Molière and *Tartuffe,* 340; credited with assisting Molière in Latin parody at end of *Le Malade Imaginaire,* 426; visits Molière at Auteuil, 428; on Racine's coaching of Mlle de Parc in *Andromaque,* 431; support of Molière during the Comic War, 432-33; entertains his intimates, 433-34; story of supper party ending in suicide pact, 435-36; gives Molière name of *Le Contemplateur,* 436; qualities which won Molière's esteem, 437; begs Molière to give up acting for authorship, 441-43; on *Amphitryon,* 450; on *L'Avare,* 454; exchange with Racine on Molière's *L'Avare,* 455-56; on *Les Fourberies de Scapin,* 458-59; on Abbé Cotin and *Les Femmes, Savantes,* 462; on Lulli, 470; verses on Molière's death, 485; praises Molière's style, 488

Boissat, and Molière, 85-86

Boisrobert, François Le Métel: influence on *L'Ecole des Maris,* 202, on *L'Avare,* 454

Bonnenfant, Nicolas: signs contract of Illustrious Theatre, 58; leaves the company, 66

Bordeaux, visits of Molière to, 76

Bores, as subject of *Les Fâcheux*, 212-14

Bossuet, Jacques Bénigne, 140, 144; on denial of sacraments to actors, 48; on *L'Ecole des Femmes*, 258; on Molière's death, 485-86

Bourdaloue, Louis: on *George Dandin ou Le Mari Confondu*, 453

Boursault, Edmé, 110; and the Comic War, 282-83, 285

Boyer, Abbé, 326-27

Boyvin, Abbé, 481

Bracciolini, *see* Poggio Bracciolini

Breteuil, Comte de, 82

Brissart: prints for Thierry-Rabouillet-Barbin edition of *Oeuvres de Molière*, 288 (plate)

Brossette: quotes Boileau on Molière's relations with Madeleine Béjart and Mlle de Brie, 89; on Visé's preface for *Le Misanthrope*, 393; on Armande Béjart Molière's complaint over delay of her husband's burial, 480; on intervention of Louis XIV in matter of Molière's burial, 480-81

Broussin, Comte du, 266

Brunetière: on *L'Ecole des Femmes*, 258

Bruscambille, Jean Deslauriers: epigram on life of comedian, 45

Bussy Rabutin, 140; on Desfougerais, 415

C

Calderon de la Barca, Pedro: possible source for *Le Sicilien*, 306

Calvimont, Madame de, 91-93

Carcassonne, visits of Molière to, 76, 86

Cercle des Femmes Savantes, Le (de la Forge), 151

Cervantes Saavedra, Miguel de: influence on *Le Bourgeois Gentilhomme*, 320

Chair, associated with Molière, 83

Chalussay, Le Boulanger de: slanders on Molière, 27, 39, 419-20; see also *Elomire Hypocondre*

Chanvallon, Harlay de, Archbishop of Paris, and burial of Molière, 479-81

Chapelain, Jean: on Rotrou, 109; letter to Bernier on Molière's translation of Lucretius, 181; hears private reading of *Tartuffe*, 338; opinion of Boileau and his circle on, 434

Chapelle: friendship with Molière, 31-32; influence of Gassendi on, 32; letter to Molière consoling him for his troubles, 134, 235; imaginary interview with Molière on his marriage, 238; at Auteuil with Molière, 427, 428, 436-37; story of supper party ending in suicide pact, 435-36; philosophical argument with Molière, 439-40

Chappuzeau, Samuel, 151; on tragedies performed at Clermont, 28; on intrusion of audience upon stage, 326

Character, as chief concern of Molière, 362-63

Characters (Molière):
Agnes (*L'Ecole des Femmes*), 255-60, 271-73 *passim*
Alceste (*Le Misanthrope*), 389-408, 458
Alcmene (*Amphitryon*), 446-50 *passim*
Amphitryon (*Amphitryon*), 449-50
Angelique (*George Dandin ou Le*

Mari Confondu), 451-54

Anselm (*L'Etourdi*), 113

Argan (*Le Malade Imaginaire*), 413, 422-25, 473-75

Ariste (*L'Ecole des Maris*), 196-98, 201-2, 205

Armande (*Les Femmes Savantes*), 463, 466-67, 468

Arnolphe (*L'Ecole des Femmes*), 254-63 *passim*, 271-73 *passim*, 458

Beggar (*Don Juan ou Le Festin de Pierre*), 371-72

Bélise (*Les Femmes Savantes*), 463, 468

Béralde (*Le Malade Imaginaire*), 423-24

Cathos (*Les Précieuses Ridicules*), 149, 156, 191

Célie (*L'Etourdi*), 111-13 *passim*

Célie (*Sganarelle ou Le Cocu Imaginaire*), 172, 177

Celimène (*Le Misanthrope*), 242-43, 398-403, 405, 407

Charlotte (*Don Juan ou Le Festin de Pierre*), 367-68

Chrysalde (*L'Ecole des Femmes*), 254-55, 260-62

Chrysale (*Les Femmes Savantes*), 464-65, 467, 468

Cléante (*L'Avare*), 456-57

Cleanthis (*Amphitryon*), 448-49

Cléonte (*Le Bourgeois Gentilhomme*), 319

Climène, a prude and exquisite (*La Critique de l'Ecole des Femmes*), 270-73 *passim*

Clitandre (*Les Femmes Savantes*), 464, 465, 467, 468-69

Clitidas (*Les Amants Magnifiques*), 314

Damon (*La Critique de l'Ecole des Femmes*), 436

Dandin, George (*George Dandin ou Le Mari Confondu*), 451-54

Don Carlos (*Don Juan ou Le Festin de Pierre*), 371-72

Don Garcie (*Don Garcie*), 186-90 *passim*

Don Juan (*Don Juan ou Le Festin de Pierre*), 93, 97, 339-40, 361-87, 409, 412

Dorante (*Le Bourgeois Gentilhomme*), 317, 319, 468

Dorante (*La Critique de l'Ecole des Femmes*), 272-77

Dorimène (*Le Bourgeois Gentilhomme*), 319

Dorimène (*Le Mariage Forcé*), 284

Eliante (*Le Misanthrope*), 396, 400-1, 402, 404

Elise (*L'Avare*), 457

Elise (*La Critique de l'Ecole des Femmes*), 272

Elmire (*Tartuffe*), 352

Elvire (*Don Garcie*), 187-90 *passim*

Elvire (*Don Juan ou Le Festin de Pierre*), 366, 375, 378

Filerin, Monsieur (*L'Amour Médecin*), 418

Geronte (*Les Fourberies de Scapin*), 459

Gorgibus (*Les Précieuses Ridicules*), 155

Harpagon (*L'Avare*), 456-57

Harpin, M (*La Comtesse d'Escarbagnas*), 331

Henriette (*Les Femmes Savantes*), 466-67, 468

Horace *(L'Ecole des Femmes),* 256-60 *passim,* 271-72 *passim*

Isabelle *(L'Ecole des Maris),* 196-203

Jourdain, M *(Le Bourgeois Gentilhomme),* 315-20, 468
Jupiter *(Amphitryon),* 446-50

Lélie *(Sganarelle ou Le Cocu Imaginaire),* 177
Léonor *(L'Ecole des Maris),* 196-98, 203, 205
Lucile *(Le Bourgeois Gentilhomme),* 245, 320
Lucile *(Le Dépit Amoureux),* 120
Lysidas *(La Critique de l'Ecole des Femmes),* 271-72, 276-77

Madelon *(Les Précieuses Ridicules),* 149, 155-56, 157
Marinette *(Le Dépit Amoureux),* 120
Marphurius *(Le Mariage Forcé),* 294, 411
Marquis *(La Critique de l'Ecole des Femmes),* 270-76 *passim*
Mascarille *(L'Etourdi),* 111-15 *passim*
Mascarille *(Les Précieuses Ridicules),* 156-57, 191
Mercury *(Amphitryon),* 449
Metaphraste *(Le Dépit Amoureux),* 411
Moron *(La Princesse d'Elide),* 302

Nerine *(Monsieur de Pourceaugnac),* 312
Night *(Amphitryon),* 447-48

Organ *(Tartuffe),* 351-59 *passim,* 377, 423

Oronte *(Le Misanthrope),* 396, 401

Pancrace *(Le Mariage Forcé),* 294, 411
Pandolfe *(L'Etourdi),* 114
Panulphe *(L'Imposteur),* 342; *see also* Tartuffe
Philaminte *(Les Femmes Savantes),* 463-64, 467, 468
Philinte *(Le Misanthrope),* 394-405 *passim*
Pierrot *(Don Juan ou Le Festin de Pierre),* 367
Pourceaugnac *(Monsieur de Pourceaugnac),* 310-13
Princess *(Les Amants Magnifiques),* 313
Purgon, Dr. *(Le Malade Imaginaire),* 424-25

Sbrigni *(Monsieur de Pourceaugnac),* 312
Scapin *(Les Fourberies de Scapin),* 458-59
Sganarelle *(Don Juan ou Le Festin de Pierre),* 364-65, 369-70, 374-77, 380, 409, 412
Sganarelle *(L'Ecole des Maris),* 196-202, 205-6
Sganarelle *(Le Mariage Forcé),* 294, 411
Sganarelle *(Le Médecin Malgré Lui),* 422
Sganarelle *(Sganarelle ou Le Cocu Imaginaire),* 170-77 *passim*
Socie *(Amphitryon),* 447-49
Sostrate *(Les Amants Magnifiques),* 313

Tailor *(Don Juan ou Le Festin de Pierre),* 374
Tartuffe *(Tartuffe),* 351-59 *passim*
Thomas Diafoirus *(Le Malade*

Imaginaire), 423, 425

Tibaudier, M (*La Comtesse d'Escarbagnas*), 331

Trissotin (*Les Femmes Savantes*), 460-62, 467

Trufaldin (*L'Etourdi*), 111

Uranie (*La Critique de l'Ecole des Femmes*), 218-19, 272

Vadius (*Les Femmes Savantes*), 460-62, 467

Valère (*L'Avare*), 457

Charpentier: replaces Lulli as Molière's collaborator, 470

Chateaubriand, Vicomte François René de: on the Jesuits, 25

Chateauneuf: reputed to act as procuress for Armande Béjart, 238

Chevalier (actor at Théâtre du Marais): on Molière's reaction to *Le Portrait du Peintre ou la Contre Critique de l'Ecole des Femmes*, 283

Chigi, Cardinal: hears reading of *Tartuffe*, 337

Chorier, Nicolas: On Molière's visit to Boissat at Vienne, 85

Christina, Queen of Sweden, 340-41

Church, attitude of, toward the theatre and actors, 47-48

Cicognini, Giacinto Andrea, 186; possible source of *Don Juan ou Le Festin de Pierre*, 382

Cinq Mars, Marquis de, 51

Ciron, Abbé de, 98

Cizeron Rival: story of incomprehensible passage in Corneille's *Tite et Bérénice*, 438-39

Clerin, Germain: signs contract of Illustrious Theatre, 58; finds guar-antor for debt, 65-66

Clermont, college of, 24-33 *passim; see also* Collège Louis-le-Grand

Clothing of Duc de Guise, divided among the actors of Paris, 65

Colbert, Jean Baptiste, 469

Collège Louis-le-Grand, 28

Comédie de Sganarelle avec des Arguments sur Chaque Scène, 175

Comédie Francaise, 40; abridged version of *Le Dépit Amoureux*, 119-20; presents Corneille's version of Molière's *Don Juan ou Le Festin de Pierre*, 386-87

Comedian, Molière's gifts as, 129

Comédiens de Monsieur le Dauphin, 246-47

Comic war, 265-92

Comedy: development of, 105 ff.; of manners, Molière's introduction of, 138, 147; Molière's view of, as presented in *La Critique de l'Ecole des Femmes*, 273-74; modern realist, 331

Comedy-ballets: of Molière, 212-21 *passim;* development of, 295

Commedia dell' arte: analysis of, 103-4; influence on Molière, 102, 411-12; influence on *Le Mariage Forcé*, 294

Common sense, and spiritual matters, 358-60

Compagnie du Saint Sacrement, 332-33; and *Tartuffe*, 333-59 *passim*

Condé, Prince de, 289-90; and private performances of *Tartuffe*, 339, 346; comment on poet's epitaph for Molière, 484; *see also* Enghien, Duc d'

Confrérie de la Passion, 39-40

Constantin, Angelo: on Scaramouche and Molière, 132

Conti, Prince de: student at Clermont, 25-27; patron of Molière, 75, 91-98; marriage of, 93-94; possible model for character of Don Juan, 93, 97; religious conversion of, 97-98; *Traité de la Comédie*, 97; repudiation of Molière's company, 98; and Compagnie du Saint Sacrement, 333

Coqueteau de la Clairière, 136

Cormier (mountebank), 92

Corneille, Pierre: and the Théâtre du Marais, 42; tragedies always in repertoire of Molière's company, 63; and Mlle du Parc, 90, 122-23; and the profession of playwriting, 107-8; author of first important French comedy, 114; Molière's unsuccessful performances of, 126-30 *passim*, 133; and the Exquisites, 140, 144; collaboration with Molière on *Psyché*, 321-22; plays performed at Hôtel de Bourgogne, 324, 325; relationship with Molière, 438-39

Corneille, Thomas: and Mlle du Parc, 90, 122-23; on *Les Précieuses Ridicules*, 151, 153-54; buys Don Juan ou Le Festin de Pierre from Molière's widow, 243; verse version of *Don Juan ou Le Festin de Pierre*, 386-87

Cortenvaux, Marquis de, 17

Corvisat (physician): abandons use of wig, 417

Cosnac: invites Molière's company to perform before Prince de Conti, 91-92

Cotin, Abbé, as possible model for Trissotin, 460-62

Cream tarts, 271, 276

Credulity, as theme for comedy in *Tartuffe*, 351-60

Crespy, Daniel, 12

Cressé, Louis (maternal grandfather of Molière), 11, 23

Croix de Lorraine, La (cabaret), 434

Cuckoldry, as theme of comedy for Molière, 171-74, 445-53

Cyrano de Bergerac, Savinien: friendship with Molière, 32; influence of Gassendi on, 32; and *Les Fourberies de Scapin*, 106, 458-59; influence, on *Le Dépit Amoureux*, 119; on *L'Amour Médecin*, 413

D

Daquin (physician), 414-15, 416

De Brie, Mlle: joins Molière's company, 87-88; Molière's relations with, 88-89; continued popularity of, 90-91; appears in *Les Facheux*, 216; Molière's supposed infatuation for, 235; appears in *Les Plaisirs de l'Ile Enchantée*, 299, 303

De la Croix, Philippe, 291

De la Forge, J., 151

Descartes, René: influence on Molière, 29; Gassendi's 'criticism of, 30

Desfontaines, Nicholas, 64, 78

Desfougerais (physician), 415

Devil, the, as hero, 379-80

Dialogue de Deux Précieuses sur les Affaires de Leur Communauté (Somaize), 152

Dijon, visits of Molière to, 76, 98

Divinity, and medicine, 414

Doctors: as themes of comedy for Molière, 101, 129, 310-11, 409-26, 473-75

Documents, contemporary, as sources of information on Molière, 22, 75-76, 79

Dominique (Giuseppe Domenico),

104, 164

Donneau de Visé, *see* Visé, Sieur de
(Jean Donneau)

Dorimond, Nicholas Drouin: influence on *L'Ecole des Maris,* 202;
possible source of *Don Juan ou Le
Festin de Pierre,* 382

Dubourg, M (linen-draper): prosecutes Molière for debt, 67

Du Croisy, Philibert Gassot: joins
Troupe de Monsieur, 137; appears
in *Les Plaisirs de l'Ile Enchantée,*
299

Duel, suppression of, 333

Du Fresne, Charles: leader of Duc
d'Epernon's company, 78, 80-81;
performance in *Nicomède,* 127; retirement, 134

Du Parc, Mlle: joins Molière's company, 88; Molière's relations with,
88-89, 235; at Théâtre du Marais,
90; at Hôtel du Bourgogne, 90,
430, 431; and the Corneilles, 90,
122-23; and Racine, 90; death of,
90; performance in *Nicomède,*
127; goes to Théâtre du Marais,
134; appears in *Les Fâcheux,* 216;
appears in *Les Plaisirs de l'Ile
Enchantée,* 299, 303; Grimarest's
account of quarrel with Armande,
409-10; appears in Racine's *Alexandre le Grand,* 430; follows Racine to the Hôtel de Bourgogne,
430-31

Du Parc, René Berthelot: appears in
Les Plaisirs de l'Ile Enchantée,
299

Durval (dramatist), 324

Du Ryer, Pierre, 63

Du Trallage: on Duc d'Epernon's
esteem for Molière, 77

E

Education of women, as theme of
comedy for Molière, 196 ff., 253
ff., 460 ff.

Egoism, as theme of comedy for
Molière, 196 ff., 392 ff.

Elomire Hypocondre (Chalussay),
27, 39, 58, 224; on first performance of Illustrious Theatre in Paris,
63; on Molière's failure as a tragic
actor, 135; on *Sganarelle ou Le
Cocu Imaginaire,* 174; on wife of
Molière, 224; on *L'Amour Médecin,* 419-21

Enghien, Duc d', 25, 289

Epernon, Duc d': patron of Molière,
71, 76-78, 81-83; and Madeleine
Béjart, 76-77; and Magnon, 76-77;
and Mareschall, 77; at Dijon, 98

Epicharis, played by Madeleine Béjart, 64

Epicurus: influence on Molière, 29;
Gassendi's defense of, 30

Erasmus: influence on *Le Dépit
Amoureux,* 119

Estates of Languedoc, as patrons of
Molière's company, 83, 94-95

Estriché, Guerin d', 243

Eurymédon ou l'Illustre Pirate (Desfontaines), 64

Excommunication, threat of, against
actors, readers, or audiences of
Tartuffe, 345

Exquisites, the, 141 ff.

F

Fagon (physician), 416

Fameuse Comédienne, La (anon.):

on Molière's relations with women, 88-89; libels on Armande Béjart, 225, 235-49 passim; libels on Madeleine Béjart, 225

Farce: as afterpiece to tragedy, 44-45, 129; early, of Molière, 102 ff.; as logical development of comedy in Molière, 368-69; return to, in Fourberies de Scapin, 458-59

Fausser, Antoine: prosecutes Molière for debt, 66

Félibien: on Versailles fête (July, 1688), 308-10

Feminism, as theme for Molière, 253-62 passim, 463 ff.

Femme Industrieuse, La (Dorimond), as source of L'Ecole des Maris, 202

Fénélon, François de Salignac de La Mothe-: on astrologers, 314

Festivals, of Louis XIV: Molière's organization of, 165-66, 293 ff.

Fiorelli, Tiberio, see Scaramouche

Fleurette, Eustache, 14

Folle Gageure, La (Boisrobert), as source of L'Ecole des Maris, 202

Fornaris, Fabritio de: influence on L'Etourdi, 112

Fouquet, Nicolas, 209-11

Fracasse, Capitaine, 45-46

Friends of Molière, 428 ff.

G

Gamard, Marin, 12

Gassendi, Pierre, 30-33

Gaston de France, 64-65

Gaultier-Garguille (Legrand), 45

Gazette, see Loret, Jean

Gély (barber), 83

Golden mean: departure from, as source of comedy in Molière, 388 ff.

Gorla, Marquise Thérèse de, see Du Parc, Mlle

Grammont, Chevalier de, 147

Grand Dictionnaire des Précieuses (Somaize), 146-47, 152

Grangier, Jean, 32

Grenoble, visits of Molière to, 76

Grimarest: Vie de Molière, 22; unreliability of, 22, 23-33 passim; on the Illustrious Theatre group, 59; on early farces of Molière, 102; on Les Précieuses Ridicules, 150; on Louis XIV's esteem for Molière and Lulli, 165; on granting of second share in the company to Molière, 195; on marriage of Molière, 234, 240-42, 249-50; on Le Bourgeois Gentilhomme, 316; on Le Misanthrope, 390-91; accounts for Molière's attitude to doctors, 409-10; on the supper party at Auteuil, 435-36; quotes Molière on Chapelle, 437; imaginary conversation of Molière with young would-be actor, 444; on L'Avare, 455; on death of Molière, 474, 476-77; reticence concerning aftermath of Molière's death, 483

Gros Guillaume (Guérin), 45

Groto, Luigi: influence on L'Etourdi, 112

Guénégaud, M de, 147

Guénot (physician), 415

Guerin, Nicolas (Guérin d'Étriché, Isaac François): marries widow of Molière, 243-44; completes Mélicerte, 305

Guérin, Robert, 45

Guerre Comique, La, see Comic war

Guerre Comique ou la Défense de

l'Ecole des Femmes, La (de la Croix), 291

Guéru, Hugh, 45

Guichard (official in service of Monsieur), 224

Guiche, Comte de: reputed to be lover of Armande Béjart, 236-37

Guillot-Gorju, 152

Guise, François Joseph, Duc de, 64-65, 99

Guyenne, Grand Provost of, 94

H

Hardy, Alexander, 44, 105, 107, 324

Hauteroche, Noël Jacques le Breton de, 284

Hell, properties for: existence of asserted to be source of Psyché, 320-21

Henrietta of England: dedication of L'Ecole des Femmes to, 262; death, 415

Henry IV, and the theatre, 41

Hervé, Marie, see Béjart, Marie Hervé

Heureuse Jalousie du Prince Rodrigue, L' (Cicognini), as source of Don Garcie, 186

Honesty, excessive, as theme for Molière, 392 ff.

Horace: influence on Le Dépit Amoureux, 119

Hôtel de Bourgogne (theatre), 39, 40-41; typical performance at, 42-46; position of at time of Molière's Paris debut, 125-26; rivalry with Molière, 167-69; Molière's attacks on, 191, 284; in the Comic War, 282-91

Hôtel de Rambouillet, 139 ff.

House of the monkeys (childhood home of Molière), 9-10; inscription on site of, 10; column of, 32 (plate)

Hugo, Victor: on L'Etourdi, 117; fondness for Le Sicilien, 306; praises style of Molière, 488

Hurtado de Mendoza, Antonio: influence on L' Ecole des Maris, 202-3

Hypocrisy, as theme for comedy in Tartuffe, 336-60 passim

I

Illusion Comique (Corneille), sets and properties for, 325

Illustre Comédien ou le Martyre de Saint Genest, L' (Desfontaines), 64

Illustrious Theatre: founding of, 56 ff.; provisions of articles in contract, 56-58; signatories of contract, 58; location of a theatre, 61-62; first performance in Rouen, 62; return to Paris, 62; first performance in Paris, 63; repertoire of, 63-64; Gaston de Paris and, 64; Duc de Guise and, 65; financial embarrassment of, 65-68

Immorality: charges of, against Molière, 253, 258, 262, 453-54

Impiety: charges of, against Molière, 253, 258, 262, 333-60 passim, 384-86

Impromptu de l'Hôtel de Condé, L' (Montfleury, fils), 192-93, 290-91

Inavvertito, L' (Beltrame), as source of L'Etourdi, 112

Interresse, L' (Secchi), as source of Le Dépit Amoureux, 118

J

Jealousy: as theme of comedy, 170-

74, 176, 253-62; as theme of trag-
edy, 186-90
Jesuits, 24-25
Jeu de Paume des Mestayers: chosen
as home of the Illustrious Theatre,
62; first performance in, 63
Jodelet, Julien Bedeau, 126; joins
Troupe de Monsieur, 137; dies,
137
Joguenet ou les Viellards Dupés, 101
Josaphat (Magnon), 76-77
Jouvency, Father: prohibits dramatic
performances at Clermont, 29

L

La Grange, Charles Varlet de: joins
Troupe de Monsieur, 137; appears
in *Les Plaisirs de l'Ile Enchantée,*
298; mission to Louis XIV to beg
protection for *Tartuffe,* 344; preface to collected edition of Molière's plays, 21, 22; Register,
21-22; on Molière's choice of acting as a profession, 38; on the
Illustrious Theatre group, 58-59;
on early plays of Molière, 101; on
Molière's return to Paris, 123-34;
on Molière's speech at Paris début,
128; on the début of the *Troupe
de Monsieur,* 130; on *Les Précieuses Ridicules,* 150; on demolition of Salle du Petit Bourbon,
168; on advances made by rival
theatres to members of Molière's
company, 169; on Molière's relation to Louis XIV, 169-70; on
personality of Molière, 179; on
Racine's unethical behavior regarding *Alexandre le Grand,* 430; **on**
death of Molière's father, 441; on
death of Molière, 474, 475, 476
La Beaupré, Mlle: on Corneille, 108

La Bruyère, Jean de: on the Exquisites, 142; on *Le Misanthrope,* 397
La Fontaine, Jean de: friendship
with Chapelle, 31; and Fouquet,
209; contributes verses to *Les
Fâcheux,* 215; verse tribute to
Molière, 220-21; *La Fameuse Comédienne* attributed to, 239; letter
to his wife concerning Limoges,
311-12; on astrologers, 313; on
public reaction to excess of scenic
effects, 329-30; visits Molière at
Auteuil, 428; early support of
Molière, 432; on gatherings of
Boileau and his friends, 433-34;
qualities which won Molière's
esteem, 437-38; on Lulli, 470;
grave of, 484; verses on Molière's
death, 484-85
La Forêt (servant of Molière), 477,
478
La Harpe, Jean François de: commends *La Comtesse d'Escarbagnas,*
331; on *L'Avare,* 454
Lamoignan, M de, and *Tartuffe,* 342-
43, 354
Language, of Molière, 117-18, 306
La Rochefoucauld, Duc François de,
142, 144
Lartigue, Nanon de, 81, 83, 98
La Serre: on Molière as heroic actor,
193
La Thorillière, François Lenoir de:
appears in *Les Plaisirs de l'Ile En-
chantée,* 299
Lauzan, Comte de: reputed to be
lover of Armande Béjart, 236-37
La Vallière, Duchesse de (Françoise
Louise de la Baume Le Blanc),
210-11, 295-96, 300
Le Brun, Charles, 209, 215
Le Clerc, Mlle, *see* De Brie, Mlle
Legrand, Henri, 45

L'Enclos, Ninon de, 426; hears private reading of *Tartuffe*, 338
Lenoir, Alexandre: monuments to Molière and La Fontaine, 484
Le Notre, André, 209, 215
Le Pautre, Jean: engraving of scene from *Le Malade Imaginaire*, 384 (plate)
Le Sage, Alain René, 331, 443; on Abbé Boyer's production of *Judith*, 326-27
Le Tellier, M, 147
Letter, anonymous, to Abbé Boyvin, on interment of Molière, 481
Lettre écrite sur la Comédie du Misanthrope (Visé), 392-93
Le Vasseur, Abbé, 287
Levis, Henri de, Duc de Vendatour, 332
Libels, contemporary, as sources of infromation on Molière, 22-23
Life of the Saints for Every Day of the Year (Rosimont), 48
Limoges, man of, as figure of fun, 311-12
Locke, Thomas: on induction of doctor, 425
Lope de Vega: influence, on *L'Ecole des Maris*, 202, on *Le Mariage Forcé*, 294, on *Tartuffe*, 358
Loret, Jean: on performances of the *Troupe de Monsieur*, 135-36; on *Les Précieuses Ridicules*, 146, 166-67; on *L'Etourdi*, 166-67; on *L'Ecole des Maris*, 207; on *Les Fâcheux*, 216; on Armande Béjart, 244; on *L'Ecole des Femmes*, 266; on *Le Mariage Forcé*, 294; on *Tartuffe*, 334-46 *passim*; on *Don Juan ou Le Festin de Pierre*, 383
Louis XIII: becomes protector of *Troupe Royale*, 46; edict concerning theatre and actors (1641), 46-47

Louis XIV: attends performance of tragedy at Clermont, 28; present at Molière's début in Paris, 125 ff.; command performances for, 135-36; character and personality of, 159-62; and Molière, 162 ff.; suggests new character for *Les Fâcheux*, 211-13; passion for ballet, 214-15; support of Molière during the Comic War, 266-91 *passim*; appearances on stage, 293-94, 298, 304, 313; and *Tartuffe*, 334-56; becomes protector of Molière's company, 340, 385; and *Don Juan ou Le Festin de Pierre*, 384-86; and *Amphitryon*, insinuations concerning, 446-48; establishment of "Academy of Opera or Musical Performances in the French Language," 469; order prohibiting free theatre-going by members of his household, 472-73; intervenes with Archbishop of Paris in matter of Molière's burial, 480-81; receipt of news of Molière's death, 484
Lucifer, 379
Lucretius: influence on Molière, 29; Molière's translation of, 29-30, 181-82
Lulli, Giovanni Battista (Jean Baptiste Lully): services to Louis XIV, 162, 164, 215, 295, 296, 299, 309, 310, 321; appears as Pourceaugnac, 312; story of supper party ending in suicide pact, 435-36; acquires monopoly on musical performances, 469-70
Lullier, François, 31
Lyon, visits of Molière to, 76, 86, 94, 96

M

Madame, and *Tartuffe*, 342-43

Magnon, Jean, 63, 136; dedication of *Josaphat,* quoted, 76

Mahelot (sceneshifter): list of plays performed at Hôtel de Bourgogne, 324-25

Malherbe, François de, 141

Malingre, Madeleine: signs contract of Illustrious Theatre, 58

Map of the Tender Passion, 141-42, 144

Marchand-tapissier (upholsterer), 10-11

Mareschall, André, 58; dedication of *Papyre,* quoted, 77

Marido Hace Mujer, El (Hurtado de Mendoza), as source of *L'Ecole des Maris,* 202-3

Marie-Thérèse, Queen: presentation of *Les Plaisirs de l'Ile Enchantée* in honour of, 295 ff.

Marigny, de: letter to a friend on *Les Plaisirs de l'Ile Enchantée,* 298

Marivaux, Pierre Carlet de Chamblain de, foreshadowed in *Les Amants Magnifiques,* 313; in *Princesse d'Elide,* 331

Marmontel, Jean François: on intrusion of audience on stage, 327; on *George Dandin ou Le Mari Confondu,* 453

Marolles, Abbé de: on Molière's translation of Lucretius, 181; hears private reading of *Tartuffe,* 338

Marriage, as theme of comedy for Molière, 253ff., 448-53

Mauvillain, Monsieur de, 410, 413

Mayor Impossible, El (Lope de Vega), as source of *L'Ecole des Maris,* 202

Mazarin, Jules, Cardinal, 124, 166-67, 178, 415

Mean, golden, *see* Golden mean

Médicin Volant, Le (Boursault), 110

Medicine, dangers of, in seventeenth century, 414 ff.

Medico Volante, Il (Dominique), 104

Melite (Corneille), 42

Ménage, Gilles, 140, 144; on *Les Précieuses Ridicules,* 145; criticism of *Le Sicilien,* 306; hears private reading of *Tartuffe,* 338; as possible model for Vadius, 460-62

Menou, Mlle, 235

Menteur, Le (Corneille), 114

Mestayer, Noel, 12

Michelet, Jules: on *Amphitryon,* 446

Misalliance, as theme of comedy for Molière, 450-54

Misanthropy, as theme of comedy for Molière, 200-2, 392 ff.

Modène, Comte de, 99, 234; and Madeleine Béjart, 36

Moderation: Jean Poquelin as example of, 19-20; *see also* Golden mean

Molière, Jean Baptiste Poquelin: childhood home, 9-10; ancestry, 10; parents, 11-20; birth, 11; middle-class status, 12-13; stepmother, 14, 15; recognized as his father's heir, 17-19; education, 23-34; friends, 31-33, 428 ff.; autograph, 32 (plate); law studies, 33-34; first evidence of interest in theatre, 38-50; sent by father to Narbonne as deputy *valet-tapissier* to Louis XIII, 50-53; informs father of his decision to go upon the stage, 53; renounces reversion of father's post, 55; founds Illustrious Theatre, 56 ff.; provision concerning in contract of Illustrious Theatre, 58; moves to Madeleine Béjart's house, 59; rents *Jeu de Paume des Mestayers,* 62; portraits of, attributed to Pierre Mignard, 64 (plate), 98, 192 (plate); cancels lease for

Jeu de Paume des Mestayers, 66; rents *Croix Noire* tennis court, 66; is imprisoned for debt, 66-67; enters service of Duc d'Epernon in Narbonne, 70-71; provincial career, 75-99; visit to Paris, 84; friendship with Mignard, 98-99; return to Paris, 123-24; enters service of Monsieur, 124; shares Salle du Petit Bourbon with Scaramouche, 130 ff.; difficulties with his company, 133-34; growing popularity of, 135-36; first comedy of manners, 138-58; and Louis XIV, 162-70; assignment of Salle du Palais Royal to, 169; failure in heroic tragedy, 179-94; return to comedy, 196 ff.; first venture in comedy-ballet, 209-21; marriage to Armande Béjart, 222-52; children of, 245, 250-51; and Baron, 246-49; engages in the Comic War, 265 ff.; thanks Louis XIV for patronage, 269-70; organizes the festivals of Louis XIV, 295 ff.; appears in *Les Plaisirs de l'Ile Enchantée,* 299-30; appears in *La Princesse d'Elide,* 302; first performance of *Tartuffe,* 303; appears as Pourceaugnac, 313; appears as Clitidas in *Les Amants Magnifiques,* 314; three conventions of stagecraft used by, 328-29; *Tartuffe* attacked and suppressed, 333 ff.; *placets* to Louis XIV, 337-38, 344, 346; company becomes *Troupe du Roi,* 340; vindication of *Tartuffe,* in revised version, 346 ff.; attacks on, following production of *Don Juan ou Le Festin de Pierre,* 380-86; and his physician, 410; influence of his illness on choice of themes, 413 ff.; appearance in *L'Amour Médecin* interrupted by illness, 419; at Auteuil, 427-59; presents skit on Racine's *Andromaque,* 432; defends *Les Plaideurs,* by Racine, 432; on form and freedom, 433; dissuades his inebriated friends from carrying out suicide pact, 435-36; philosophical temperament of, 435 ff.; relationship with Corneille, 438-39; attitude to the live stage, 441 ff.; and *l'Académie Française,* 443-44; return to Paris, 460; reunion with his wife, 460, 470; death of his sons, 471; involved in play house riots, 472-73; illness and melancholy of, 471 ff.; writes *Le Malade Imaginaire,* 473-74; plays lead in *Le Malade Imaginaire,* 474 ff.; death of, 474-79; denied Christian burial, 479-80; his widow's appeal to Louis XIV, 480; interment, 481-82; scandal surrounding circumstances of his death and burial, 481 ff.; posthumous judgments of, 484 ff.; appearance and character of, 488-89; *see also* Characters (Molière); Plays (Molière); Prefaces to plays (Molière); Publication of plays (Molière)

Molière, Mlle de (Armande Béjart): appears in *Les Plaisirs de l'Ile Enchantée,* 298-99, 303; *see also* Béjart, Armande-Grésinde-Claire-Elizabeth

Molina, Tirso de: possible source of *Don Juan ou Le Festin de Pierre,* 365, 381-82

Mondory (Montdory), Guillaume Desguilberts, 41, 44

Money, value of, in seventeenth-century France, 11n

Monsieur (brother of Louis XIV):

becomes patron of Molière, 124 ff.; marriage of, 330; private performance of *Tartuffe* for, 339; relinquishes Molière's company to Louis XIV, 340

Montaigne, Michel Eyquem de: possible influence on *L'Amour Médecin*, 418

Montausier, Monsieur de, 141, 142, 392, 461

Montespan, Mme de (Françoise Athénaïs Rochechouart, Marquise de Montespan), 446, 469

Montfleury, Zacharie Jacob, 44; reaction to debut of Molière, 125-30; Molière's allusion to obesity of, 192, 284; slanderous letter to Louis XIV on Molière's marriage, 233, 290-91

Montfleury, Antoine: on Moliére in rôle of Caesar, 192-93; and the Comic War, 289-90

Montpellier, visits of Molière to, 76, 93-94

Morin (mathematician and astrologer), 314

Mort de Chrispe, La (Tristan l'Hermite), 63, 137

Mort de Sénèque, La (Tristant l'Hermite), 64

Multiple stage system, 324-25

Muse Historique (Loret), 135-36, 166-67

Musset, Alfred de, foreshadowed by *Le Sicilien*, 331

N

Nantes, visits of Molière to, 76, 78-79, 82

Narbonne: denial of sacraments to theatre-goers (1666), 47-48; visits of Molière to, 76, 95-96

P

Palais Royal, 182-83; rebuilding of, 323; performance of second version of *Tartuffe*, 342; temporary closing of, 428

Palaprat, M de: on Moliére and the Italians, 132

Panégyrique de l'Ecole des Femmes, La (Robinet), 288-89

Papyre ou le Dictateur (Mareschall), 77

Paradoxes: in life and work of Molière, 195-96

Parasite, Le (Tristan l'Hermite), as source of *L'Etourdi*, 112

Paris, Archbishop of: denial of sacraments and Christian burial to actors (1624), 48; *see also* Péréfixe, Hardouin de; Chanvallon, Harlay de

Patin, Guy: on *L'Amour Médecin*, 412, 420; on his colleagues, 414-15

Pédant Joué, Le (Cyrano de Bergerac), 32

Pedants, as themes for comedy, 101, 294, 411 ff.; 460 ff.

Pellison (author of prologue to entertainment given by Fouquet), 210, 215

Perault, Charles, law examination of, 33

Péréfixe, Hardouin, Archbishop of Paris: and *Tartuffe*, 301, 334, 344-45, 348

Père-Lachaise, monuments to Molière and La Fontaine in, 484

Perier, Toussaint, 12

Perrault, Charles: on début of *Troupe de Monsieur*, 130

Perrin, Abbé, 469

Perside ou la Suite de Illustre Bassa (Desfontaines), 64

Pézenas, visits of Molière to, 76, 83, 87, 94-95

Philosophy, Molière's study of, 28, 29-32

Phormio (Terence): influence on *Les Fourberies de Scapin*, 458

Physicians, of Louis XIV, 412, 414-16

Pinel, Georges: joins Molière's troop, 54, 58

Piracy: responsible for preservation of original version of *Don Juan ou Le Festin de Pierre*, 386; *see also* Ribou, Jean; Somaize

Pirandello, Luigi: anticipated by *Amphitryon*, 449

Plagiarism, and seventeenth-century theatre, 106 ff.

Plaisirs de l'Ile Enchantée, Les, 295-303

Plapisson, Comte de, 266

Plautus: adaptations of performed at college of Clermont, 28; influence, on *L'Etourdi*, 112, on *Le Dépit Amoureux*, 119, on *Monsieur de Pourceaugnac*, 312, on *L'Amour Médicin*, 413, on *Amphitryon*, 445, 448, 450, on *L'Avare*, 454, on *Les Fourberies de Scapin*, 458

Plays (Molière):

Amants Magnifiques, Les, 313-14

Amour Médecin, L', 410-13, 417-21, 422, 427; frontispiece, 256 (plate)

Amphitryon, 306, 445-50; fragments of Don Garcie in, 184

Avare, L', 445, 454-58; Brissart print for, 288 (plate)

Bourgeois Gentilhomme, Le, 314-20

Comtesse d'Escarbagnas, La, 330-31

Critique de l'Ecole des Femmes,

La, 218-19, 265, 269-77, 281

Dépit Amoureux, Le, 106, 111, 118-21, 133, 135, 136, 411

Docteur Amoureux, Le, 101; presentation at Paris début, 129

Docteur Pédant, Le, 101

Don Garcie de Navarre ou le Prince Jaloux, 180-94

Don Juan ou Le Festin de Pierre, 243, 339-40, 361-87, 409, 412; Prince de Conti as possible model for, 93, 97

Ecole des Femmes, L', 253-64, 265-66; frontispiece, 256 (plate)

Ecole des Maris, L', 195-208; frontispiece, 256 (plate)

Etourdi ou les Contretemps, L', 106, 110-17, 133, 135, 136, 166, 411

Fâcheux, Les, 212-21, 303

Fagotier, Le, 101, 422; see also Médecin Malgré Lui, Le

Femmes Savantes, Les, 460-69; fragments of Don Garcie in, 184

Festin de Pierre, Le, see Don Juan ou Le Festin de Pierre

Fourberies de Scapin, 106, 445, 458-59; see also Gorgibus dans le Sac; Joguenet ou les Vieillards Dupés

George Dandin ou Le Mari Confondu, 308, 450-54; anticipated by Le Mariage Forcé, 294; see also Jalousie du Barbouillé, La

Gorgibus dans le Sac, 101, 196, 458

Gros-René Ecolier, 136

Gros-René jaloux, 450

Hypocrite, The, see Tartuffe

Imposteur, L', 342; see also Tartuffe

Impromptu de Versailles, L', 185, 191-92, 219, 264, 265, 283-86,

289-90

Jalousie du Barbouillé, La, 102, 105-6, 411, 450

Jalousie de Gros-René, La, 450

Maître d'Ecole, Le, 101

Malade Imaginaire, Le, 422-25, 473-75; Brissart print for, 288 (plate); scene from, 384 (plate)

Mariage Forcé, Le, 293-95, 303, 411

Médecin Malgré Lui, Le, 391, 392, 421-22; Brissart print for, 288 (plate); see also *Fagotier, Le; Médecin Volant, Le*

Médecin Volant, Le, 102-3, 104, 105-6, 136, 196, 411

Mélicert, 248, 304-5

Misanthrope ou l'Atrabiliaire Amoureux, Le, 389-408; fragments of *Don Garcie* in, 184; frontispiece, 256 (plate), Brissart print for, 288 (plate)

Monsieur de Pourceaugnac, 310-13, 422

Pastorale Comique, 304, 305

Pédant Joué, Le, 459

Précieuses Ridicules, Les, 145-58, 166, 191, 460, 462-63

Princesse d'Elide, La, 236-37, 245, 296, 302-3, 336

Psyché, 249, 320-23, 330, 438

Sganarelle ou Le Cocu Imaginaire, 170-77

Sicilien ou l'Amour Peintre, Le, 304, 305-8

Tartuffe ou l'Imposteur, 300-1, 332-60; Louis XIV's defense of, 163, 334-56 *passim;* fragments of *Don Garcie* in, 184; Molière's *placets,* 337-38, 344, 346; preface to published version, 347-50; anticipated by *Le Mariage Forcé,* 294

Trois Docteurs Rivaux, Les, 101, 196

Playwrights 107 ff.

Pliny the Elder: possible influence on *L'Amour Médecin,* 418

Poet, hired, 107-9

Poggio Bracciolini, Giovanni Francesco: influence on *Le Dépit Amoureux,* 119

Poisson, Mlle: description of Molière, 488

Pommier, François: loan to Molière's company, 65; prosecution of Molière for debts, 66-67

Pompe Funèbre de Scarron (anon.), on Molière, 179

Pompe Funèbre d'une Précieuse, La (Somaize), 152

Poquelin, Catherine Fleurette (stepmother of Molière), 14, 15

Poquelin, Jean (great grandfather of Molière), 10

Poquelin, Jean (grandfather of Molière), 10

Poquelin, Jean (father of Molière): becomes upholsterer, 10-11; marries Marie Cressé, 11; marriage contract of, 11-12; home and furniture of, 13; clothing of, 13; second marriage of, 14; sends son to Clermont, 16; becomes *tapissier ordinaire du roi,* 17; secures reversion of his post for his son, 17-18; prosperity of, 18-19; professional duties of, 19; alarmed by Molière's interest in the theatre, 50; sends Molière to Narbonne as deputy *valet-tapissier,* 50-53; reaction to Molière's decision to go upon the stage, 54-55; legal document concerning Molière's reversion of father's post in exchange for sum of money, 55; guarantees and pays off Molière's debts, 68; fails to make effective Molière's renunciation of reversion of father's post, 68-69; becomes reconciled to son's theatrical career, 74, 124-25; continued prosperity of, 84; at signing of Molière's marriage contract, 222; death, 440-41

Poquelin, Jean Baptiste, *see* Molière, Jean Baptiste Poquelin

Poquelin, Marie Cressé (mother of Molière): marriage of, 11-12; literacy of, 12, 14; home and furniture of, 13; clothing and jewelry of, 13-14; children of, 14; death of, 14; biographers' theories on, 14-15

Poquelin, Marie-Madeleine, 222

Poquelin, Nicolas (uncle of Molière), 17

Portrait du Peintre ou le Contre Critique de l'Ecole des Femmes, Le (Boursault), 282; Molière at performance of, 282-83

Précieuses en Vers, Les (Somaize), 152

Prefaces to plays (Molière), cited, 147, 148-49, 207, 212, 215, 268-69, 347-50

Preux d'Aubray, 67

Producer: Molière as: self-portrait in *L'Impromptu de Versailles,* 286

Prometheus, 379

Prose and verse, Molière's experiments in combining, 306

Psyché (Boileau), 433-34

Publication of plays (Molière): *Les Précieuses Ridicules,* 147-49; *Sganarelle ou Le Cocu Imaginaire,* 175; *L'Ecole des Maris,* 207; *Les Fâcheux,* 216; *L'Ecole des Femmes,* 262, 268; *La Critique de l'Ecole des Femmes,* 281; *Tartuffe,* 346; *see also* Piracy; Ribou, Jean; Somaize

Pucelle, La (Chapelain), 434

Pure, Abbé de, and the exquisites, 144: supposed author of scenario on which *Les Précieuses Ridicules* was based, 153-54

Pylade and Oreste (Coqueteau de la Clairière), 136

Q

Queen mother: Molière's dedication of *La Critique de l'Ecole des Femmes* to, as reply to *Zélinde,* 281; presentation of *Les Plaisirs de l'Ile Enchantée* in honour of, 295 ff.; and Companie du Saint Sacrement, 333; present at private performance of *Tartuffe,* 339; death of, 390

Quinault, Philippe, 162, 321

R

Rabelais, François: influence on *Le Mariage Forcé,* 294; use of man from Limoges as comic figure, 311

Racine, Jean Baptiste: friendship with Chapelle, 31; letter to Abbé Le Vasseur on Louis XIV's praise of Molière, 287; expresses Court disapproval of Louis XIV's appearance on stage, 293-94; Molière's appreciation of, 336; relationship with Molière, 428-32; snubs detractor of Moliére's *Le Misanthrope,* 432; exchange with Boileau on Molière's *L'Avare,* 455-56

Racine, Louis, 433; story of supper party at Auteuil, 435-36; between Molière and *l'Academie Française,* 443

Raisin (organist of Troyes), 246-47

Raisin, Mme, 247

Rambouillet, Marquise de, 139 ff.; invites Molière to perform *Les Précieuses Ridicules,* 145

Ratabon, M de, 168

Realism, slavish: accusations of against Molière, 204-5, 212, 216-20; Molière's defence against charges of, 218-20

Reason, and medicine, 414

Réaux, Tallemant de: on Molière and Madeleine Béjart, 37; on Madeleine Béjart as Epicharis, 64; on intrusion of audience upon stage, 326

Régnier, Mathurin: influence on *Tartuffe,* 358

Relation de la Fête de Versailles (Félibien), 308-10

Réveillon, Pierre, 79

Ribou, Jean: plans to pirate *Les Précieuses Ridicules,* 148; pirates *Sganarelle ou Le Cocu Imaginaire,* 175; and publication of *Le Misanthrope,* 392-93

Richelieu, Cardinal: patron of Mondory and Théâtre du Marais, 42, 126; as playwright, 46, 124-25; builds Palais du Cardinal (later known as Palais Royal), 46; and the Marquise de Rambouillet, 140; reputed to be lover of Armande Béjart, 235-37

Rights: of authors, 108, 109-10, 430-31; of managers, 430-31; *see also* Piracy; Plagiarism

Riots, in playhouses, 471-72

Robinet de Saint-Jean, Charles: on Armande Béjart, 244; attack on Molière, 288-89; on *Le Sicilien,* 307-8; reports gossip concerning "original" of Monsieur de Pour-ceaugnac, 311; on *Monsieur de Pourceaugnac,* 312; on *Psyché,* 323; defense of *Don Juan ou Le Festin de Pierre,* 385; on production of *Alexandre le Grand* (Racine), 430; on royal reception of *George Dandin ou Le Mari Confondu,* 454; on *L'Avare,* 456

Rochemont, Sieur de: on *Don Juan ou Le Festin de Pierre,* 380-81, 384-85

Rohault: imaginary conversation with Molière on his marriage, 241-42

Roman Comique (Scarron), 79-80

Rosé, Catherine de, *see* De Brie, Mlle

Rosimont (actor): piety of, 48; denied Christian burial, 48

Rotrou, Jean de, 35-36; influence, on *Le Dépit Amoureux,* 119, on *Le Bourgeois Gentilhomme,* 320, on *Amphitryon,* 446, on *Les Fourberies de Scapin,* 458; *Les Sosies,* produced at Marais Theatre, 446, influence on Molière's *Amphitryon,* 446

Rouen, visits of Molière to, 76, 99

Roullé, Pierre: on first version of *Tartuffe,* 334-36

Rousseau, Jean-Jacques: on *L'Ecole des Femmes,* 258; on *Le Misanthrope,* 392, 397; on *George Dandin ou Le Mari Confondu,* 453; on *L'Avare,* 456

Royalties, 108, 109

S

Sablière, Madame de la, 426

Saint Aignan, Duc de, 296

Saint Alexis ou l'Illustre Olympie (Desfontaines), 64

St. Barthélemy, Vicar of, *see* Roullé, Pierre

St. Evremond, Seigneur de Charles de Marguetel de Saint Denis, 144
St. Joseph, cemetery of: unknown place of Molière's grave in, 482 ff.
Saints: Molière on, 349-50
Salle du Petit Bourbon, 130-36 *passim;* demolition of, 167-68
Salon of Marquise de Rambouillet, 139 ff.; *Les Précieuses Ridicules* a satire on, 145 ff.
Sapho (Scarron), 144
Sauvé, F.: engravings of Brissart prints, 288 (plate)
Scaramouche, and Molière, 130-33
Scarron, Paul: on life of wandering players, 79-80; and the exquisites, 144; influence on *Tartuffe,* 358
Scévole (du Ryer), 63
Scudéry, Madeleine de, 141-44 *passim*
Secchi, Nicolo: influence on *Le Dépit Amoureux,* 118
Section de Molière et de La Fontaine, La: attempt to locate grave of Molière, 483-84
Segrais, Jean Regnault de, 140, 144; on *Les Précieuses Ridicules,* 147
Seneca: adaptations of performed at college of Clermont, 28
Sets, theatrical, 324-25
Sévigné, Madame de (Marie de Rabutin-Chantal), 139, 140, 144, 479
Shaw, Bernard, anticipated by Molière, 307
Silvestre, Israel: engraving of scene from *Princesse d'Elide,* 352 (plate)
Sisters of charity, at death of Molière 477
Sketches, earliest, of Molière, 100 ff.
Snobbery, as theme of comedy for Molière, 315 ff., 451 ff.
Soeur, La (Rotrou), 458
Somaize: on *Le Médicin Volant,* 104; on *Les Précieuses Ridicules,* 146-47; and plans to pirate *Les Précieuses Ridicules,* 147-48; attacks on *Les Précieuses Ridicules,* 151-54; attacked in *Songe du Rêveur,* 177-78
Songe du Rêveur (anon.): attack on Somaize and defence of Molière, 177-78
Sonnet on the Burial of Jean Baptiste Poquelin, known as Molière, an Actor, in the Cemetery of the Stillborn in Paris, quoted, 483
Sosies, Les (Rotrou), 446
Souvré, Monseigneur de, 17
Soyecourt, Marquis de, 212-13
Stagecraft, 323-30
Subligny, Perdou de, 432
Supper-tray, apocryphal story of, 164-65

T

Talhouet, Comte Louis de, 124
Tapissier ordinaire (or *valet-tapissier) du roi:* duties of, 19, 51-52
Tennis courts: use of as theatres in Paris, 61
Terence: adaptations of performed at college of Clermont, 28; Molière's study of, 28; influence, on *L'Etourdi,* 112, on *Le Dépit Amoureux,* 119, on *L'Ecole des Maris,* 202
Theatre: monopoly of, by *Confrérie de la Passion,* 40-41; transitional period in early seventeenth century, 46-47; provincial, 79-81; and religion: Molière on, 349
Théâtre du Marais, 41-42; permanent quarters of, 61; position of at time of Molière's Paris debut, 124-25; withdraws from Comic War, 291

Thébaïde, La (Racine), 336; presented at the Palais Royal, 429
Tite et Bérénice (Corneille), 438
Torelli, Giacomo, 215
Tostere, Denis, 12
Toulouse, visits of Molière to, 76
Tragedies: presentation of, at college of Clermont, 24, 28-29
Tragedy: Molière's ambition to play, 64
Traité de la Comédie (Conti), 97
Tristan l'Hermite, François, 63, 64-65; anecdote of hired poet, 109; influence on *L'Etourdi*, 112
Troupe de Monsieur: first appearance, 125-30
Troupe du Roi, conversion of *Troupe de Monsieur* to, 340
Troupe Royale, establishment of, 41
Turcaret (Le Sage), Molière's Harpin as model for, 331
Turlupin (Guéru), 45
Turquerie, Louis XIV's demand for, as basis of *Le Bourgeois Gentilhomme*, 314-15

U

Unbelief, as theme in *Don Juan ou Le Festin de Pierre*, 361-87 *passim*
Unities, and stagecraft, 325 ff.
Urlis, Catherine des: signs contract of Illustrious Theatre, 58; leaves the company, 66

V

Valet-tapissier, see *Tapissier ordinaire du roi*
Valise, lost, legend of, 100
Vallot (physician), 415, 416
Valville: abridgement of *L'Etourdi*, 119-20
Vario (painter), 132

Véritables Précieuses, Les (Somaize), 148, 152
Verneuil, Duc de, 109
Verse and prose, Molière's experiments in combining, 306
Vienne, visit of Molière to, 85-86
Vigarani, Sieur de, 169
Villequin ou de Brie, Edmé, 88
Villiers, Claude Deschamps de: possible source of *Don Juan ou Le Festin de Pierre*, 382
Virtue, excessive, as theme of comedy for Molière, 388-408 *passim*
Visé, Sieur de (Jean Donneau): on early farces of Molière, 102; on *Sganarelle ou Le Cocu Imaginaire*, 174; on *Les Fâcheux*, 217-18; on *L'Ecole des Femmes*, 266-68; on *La Critique de l'Ecole des Femmes*, 277-81; reconciliation with Molière, 278, 287-88; *La Réponse à l'Impromptu de Versailles ou la Vengeance des Marquis*, 286-87; on Court reception of *Le Misanthrope*, 390-91; *Lettre écrite sur la Comédie du Misanthrope*, 392-93
Vivonne, Catharine de, see Rambouillet, Marquise de
Voisin, Abbé: criticizes dramatic performances at Clermont, 29
Voiture, Vincent, 140
Voltaire, François Marie Arouet: on Chapelle, 31; on *L'Etourdi*, 117; on *Les Plaisirs de l'Ile Enchantée*, 295; on *Le Médecin Malgré Lui*, 421; on *Amphitryon*, 450; on *L'Avare*, 454, 455; on Molière's use of living models, 460 charges that Abbé Cotin's death was result of Molière's satire, 462
Voyage dans la Lune (Cyrano de Bergerac), 32

W

Wig, worn by physicians, 416-17
Women, education of, *see* Education
  of women
Writing, Molière's method, as explained in *La Critique de l'Ecole
  des Femmes,* 273-74

Z

*Zélinde, Comédie, ou la Véritable
  Critique de l'Ecole des Femmes et
  Critique de la Critique* (Visé),
  277-81
Zénobie (Magnon), 136